RULES

THE LAWRENCE STONE LECTURES

Sponsored by

*The Shelby Cullom Davis Center for Historical Studies
and Princeton University Press*

A list of titles in this series appears at the back of the book.

RULES

A SHORT HISTORY
OF WHAT WE LIVE BY

LORRAINE DASTON

PRINCETON UNIVERSITY PRESS

PRINCETON & OXFORD

Published by Princeton University Press
41 William Street, Princeton, New Jersey 08540
99 Banbury Road, Oxford OX2 6JX

press.princeton.edu

Library of Congress Cataloging-in-Publication Data

Names: Daston, Lorraine, 1951– author.
Title: Rules : a short history of what we live by / Lorraine Daston.
Description: Princeton : Princeton University Press, [2022] |
    Series: The Lawrence Stone lectures | Includes bibliographical
    references and index.
Identifiers: LCCN 2021048090 (print) | LCCN 2021048091 (ebook) |
    ISBN 9780691156989 (hardback ; alk. paper) | ISBN 9780691239187 (ebook)
Subjects: LCSH: Authority. | Order (Philosophy) | Algorithms. | Law. |
    Natural law.
Classification: LCC HM1251 .D37 2022 (print) | LCC HM1251 (ebook) |
    DDC 303.3/6–dc23/eng/20211013
LC record available at https://lccn.loc.gov/2021048090
LC ebook record available at https://lccn.loc.gov/2021048091

British Library Cataloging-in-Publication Data is available

Editorial: Eric Crahan and Barbara Shi
Production Editorial: Kathleen Cioffi
Text Design: Karl Spurzem
Jacket Design: Faceout Studio, Molly von Borstel
Production: Danielle Amatucci
Publicity: Maria Whelan and Kate Farquhar-Thomson
Copyeditor: Martin Schneider

Jacket images: Shutterstock

This book has been composed in Arno Pro with Trade Gothic LT Std

Printed on acid-free paper. ∞

Printed in the United States of America

10 9 8 7 6 5 4 3 2 1

To Wendy Doniger, who honored every breach.

CONTENTS

ILLUSTRATIONS

RULES

1

Introduction

THE HIDDEN HISTORY OF RULES

Clues to a Hidden History

This is a short book about a vast topic. We are, all of us, everywhere, always, enmeshed in a web of rules that supports and constrains. Rules fix the beginning and end of the working day and the school year, direct the ebb and flow of traffic on the roads, dictate who can be married to whom and how, situate the fork to the right or the left of the plate, score the runs and walks of baseball games, tame debate in meetings and parliaments, establish what can and cannot be taken on a plane as hand luggage, specify who can vote and when, parse the grammar of a sentence, channel customers into the proper lines at the grocery store, tell pet owners whether their animals are welcome or not, lay down the meter and rhyme scheme of a Petrarchan sonnet, and order the rites of birth and death. And these are just examples of explicit rules, the sort to be found written down on signs and in manuals, handbooks, sacred texts, and legal statutes. Add implicit rules, and the web becomes so densely woven that barely any human activity slips through the mesh: there are the unwritten rules about whether to greet with outstretched hand or two pecks on the cheek *à la française* (or one, *à la belge*), how many miles per hour over the posted speed limit will be tolerated without incurring a traffic ticket, how much to tip at what kind of restaurant, when to raise (and lower) one's voice in conversation, who should open doors for whom, how often and how loudly an opera may be interrupted with cheers and boos, when to arrive at and when to leave a dinner party, and how long an epic should be. Cultures notoriously differ as to the content of their rules, but there is no culture without rules, lots of them. A book about all of these rules would be little short of a history of humanity.

Rules are so ubiquitous, indispensable, and authoritative that they are taken for granted. How could there ever have been a society without rules, a time before rules? Yet the universality of rules does not imply their uniformity, either across cultures or within historical traditions. Rules exhibit vertiginous variety not only in their content but also in their forms. The former has been grist for the mill of travelers and ethnographers ever since Herodotus's (c. 484–c. 425 BCE) tales of how, from an ancient Greek perspective, in Egypt everything is reversed (though no less regular): the men stay home and weave, while the women go to the market; women urinate standing up, men sitting down; even the Nile runs backwards, from south to north.[1] The latter unfurls in the long list of species that belong to the genus of rules: laws, maxims, principles, guidelines, instructions, recipes, regulations, aphorisms, norms, and algorithms, to name just a few. The variety of these species of rules is a clue to a hidden history of what a rule is and does.

Since Greco-Roman antiquity, three principal semantic clusters have mapped out the meanings of rules (Chapter 2): tools of measurement and calculation; models or paradigms; and laws. The subsequent history of rules is one of proliferation and concatenation, yielding ever more species of rules and ever more exemplars of each species. The result is a cat's cradle of complexity almost as complex as culture itself. The three Ur-meanings of rules nonetheless spin out scarlet threads that wind their way through the historical labyrinth over millennia. By adopting a *longue durée* perspective and canvasing rules from many diverse sources, from monastic orders to cookbooks, from military manuals to legal treatises, from calculation algorithms to practical how-to instructions, this book traces the long career of this ancient trio of meanings in the learned and vernacular traditions that share Greco-Roman roots and that have evolved together over more than two millennia. Chapters 2 and 3 reconstruct how rules functioned as supple models from antiquity through the eighteenth century; Chapters 4 and 5 describe how algorithms of calculation worked in practice from ancient times until the rise of algorithms and mechanical calculation during the nineteenth and twentieth centuries. Chapters 6 and 7 contrast rules at their most specific, as nitty-gritty regulations, with rules at their most general, as Olympian natural laws and laws of nature, from the thirteenth through the eighteenth centuries. Chapter 8 examines how moral, legal, and political rules bend and break in the face of recalcitrant exceptions, from the sixteenth through the twentieth centuries.

Three oppositions structure this long history of rules. Rules can be either thick or thin in their formulation, flexible or rigid in their application, and general or specific in their domains. These oppositions can overlap, and some are more relevant than others, depending on which of the three kinds of rule is in question. Rules understood as models tend to be thick in formulation and flexible in application (Chapters 2 and 3). A thick rule is upholstered with examples, caveats, observations, and exceptions. It is a rule that anticipates wide variations in circumstances and therefore requires nimble adaptation. Thick rules incorporate at least hints of this variability in their very formulation. In contrast, rules understood as algorithms tend to be thinly formulated and rigidly applied, though they too can sometimes thicken (Chapters 4 and 5). An algorithm need not be brief, but it is seldom designed to deal with unusual or simply diverse cases. Because thin rules implicitly assume a predictable, stable world in which all possibilities can be foreseen, they do not invite the exercise of discretion. This is unproblematic when the thin rules are confined to solving textbook problems—for example, in simple arithmetic. But the annals of computer algorithms are by now full of cautionary tales about programs for everything from facial recognition to paying your taxes that were tailored too thinly and enforced too rigidly to fit a more variegated reality.

Both thick and thin rules can be either minutely specific—a model for making this kind of table out of this kind of wood, or an algorithm for computing the area of this irregular polygon only— or sweepingly general. Rules understood as laws can also run the gamut from specific regulations governing parking on this street on Sundays to the generality of the Decalogue or the second law of thermodynamics (Chapters 6 and 7). Both specific and general laws can be applied either rigidly or flexibly. Rules that teem with specifics, like the sumptuary regulations discussed in Chapter 6, may need some give in application, if only because the specifics change so quickly. And even the most general laws of all, understood as divine commands that are eternally and universally binding, may also on occasion be bent (Chapter 8).

These oppositions should be understood as marking the extremes of a spectrum of possibilities rather than as all-or-nothing complements. The chapters that follow illustrate how rules, whether conceived as models, algorithms, or laws, differ by degrees in thinness and thickness, rigidity and flexibility, specificity and generality. Although not all combinations are equally possible, a long history like this one can stretch the present-day imagination with examples of rule regimes that have become rare, such as algorithms formulated thickly and applied flexibly (Chapter 4).

Rules are a betwixt-and-between category. In ancient and medieval schemes of knowledge, they occupied the middle territory between lofty sciences like natural philosophy, which aimed at certain knowledge of universal causes, and the most lowly, mindless, repetitive gestures of unskilled workmen. The province of rules was the arts, those branches of practical knowledge and know-how that blended reason and experience, guidelines that could be taught and savvy that could only be acquired through practice (Chapter 3). In early modern polities, rules were situated between local regulations overflowing with local specifics and universal natural laws valid for everyone, everywhere, always. Analogously, rules in early modern science were regularities too specific to qualify as grand laws of nature but too general to count as isolated observations: for example, the rule that water expands rather than contracts when it freezes versus the law of universal gravitation, as valid for the remotest planets as for the apple that falls from this tree (Chapters 6 and 7). Rules define both social and natural orders of a middling sort, always mediating between extremes of certainty and chance, generality and specificity, perfect order and utter chaos.

All of these contrasts boil down to one big contrast: a world of high variability, instability, and unpredictability versus one in which the future can be reliably extrapolated from the past, standardization insures uniformity, and averages can be trusted. Although the episodes recounted in this book trace a rough historical arc from the former world to the latter, there is no inexorable dynamic of modernity at work here. An island of stability and predictability in a tumultuous world, no matter what the epoch or locale, is the arduous and always fragile achievement of political will, technological infrastructure, and internalized norms. At any moment it can be suddenly overwhelmed by war, pandemic, natural disaster, or revolution. In such emergencies, thin rules suddenly thicken, rigid rules become rubbery, general rules wax specific. It is telling that such explosions of uncertainty are called "states of exception" (Chapter 8)—states in which rules temporarily lose their hold. If rules are changed too often and too quickly to keep up with dynamic circumstances, the very idea of a rule can start to wobble (Epilogue).

Rules as Both Paradigms *and* Algorithms

Rules provide a rich vein to be mined for philosophical problems and projects. The most ancient and enduring problem inspired by rules is how universals can be made to fit a potential infinity of particulars that cannot be foreseen by the rule-maker. This problem is as old as philosophy itself and still very much with us. All the chapters in this book describe how this problem was addressed in different settings and in different periods, whether in the law court, the artisan's workshop, or the confessional. I turn to this problem in the next section. But first I must answer a question key to understanding a second, more modern philosophical problem about rules that readers will have no doubt posed themselves by this point. Algorithms and laws are still central to our understanding of rules, but whatever happened to the third member of the ancient trio, models or paradigms?

Right through the end of the eighteenth century, this now-extinct meaning of rules was robust in both precept and practice. In the course of the nineteenth and twentieth centuries, however, rules-as-algorithms increasingly edged out rules-as-paradigms. This shift spawned a second modern philosophical problem about thin rules: can rules be followed unequivocally, without interpretation or contextualization, and if so, how is this possible? As we shall see in Chapter 5, this is a problem that can hardly even be formulated until the prototypical rule shifted from being a model or paradigm to being an algorithm, especially an algorithm executed by a machine. This shift is remarkably recent, and its consequences are still reverberating in philosophy, administration, military strategy, and the ever-expanding domains of daily life conducted online.

Although algorithms are as old as the operations of arithmetic and the associations of rules with quantitative exactitude stretch back to Greco-Roman antiquity and beyond, algorithms were rarely the primary sense of rule in the intellectual traditions stemming from ancient Mediterranean cultures, even in mathematics. When dictionaries of European vernaculars began to be published in the seventeenth and eighteenth centuries, algorithm featured as the third or fourth definition under the lemma "Rules"—if it appeared at all. The most comprehensive mathematical encyclopedia of the nineteenth century, a seven-volume German behemoth, did not even contain an entry for "Algorithm."[2] Yet only a few decades after its publication, algorithms had become central to understanding the essence of mathematical proof, and by the mid-twentieth century they were powering the computer revolution and conjuring dreams of everything from artificial intelligence to artificial life. We are now all subjects of the empire of algorithms. This empire was barely a dot on the conceptual map until the early nineteenth century. Algorithms play an important role in many mathematical traditions all over the world, some quite ancient, and material aids to calculation such as pebbles, counting rods, and knotted strings are also widespread (Chapter 4). But the idea that many forms of human labor, including mental labor, might be reduced to algorithms, much less algorithms mechanically executed, seems to have taken hold only in the nineteenth century (Chapter 5). Before remarkable experiments applied the economic principles of the division of labor to monumental calculation projects during the French Revolution, the mechanization of rules, even the humble algorithms of arithmetic, had seemed a doomed project. The calculating machines invented by Blaise Pascal (1623–1662), Gottfried Wilhelm Leibniz (1646–1716), and others in the seventeenth century remained little more than ingenious toys, finicky and unreliable.[3] The improbable rise of the algorithm and its transformation from trivial arithmetic operation to safeguard of mathematical rigor to endlessly adaptable programming language for computers is a story that has been told often and well.[4] However, the triumph of algorithms-for-everything has obscured how narrowly algorithms were still associated with calculation as late as the mid-twentieth century, even by computer pioneers such as the American physicist Howard Aiken (1900–1973), who famously opined that a few computers ought to suffice for the needs of the nation—by which he meant the needs of massive calculation for undertakings like the U.S. census.[5] One aim of this book is to throw light on a crucial earlier episode in this rags-to-riches history: how mathematical algorithms intersected with political economy during the Industrial Revolution, a story that is as much about the history of work and machines as it is about the history of calculation.

Rules were many things before they became first and foremost algorithms, i.e., instructions subdivided into steps so small and unambiguous that even a machine could execute them. Some of these earlier genres of rules would still be readily recognizable as such, including laws, rituals, and recipes. But perhaps the most central meaning of rule from antiquity through the Enlightenment is no longer associated with rules at all: the rule as model or paradigm. Indeed, in twentieth-century philosophy, this once-primary sense of rule, listed first in dictionary entries well into the eighteenth century and still invoked by Immanuel Kant (1724–1804), is diametrically *opposed* to rules.

What kind of model could serve as a rule? The model could be a person who embodies the order rules sustain, such as the abbot of a monastery in the Rule of Saint Benedict (Chapter 2), or a work of art or literature that defines a genre by exemplum, in the way that the *Iliad* defined the epic in the tradition from the *Aeneid* to *Paradise Lost*, or a well-chosen example in grammar or algebra that teaches the salient properties of a much larger class of verbs or word problems. Whatever form the model takes, it must point beyond itself. Mastering the competence embodied by the model goes well beyond being able to copy the model in all its details. Models are to be emulated, not imitated. A writer who reproduced a famous work of literature word-for-word, as in the Borges story in which the protagonist attempts to produce parts of Miguel de Cervantes's *Don Quixote* verbatim,[6] would not be following but rather repeating the rule-as-model. To follow such a rule involves understanding which aspects of the model are essential and which are merely accidental details. Only the essential features can forge a reliable analogical chain between the rule-as-model and new applications. Reasoning from precedent in common law traditions supplies a familiar example of rules-as-models in analogical action. Not every past case of manslaughter can be plausibly presented as a precedent for the one at hand, and not every detail of even a convincing precedent will match up with the present case. The way seasoned jurists deliberate over legal precedents highlights the difference between a mere example (this or that manslaughter case) and a model or paradigm (a load-bearing precedent with broad implications for many manslaughter cases). The serviceable paradigm must exhibit a high ratio of essential to accidental details and radiate as many analogies as a porcupine does quills.

The modern locus classicus for the opposition between rules and paradigms in philosophy is historian and philosopher of science Thomas Kuhn's (1922–96) influential *Structure of Scientific Revolutions* (1962), a book that sold hundreds of thousands of copies and was once a fixture in university courses across the disciplines.[7] It was also the book that turned *paradigm* into a household word and the stuff of *New Yorker* cartoons. (Fig. 1.1.) According to Kuhn, a science becomes worthy of the name when it acquires its first paradigm; scientists learn how to solve problems and indeed what constitutes a problem by textbook paradigms; scientific revolutions are nothing more or less than the dethronement of one paradigm by another. Just because it was such an all-purpose tool, the word *paradigm* had many meanings in Kuhn's book, twenty-one by one count.[8] There was, however, one sense of *paradigm* that Kuhn himself consistently underscored as the most important, namely paradigms as exemplars, as *opposed* to sets of rules. In his 1969 postscript to *The Structure of Scientific Revolutions*, Kuhn described this sense of paradigm as "models or examples, [that] can replace explicit rules as a basis for the solution of the remaining puzzles of normal science" as philosophically "deeper" than the others,[9] even though he was at a loss to explain exactly how it worked. Forestalling charges of irrationalism and woolly-mindedness, he stoutly defended the knowledge transmitted by paradigms as genuine knowledge: "When I speak of knowledge embedded in shared exemplars, I am not referring to a mode of knowing that is less systematic or less analyzable than knowledge embedded in rules, laws, or criteria of identification." But to date, neither Kuhn nor anyone else has succeeded in clarifying that

"I'm afraid you've had a paradigm shift."

FIGURE 1.1. Kuhn's paradigm shifts become proverbial, *The New Yorker* (17 December 2001). J. C. Duffy / The New Yorker Collection / The Cartoon Bank.

alternative mode of knowing, a "perplexity," philosopher Ian Hacking concluded, "in the nature of the beast."[10]

Kuhn's perplexity about how to reconcile the knowledge of paradigms with that of explicit rules already had an illustrious philosophical pedigree by 1969. In his *Philosophical Investigations* (1953), Ludwig Wittgenstein (1889–1951) famously argued for the incorrigible ambiguity of even mathematical rules: how is it possible to follow rules, he asked, even the most formal and algorithmic rules, without setting off an infinite regress of interpretations of the rule? Wittgenstein concluded that to follow a rule is a practice, taught by example rather than by precept within a community of users: "To obey a rule, to make a report, to give an order, to play a game of chess, are *customs* (uses, institutions)."[11] Ironically (and possibly unwittingly), Wittgenstein's proposal returns the rule back to its original meaning as a model taught by practice rather than by precept. But for his many readers, including Kuhn, explicit rules, epitomized by the mathematical algorithm, were the polar opposite of paradigms and practices.

So it comes as something of a shock to learn that for most of its history, the word for "rule" and its cognates in ancient and modern European languages, from ancient Greece and Rome through the Enlightenment, were synonymous with *paradigm*.[12] Here, for example, is the Roman encyclopedist Pliny the Elder (c. 23–79 CE), upholding the Greek sculptor Polykleitos's (c. 480–c. 420 BCE) statue *Doryphoros* (*The Spear Bearer*) as the *canona* (the Latinized version of the Greek word for rule, *kanon*), the model of male beauty worthy of imitation by all artists: "He also made what artists call a 'Canon' or 'Model Statue,' as they draw their artistic outlines from it as from a sort of standard."[13] (Fig. 1.2.) Or Dionysius of Halicarnassus (c. 60–c. 7 BCE) praising the fifth-century BCE Attic orator Lysias (c. 445–c. 380 BCE) as the *kanon* of rhetoric, immediately glossed in the next sentence as the paradigm (*paradeigma*) of excellence.[14] Or, fast-forwarding almost two thousand years to Enlightenment France, here is the *Encyclopédie*'s sample sentence for its first definition of the entry "*Règle, Modèle*": "the life of Our Savior is the *rule* or the *model* for Christians."[15] In both ancient Greek and Latin grammars, the words *kanon* and *regula* were used along with *paradeigma* to denote that paradigm of paradigms, the patterns of inflections such as verb conjugations intoned by schoolchildren over the centuries: *amo, amas, amat*, etc.

At first glance, this may seem to be yet one more intriguing example of the *bizarrerie* of languages, in which words occasionally flip-flop into their opposites, but no more than that. Once upon a time, long ago, a word meant *A*; now it means not-*A*. Rule (*kanon, regula*) once meant model or paradigm; now it means exactly the opposite: hence Kuhn's conundrum of how to clarify paradigms without reducing them to rules, i.e., without reducing *A* to not-*A*—and also the provocatively paradoxical quality of Wittgenstein's equation of rule-following with usage and custom.

FIGURE 1.2. Roman copy of Polykleitos's *Doryphoros* (The Spear Bearer,
1st c. BCE), called the "canon" of artists by Pliny the Elder. Courtesy of the Ministry
of Culture, National Archaeological Museum of Naples. Photo by Giorgio Albano.

But the etymology of the pre-modern cognates for "rule" is both richer and more unsettling than this developmental account from meaning *A* to meaning not-*A* would suggest: the more familiar modern associations of the word are *also* part of the definition of the pre-modern cognates of "rule." The ancient Greek word *kanon*, for example, connoted painstaking exactitude, especially in connection with the arts of building and carpentry, but also in a figurative sense when applied to other domains such as art, politics, music, and astronomy. The same Polykleitos who fashioned the *Doryphoros* statue was the author of a lost treatise entitled *Kanon* in which he allegedly specified the exact proportions of the human body to be followed by artists; such prescriptive measurements of classical statues were still on display in the eighteenth century. (Fig. 1.3.) Via Greek physician and philosopher Galen's (129–c. 210 CE) reference to Polykleitos, the word and concept of a canonical body was taken up by Andreas Vesalius (1514–1564) and other early modern anatomists.[16] (Fig. 1.4.) Variants of the word *kanon* also turn up in ancient astronomy and harmonics, both mathematical sciences. The range of the Latin *regula* followed that of the Greek *kanon* closely.[17] This cluster of meanings evokes the rigor of mathematics, both as the geometric doctrine of proportions and as the tool of measurement and computation—meanings that happily co-existed with the cluster centered on models and paradigms. In short, for several millennia, in various ancient and modern European languages, the word *rule* and its cognates meant, at least according to modern lights, *A* and not-*A* simultaneously. This is no longer just a linguistic curiosity; it is mind-boggling.

A second aim of this book is to reconstruct the lost coherence of the category of rule that could for so long and apparently without any sense of contradiction embrace meanings that now seem antonymical to each other (Chapters 2 and 3). In many ways, this is the obverse of the first aim, namely to follow the spectacular career of the algorithm since the nineteenth century. Algorithms not only replaced paradigms as the quintessential rules; they also increasingly made the workings of paradigms seem inscrutable,

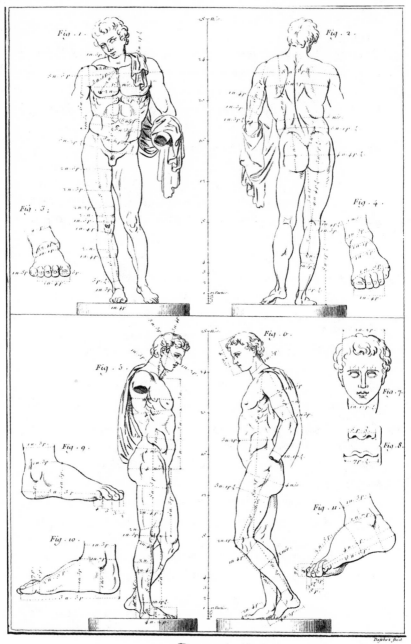

Dessein,
Proportions de la statue d'Antinoüs.

FIGURE 1.3. Measured proportions of the statue of Antinous (article "Dessein"), *Encyclopédie, ou Dictionnaire raisonné des sciences, des arts et des métiers* [Encyclopedia, or systematic Dictionary of sciences, arts, and trades], ed. Jean d'Alembert and Denis Diderot, vol. 3 (1763).

intuitive, and opaque to rational scrutiny. These were the disreputable associations against which Kuhn struggled as he defended the centrality of paradigms to successful science, and they continue to vex all attempts to defend the prerogatives of judgment against more mechanical modes of assessment. It is extraordinary that the faculty Kant asserted to be the precondition for understanding the unity of nature in time and space[18] should instead come to be belittled as "merely subjective." In contemporary parlance, a "judgment call" is one without firm grounding in public reason, only a step away from private whim. The flexible rule became the flabby rule—or no rule at all. Seen in the broader context of the demotion of judgment from exercise in reason to indulgence in darkling subjectivity, this episode in the history of rules forms part of the modern history of rationality, itself now defined by rules.[19]

Universals and Particulars

Rules rally judgment because their application must bridge universals and particulars. First, we must judge whether *this* rule subsumes *this* particular—or should we apply another rule altogether? This is the dilemma confronted by a judge seeking apposite precedents in the common law legal system or the doctor making a diagnosis from equivocal symptoms or even the math student seeking the integral of a novel function. Although in many cases the choice of which rule fits this instance is clear-cut (meter maids are seldom in doubt as to which traffic law applies to which parking violation), in many other cases there is an *embarras de règles*— and still more frequently, a welter of particulars that don't seem to fit any rule. Second, even if rule and particular clearly match, they almost never align perfectly. To a greater or lesser extent, tailoring and tweaking will be necessary to smooth over the gap between universal and particular. Whole specialties of learned practice have taken root and blossomed in this gap: equity in the law, casuistry in theology and ethics, case histories in medicine, discretion in administration.

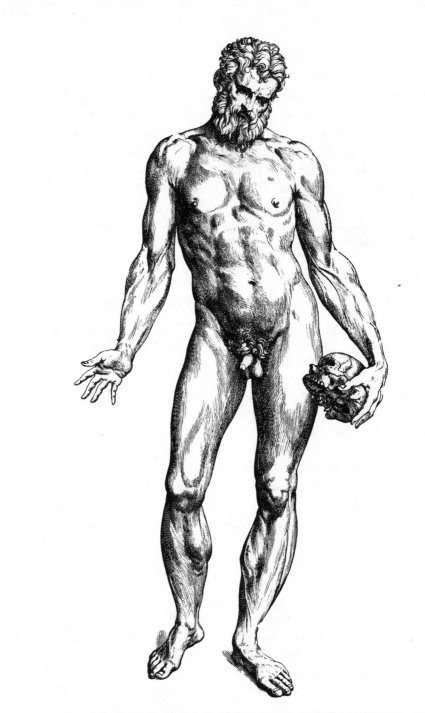

FIGURE 1.4. Andreas Vesalius's canonical male and female bodies, *De humani corporis fabrica. Epitome* [Brief summary of *On the fabric of the human body*] (1543).

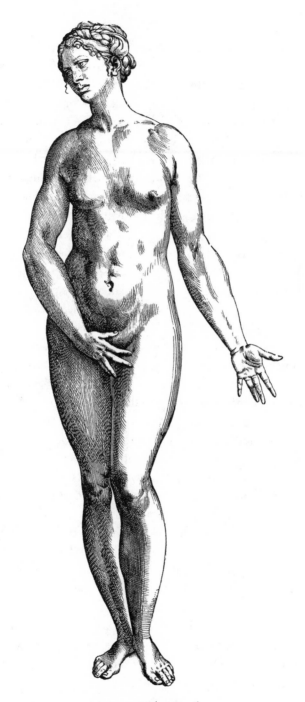

FIGURE 1.4. (*continued*)

The third aim of this book is to examine how rules were framed in order to anticipate and facilitate bridge-building between universal and particulars. This investigation calls for casting nets wide in order to catch many different kinds of rules for the sake of comparison: rules for monastic orders, games, parliamentary procedure, cooking, waging war, composing rondos and canons, converting weights and measures, etiquette, traffic circulation, who can wear what kind of luxury garment and when. In addition, there are the laws of nations and the laws of nature, both significant ideals but also counter-ideals to the more mundane and less general rules known as regulations. In contrast to the remote majesty of laws, both human and divine, regulations hug the terrain of practice, which is parceled into distinct domains of application. This rainbow of rules—from the laconic to the loquacious, the local to the global, the specific to the general—applies pressure to the bland philosophical categories of "universals" and "particulars." Some universals are more universal than others, and some particulars more particular. Both *modus ponens* in logic and the sumptuary laws promulgated by the Italian city-state of Ferrara in 1460 are rules, but whereas "if p, then q; p; therefore q" holds everywhere and for any and all p's and q's, the Ferrarese ban on silk and ermine in women's clothing is at once more specific, local, and lengthy than the terse generalities of propositional logic.[20] We will need a more refined taxonomy of both universals and particulars in order to understand the differences between the bridges that span them, some as simple and supple as rope bridges and others as rigid and sturdy as a steel-girdered monument to modern engineering.

More specifically, close attention to just what kind of bridge connects what variety of rule to what manner of case will illuminate the contrasting intellectual and cultural preconditions for rules-as-paradigms and rules-as-algorithms. Because these kinds of rules coexisted for so long—and arguably still do so today, despite the ascent of the algorithm—these preconditions cannot be mutually exclusive. Nonetheless, certain historical trends, such as the standardization of everything from weights and measures to spelling to time zones, have also favored the standardization of rules: artificially imposed uniformity can mimic natural universality, at least under the historically exceptional conditions of stable infrastructure and sturdy international agreements. Other trends, such as the increasing rationalization of work in industrialized societies, as well as ideals of natural law imported from theology into natural philosophy and from there into jurisprudence and ethics, have also promoted rules of ambitious globality and exactitude. Proliferating especially (but not exclusively) in urban settings in the modern era, these rules appeal ever more to universal principles (whether of the market or the rights of man) and ever less to local context and background knowledge. Not coincidentally, the rise of such ambitious rules begins with the expansion of trade and empire to global dimensions in the sixteenth century, which created both the need for and the means to enforce rules that transcended any one locality.

Whether such rules actually achieve the universality and precision to which their framers aspire is a question furiously debated within the human sciences, the economists and many sociologists arguing forcefully for the affirmative and the historians and anthropologists just as vehemently for the negative.[21] My position is that even if the historians and anthropologists are correct in their claim that the efficacy of rules that purport to transcend context and interpretation is an illusion, it is undeniably a mighty and widespread illusion, one that cries out for explanation—all the more so if it is indeed contradicted by reality. This book gives both sides of the argument their due by showing that the degree to which rules can (or cannot) transcend local context depends on the historical preconditions that do (or do not) sustain islands of stability, uniformity, and predictability in an intrinsically uncertain world. The historical preconditions that link these islands into a far-flung archipelago, whether by empire, treaty, or trade, are even more precarious. Even the most routinized and reliable global rules can without warning shrink to local dimensions, as the havoc wrought with international air travel during the outbreak of the SARS-CoV-2 pandemic in 2020 illustrates. When rule-governed world orders do come into being, the rules depend on the order just as crucially as the order does on the rules.

A History of the Self-Evident

Debates about rules overflow the academy. We fret endlessly about whether there are too many rules or not enough, whether rules are too stringent or too lax, when they apply and who decides, and the optimal balance between predictability and spontaneity. The varying frequency and intensity of such debates are themselves historical phenomena, prima facie evidence for the multiplication and stiffening of all kinds of rules in societies that depend on the intricate coordination of innumerable actors, whether drivers on the highway, voters in national elections, or everyone from meteorologists to farmers to truckers to salespeople in long-distance commerce. Rules choreograph what ought to be a ballet but sometimes looks more like a free-for-all—or a tableau vivant of figures frozen into position like statues. Sociologists of bureaucracy have invented terms like "rule strain" and "rule drift" to describe pathologies of highly regulated polities;[22] ingenious public sector employees have exploited those same pathologies by the work-to-rule strike, in which scrupulous adherence to all the rules brings all business to a screeching halt.[23]

No doubt there have always been complaints about specific rules and their enforcement. What is novel about the modern predicament are complaints about the sheer number and inflexibility of rules, whether the rules in question are the overt regulations of government or the covert algorithms of computer search engines. We moderns cannot live without rules. But we also cannot live with them, at least not comfortably. Twentieth-century imaginative literature has given us adjectives like *Kafkaesque*; social theory, images like Max Weber's "iron cage," both referring to modern bureaucracies. Twenty-first-century writers and theorists fantasize about a brave new world run by computer algorithms that infiltrate every aspect of life, down to our very thought processes.[24] Are there qualities of modern rules—their alleged complexity, inflexibility, inefficiency, and sheer prolixity—that notch up the ubiquitous tensions between imperious universals and recalcitrant particulars, between order and freedom? And whether or not this is fact or simply perception, what historical shifts in how we make rules and think about them explain our current anxious preoccupation with them? The shift from rule-as-model to rule-as-algorithm offers at least partial answers to these questions: by driving the exercise of discretion underground, rules-as-algorithms blow up the bridges that connected universals to particulars in rules-as-models.

This book is a history in both ancient and modern senses of the word.[25] It is an inquiry, in the far-ranging sense in which Herodotus used the term *historia*. Moreover, despite the universal pretensions of its subject matter, it teems with particulars, as in Aristotle's (384–322 BCE) sense of *historia*, which he opposed to the universals of philosophy (and poetry). Finally, it is a history in the more familiar sense of a narrative that unfolds in time. But it is an incomplete history on all three counts. An inquiry that pursues so gargantuan a topic over more than two millennia and several languages will be of necessity selective. Even the multitude of particulars served up in these pages is only a sliver of the universe of possibilities. The scope of the narrative is regrettably and regretfully limited to what is somewhat misleadingly called the Western tradition, simply because it is the one I know best. But I have tried to draw upon comparative scholarship about other traditions, rich in their own fascinations, wherever it seems illuminating to do so. If readers are prompted to ask about rules of other kinds, in other times and places, so much the better: the book is an invitation to further inquiry and debate about rules at their most diverse. Chronological coverage is also spotty, for much the same reasons. In order to discern the arc of *longue durée* developments, I have been obliged to hopscotch among centuries and genres in a fashion that will probably induce a certain queasy motion sickness among my fellow historians, accustomed for good reason to settle into one period and place. I must, however, crave their indulgence. Only by taking a panoramic view can I sharpen contrasts, pinpoint moments of transition, and, most important, use the resources of history to query the self-evidence of our contemporary habits of thought.

One of the uses of history, especially history pursued on a longer time scale, is to unsettle present certainties and thereby enlarge our sense of the thinkable. It is a curious property of the reigning conceptual milieu to appear coherent and inevitable to its inhabitants, in much the way that local customs seem self-evident to provincials who never leave home. Simply knowing in principle that the way we think now is the product of historical contingency rather than of logical necessity is rarely sufficient to lift the blinders imposed by history and habit. The mental world we happen to inhabit contracts the imagination to its own cramped dimensions. One epoch's self-evidence—how could anyone think otherwise?—is another's perplexity—what *were* they thinking? Vivid counter-examples drawn from other times and places must often be enlisted to drive a wedge between concepts that are routinely conflated in current usage: between the universal and the uniform, the specific and the rigid, the algorithmic and the mechanical, the mechanical and the mindless, the discretionary and the subjective. Examples can also help to reunite what modern philosophy has put asunder: rule and paradigm. Here history makes common cause with philosophy in the work of clarifying, expanding, and opening up conceptual possibilities. Philosophy faces the further daunting challenge of originating new concepts, not just criticizing old ones. The concepts of the past can seldom be stretched far enough to cover the needs of the present, just because they are the creations of and for the past. But although history can no more resurrect dead concepts than it can dead people, it can briefly reanimate them: revenants, who trouble the complacency of the living with their revelations.

2

Ancient Rules

STRAIGHTEDGES, MODELS, AND LAWS

Three Semantic Clusters

In the wetlands of the Mediterranean and the dunes of the Middle East grows the giant cane plant (*Arundo donax*), tall as a tree and arrow-straight. (Fig. 2.1.) For thousands of years in this region its ramrod stalks have been used to make baskets, flutes, balance scale beams, and measuring rods.[1] The ancient Greek word for "rule," *kanon*, derives from the Semitic word (cognate with the ancient Hebrew *qaneh*) for this plant, and its earliest attested uses refer to rods of various kinds and later to straightedges. Its ancient Latin equivalent, *regula*, has analogous associations with straight planks and wands and, more metaphorically, to that which upholds and directs (as in *regere*, to rule, or *rex*, king), juxtapositions still audible in the ambiguities of the English word *ruler*.[2] In archaic Greek sources, the earliest surviving occurrences of *kanon* appear in the context of all kinds of construction work: masons, carpenters, stonecutters, and architects all use a *kanon*, or straightedge, to make sure that building materials are straight and fit together neatly. The *kanon* served the painstaking exactitude needed to put together a solid, straight, symmetric house, temple, wall, or other structure. The straightedge or ruler (which may or may not be marked with

FIGURE 2.1. Giant cane plant (*Arundo donax*). Otto Wilhelm Thoma, *Flora von Deutschland, Österreich und der Schweiz* [Plants of Germany, Austria, and Switzerland] (1885).

measuring units) and the compass were the emblematic tools of the builder and the geometer and remained so for millennia. (Fig. 2.2.) So strong was this Ur-sense of rule as straightedge, literally and metaphorically unbending, that the comic ancient Greek playwright Aristophanes could bank on getting a laugh from his audience by having an astronomer use a "curved *kanon*"—a patent absurdity.[3]

Three principal semantic clusters branched from this reedy stem *kanon* in ancient Greek: meticulous and often mathematical exactitude; models or patterns for imitation; and laws or decrees.

GEOMETRIA.

Ioan. Sadler scalp.
et excudit.

M. de Vos figura.

Terrarum spatia & metas Geometria ponit
Distinguitq̃ plagas, montesq̃ ac flumina lustrat.

FIGURE 2.2. Allegorical representation of Geometry, with her emblemata of
straightedge and compass (c. 1570–1600). Johann Sadeler, *Geometria*,
Metropolitan Museum of Art, New York.

Because the meanings of the Latin word *regula,* and through it, also of the words for "rule" in modern European vernaculars (Italian *regola,* Spanish *regla,* French *règle,* German *Regel,* Dutch *regel*), track those of the Greek *kanon* for many centuries, it is worth examining each of these three clusters in more detail.

It is a short step from the straightedges and measuring rods of builders and carpenters to other applications of geometric proportions and calculations, especially in the ancient exact sciences of astronomy and harmonics. The Pythagorean musical doctrine of harmonic intervals was known as *kanonike,* specifying the ratios of the lengths of strings that produce various chords; the monochord, a single-stringed musical instrument with a movable bridge that demonstrated these principles, was sometimes called a *kanon harmonikos.*[4] As we saw in Chapter 1, a lost treatise by the Greek sculptor Polykleitos titled *Kanon* allegedly specified the exact proportions of the ideal male body, inspiring speculative reconstructions for centuries thereafter.[5] Closer to arithmetic and calculation rather than to geometric proportions were the uses to which the word *kanon* was put in astronomy. The tables supplied by the Alexandrian astronomer Ptolemy (2nd c. CE) in his *Mathematical Syntaxis* (also known as the *Almagest*) and later republished separately as "Handy Tables" (*Procheiroi Kanones*) offered tools for the computation of astronomical values (e.g., planetary positions) based on the models of the *Almagest.*[6] Ptolemy's *kanones* were enormously influential in medieval and early modern astronomy in both the Christian and Islamic worlds and lent their name to all astronomical and astrological tables thereafter. The Greek word *kanon* was adopted in medieval Arabic and Persian astronomical treatises as *qanun* (as in the *Al-Qānūn al-Mas'ūdi* of the great Persian polymath Abu Rayhan al-Biruni [973–c. 1050], a compilation of astronomical knowledge)[7] and was still in use in English (canon) to refer to an astronomical table in the late seventeenth century.[8] Since astronomy was probably the most calculation-intensive activity until the rise of mathematically based insurance in the nineteenth century, and since tables such as Ptolemy's and their many imitators were primarily intended to facilitate calculation, this use of the word *kanon* had already attached it firmly to computation in late antiquity and throughout the medieval and early modern periods—but to computation done by astronomers and mathematicians, not machines.

The second cluster of meanings also leans on the core meaning of *kanon* or *regula* as a standard that assesses straightness or, in a metaphorical sense, rectitude or correctness. But in this case the standard is to be imitated, not measured. Whereas Galen understood Polykleitos's *Kanon* as a (by then lost) treatise providing proportions of the ideal male body to guide sculptors, Pliny the Elder, as we have also seen in Chapter 1, interpreted Polykleitos's actual sculpture of a male nude, the *Doryphoros* (*Spear Bearer*) as the *kanon* of artists, the model for them to imitate.[9] The meaning of *kanon* as imitation of a model, especially of a human being, emerges during the Hellenistic period (4th–1st cs. BCE) first in connection with rhetoric, upholding one or another orator as the pinnacle of eloquence, a sense that Pliny carries over to Polykleitos's *Doryphoros*, the very model of artistically rendered male beauty. In a similar vein, the ancient Greek biographer Plutarch (1st–2nd cs. CE) warns young readers against emulating characters in poetry as models of virtue, contrary to the intention of the poet.[10] In these contexts, *paradeigma* (example) often shadows *kanon*: *paradeigmata* could simply be "examples," the sense in which Aristotle uses the word in the *Rhetoric*,[11] but they could also be physical models, especially in the context of architecture.[12] (Fig. 2.3.) Plato (5th–4th cs. BCE) used the word in this sense in the *Timaeus* when he compared the eternal models of the divine craftsman and those of the human craftsmen who merely imitate them.[13] Like the link between rule and computation, that between rule and paradigm or model also proved remarkably enduring, playing out its grand final scene in Immanuel Kant's 1790 account of genius as "that which gives the rule [*Regel*] to art" by means of the "models [*Muster*] . . . [that] must serve others for this, i.e., as a standard or rule [*Richtmaße oder Regel*] by which to judge."[14] Eighteen hundred

FIGURE 2.3. Ancient Etruscan architectural model of the temple Vulci
(c. 300 BCE). Museo Nazionale di Villa Giulia, Rome.

years after Pliny's elevation of the *Doryphoros* as the canon of artists, the idea of the rule as a model to imitate was still reverberating
in aesthetic theory.

The third cluster, which connects *kanon* with *nomos* in Greek
and *regula* with *lex* and *jus* in Latin, rule with law, proved even
more long-lived. In ancient Greek, both *nomos* (law or custom, but
originally land allotment or pasturage) and *kanon* (which could
refer to a rope stretched taut, a literal guideline) formed a triad
with *horos* (boundary). All three took on the figurative meaning
of a limit that could not be breached without sanction. Especially
in the context of arts such as architecture or medicine, and later
among the grammarians, *kanon* came to mean "rule."[15] Early
Christian writers such as Clement of Alexandria (2nd–3rd cs. CE)

sometimes used *kanon* to refer to the Gospels, and by the 4th century CE, Athanasius (c. 298–373 CE) and other church fathers had extended the word's meaning to a list of those books of scripture considered to be divinely inspired and therefore "canonical."[16] During the same period, the early Christian church, especially in the Greek-speaking eastern Roman Empire, began to use the word *canon* to refer to decrees made by various councils and synods to govern matters such as the liturgical calendar, the sacraments of baptism and the eucharist, and fast days. By the fifth century, these collections of rules or "canons" were systematized into "canon law."[17] Already by the late second century, patristic writers were also using the phrase "rule of truth" in Greek and later Latin (*kanon tes aletheias, regula veritatis*) to draw a bold line between orthodoxy and heterodoxy.[18]

After Roman emperor Constantine I (3rd–4th cs. CE) decreed toleration of Christianity in 313 CE, the terminology of church law began to interweave with that of Roman law. The 6th century CE *Novels* and *Digest* of Emperor Justinian I (c. 483–565 CE), for example, refer frequently to *kanones*, often equating *nomos* and *kanon*.[19] The ramifications of the Latin word *regula*, like *kanon* originally the word for straightedge and later more generally for rule, retraced many of the wider associations of its Greek equivalent. In association with the Latin word *norma* (perhaps from the Greek word *gnomon*, a vertical staff perpendicular to the horizon and later a carpenter's tool to make right angles), *regula* expanded its connotations from straight planks used in building construction to models in rhetoric to rules in grammar and law.[20]

In the field of Roman law, however, *regula* took on a special meaning with no close Greek equivalent but with important consequences for later understandings of rules more generally. The *regula iuris* applied to a particular case but also summarized other, similar cases. In the late Roman republic, jurists collected these *regulae* as pithy distillations of earlier cases, associated with one another by analogy. The fiftieth and final book of Justinian's *Digest* contains 211 of these rules under the rubric *De diversis regulis juris antiqui* (Diverse rules of older law); books of such rules (*libri regularum*) circulated for the use of officials with scant legal training throughout the Roman Empire. Chapters of Book 50 dealt with topics such as citizenship of cities, taxes, and administration of public property, all relevant to the duties of provincial governors. Medieval commentators on Roman law treated these rules as general maxims and wrote copious glosses on them.[21] Several aspects of these rules for practitioners were pregnant with things to come: first, the attempts to derive a rule of thumb from precedents linked by analogy; second, the explicitly inferior status of rules with respect to law, both in dignity and generality; third, the prominently featured exemplary individual case (as opposed to the general principle); and fourth, the emphasis on brevity and practice.[22] As the Roman jurist Paulus (3rd c. CE) explained in a passage excerpted in the last book of the *Digest*: "A rule is a statement, in a few words, of the course to be followed in the matter under discussion. The law, however, is not derived from the rule, but the rule is established by the law."[23] Common law, casuistry, and the liberal and mechanical arts all came to inhabit the territory staked out by the Roman *libri regularum*. They all depended on rules that got things done in the world, consistent with but not deduced from higher principles and often in the form of an example extended by analogy.

The first and third semantic clusters that in Greco-Roman antiquity connected rules with exactitude and laws, respectively, are still recognizable in broad outline to denizens of the twenty-first century. Although we may no longer call astronomical tables and straightedges by the same name, we immediately understand how rules relate to measurement and computation and, in a more figurative sense, to all activities that demand punctilious attention to detail and accuracy in their execution. Similarly, rules and laws still flock together in modern law and administration, still honoring the rough-and-ready hierarchy defined by Paulus and other Roman jurists. Moreover, we have no difficulty retracing the links in the chain of associations that bound the rules of the architects and carpenters with those of astronomers and grammarians and ultimately with those of judges and lawyers. Rules of all sorts govern, constrain, specify, guide, and otherwise order action into rituals and routines. Rules dictate what to do when with whom and how, and they do so down to the last comma, in the imperative. Emblem of the strait and narrow, the image of the giant cane plant might still serve, thousands of years later, to symbolize the essence of rules. Rules rule.

Only the second cluster, connecting rules with imitation, models, and paradigms, mystifies us, although, as we have seen, Kant could still invoke this sense of rule at the end of the eighteenth century in his *Critique of Judgment*. What finally snapped the thread of historical continuity, so sturdily spun in the case of the first and third clusters? Why did model and paradigm not only disappear from the list of synonyms for rule but actually become its antonyms? How did it become possible, indeed self-evident, to oppose rules and paradigms as immiscible ways of knowing, a leitmotif of twentieth-century philosophy? The eclipse of the second cluster will occupy us for much of the rest of this book, especially in Chapters 5 and 8. But before charting its decline, we must pay homage to its rise: the spectacular career of rule-as-model in late antiquity and the Latin Middle Ages, epitomized by the success of the Rule of Saint Benedict as a blueprint for Christian monastic communities.

The Rule Is the Abbot

It is midday, the hour of sext, at the Benedictine monastery of Monte Cassino in what is now southern Italy. (Fig. 2.4.) It could be the mid-sixth century, soon after Benedict of Nursia (480–547 CE) had founded the monastery, or hundreds of years later, or at a Benedictine monastery in Canterbury or Arizona: much the same order would govern the monks' day anywhere, any century.[24] At the sixth hour of the day from Easter to Pentecost and the ninth hour on Wednesdays and Fridays for the rest of the summer until

FIGURE 2.4. Saint Benedict eating with the monks (Giovanni Antonio Bazzi [Il Sodoma], detail of fresco *Life of Saint Benedict* at the Benedictine abbey of Monte Oliveto Maggiore, Abbazia, Italy, 1505).

September 13, the monks gather for the main meal of the day: two cooked dishes, supplemented by a daily ration of a pound of bread, all washed down with one, and only one, *hemina* of wine.[25] They eat in silence, except for the voice of the monk reading aloud from the Bible—four or five pages, but not from the Heptateuch or the Book of Kings (too exciting for monks of weak character). Those who arrive too late or depart too early at meals are twice chided; recalcitrant offenders must sit by themselves and are denied their cup of wine. No one may eat or drink except at mealtimes. In winter, the monks must rise from their beds at the eighth hour of the night to celebrate vigils; each monk sleeps in his own bed, clothed and belted, in a common dormitory in which a light burns until morning. All the monks must perform kitchen duties once a week, including washing all the towels and serving the other monks at the single meal of the day. Equally specific is the graduated scale of punishments for infractions, from being excluded from mealtimes to ejection from the monastery.[26] The seventy-three chapters (*praecepta*) of the Rule of Saint Benedict seem to regulate every moment and every aspect of monastic life in maniacal detail. If micro-managers have a patron saint, it is surely Saint Benedict.

The Rule of Saint Benedict, written circa 535–545 CE, was not the first set of regulations governing monastic communities. Cenobite or communal monasticism, in contrast to the anchorite variety practiced by solitary ascetics in the Egyptian desert, originated in the Greek-speaking eastern Christian church in the 4th century CE and was brought to Marseilles and other parts of western Europe by theologian and mystic John Cassian (c. 360–c. 435 CE). Benedict's Rule drew upon several earlier sets of cenobite regulations, including the Rules of Saint Basil (330–379 CE), Saint Augustine (354–430 CE), and, especially, the anonymous *Regula Magistri* (Rule of the Master, probably composed c. 500–530 CE in Provence). These earlier guidelines varied greatly in length, format, and degree of detail, from the catechism-like Rule of Saint Basil to the ninety-five chapters of the Rule of the Master.[27] There is no indication that Benedict considered his Rule to be either original or definitive. On the contrary, he concluded with the modest caution that his precepts were intended for beginners in monastic life, to be supplemented by the Rule of Saint Basil and the writings and lives of the church fathers. Yet it was the Rule of Saint Benedict that was to become the founding constitution of all monastic communities in western Christendom down to the present day.[28] Its longevity and broad diffusion are almost without parallel in the history of institutions, in stark contrast to the notoriously short life spans of most ideal communities created as retreats from society at large. What accounted for its extraordinary resilience and adaptability?

The answer lies, improbably, in the very detail of the Rule's seventy-three precepts and the discretion they invited in application. Because we moderns equate specific rules with rigid ones, this claim seems paradoxical: micro-managers (and regulators) heap up detail in order to minimize discretion. But much of the detail so minutely described in the Rule of Saint Benedict actually loosened the hold of the positive directives. Let us return to mealtime at the monastery. The monks have drained their one *hemina* of wine to the dregs; surely there is no ambiguity here about either measure or daily portion? But it is high summer, and the monks have labored long in the fields under a brazen sun: "When the work is harder, it lies in the discretion and responsibility of the abbot to give more, if it does good." Or the strict rule of silence to be observed at meals: "Anyone who violates this rule of silence will be severely punished." Both tone and content are categorical—but exceptions immediately follow: "Unless talking is necessary because of a guest, or the abbot gives someone permission."[29] The Rule of Saint Benedict is peppered with provisos and exceptions, following hard on the heels of the precepts and articulated in almost as much detail. There is no precept so firm—and no infringement so heinous—that it cannot be commuted if the abbot judges that circumstances so warrant.

Monastic life revolved around the person of the abbot, who was as it were the rule of the Rule: the living model of a holy life, mentioned 120 times in the text, and responsible for every monk and every aspect of monastery activity. The abbot, whose name derives from the New Testament Aramaic word *abbas* or "father," is invested with vast amounts of discretion, a faculty praised by Benedict as the mother of all virtues (64.17–19). *Discretio* (not a classical Latin word) means the ability to draw distinctions (*discenere*) and to consider each case on its merits.[30] Over and over again the precepts of the Rule of Saint Benedict are firmly and sharply enunciated, only for the abbot's discretion to be invoked in the next sentence. For example, in Chapter 33 we are told in no uncertain terms: "No monk may possess any property, nothing whatsoever, neither book nor writing tablet nor stylus—absolutely nothing"— unless the abbot wills otherwise. Or, in Chapter 63, concerning rank in the monastery, Benedict begins in his usual unequivocal tone: "In no case may age determine rank, for did not Samuel and Daniel, albeit young, stand in judgment over the eldest?" But then, in the very next sentence, comes the usual qualification: "Unless the abbot after considered deliberation or for particular reasons" should decide to alter the usual order defined by date of entry in the monastery (63.5–7).

The abbot's discretion is by no means arbitrary. Rather, he is enjoined to adapt the rigor of the Rule to particular circumstances and to the individual capacities of the monks, for whom he will be held responsible in the eyes of God: "He represents Jesus Christ in the monastery" (2.2). At every point, he is explicitly called upon to adjust the Rule as situation dictates, e.g., with respect to food and drink: the strict portions and mealtimes may be relaxed "out of consideration for the weak" (39.1); no one may eat the flesh of four-footed animals—except the sick (39.11); everyone must take his turn in the kitchen, but the weak may receive extra help (35.3); a monk who makes a mistake in his work or who breaks or loses the monastery's property and does not immediately confess his guilt should be severely punished—unless it is a question of hidden sin, in which case the abbot may minister to the wounded soul without exposing the mistake (46.5–6). For almost every precept of the Rule, exceptions are foreseen; discretion is exercised; specific circumstances are weighed.

Accustomed as we are to the peremptory tone of modern rules, which strongly discourage the exercise of discretion at a red light or in reporting one's taxable income or paying the subway fare, we are likely to find the characteristic diction of the Rule of Saint Benedict somewhat comical, reminiscent of the pet owners who stipulate that their new puppy may under absolutely no circumstances—no, never—come sleep in their bed—unless it whines or begs prettily or scratches long enough at the door. But there is nothing weak-willed or wavering about Benedict's Rule. What to modern eyes reads as a pendulum swing between stringency and indulgence was to pre-modern sensibilities the only way to formulate a complete rule, both specific and supple. The abbot does not simply enforce the Rule; he exemplifies it, just as the *Doryphoros* statue exemplifies the canon of male beauty.

Because discretion will figure so prominently in the history of how rules are formulated and applied, it is worth briefly pausing to examine its meaning and history. Discretion is one form of judgment, though not the whole of judgment, which embraces not only knowing when to temper the rigor of rules but also matters of taste, prudence, and insight into how the world works, including the human psyche. Although the word *discretion* has a Latin root, *discretio*, derived from the verb *discerne*, meaning "to divide or to distinguish," and related to the adjective *discretus*, the root of the word *discrete*, its meanings in classical Latin hew to the literal definition.[31] But in post-classical Latin, starting in the 5th or 6th century CE, *discretio* begins to take on the additional meanings of prudence, circumspection, and discernment in weighty matters—perhaps in connection with the biblical passage 1 Corinthians 12:10, in which Saint Paul enumerates different spiritual gifts, including that of distinguishing good from evil spirits (*discretio spirituum* in the fourth-century Latin translation by Saint Jerome, a phrase that was later to become important in the persecution of false prophets, heretics, and sorcerers).[32] The sixth-century Rule of Saint Benedict exploits this extended range of meanings to the hilt. Once entrenched in usage, the meanings of the late Latin root *discretio* and its derivatives in other European languages seem to have remained remarkably constant, always associated with marking and making significant distinctions. *Discretio* accordingly flourished in the Latin of medieval scholastics, whose disputatious style of argument, framed in questions, objections, and replies, favored a sharp eye for subtle distinctions. For example, the index of the works of the great medieval theologian Thomas Aquinas (1225–1274) lists at least two hundred appearances of the word, in contexts ranging from the distinction between good and evil, the hierarchy of venal and mortal sins, and kinds of tastes and smells, as well as in connection with the virtues of prudence and modesty, the judgments of the common sense (*sensus communis*) that integrates impressions from the various sense organs into a unified object of perception in Aristotelian psychology—and also the distinction between good and evil spirits in 1 Corinthians 12:10.[33] The *Lexicon philosophicum* (1613), compiled by German philosopher Rudolph Goclenius the Elder (1547–1628) and a standard reference work for most of the seventeenth century, still covered much the same semantic territory four hundred years later: the primary meaning of *discretio* is "discrimination or distinction of one thing from another."[34]

Discretio and its vernacular cognates had two sides, already evident in the abbot's role in the Rule of Saint Benedict, the one cognitive and the other executive. To be able to distinguish between cases that differ from one another in small but crucial details is the essence of the cognitive aspect of discretion, an ability that exceeds mere analytical acuity. Discretion draws additionally upon the wisdom of experience, which teaches which distinctions make a difference in practice, not just in principle. A hypertrophy of hairsplitting is the besetting sin of scholasticism, and a mind that makes too many distinctions risks pulverizing all categories into the individuals that compose them, requiring as many rules as there are cases. In contrast, discretion preserves the classificatory scheme implied by rules—in the case of the Rule of Saint Benedict, categories such as mealtimes or work assignments—but draws meaningful distinctions within those categories—the sick monk who needs heartier nourishment; the weak monk who needs a helping hand on kitchen duty. What makes these distinctions meaningful is a combination of experience, which positions discretion in the neighborhood of prudence and other forms of practical wisdom, and certain guiding values. In the case of the Benedictine monastery these are the Christian values of compassion and charity; in the case of legal decisions, these may be values of fairness or social justice or mercy. Discretion combines intellectual and moral cognition.

But discretion goes beyond cognition. The abbot's discernment would count for naught if he could not act upon those meaningful distinctions. The executive side of discretion, already present in the Rule of Saint Benedict, implies the freedom and power to enforce the insights of the cognitive side of discretion. Discretion is a matter of the will as well as the mind. As we shall see in Chapter 8, the willfulness of discretion had by the seventeenth century come to be tarred with the same brush as arbitrary caprice, a sign that the cognitive and executive sides of discretion had begun to split apart. The practical wisdom of those exercising power no longer commanded trust and therefore undermined the legitimacy of their prerogatives. Without its cognitive side, the executive powers of discretion became suspect. The history of the English word *discretion* roughly parallels this evolution. Originally imported from the Latin via French (*discrecion*) in the twelfth century, the meanings of *discretion* relating to cognitive discernment and to executive freedom coexist peacefully from at least the late fourteenth century.[35] Whereas the cognitive meanings are however now listed as obsolete, the executive meanings endured—and became increasingly controversial, as every contemporary argument about the abuse of the discretionary powers of the courts, the schools, the police, or any other authority testifies. Cognitive discretion without executive discretion is impotent; executive discretion without cognitive discretion is arbitrary.

Exercising discretion in the modern sense stands opposed to following rules faithfully. In contrast, the abbot's discretion is *part* of the Rule, neither contravening nor supplementing its stern imperatives. In modern jurisprudence, both Anglo-American and continental, the discretion of the judge to interpret and enforce the law is subsumed under the ancient concept of equity, often interpreted as an emergency brake to be pulled if the application of the letter of the law in a particular case would not only betray its spirit but also result in patent injustice.[36] There is good reason to believe that Benedict was familiar with at least the Roman law practice of equity; he invokes "reasons of equity" to justify both greater severity and lenience in the observance of the Rule (discretion in the contexts of legal equity and moral casuistry will be addressed in Chapter 8).[37] For the moment, however, it is important to flag how the abbot's role in Benedict's Rule exceeds that of the equitable judge in at least one crucial respect. It belongs to the wisdom of the judge to decide whether or not and how much the general law or rule should be bent to the contours of a particular case in order that justice be served. For Aristotle, who laid the cornerstone of the concept of equity (*epieikeia* in Greek) in the Greco-Roman tradition, the judge who exercises discretion in such cases in effect completes the work of the legislator, who cannot foresee all possible eventualities. "When therefore the law lays down a general rule, and thereafter a case arises which is an exception to the rule, it is then right, where the lawgiver's pronouncement because of its absoluteness is defective and erroneous, when the legislator fails us and has erred by over-simplicity, to correct the omission—to rectify the defect by deciding as the lawgiver would himself decide if he were present on the occasion, and would have enacted if he were cognizant of the case in question."[38] This view still finds a home in some schools of constitutional law, which hold that it is the duty of the judge to plumb the intentions of the original framers of the Constitution and interpret its dictates accordingly.[39] Comparing such adjustments to the law to the pliable leaden ruler used by the builders of island of Lesbos to measure curved solids, Aristotle attempted to correct the deficiencies of the too-general law. Aristotle's ideal judge personifies the legislator, not the law itself. In contrast, Benedict's ideal abbot personifies the Rule.

Even a rule curved by discretion cannot quite capture the quality of exemplification. A judge may display practical wisdom in jiggering general laws to fit particular cases but need not model the qualities of justice and rectitude in private life. Indeed, the maxim that elevates the rule of law over the rule of persons instills caution whenever rules are personalized, much less personified. Obedience to the law does not require that citizens model their conduct on that of judges and lawyers, however learned they may be in legal matters. But the monk who submitted himself to the Rule of Saint Benedict embraced the living standard of the abbot, who in turn represented Christ and was therefore addressed as "Abba, Father!"[40] The Rule was read to novice monks at regular intervals, and its detailed precepts were to be heeded and internalized. But without the animating presence of the abbot, the Rule would have been a mere list of do's and don't's, not a way of life. That punctilious obedience alone did not suffice to master the monastic way of life is indicated by the number of precepts that chastise those who obey, but without conviction: an order is to be carried out without foot-dragging, negligence, or listlessness (5.14) and above all with "no grumbling" (4.39, 23.1, 34.6, 40.8–9, 53.18). The "rule" of the Rule of Saint Benedict refers not to the detailed precepts (though these more closely resemble rules in the modern sense), nor even to precepts tempered with discretion, but to the entire document, a "rule" in the singular and a model to be emulated.

Following Models

Emulation and discretion are distinct but related abilities. Discretion, the ability to distinguish, tweaks the universal law or rule to the particular case, the classical exercise of judgment. Emulation, in contrast, enlists judgment to move from particular to particular. The monk who emulates the abbot or the artist who emulates the *Doryphoros* does not copy these models down to the last detail but rather translates their lessons to a new case by analogy. Emulation is not imitation. A monk who mimicked the abbot down to the last details of gait and gesture would render himself ludicrous, not virtuous; an artist who turned out nothing but exact replicas of the *Doryphoros* would not be celebrated by posterity. Both discretion and emulation involve reasoning by analogy, understood in the capacious sense of discerning significant differences as well as similarities: reasoning under the motto of *mutatis mutandis*. Styles and genres pick out lineages of emulation in art and literature; personae, as opposed to individual persons, do the same in the realm of ethics and religious observance. However, it is paradigmatic cases rather than definitions that do the heavy lifting of inclusion and exclusion. "Is this an epic?" is the sort of mind-stunning question that silences discussion. "In what ways does this resemble or differ from *Gilgamesh* or the *Chanson de Roland*?" in contrast sends analogical sparks flying.

Current discussions of rule-following focus on the distinction between rules and principles. Systems governed by explicit rules—for example, those that specify how many articles must be published in order to qualify for academic promotion—are glass-clear and just as transparent. But they are notoriously susceptible to gaming, and for the very same reason: the more transparent the rule, the more mechanical its application, and the more mechanical the application, the easier to trick the mechanism—for example, by slicing apart what ought to have been one coherent article into several slighter publications, thereby upping the tally but betraying the spirit of the rule. Adding more stipulations to the rules only fuels a never-ending arms race with the gamers. Advocates of principles argue that it would be better simply to announce the desired goal—in this example, an excellent publication record of original and significant research—and let those reaching for a higher rung on the academic ladder be guided by this principle rather than by rules. Countering those who object that principles leave unclear both how to reach the goal and also when it has been achieved, the champions of principles over rules retort that transparency is a lesser value than the integrity of the system—here, the system of academic evaluation.

Because both principles and models stand opposed to explicit rules mechanically applied and because both require judgment, it is tempting to assimilate one to the other. But the emulation of a model mobilizes judgment in a different way than honoring a principle does. The principle is abstract and general; the model is concrete and specific. A principle such as "Honesty is the best policy" or "Be kind to others" must be translated into the specifics of each new situation: what would constitute honesty (or kindness) in this particular context? Here judgment throws down a grappling line from the universal to the particular. But in the case of emulating a model, judgment hops from particular to particular, charting its path by analogy. There's no need for judgment to descend from the general to the specific and to solidify the abstract into the concrete. Instead, its role is to connect two equally concrete, specific instances by carefully assayed analogies. Which similitudes are strongest and just how far can they be pushed? Judgment enlisted in following rules-as-models, whether in discretion or emulation, is not the same judgment that anchors principles to particulars.

Both discretion and emulation stand opposed to induction over identical cases or deduction from first principles, and the workings of both are often opaque to conscious scrutiny. Yet both abilities, honed to a greater or lesser degree, are ubiquitous. Children understand intuitively how to follow but not ape their parents' example; daily social interactions demand that rules of ethics and etiquette be constantly adjusted to the situation at hand. Following the rule in this sense, understood as an inference from exemplum to example, from paradigm to particular, could not be more humdrum. The mystery is not *that* we do it but *how* we do it. This is a quintessentially modern mystery, and one that turns on the multiple senses of the word *rule*: how is it possible to follow a rule like the Rule of Saint Benedict without being able to analyze that ability into explicit steps like the rule for finding the square root of a given number? In other words, how can following a model be turned into executing an algorithm?

That this question does not arise until the turn of the nineteenth century, as we shall see in Chapters 4 and 5, is prima facie evidence that the several semantic clusters revolving around the word *rule* were not earlier perceived to be on a collision course with each other. All referred in literal and figurative senses to standards to be followed as faithfully as possible, whether as astronomical calculation, grammatical paradigm, or legal decree. As we shall see in Chapter 3, both the forms that most rules took, larded with examples and exceptions, and the obvious fact that all required a generous pinch of judgment in application would have further blurred distinctions between implicit and explicit modes of rule-following. Far more salient were differences in scope and validity: which rules held everywhere and always (precious few), which most of the time, and which only sometimes, in some places, for some people.

The authority of the Rule of Saint Benedict expanded the realm of the rule as model beyond its ancient applications in art, grammar, and rhetoric and raised its standing among the other semantic clusters stemming from the Greek *kanon* and the Latin *regula*—the meaning of which in medieval Latin embraced older meanings such as straightedge and arithmetic procedures but also precepts governing matters of faith and monastic orders, including guidance provided by a model.[41] The dictionaries of the seventeenth and eighteenth centuries in most major European languages still listed this meaning among all those given under the lemma *rule* and treated *rule* (in this context often used in the singular, another bow to the Rule of Saint Benedict) and *model* as synonyms.[42] Not accidentally, the sentences provided to illustrate usage referred either to the arts or religious observance, traces of a genealogy that reached back to Pliny and Benedict. But by the mid-nineteenth century, this sense of the world *rule* had begun to fade from dictionaries and soon disappeared altogether.[43] To call anyone the "rule" of anything must already have rung quaint in late nineteenth-century ears: Major General Stanley does *not* sing "I am the very rule of a modern Major-General" in Gilbert and Sullivan's *The Pirates of Penzance* (1879).

Although we may no longer refer to them as "rules" and no longer seek them in Plutarch's *Lives* and saints' *vitae*, models of how to live (as in the phrase "role models") crowd the biography and self-help sections of every bookstore. Does it really matter that word and concept have drifted apart? Every word of ancient lineage and wide application will have its dead branches as well as its green shoots, or extinct usages fossilized in a single surviving phrase (e.g., "after the fact," meaning "after the deed," or "natural history," meaning the study of natural particulars). That a once-vibrant usage has been stamped "archaic" in the latest edition of the dictionary is as much the way of the world as the disappearance of bustles and antimacassars.

But the case of the rule as model is somewhat different. First, the concept is alive and well, just living under a new name. Second, the divorce between word and concept was not amicable: the word *rule* no longer just happens not to mean model or paradigm anymore; its primary meanings now seem incompatible with those of its former boon companion. The meanings of model and paradigm have remained notably steadfast: almost every ancient Greek use of *paradeigma* in architecture, grammar, or art could be translated without friction into the modern English *paradigm* or *model* or *example*. It is the meaning of rule that has strayed, and the whys and wherefores of its wanderings will be the subject of Chapters 5, 6, and 7, which examine various attempts to formulate explicit, rigid rules in the domains of calculation, regulation, and universal laws, respectively. For now, it is enough to mark the discontinuity and to hold fast to the insights yielded by the Rule of Saint Benedict: specificity does not imply rigidity; exceptions can be part of rules; and emulation and discretion are not identical.

Conclusion: Rules between Science and Craft

Let us return to the concrete contexts that seeded the semantic clusters attached to the word *rule* and its cognates in other European languages. All involve getting things done in the world: the straightedge that measured wood and stone in the hands of the carpenter or mason; the dollhouse-sized architectural model that won the patron's approval and guided the builders; the brief directives that instructed priests on how to perform a baptism and provincial officials on how to levy taxes. The ample modern category of rules embraces the inferences of logic and the natural laws of science, but the original home of rules was what was known as *technê* in Greek and *ars* in Latin: medicine, rhetoric, architecture, navigation, military strategy, and other fields guided by precepts but responsive to the vicissitudes of practice. Whereas *epistêmê* in Greek (*scientia* in Latin) dealt with universal and necessary truths, the arts could never escape the realm of the particular and the contingent. The doctor healed this individual patient, not sick people in general; the orator must persuade this particular audience, not audiences in general. Even the most experienced navigator would eventually confront a freak storm or deviating current; architects constantly adapted themselves to the specificities of site and materials and the whims of their patrons. Poised between the ethereal sciences and the banausic crafts, the arts were reasoned but not demonstrative, reliable but not infallible, regular but not universal. They engaged the head as well as the hand; they manipulated both form and matter.

Perhaps because he was the son of a physician schooled in the citadel of Platonic dialectic, Aristotle was exquisitely sensitive to the in-between predicament of the arts. His discussions of the distinctions between *epistêmê* and *technê* in various works suggest that he regarded these pursuits as points along a continuum rather than as watertight compartments. Ideally, *epistêmê* deals with unchanging forms governed by necessary universals (identifying those axioms, however, returns the investigation to experience).[44] But Aristotle occasionally admits that *epistêmê* must also deal with mutable matter as well as immutable form and softens its universals to "that which happens always or for the most part."[45] Just as he dilutes the certainty of *epistêmê*, Aristotle fortifies that of *technê*. Although it cannot avoid contingency and accident, *technê* nonetheless involves reasoning from causes and achieving some degree of generality: the cure that works for this bilious patient will also work for others of that complexion—most of the time.[46] Crucially, both *epistêmê* and *technê*, as opposed to the handicrafts based wholly on experience, are in Aristotle's account articulate: those who cultivate them can offer an account of why they do what they do, and they can transmit their knowledge through teaching, not just pointing.[47]

Epistêmê is usually translated as *science* and *technê* as *craft*, but these are misleading approximations for our purposes. Science in the modern sense is neither deductive nor logically necessary, and it most certainly deals with matter and change; craft lumps together activities Aristotle and many other ancient, medieval, and early modern thinkers would have firmly distinguished. Medicine and ethics might not attain to the certainty of geometry but were in an entirely different class, both intellectually and socially, from menial handiwork. In modern (and also medieval) terms, the rough-and-ready distinction would be between subjects that formed part of the university curriculum (including arts like practical medicine and rhetoric) and those learned as an apprentice in the artisan's workshop. Marching under the Ciceronian banner "reduce to an art" in the sixteenth and seventeenth centuries, practitioners of mining, engineering, farming, dyeing, and other crafts took advantage of the opportunities offered by the printing press to elevate their status and salaries by publishing manuals that purported to formalize their knowledge into rules.[48] During the same period, and not coincidentally, the sciences and arts cross-fertilized one another in ways that transformed both categories.[49] By the mid-eighteenth century, the sciences had adopted and refined empirical practices originally developed in the arts and crafts, such as observation and experiment; lowered their sights from certain to merely probable knowledge; embraced utility alongside understanding as a goal; and abandoned logic for mathematics as their ideal of demonstration. Conversely, the arts boasted more robust rules, "positive rules [that are] invariable and independent of caprice and opinion."[50] These developments gradually eroded the identity of the arts as a distinct form of knowledge, and the term itself became affixed to painting, sculpture, music, and imaginative literature.

In order to understand the in-between status of rules, close to practice and particulars yet aspiring to generality, we must revisit their traditional home, the lost category of the arts. Already in antiquity, the arts were an accordion-like category, expanding and contracting to serve the ends of different philosophical schools. Plato and Aristotle diverged in their views on *technê*, for example, and the Stoics sometimes equated *technê* with the reason and the order of the universe.[51] *Ars* in medieval and Renaissance Latin was equally sprawling, embracing the more theoretical liberal arts (which subsumed not only grammar and rhetoric but also logic, astronomy, harmonics, arithmetic, and geometry, all disciplines Aristotle would have classified under the rubric *epistêmê*) as well as the practical mechanical arts, including everything from cookery to fortifications.[52] It is the arts that became a bustling factory of rule-making from roughly the late fifteenth through the eighteenth centuries, as practitioners proudly staked their claims to intellectual prestige as well as manual skill in book after book of how-to instructions. Aristotle's dictate that a *technê* must be teachable in terms of precepts and maxims, however circumscribed in application, animated these so-called *Kunstbüchlein* ("little books about the arts") throughout the Renaissance and early modern periods.[53] Whether readers actually could learn how to smelt metals or besiege a city or convert currencies or play a rubber of whist from these handbooks is another question. In the next chapter we turn to the multiple strategies used to make the arts learnable by rules.

3

The Rules of Art

HEAD AND HAND UNITED

The Understanding Hand

Nuremberg, 1525: The artist Albrecht Dürer (1471–1528) dedicates
a manual on geometry for the use of painters, goldsmiths, sculptors, stonemasons, carpenters, and "all those who use measurement" to his humanist friend Willibald Pirckheimer (1470–1530). As
befits its intended readership of craftsmen and Dürer's own background as the son of a goldsmith, the book is written in the German
vernacular, not Latin. But the dedication to a renowned classical
scholar and the allusions to the lost "art of the Greeks and Romans"
signal Dürer's ambitions to elevate handiwork to the level of an art
by teaching its principles systematically. Painters and artisans who
had learned their craft solely through "daily practice" had "in their
ignorance [*Unverstand*] grown up like a wild, unpruned tree" and
were rightly laughed at by connoisseurs. By mastering the geometry of compass and straightedge, such "art-hungry youths" would
improve their minds as well as their handiwork.[1] (Fig. 3.1.)

Dürer's dedicatory epistle rang the changes on themes that were
endlessly repeated in the burgeoning early modern how-to literature. Hundreds if not thousands of books aimed to turn all manner
of handicrafts into arts: not only painting and carpentry but also
dredging and dyeing, gunnery and cookery, composing a musical

FIGURE 3.1. Albrecht Dürer's polygon construction,
*Unterweysung der Messung, mit dem Zirckel und
Richtscheyt* [Instructions on measurement with
compass and ruler] (1525) fig. 11. SLUB, digital.
slub-dresden.de/id27778509X.

canon and measuring a stack of wood. Following the Ciceronian
dictum that a true art can be "reduced to rules," these compact
books, like Dürer's mostly written in the vernacular and often illustrated, offered instructions, maxims, precepts, tables, and diagrams to literate artisans intent on bettering their lot—and also to
the princes interested in hiring them.[2] Competition among early
modern courts for artists, engineers, doctors, alchemists, cooks, and
other practitioners of the arts whose skills could be used to defend,
enrich, and embellish the court created new opportunities for social
and economic advancement. As Dürer's own career shows, virtuoso

Ars

Vsus

Quisquis amore bonas exercet sedulus arteis,   /   Diemet staden bemind Consten t'Exereeren
Congeret obryzum multa cum laude metallum. Hem beladen beunt met veel Ryckdom in Eeren

FIGURE 3.2. Hendrik Goltzius, *Ars et Usus* [Art and practice] (1583).
© The Trustees of the British Museum, London.

artisans were mobile in every sense of the word, invited to courts all over Europe and cosseted by popes and princes.[3]

Such success stories and rising literacy rates among urban artisans stoked ambitions and opened up markets for authors who promised to divulge trade secrets and "reduce"—i.e., collect and order—haphazard practice into clear, reliable rules.[4] To formalize craft knowledge into rules was to give it voice and dignity but not to remove it from the workshop. Dürer intended his instructions as a "thorough introduction" to be expanded by "daily use," which in turn would deepen understanding and kindle invention.[5] Books like Dürer's addressed practitioners of the "mechanical arts" (*artes mechanicae*), which included all kinds of handiwork, from carpentry to cookery.[6] Originally opposed to the more prestigious liberal or "free" arts (*artes liberales*) that constituted the core of the university curriculum, the stock of the mechanical arts rose sharply in early modern Europe. The *Nova reperta* (New inventions), a famous series of engravings printed in Antwerp around 1600, celebrated the ingenious innovations of skilled artisans, from oil pigments to the printing press.[7] Almost all of the early modern *Kunstbüchlein* and books of secrets that claimed to induct novices into the tricks of the trades assumed that readers would shuttle back and forth between reading rules and recipes and trying them out in practice.[8] A 1583 engraving of *Ars et Usus* (Art and practice) by artist Hendrik Goltzius (1558–1617) allegorizes this relationship: the winged female figure of Art, crowned with laurels, seated on a globe, and surrounded by books and mathematical instruments, guides the hand of the male figure of Practice as he draws— another emblem, like the books and instruments, of careful advance planning in handiwork. The caption, in Latin and Dutch, promises that the partnership of Art and Practice would bring "riches and fame." (Fig. 3.2.) Goltzius's own celebrity and prosperity as an artist in several media, despite a severely crippled right hand, lent credence to the formula.

Artisans keen on bettering their lot were not the only readers and writers of these books. Brisk traffic between scholar's study and artisan's workshop ultimately transformed scientific theory as much as artisanal practice: Galileo's (1564–1642) involvement with engineers and shipbuilders is only the most famous example of such fruitful hybrids.[9] Ballistics, fortifications, mining, and metallurgy—all areas of intense interest to early modern princes—attracted the learned scrutiny of Galileo, Isaac Newton (1642–1727), and Leibniz, among others.[10] But to reduce practice to rules did not necessarily imply a further reduction of rules to theory. Like the betwixt-and-between status of the arts themselves, suspended between handicraft and science, rules hovered between head and hand.

Or rather, rules wed head and hand, dexterity with understanding. This may have begun as an unequal partnership, with the lion's share of the prestige accorded to precepts rather than practice. Dürer's early sixteenth-century audience of autodidacts were on his account skilled but unrefined and therefore the butt of ridicule among those who knew better. By the mid-seventeenth century, however, the laughter of the learned had become fainter. The accomplishments of engineers such as Simon Stevin (1548–1620) and Isaac Beeckman (1588–1637), goldsmiths such as Wendel Jamnitzer (1507/8–1585), potters such as Bernard Palissy (1510–1589), and clockmakers such as Conrad Dasypodius (c. 1532–c. 1600) commanded the patronage of princes and the admiration of reforming natural philosophers such as Francis Bacon (1561–1626), René Descartes (1596–1650), and Robert Boyle (1627–1691). In his 1620 treatise on the "new logic" of science, Bacon famously contrasted the stagnation of natural philosophy since antiquity with the progress of the modern mechanical arts, "which are continually thriving and growing,"[11] and elsewhere called for a "history of the mechanical arts," a project later undertaken (though never completed) by the Royal Society of London and the Académie royale des sciences of Paris soon after their foundation in the 1660s.[12] Some of Descartes's *Regulae ad directionem igenii* (Rules for the direction of the mind, composed c. 1626), especially Rules XIV–XXI dealing with how to solve mathematical problems, more closely resemble the heuristics of the artisans' handbooks than the humanist treatises on method by Jacopo Zabarella (1533–1589) or Petrus Ramus (1515–1572).[13] For authors like Bacon and Descartes, the mechanical arts had become tools to think about and think with: their inventions served as a source of metaphors and models, their steady improvements and empirical methods as a source of inspiration, and their circumscribed rules of practice as a target of emulation. The rules of art eventually transformed the methods and aims of science.

What exactly were these rules, and how did they in fact guide practice? Here is Sébastian Le Prestre de Vauban (1633–1707), field marshal to King Louis XIV of France (1638–1715, r. 1643–1715), describing in 1704 how to open the trenches dug in secret by the attacking army:

> The day of the opening having arrived, the guards assemble around two or three o'clock in the afternoon and array themselves in battle formation, after having said a prayer; the general inspects them on parade, as he deems good. The workers also gather close by, all equipped with fascines [bundles of wood bound together to protect sides of trenches] and spades, and each of them with pick and shovel. As night approaches and daylight begins to fade, the guards begin to march, each soldier carrying a fascine with his weapons; this should be repeated with all the guards.[14]

Or English practical mathematician Leonard Digges (c. 1515–c. 1559) instructing land surveyors in 1556 on the use of a cross-staff: "Ye must stande right up wyth your bodye and necke, your fete iust together, your handes not much moving, the one eye closed, and ever marke your standynge ryght with the myddles of your fete."[15] Or man-about-London Charles Cotton (1630–1687) explaining in 1687 how to prepare your horse for a race: "Lead your Horse to his course with all gentleness, and give him leave to smell to other Horses dung, that thereby he may be enticed to stole and empty his body as he goes."[16] Or advice from an anonymous

French chef of a lordly household in 1689 to aspiring chefs on the secrets of dressing a lettuce salad: "To festive lettuce salads add sugar, musk, and ambergris, enriched with flowers."[17]

These examples of rules, culled more or less at random from early modern handbooks on how to besiege a city, measure wood and land, win at games and races, or prepare a sumptuous meal could easily be supplemented by thousands more from the same period: how to make jams, build a house, pump water out of mines, cure warts, garrison a defending army, compose a musical canon, start a pig farm, draw in perspective, pass a bill in parliament, and in general go about the business of daily life in a regulated and orderly fashion. The genre of how-to books has been booming ever since, but in the early days of printing and in a period in which handiwork had to prove its credentials as a proper art, conventions were still fluid. The rules in question might be long or short, delivered as maxims or instructions, teem with detail or float above specifics, be spelled out in prose or parceled into tables. Most such rules took the form of numbered lists, although recipes preserved their own sequential, discursive format. Despite this swarming variety, a few regularities among the rules and regulations emerge from the hodgepodge of these early modern how-to's.

First, rules were always framed in the imperative mood. Whether the addressee was the heir to the French throne (as in Vauban's case), carpenters and masons ignorant of geometry (Digges), a gamester who "knows no Judge but the Groom-Porter, no Law but that of the Game" (Cotton), or a scullery boy aspiring to oversee the kitchen of a nobleman (the French chef), the reader was implicitly placed in the position of an apprentice under a master. The author's voice was authoritative, and the title to that authority was superior knowledge.

Second, the knowledge in question was often gleaned from personal experience, but it was knowledge cast in the form of generally applicable rules. In today's parlance, to call an activity an "art" is to draw attention to its implicit, intuitive aspects ("medicine is an art as well as a science") as well as to individual virtuosity attained in some usually minor pursuit ("he made an art of impromptu toasts"). In contrast, the early modern mechanical arts proudly distinguished themselves from mere crafts, the latter allegedly governed by unthinking routine and at the mercy of chance, by being teachable via explicit rules to all readers who applied them (and themselves) diligently. One way of thinking about the medieval and early modern distinctions among the sciences, the arts, and the crafts is to focus on the degree of certainty each promised. True science attained demonstrative certainty; an art achieved at least regularity in most cases; a mere craft was haphazard. Chance played the greatest role in the banausic crafts and the least in the sciences, with the arts somewhere in between. Many titles and subtitles of early modern how-to books advertised their clear, methodical exposition: "Wherein the whole ART is revealed in a more easie and perfect Method, than hath been publisht in any Language."[18]

Third, the sixteenth- and seventeenth-century how-to books, in contrast to their successors, were seldom addressed to rank beginners. An apprenticeship and some previous experience in the craft was assumed. Fourth, the promised payoff of mastering the rules was improvement, first and foremost of the arts themselves but also of the artisan. Practicing a rule-governed art rather than a slapdash trade would, so the lure, polish both practitioner and product. In the late seventeenth and eighteenth centuries, the discourse of improvement and self-improvement in the mechanical arts merged with that of public utility, as mercantilist governments across Europe sought to fill their coffers by raising the quality of exportable manufactures—once again by issuing rules.[19]

Great hopes and grand promises were invested in rules: they would raise up trades to arts, lowly workers to respected and prosperous artisans, shoddy wares to up-market commodities, government debt to surplus, mute intuition to articulate precept, endless particulars to sturdy generalizations. These early modern great expectations—at once social, economic, and epistemic—invite modern skepticism. We associate rules with red tape, overbearing bureaucracy, know-it-all, know-nothing academics, and all the other forces alleged to stifle initiative, gum up the machinery of markets, and sickly o'er hands-on know-how with the pale cast of theory. Our eyebrows arch at the very idea that the implicit knowledge of practice could be rendered explicit in rules.[20] Familiar oppositions in several languages sharpen the boundary between the knowledge of how (associated with the unconscious skills exercised by the body) and the knowledge of why (associated with the conscious deliberations of the mind): *connaître* versus *savoir*, *kennen* versus *wissen*, tacit versus explicit knowledge. How exactly was practice to be translated into precept—and back again?

Thick Rules

Let us return to the early modern rules themselves. Although they vary considerably in subject matter, length, format, and detail, all come enriched with copious advice on how to apply them: examples, exceptions, problems, provisos, models, caveats, and, in almost all cases, an appeal to what Saint Benedict had deemed the abbot's cardinal virtue, discretion. They are thick rules, in contrast to thin rules that articulate only the imperative to be executed, with no further elaboration. Recall that in the Rule of Saint Benedict not only are exceptions foreseen as part of the formulation of the rule; the interpreter of the rule, the abbot, is also its exemplification. Another way of putting this is that the text of the Rule was not free-standing; without an abbot worthy of his office, it remained incomplete. But however influential the Rule of Saint Benedict may have been in Latin Christendom, it would be reasonable to object that its discipline hardly compares with the rigor of mathematics. Mathematical rules—for example the algorithms for solving a quadratic equation or finding the first derivative of a function—are nowadays the thinnest of rules, terse and unembellished. What about their early modern equivalents, rules closer to the original meaning of the Greek *kanon* and the Latin *regula* as straightedges, rules about exact measurement and calculation?

The association of rules with exactitude, especially mathematical exactitude, stretches as far back as sources reach and is still present—indeed, omnipresent—in modern reflections about what rules are and how they work. Although it may not have been the primary early modern definition of *rule*, it was never absent. I therefore turn to some of the best-known rules of medieval and early modern commercial arithmetic and measurement. In this domain, there is no single text that can compare in authority and influence with the Rule of Saint Benedict, so my evidence will be more statistical and scattershot. Some regularities do nonetheless emerge.

In late medieval and early modern commercial arithmetic, the most frequently used of all reckoning rules was the Rule of Three. Here is how the *Kadran aus marchans* (*Dial of merchants*, 1485) explains it:

> The rule of three: called the rule of three because there are always three numbers, viz. two similars and one contrary and if there are more all must be reduced to these three.

None the wiser? The fifteenth-century merchant reading this explanation was probably also scratching his head. But then comes the example:

> That is to say, if 3 Avignon florins are worth 2 royal francs, how much would 20 Avignon florins be worth?[21]
> [Answer: $(2 \times 20) \div 3 = 13\ 1/3$.]

After working through the half-dozen examples of this sort provided by the text, the merchant was probably able not only to convert currencies but also to find prices: if 4 ells of silk cost 20 florins, how much would 10 ells cost? He would have needed neither algebra nor the Euclidean doctrine of proportions in order to generalize from one example to another; nor would he have been fazed by a shift in subject matter, from currency exchanges to the price of silk or the conversion of weights and measures. The generality of the rule lay less in its bare enunciation (which was, as often as not, unintelligible on its own) than in the enunciation read in light of the examples. Anyone who has recently looked at an elementary mathematics textbook will recognize the format. As in the case of the Rule of Saint Benedict, what we would identify as the rule proper was not free-standing: the examples were part of the rule, and the rule owed its generality to the accumulation of specifics in the various examples that could be analogized to still further cases.

Let us take another example from the realm of calculation and measurement, revisiting Digges's 1556 English treatise on measurement, which promised to teach "diverse most certayne and sufficient rules, touching the measuring of all manner Superficies" of timber, stone, glass, and land.[22] Digges reproached "heady and selfwylled" craftsmen for adhering to false rules for measuring stands of timber and wrapped himself in the mantle of the "infallible grounds" of geometry. Yet not only are his alternative rules expressed almost entirely by means of examples; he also cautions that discretion must be exercised in order to simplify calculations: "It were intolerable tediousness, yea impossible, to sette foorth the true quantities of timber measure, to all odde quantities of squares. The discrete handlynge of these, the wittye shall brynge to a sufficient exactnesse."[23]

In a similar vein, the early seventeenth-century Welsh composer Elway Bevin (1554–1638) explained how to write musical canons, the most mathematical form of what was at the time still considered a branch of mathematics, namely harmonics. Bevin also instructs the would-be composer via heaps of examples. Canons are now considered the most rule-bound, even algorithmic, form of musical composition, but Bevin proceeds from simple examples (varying plainsong just by altering the rests) to ones so complex that he compares them to "the frame of this world, for as the world doth consist of the four Elements, viz. Fire, Ayre, Water and the Earth . . . so likewise this canon consisteth and is devided into foure severall Canons. . . ."—all without so much as a feint at formalization.[24] (Fig. 3.3.) Even the mathematical sciences—

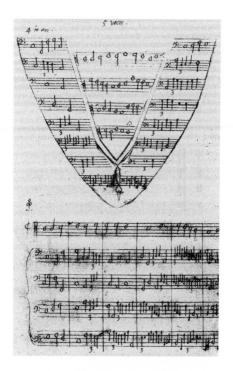

FIGURE 3.3. Elway Bevin's score for a canon,
Briefe and Short Instrvction of the Art of Mvsicke,
to teach how to make Discant, of all proportions
that are in vse (1631).

arithmetic, measurement, harmonics—were codified as much by
examples as by rules in these handbooks.

Or rather, the examples were part and parcel of the rules, a necessary supplement and sometimes even a substitute. Although no
single example may have exemplified the rule as the abbot of the
monastery ideally exemplified the Rule of Saint Benedict, such
repertoires of examples served to teach and generalize the rule
much as a paradigmatic model did. Consider Cotton's compendious treatise *The Compleate Gamester*, which in addition to tips on
horse racing offered instruction on billiards, chess, all manner of
card games, cock fighting, and just about any other form of what

he calls the "enchanting witchery" of gaming might take in the more louche sections of London. Cotton was profligate in details of all kinds: descriptions of how cheats can strip a player's coat of its gold buttons while he is preoccupied with the throw of the dice; admonitions not to let sleeves drag and pipe ashes spill onto the billiard table; instructions on how to judge the courage of a fighting cock by its frequent crowing in the pen. Sundry "orders," "laws," and "rules" are set forth for the various games, many of which we would readily recognize as rules of the game: e.g., if you touch a chess piece, then you must play it. But Cotton warned his reader that some games can be mastered only by experience—e.g., the fiendishly difficult game of "Irish," which "is not to be learn'd otherwise than by observation and practice," or even chess, the subject of one of the book's longest chapters. Cotton toyed with the idea that "Chess as well as Draughts may be plaid by a certain Rule" but, after some twenty pages of detailed instructions, concluded that "[m]any more Observations might be here inserted for the understanding of this noble Game, which I am forced to wave to avoid prolixity."[25]

Not only Cotton's treatise but the successive eighteenth-century editions of Edmond Hoyle's (1672–1769) guides to whist and other card games aimed at making the reader not just competent but proficient. For that reason, the line between what we would call the rules of the game proper (e.g., how many cards each player is dealt at the beginning of a hand of whist) and tips on how to win (e.g., "If you have Queen, Knave, and three small Trumps, with a good Suit, trump out with a small one") is deliberately blurred. Hoyle supplied his readers not only with the calculations of odds of a player's partners having certain cards; he also included a set of rules "to endeavour to deceive and distress your Adversaries, and demonstrate your Game to your partner."[26] Psychology and calculation conspire to best one's opponent, even in chess. Cotton duly supplies the values of each piece, from pawn to queen, but in the next breath counsels the reader: "besides you are to note, that whatsoever piece your adversary plays most or best with

effects in the workshop.[29] In other undertakings, most obviously games but also war, commerce, and politics, chance was built in. The goddess Fortuna loomed large in the early modern imagination. Allegorized with her emblems of instability—the turning wheel or the fragile bubble—she threatened to overturn the best-laid plans and proclaim the rule of unrule. (Fig. 3.4.)

Rules at War

The specter of Fortuna haunted early modern treatises like Vauban's on how to wage war. In no other sphere of human activity is the risk of cataclysmic chaos greater; in no other sphere is the role of uncertainty and chance, for good or ill, more consequential. Yet of the many early modern treatises that attempted to reduce this or that disorderly practice to an art, none were more confident of their rules than those devoted to fortifications. This was in part because fortifications in the early modern period qualified as a branch of mixed mathematics (those branches of mathematics that "mixed" form with various kinds of matter, from light to cannonballs). Like mechanics or optics, it was heavily informed by geometry and, increasingly, by the rational mechanics of projectile motion. Indeed, many treatises on the subject began with an introduction to plane geometry and treated the stellated polygon form characteristic of early modern fortresses as just another straightedge-and-compass construction, as in the 1596 treatise by the Florentine military engineer Buonaiuto Lorini (c. 1547–1611), architect of the fortifications at Palmanova.[30]

However, the affinity between siege warfare and rules went well beyond the starfish geometry of early modern fortified cities. (Fig. 3.5.) In contrast to the field warfare dominated by cavalry and, by the late Middle Ages, infantry armed with long bow and pike, the advent of artillery (especially cannonry and mines) in the late fifteenth and early sixteenth centuries proved devastating to medieval walled cities and shifted the locus of European warfare from the field to the fortress. Wars of position, as such sieges were

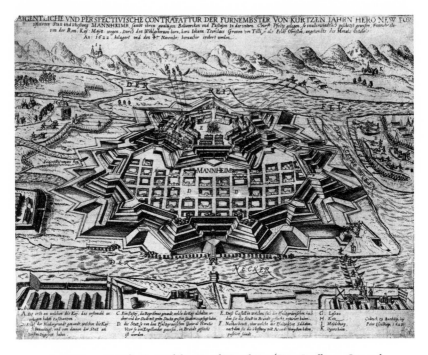

FIGURE 3.5. Fortifications of the city of Mannheim (Peter Isselburg, *City and Fortifications of Mannheim*, 1623), Landesarchiv Mannheim.

called, not only permitted but positively demanded detailed planning, from the logistics of provisioning garrisons for the long haul and the transport of cannons that weighed into the tons (plus many times that weight in gunpowder and shot) to the physics and mathematics of attack and defense. The precision of the latter would be easy to exaggerate. Despite numerous tables in early modern treatises on warfare purporting to compute the angle at which a cannon must be positioned in order to hit ramparts at a given distance, the reality was that seventeenth-century cannonry was accurate only at point-blank range.[31] Nonetheless, when compared to the mayhem of field warfare, where even deciding which side had been victorious could be a challenge, wars of position were models of order. As Vauban wrote, even the greatest commanders were at the mercy of "Dame Fortune, who is fickle and often decides against them; but in the attack and defense of fortifications fortune plays a far lesser role than prudence and dexterity."[32]

Everywhere in the early modern literature of reducing practice to an art, the theme of minimizing the role of chance crops up. As in the case of the "low sciences" of practical medicine and astrology, practitioners of the arts and crafts confronted not just the compliant regularities of form but the recalcitrant singularities of matter: this individual patient with this particular phlegmatic complexion and sedentary regimen; this particular block of walnut wood with this distinctive grain, knots, and warp. In both medicine and carpentry—and fortifications—the reasons for the predominance of particulars were the same: the resistance of matter to form. As Vauban's master, Blaise de Pagan (1604–1665), wrote on the limits of applying mathematics to fortification, "if the science of fortifications were purely mathematical, its rules would be purely demonstrable, but as it [fortifications] has matter as its object and experience as its principal foundation, its most essential maxims depend on conjecture."[33] In the kingdom of particulars, chance was mighty and rules were weak. On the basis of his forty-eight successful sieges, Vauban aimed to distill his long years of military experience into, if not rules, then at least general maxims. Dame Fortune could not be banished from the battlefield, but she could be restrained.

Vauban's efforts to rein in chance covered every aspect of the preparation for and conduct of the siege, from the first reconnaissance (best done alone on horseback by the chief engineer himself, who should also loosen the tongues of locals with a few bribes) to the laborious digging of the trenches (how many peasants with what kind of shovels should dig for how long) to the moment of assault.[34] Elaborate tables specify how many inches deep the trenches should be, how many pounds of gunpowder are needed to blow up ramparts of specified height and depth, and how many pounds of lentils, rice, beef, cheese, salted herring, butter, cheese, cinnamon, not to mention cannons, bombs, mortars, hammers, scissors, cords of wood, ovens for baking bread, and much, much else are required to defend a fortress, expressed as a function of the number of bastions (from four to eighteen). Thirty-one watercolor images supplemented the detailed descriptions on exactly how to dig the trenches, with close-ups and detailed illustrations of which tools to use.

In his thirty numbered "General Maxims," Vauban hammered away at the responsibility of the engineer to superintend every detail of the trenches and the positioning of the cannons and other artillery. He warned that if these instructions were not obeyed at the correct time and to the letter, "all turns to confusion."[35] Vauban knew firsthand what confusion in battle looked like, acknowledging that his own sieges had been far from tidy: "Let us honestly admit that most of our sieges are very imperfectly conducted, that most of our attacks are terribly disorderly, and unnecessarily and unreasonably endanger, the King's subjects, his honor, and his state." But Vauban did not give up on rules of sieges as a lost cause. Instead, he called for "more certain and more realistic rules" that would "make siegecraft more orderly and less bloody."[36]

Yet although Vauban was a demon of detail, he was neither an a priori systematist nor a stickler for superfluous exactitude. The peasants who had been conscripted to dig the trenches had to be watched like hawks lest they not dig deep enough, but it sufficed to eyeball the inclination of the trench walls, "which, serving only for a short time, need not be made in a polished manner."[37] Special attention should be paid to the peculiarities of local topography; regularly built fortresses could be attacked and defended by the book, but irregular ones required deviations from the rules; taking precise measurements could be a dangerous distraction in the heat of battle. Even the maniacally detailed tables were not meant to be followed to the letter but to serve as aides-mémoires and checklists.[38] By unburdening memory, rules and tables freed the mind to exercise judgment and ingenuity as the specific situation demanded. Having begun his own career as a military engineer, Vauban was proudly aware that the words *engineer* and *genius* shared a common root in *ingenium*, the faculty of brilliant improvisation.[39]

As in the case of other early modern rules that came complete with examples and exceptions and experience, Vauban's rules were not free-standing. Early modern rules were not statistical generalizations, summaries of what to do in the most probable case. Statistics had yet to be systematically collected; probability distributions had barely been thought of. But even if Vauban and his fellow rule-makers had had such tools at their disposal, it is arguable that they would have found them of little use. If the distribution of probabilities of possible cases approximates a flat line, with no pronounced peak or steeply tapering tails, statistical generalizations are a poor guide to practice. Any one eventuality is just about as likely as any other; averages are no guide; planning becomes a lottery. Moreover, the gathering of statistics necessarily assumes homogeneity within the category counted. For example, a national census of all citizens to determine legislative representation must abstract from those features irrelevant to voting rights, such as height and weight, however much such details might matter in other contexts. Because success or failure so often hinges on details in practical matters and because those relevant details fluctuated constantly, the practice of most early modern arts could not have afforded the coarse-grained approach of statistics—or for that matter, of Aristotelian universals. The world of early modern practitioners was too unstable and too fine-grained for such thin rules. Only thick rules, cocooned in layers of particulars that illustrated or qualified or exemplified, could cope with the ruses of Dame Fortune.

Of particulars there are no end, as Aristotle pointed out.[40] But thick rules did not aim to anticipate all particulars. Rather, they drew attention to the range and kinds of deviations and exceptions to the rules, the domains wherein the rule could be expected to work and where not, and how much trimming was needed to fit even typical examples to the rule. Thick rules alerted practitioners to the details they must heed and the latitude needed to adjust the

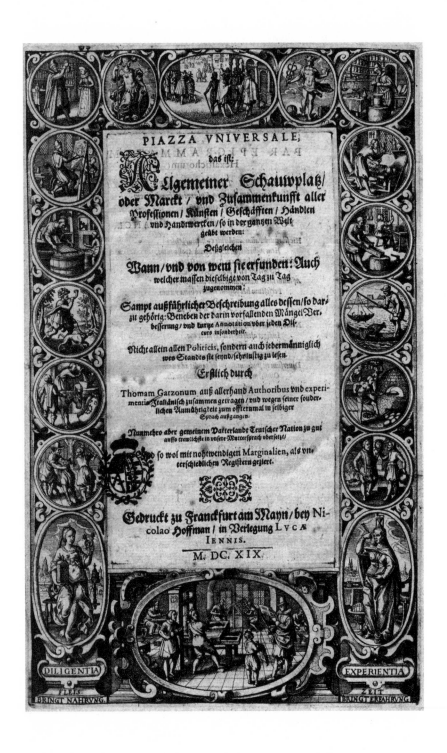

PIAZZA VNIVERSALE;
das ist:

Allgemeiner Schauwplatz,
oder Marckt, vnd Zusammenkunfft aller
Professionen, Künsten, Geschäfften, Händlen
vnd Handwercken, so in der gantzen Welt
geübt werden:

Deßgleichen

Wann, vnd von wem sie erfunden: Auch
welcher massen dieselbige von Tag zu Tag
zugenommen;

Sampt außführlicher Beschreibung alles dessen, so dar-
zu gehörig: Beneben der darin vorfallenden Mängel Ver-
besserung, vnd kurtze Annotation vber jeden Dis-
curs insonderheit.

Nicht allein allen Politicis, sondern auch jedermänniglich
wes Standts sie seynd, sehrlustig zu lesen.

Erstlich durch

Thomam Garzonum auß allerhand Authoribus vnd experi-
mentis Italiänisch zusammen getragen, vnd wegen seiner souder-
lichen Anmühtigkeit zum offtermal in selbiger
Sprach außgangen:

Nunmehro aber gemeinem Vaterlande Teutscher Nation zu gut
auffs trewlichste in vnsere Muttersprach vbersetzt;

Vnd so wol mit nohtwendigen Marginalien, als vn-
terschiedlichen Registern gezieret.

Gedruckt zu Franckfurt am Mayn, bey Ni-
colao Hoffman, in Verlegung Lucæ
IENNIS.

M. DC. XIX.

DILIGENTIA

FLEIS

BRINGT NAHRVNG.

EXPERIENTIA

ZEIT

BRINGT ERNAHRVNG.

rule to the case at hand. They put readers on their mettle by showing how agility and judgment would be in many cases required of them. To enumerate all such cases would be impossible and also pointless; it was enough to flag their existence and model a few solutions. Experience would take care of the rest. Few early modern rulebooks were written for rank beginners with no experience whatsoever, and none were written to be executed by machines. Even the arithmetic rules were not purely algorithmic, as we have seen. As in the case of the craftsmen addressed by Dürer and Digges, the envisioned audience had already undergone at least an apprenticeship. The point was not to instruct the clueless but to elevate the level of practice from routine to reflection.

Even game books were not self-contained; at some point, the would-be player of whist or Irish must plunge into the fray. Thick rules repeatedly gestured toward experience because that was both the departure point and destination of their readers. The rules could not replace experience, only systematize and extend it. But this was already a great deal: experience refracted through the lens of the rules of art was better ordered, more sharply focused, and above all broader than that of most craftsmen occupied with the pell-mell of particulars encountered in their own workshops.[41] The frontispiece of a 1619 guide to "all the professions, arts, trades, commerce, and handicrafts" summed up the foundation of them all: beneath vignettes of painters, printers, hunters, carpenters, bakers, and other workers stand two larger allegorical figures, "Diligentia" and "Experientia," the essential supplements to all rules of art. (Fig. 3.6.)

FIGURE 3.6. Frontispiece showing practitioners of the many mechanical arts, all guided by Diligence and Experience (Tommaso Garzoni, Frontispiece, *Piazza universale, das ist: Algemeiner Schauplatz oder Marckt und Zusammenkunfft aller Professionen, Künsten, Geschäften, Händeln und Handwercken* [Universal piazza, or general showplace or market and meetingplace of all professions, arts, businesses, trades, and handiwork], 1619). SLUB, digital.slub-dresden.de/id265479053.

Cookbook Knowledge

There is one genre of pre-modern rulebook that rarely aspired to any kind of universal or even partial generalization: cookbooks were almost exclusively about particulars.[42] They therefore raise a different kind of problem about applying rules in practice: how to build practice into the rules themselves. Whereas seventeenth-century cookbooks were generally addressed to readers who had already undergone an apprenticeship in the kitchen and who were looking to improve their position in an aristocratic household by learning how to prepare the latest French sauces and sweetmeats, their eighteenth-century successors were increasingly pitched to the novice scullery maid or at least her literate mistress.[43] The latter type of cookbook explicitly aimed at free-standing rules, albeit rules rooted in the particulars of eggs, flour, sugar, and butter.

Two English cookbooks, one published in 1660 and the other in 1746, will serve to make this contrast vivid. Robert May's (1588–c. 1664) *The Accomplisht Cook, Or the Art and Mystery of Cookery* is addressed "To the Master Cooks, and to such young Practitioners of the Art of Cookery" who had already completed their apprenticeship. May set forth his own credentials at length: son of a master cook in a noble household, he had apprenticed in both London and Paris before cooking for Lord Lumley in London and "various nobles in Kent, Sussex, Essex, Yorkshire" when he had been rusticated by the English Civil War. May promised his readers not only the fruits of his "long experience, practice, and converse with the most ablest men in their times" but also *"new Terms of Art,"* mostly French, to his backwards countrymen, already woefully behind continental standards of haute cuisine.[44]

May seemed just the sort of highfalutin' cookbook author Mary Kettilby (17th c.–c. 1730) had in her sights when she offered her collection of some three hundred recipes as "Palatable, Useful, and Intelligible, which is more than can be said of . . . some great Masters having given us Rules in that Art so strangely odd and fantastical, that 'tis hard to say, Whether the Reading has given more

The Fair, who's Wise and oft consults our BOOK,
And thence directions gives her Prudent Cook;
With CHOICEST VIANDS, *has her Table Crown'd,*
And Health, *with* Frugal Ellegance *is found.*

FIGURE 3.7. Frontispiece showing the mistress of the house handing her
maidservant a recipe (Mary Kettilby, *A Collection of above Three Hundred
Receipts,* 1747).

Sport and Diversion, or the Practice more Vexation and Chagrin, by following their Directions." She was writing not for aspiring master cooks of lords and ladies but rather for "Young and Unexperienc'd Dames" and "Cook-Maids at Country-Inns."[45] Yet Kettilby also assured her readers that her culinary and medical recipes conveyed "the great Knowledge, and long Experience of those Excellent Persons" who had contributed them. In contrast to May, however, Kettilby was attempting to distill experience for the inexperienced, not the somewhat experienced who had already apprenticed to a master. Her rules aimed to be free-standing—or, as a modern cookbook might put it, foolproof. (Fig. 3.7.)

How did this alleged contrast cash out in the recipes? Here are two recipes for desserts, the first from May's cookbook and the second from Kettilby's, with similar ingredients (warning: not for the lipophobic):

A boild Pudding

Beat the yolks of *three eggs* with rose water, and *half a pint of cream*, warm it with *a piece of butter as big as a walnut*, and when it is melted mix the eggs and that together, and season it with nutmeg, sugar, and salt; then put in as much bread as will make it **thick as batter**, and lay on *as much flour as will lie on a shilling*, then take a double cloth, wet it, and flour it, tie it fast, and put it in a pot; when it is boild, serve it up on a dish with butter, verjuyce [grape vinegar], and sugar.[46]

To make Fry'd Cream

Take a *Quart of good new Cream*, the Yolks of *seven Eggs*, a Bit of Lemon Peel, a grated Nutmeg, *two Spoonfuls of Sack, as much Orange-flower Water*: Butter your Sauce-pan, and put it over the Fire; **stir it all the while one way with a little white Whisk**, and as you stir, strew in Flour very lightly, 'till 'tis thick and smooth; then 'tis boil'd enough, and may be pour'd out upon a Cheese-plate or Mazarine; spread it with a Knife **exactly**

even, about *half an Inch thick*, then cut it in Diamand-squares, and fry it in a Pan of boiling sweet Suet.[47]

For the sake of ready comparison, I have marked the quantitative measures (including analogical ones like "as big as a walnut") in italics and the tips on procedure (e.g., how to tell when the pudding has boiled enough) in bold. As is clear at a glance, May and Kettilby do not differ significantly in terms of the measurements they provide (an observation confirmed by a survey of other cookbooks of this period) but rather in terms of their descriptions of techniques and how to know when the dish is done. The point here is not to deny a long-term evolution toward more (and more precise) measurements in recipes. The editor of a 1780 edition of a 1390 cookery manuscript, for example, complained that "the quantities of things are seldom specified, but are too much left to the taste and judgment of the cook"—an indication of how expectations had changed over the intervening four centuries.[48] Rather, the point of this sample comparison is to show first, that what separated the experienced from the inexperienced cook was knowledge of procedures, not amounts; and second, that this so-called tacit knowledge could be made explicit. Whether a cookbook has ever been made completely foolproof of course depends on just how foolish the fool, just as complete explicitness depends on the standardization of ingredients, measurements, cooking utensils, and ovens. But the all-or-nothing opposition between irreducibly tacit and exhaustively explicit knowledge, so characteristic of modern debates, obscures the spectrum of possibilities illustrated by this early modern comparison. Even if no rule is completely free-standing, some are more free-standing than others.

A final lesson from the early modern cookbooks: greater explicitness need not take the form of greater specificity. To take one last example in the dessert vein, this time from Hannah Glasse's (1708–1770) enormously popular *Art of Cookery, Made Plain and Easy* (first edition 1747, most recent edition 1995) addressed to "every servant who can but read,"[49] which spelled out the *general rules* for making puddings:

Rules to be observed in making Puddings & c.

In boiled puddings, take great care that the bag or cloth be very clean, and not soapy, and dipped in hot water, and then well floured. If a bread-pudding, tie it loose; if a batter-pudding, tie it close, and be sure the water boils when you put the pudding in, and you should move your puddings in the pot now and then, for fear they stick.[50]

There's no need this time to highlight the procedural instructions in bold; it's all about procedure. Glasse's rules make explicit everything that May assumed his readers would know (e.g., move the pudding around from time to time to prevent sticking) and some things even Kettilby assumed went without saying (e.g., that the bag shouldn't be soapy). Note however that the rules are also general—not about almond or orange or figgy pudding but about boiled puddings *per se*. Glasse's cookbook is well on its way to becoming a cookbook in the pejorative modern sense: a manual for dummies. Increasing specificity and quantitative precision is one way of rendering the tacit explicit, but it is not the only or even the most effective way to do so. On the contrary, anyone who has struggled through an instruction manual fat with prolix detail knows that too much specificity, too much exactitude, converts explicit back into tacit knowledge.

The early modern rules of the mechanical arts are rich in lessons for contemporary discussions about tacit versus explicit knowledge. As the distinction was originally formulated by chemist and philosopher of science Michael Polanyi in his book *Personal Knowledge* (1958), tacit knowledge embraced everything from knowing how to ride a bicycle to knowing how to read an image in X-ray crystallography and stood opposed to knowledge, especially scientific knowledge, that was objective in the sense that it could be completely and explicitly spelled out, accessible to anyone and everyone. Polanyi's aim was to carve out a middle space between objective, impersonal knowledge available to all and the purely private preserve of subjectivity, unchecked by logic or empirical evidence. In his view, this intermediate realm qualified as genuine and indeed essential knowledge but was nonetheless personal—the "personal knowledge" of his title.[51] As sociologist of knowledge Harry Collins observed in his probing analysis of the category of tacit knowledge, Polanyi's polar opposition in fact unfurls into a swathe of possibilities between the most deeply buried tacit knowledge of just the right gesture to get a finicky piece of laboratory apparatus to work properly and explicit knowledge of how to find a cube root so complete and unambiguous that it can be executed by a computer program. The stark binary of tacit versus explicit knowledge assumes that the latter is both possible—and also superior. "The idea of the tacit is parasitical on the *idea* of the explicit," Collins observed.[52]

The rules of the early modern mechanical arts provide an example of a world of thought and practice *not* bifurcated between the tacit and explicit. Thick rules blended the tacit and explicit: they assumed some hands-on experience but also the insufficiency of experience alone to produce the finest results. Rules larded with examples, observations, and even exceptions guided the attention of the practitioner to relevant details, spotlighted patterns, and staked out the limits of all rules. Early modern rulebooks contain no effusions over the ineffable aspects of skill or connoisseurship that no rule can convey, though they contain many appeals to experience. On the contrary, the authors of rulebooks for the mechanical arts insisted that the tacit knowledge learned by the apprentice in the workshop was by itself inadequate to achieve the highest level of virtuosity. Thick rules winnowed, ordered, and widened the apprentices' experience and sent them back to the workbench to acquire still more experience, this time refracted through the prism of reflection. Like those tightly folded paper flowers that blossom only if immersed in water, thick rules could take hold only if immersed in experience.

The case of the cookbooks teaches us the ambiguity of thin rules, which can be framed for those who know almost everything or for those who know almost nothing. Rule-followers who have already acquired the relevant experience and vocabulary can interpret a terse instruction like "fold the egg whites into the roux" without further explanation. Advanced cookbooks can spare expert readers the additional information thick rules would provide for novices—not because the information is tacit but because it is superfluous. But thin rules for those without any background experience—rank beginners or, in the extreme case, machines—require standardization, routinization, and a painstaking breakdown of the task at hand into simple steps. Only the latter sort of thin rules are explicit in the modern sense and presuppose a vision of mechanical labor, whether performed by humans or machines, as we shall see in Chapters 4 and 5.

Conclusion: Back and Forth, Betwixt and Between

The *artes mechanicae* were a dynamic category. Although there were various attempts to canonize seven of them, on the analogy of the seven liberal arts, they were too various and too inventive to be frozen into a static tableau like the trivium and quadrivium. Hugh of Saint Victor (c. 1096–1141) had in 1125 named wool manufacture, navigation, agriculture, hunting, weapon-making, medicine, and theater as the seven mechanical arts, but later medieval and Renaissance listings added to this rubric cooking, fishing, gardening, pharmacy, livestock herding, commerce, metal work, architecture, engineering, painting, pottery, sculpture, clockmaking, scribal copying, surveying, printing, politics, military strategy, gaming, alchemy, carpentry, and almost any other expression of the *vita activa*.[53] The proliferation of the mechanical arts in the early modern period testifies to market expansion and specialization as well as to the rising status of pursuits once stigmatized as illiberal and servile. New inventions—the magnetic compass, the printing press, and gunpowder were repeatedly cited by early modern authors—and impressive feats of engineering, architecture, painting, sculpture, and other arts that adorned piazzas and palaces displayed the fertility of the mechanical arts to best advantage.

Equally dynamic was the relationship between the mechanical arts and, on the one hand, the sciences, and, on the other, handicrafts governed by chance and routine. All three elements of this triad were in movement during this period, with the mechanical arts occupying the position of middleman, betwixt and between the necessary universals of the sciences and the happenstance particulars of the crafts. Although their immersion in the world of matter disqualified the arts from laying claim to the universality and necessity of form, their ability to formulate and follow rules elevated them above the rote bodily labor of the crafts. When Francis Bacon wanted to show how advanced his imaginary utopia of Bensalem was, he had the officials of the House of Salomon boast to the shipwrecked European sailors: "We also have diverse mechanical arts, which you have not; and stuffs made by them; as papers, linens, silks, tissues . . . many of them are grown into use throughout the kingdom; but yet, if they did flow from our invention, we have of them also for patterns and principals."[54] Bacon's "patterns and principals," both early modern synonyms for rules, emphasized that such arts were worthy of the name. Marking both an epistemological and a social distinction, the rules of art were a title to greater prestige and profits for those who mastered them.

Indicative of how fluid the relationship between the sciences, the arts, and the crafts was during the sixteenth and seventeenth centuries were the shifting connotations of the word *mechanical*. In ancient Greek and Latin, the words *mechanice/mechanica* referred to any device that multiplied human force in overcoming nature's resistance, first and foremost the basic machines of antiquity such as the lever and pulley. By the thirteenth century, however, the Latin word had also become associated with cruder forms of manual labor carried out by those at the lowest end of the social scale. Their very necessity to human survival tainted both work and workers with ignobility, with perhaps a faint echo of the curse of Adam, who had been condemned to earn his bread by the sweat of his brow when he and Eve were expelled from the Garden of Eden. Opposed to *liberal* (in the sense of "free," unbeholden to others), *mechanical* was a word increasingly attached to work that was unfree, at the beck and call of superiors. In the vernacular, its associations with coarseness and dirty hands widened to encompass all insignia of base condition.[55] In the course of the seventeenth century, however, the fusion of practical and rational mechanics as well as the ascent of the mechanical arts burnished the word to a new luster and placed it at the very center of the new science. Newton wrote of the new dignity of mechanics in the preface of the *Principia mathematica philosophiae naturalis* (Mathematical principles of natural philosophy, 1687): "He that works with less accuracy is an imperfect mechanic; and if any could work with perfect accuracy, he would be the most perfect mechanic of all; for the description of right lines and circles, upon which geometry is founded, belongs to mechanics."[56]

Finally, the mechanical arts occupied an intermediate and mobile position between head and hand, understanding and dexterity. Poised between universals and particulars, the tacit and the explicit, the rules of the arts occupied a fulcrum position, always see-sawing back and forth between the two. Because the philosophical opposition of universals and particulars is ancient and still mighty, the back-and-forth movement between general (but not universal) rule and specific (but not singular) case seems inherently unstable. But just as the point of a see-saw is not to rest in an up or down position, the purpose of a rule of art was not to gravitate to one or another pole and stay there. Thickened by examples, exceptions, explanations, models, and problems, the rule of art was all about see-sawing back and forth between reflection and practice. What it taught were mid-level generalizations that sharpened the eye of the practitioner for patterns and analogies and characteristic cases that made the salient terms of the rule memorable. Just because the generalizations were never universals and the examples and even the exceptions were never complete anomalies, the reader who absorbed these thick rules also learned the limits of their domains of application.

Discretion is perhaps too bland a term for the delicate sense of knowing just when and how to adjust a rule to circumstance or abandon it all together. Even the most categorical rules of art, trumpeted under the impressive title of "axioms," invariably gave way a few sentences later to a notable exception. For example, Vauban laid down what indeed sounds like a self-evident axiom of siegecraft: always attack a fortress at its weakest point. But barely a paragraph later he offers the counter-example of the Siege of Valenciennes, attacked at the gate of Anzin, not the weakest point in the fortifications but more easily reached by a good paved road that greatly facilitated the transport of cannons and other heavy munitions. This was the exception that proved the rule in the old-fashioned sense of *prove* as "test" (as in the proverb, "the proof of the pudding is in the eating"): it tested the limits of a serviceable rule in practice. Examples and exceptions also flagged relevant details (e.g., a decent road) to be noted, weighed, and exploited. Such details could also serve as the stepping-stones of analogy, connecting dispersed cases to a rule and—just as importantly—to each other. Like the see-saw, discretion was a balancing act.

Thick rules cast the preconditions for thin rules into relief. The domain of application must be well defined, materials and measurements must be standardized, the task must be divided into its smallest steps, and the ambit of chance must be minimized. As we shall see in Chapter 4, thin rules are not necessarily short rules. On the contrary, predictable circumstances, a micro-managing mentality, or a desire to restrain discretion can lead, singly or collectively, to rules barnacled with specifics. The key features of the thin rule are the assumptions of stability and standardization, both of conditions and users. Algorithms designed to be executed by computers are the thinnest of rules. This is not because such rules are in any sense minimalist—on the contrary, programs can be both long and complex—but because they assume complete uniformity in execution and conditions of application. Whether or not thin rules work in practice is a question of degree: whether the users and the world are more or less uniform, more or less stable.[57] Thin rules return the word *mechanical* to its older meaning of routinized, but for the opposite reason. Originally, work was mechanical because it dealt only with particulars, one damned thing after another; today, work is mechanical because it is done by machines that deal only with universals.

No rule on the page was ever thick enough to teach an art by itself. It could organize and mimic experience but not replace it. The how-to books of the sixteenth and seventeenth centuries addressed themselves to practitioners already initiated into the elements of their crafts and exhorted them to return to the workbench or battlefield or kitchen in order to translate understanding back into dexterity. Rules of art began and ended in experience. Even the eighteenth-century cookbooks written for novices had to be tempered by hands-on practice; making experience explicit could accelerate trial-and-error learning but not eliminate it. Nor can even the best-produced YouTube videos, for that matter, for the obvious reason that craft experience enlists the hands, tongue, nose, and ear as well as the eye. Orchestration of the senses, mind, and body requires time and repetition; discretion hones its edge against many and varied cases. Experience in the early modern sense was layered: many individual sensations of many different particulars eventually sedimented in memory into the experience of universals. Experience was therefore a process that took time, not a split-second event like the lightning flash of inspiration.

Let us return to Goltzius's allegory of Art and Practice one last time. (Fig. 3.2.) With her left hand, winged Art is pointing out something to Practice, focusing his attention on a telling detail, just as a thick rule would have done with its examples and exceptions. She sits astride the globe, symbol of the expansive reach of her teaching and the fame it brings. He is closer to the background landscape, which at first glance looks quite generic but upon closer inspection reveals a windmill, a local Dutch detail from Goltzius's own immediate surroundings in Haarlem. Globe and windmill bring together universal and particular. In the lower right-hand corner, at a slight distance from the scattering of books and instruments, all emblems of practice tutored by art, stands an hourglass, the symbol of time passing, grain by grain of sand. Without time and the slow sedimentation of experience, both the learning of art and the diligence of practice would be for naught. Parading examples, explanations, and exceptions before the mind's eye, thick rules recalled the passage of time and the slow fusion of head and hand.

4

Algorithms before Mechanical Calculation

The Classroom

The scene is a classroom, anywhere, anytime.[1] It could be a house in the ancient Babylonian city of Nippur circa 1750 BCE where pupils in training to become scribes bend over clay tablets written in cuneiform; it could be an academy of classical learning in Han dynasty China circa 150 CE where the sons of aristocrats solve arithmetic problems using counting rods as one of the Six Arts; it could be the home of a Renaissance *maestro d'abbaco* (French *maître d'algorisme*, German *Rechenmeister*) in a bustling commercial city like Pisa or Augsburg circa 1500 where aspiring merchants master Indian numerals[2] and the art of double-entry bookkeeping in bound ledgers; or it could be any primary school right now, where children are poring over multiplication tables, whether on paper or on screen. From the oldest surviving written documents from ancient Mesopotamia until very recently, the natural home of the algorithm was the classroom, and its natural medium was the textbook, whether written on clay, papyrus, palm leaves, bamboo slips, parchment, or paper. For thousands of years, algorithms had nothing to do with computers and with the vast majority of applications that have made the very word *algorithm* emblematic of the digital age. Algorithms were first and foremost about computation, not computers, and our sources for their long, far-flung history are overwhelmingly didactic texts.

This background must be kept firmly in mind in order to understand what algorithms were before the twentieth century, when developments in mathematical logic and computer science transformed these rules of practice, almost always attached to the solution of specific problems in surviving texts, into the highly abstract and general principles that now undergird the foundations of mathematics and computer programming. To read this recent history back into previous millennia is to risk losing aspects of algorithms that now seem incompatible with the current understanding of their essential characteristics.

Contemporary accounts of algorithms emphasize their abstract generality, but historically, algorithms have almost always been couched in concrete specificities: not an arithmetic function defined recursively such that $\varphi\left(k+1, x_{2,\ldots} x_n\right) = \mu\left(k, \varphi(x_2, \ldots x_n)\right.$ $\left. x_2, \ldots, x_n\right)^3$ but rather a method to calculate the area of a circular field given the diameter or to distribute a given number of loaves of bread in unequal amounts. Algorithms have been central to standards for mathematical demonstration since 1928, when mathematician David Hilbert (1862–1943) posed the *Entscheidungsproblem* (decision problem), which challenged mathematicians to specify a procedure that could determine in a finite number of steps whether any expression could be deduced from a given set of axioms.[4] But historically, algorithms have been contrasted to axiomatic ideals of demonstration, often with a deprecatory "mere" attached to emphasize the contrast between Euclidean-style demonstration and "mere algorithms." And for most of their long history, algorithms formed the bedrock, not the pinnacle, of the mathematical curriculum. They were fundamental, in the sense of being the precondition for all subsequent mathematical study. Algorithms were what students learned first and best.

There is one further contrast between the pre-modern and modern views of algorithms that will be central to this chapter's account of algorithms before the computer. They were executed by people, not machines. The mechanization of calculation was a gradual process that began in the late eighteenth century with the application of the principles of division of labor to human calculators and by no means ended when reliable, mass-manufactured calculating machines like the Thomas Arithmometer became available in the mid-nineteenth century.[5] For almost a century thereafter, in astronomical observatories, insurance offices, census bureaus, and war-time weapon projects, wherever calculations had to be done on an industrial scale, humans and machines worked in tandem to apply algorithms, as we shall see in Chapter 5. Only in the final quarter of the twentieth century was near-full automation of the execution of computational algorithms achieved by pre-programmed electronic devices. Yet already in the early nineteenth century, even before algorithms could be reliably executed on counting machines, much less computers, these sorts of computations began to be described as "mechanical," a word that flags a new way of viewing algorithms as rules that can be followed with little or no understanding—and followed in a completely standardized fashion, without adjustments to specific context. In the course of the nineteenth and twentieth centuries, algorithms became, in the terminology of "thin" and "thick" rules introduced in Chapter 3, the model of the thinnest rules of all—and thin rules in turn became the model of all rules.

The aims of this chapter are first, to reconstruct what premodern algorithms were and how they worked in practice, and second, to trace how algorithms became mechanized even before they became computerized. The temporal and geographic frameworks of these inquiries are not symmetric: algorithms have been in use for thousands of years in many cultures; the mechanization of algorithms took place over two centuries, mostly in the context of economic, political, and scientific modernization. Despite their different timelines, both inquiries track moving targets: neither the category of "algorithmic" nor that of "mechanical" remained constant, and their eventual convergence explains how thin rules became thinkable.

What Was an Algorithm?

The English word *algorithm* (and its cognates in other European vernaculars) is the latinized version of the name of Muhammad ibn Musa al-Kharizmi (c. 780–c. 850 CE), a Persian mathematician, astronomer, and geographer whose treatises on Indian numerals, algebra, the astrolabe, and astronomical tables and revisions of Ptolemaic geography greatly influenced these sciences in medieval Europe and the Middle East. In the twelfth century his treatise on calculation with Indian numerals was translated into Latin; the oldest surviving such Latin manuscript begins with the words "Dixit Algorizmi" (Thus spoke Algorizmi), and variants of "Algorizmi" became the term first for calculations conducted with Indian numerals (0,1,2,3,4,5,6,7,8,9) and eventually for arithmetic calculations more generally.[6] Popular elementary thirteenth-century Latin textbooks on arithmetic, such as Alexander de Villa Dei's (1175–1240) *Carmen de algorismo* and John de Sacrobosco's (c. 1195–c. 1256) *Algorismus vulgaris*, were used as standard university texts and helped to naturalize the Arabic loan-word as a synonym for the four basic operations of addition, subtraction, multiplication, and division.[7]

Current dictionary definitions vary according to area of application (mathematics, medicine, informatics), but in contrast to the original narrow associations of the word with reckoning by Indian numerals, most modern definitions broaden its meanings to include any step-by-step procedure used in calculation or problem-solving. A standard reference work on computer programming captures both the colloquial and the technical senses of the word in its definition of the word *algorithm*: "The modern meaning of algorithm is quite similar to that of *recipe, process, technique, procedure, routine, rigmarole*, except that the word 'algorithm' connotes something just a little different. Besides merely being a finite set of rules which gives a sequence of operations for solving a specific type of problem, an algorithm has five important features [finiteness, definiteness, input, output, effectiveness]."[8] The formal specification of each of those five desiderata has generated a large technical literature in logic, mathematics, and informatics, and the approaches of these fields are not always convergent: for example, a sequential procedure that terminates in n steps, where n is a very large number but less than infinity, may satisfy the mathematician's criterion for finiteness but leave a computer programmer who must take into account computation time dissatisfied. However, from a historical perspective, such technical debates played a minor role before the twentieth century. For preceding centuries, the core meaning of the word *algorithm* was the solution of specific problems by step-by-step procedures of calculation.

But long before the word there was the thing. From ancient mathematical traditions in Babylonia, Egypt, India, China, and elsewhere, texts survive that contain numerical problems and sophisticated solutions that are clearly algorithmic in the sense that crystallized around the word as it came to be assimilated into medieval Latin and other languages after circa 1200 CE. A brief and incomplete sampling of the kinds of problems to which the term *algorithm* is retrospectively applied might include: ancient Egyptian problems (c. 1650 BCE) on how to distribute 100 loaves of bread among 10 men if 50 are to be distributed among 6 men and the other 50 among the remaining 4;[9] Old Babylonian prediction rules (c. 1100 BCE) for the length of the lunar month;[10] Chinese procedures for the extraction of square and cube roots (1st c. CE);[11] and medieval Sanskrit problems (12th c. CE) on how to determine the purity of gold compounded of four parcels of gold, all of different weights and degrees of fineness.[12] All of these problems and the methods used to solve them—which often require great erudition and insight on the part of modern scholars to reconstruct—fit neatly into at least the broader modern category of algorithms: a step-by-step procedure to solve mathematical problems by calculation.

Was this also the category to which such problems belonged in the learned cultures that posed and solved them? Scholars who have painstakingly reconstructed these traditions have expressed doubts on this score, even if they are convinced that the methods qualify as algorithms in the modern sense. Historian of Babylonian mathematics Jim Ritter points out that the canon of ancient mathematical texts was first constituted by European scholars in the nineteenth century, when the prevailing assumption was that mathematics was mathematics was mathematics, regardless of context, and that modern definitions (and algebraic notation) could be applied unproblematically to diverse past traditions. In the case of Old Babylonian problem texts, Ritter suggests that it may be illuminating to interpret surviving cuneiform problem texts not only in the context of other mathematical texts but also in that of other "rational practice" texts from the ancient Near East, including Akkadian tablets about medicine, divination, and jurisprudence. Why? Because all of these texts exhibit striking semantic and syntactical similarities, and all would have been rooted in the practices of the same professional class of scribes. Modern historians of mathematics might not recognize the broader category of procedural texts, but perhaps "the grouping would have made sense to the ancient Babylonians."[13]

Historians of other mathematical traditions express analogous concerns about reading the past through the lens of the present. In the case of ancient Chinese and Sanskrit problem texts, autonomous mathematical canons seem to have crystallized around algorithms, although their forms and contents do not comfortably align with modern categories. For example, ancient Sanskrit texts presented mathematical rules in verse and problems cast as riddles; astral knowledge, both astronomical and astrological, formed part of many such canons. Moreover, combinatorial algorithms can also be found in Sanskrit texts devoted to topics that fall outside the bounds of the modern category of mathematics, including music, architecture, prosody, and medicine.[14] Old Babylonian (2000–1650 BCE) algorithms were embedded in practices of land surveying that served "to deliver social justice through the equitable distribution and fair management of assets."[15] Chiseling these pre-modern algorithms out of their original contexts often has the paradoxical effect of rendering them at once more familiar—they are recognizably mathematical in the modern sense—and more cryptic.

Ancient Egyptian, classical Chinese, and medieval Sanskrit, Arabic, Persian, and Latin texts all provide examples of algorithms that can be translated into modern algebraic notation. But did the scribes and sages who wrote these texts understand them in this fashion? Or to reverse the perspective, why are their formulations, notation, and procedures so opaque to modern eyes that such algebraic translations—which are anything but straightforward and were made possible only by decades of specialist scholarship—become necessary for *our* understanding? Even the context of actual computation is elusive: although the problem solutions are sequential, the exact path from step A to step B is rarely spelled out. Historian of Sanskrit mathematics Agathe Keller underscores the inherent "complexity of the relationship between what is stated about an algorithm, and the algorithm's execution," which results in multiple possible reconstructions of steps that would probably have been supplied orally in a pedagogical setting.[16] Also mostly missing are the physical traces of how numbers, however represented, were manipulated. Rare prodigies might have done all reckoning in their heads, but most mathematical calculations relied on some material equivalent of pencil and paper: symbols traced in the dust or on a wax tablet, beads moved on an abacus, knots tied in string, or more ephemeral tabular arrays. Long before there were calculating machines, there were calculating technologies. Occasionally, the handiwork of calculation left a faint clue in the text: historian of classical Chinese mathematics Karine Chemla remarks that the verb form "one puts" frequently used in even the oldest sources refers to the surface upon which calculations were carried out with counting rods; it is presumed that "the practitioner knows how to lay out the values on the surface."[17] (Fig. 4.1.)

What difference does it make how an algorithm is physically carried out? Since the proliferation of cheap handheld calculators in recent decades, algorithms have been largely blackboxed. Our

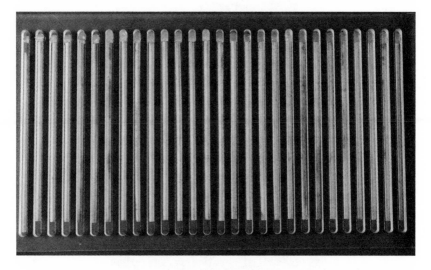

FIGURE 4.1. Chinese counting rods (Han Dynasty, 202 BC–220 CE).
© Shaanxi History Museum.

hands do no more than punch keys. But if there is one point upon which teachers of algorithms in all epochs and in all cultures seem unanimously to concur, it is that understanding an algorithm means working through it, step by step, with the hand as well as the head. Whether the kind of handiwork involved—for example, abacus versus pencil and paper, or manipulating words versus numerals—makes a significant difference to how an algorithm is understood remains open to debate, although some suggestive psychological studies show marked effects.[18] However, that a new word—*algorithm*—was coined to designate calculation using Indian numerals and that a new profession—reckoning master—emerged to teach how to calculate with the new symbols suggest that the cognitive transition between reckoning systems was not trivial. The oldest surviving Latin translation of al-Kharizmi's treatise, the *Dixit Algorismi*, opens with an explanation of the novel Indian numerals, only to revert immediately back to the more familiar Roman numerals for the remainder of the treatise.[19] Anyone who has ever had to update a computer program will sympathize

FIGURE 4.2. Old Babylonian cuneiform clay tablet of a mathematical problem
solution (1650–1000 BCE). bpk / Vorderasiatisches Museum, SMB / Olaf M. Teßmer.

with this reversion to the familiar, however shortsighted it may be in terms of calculating power and efficiency.

The difficulty and necessity of translating pre-modern algorithms into modern algebraic notation shows just how much the original historical context mattered to understanding them. The word *translation*, with its associations of transparency and fidelity, hardly does justice to this process. Knowing the relevant languages and symbol systems is merely the beginning; whole modes of thought and calculation must be pieced together like mosaic stones from surviving texts that are themselves often fragmentary. The original oral context of the classroom must be intuited and inferred and gaping ellipses filled in by plausible conjecture. In almost no case do the pre-modern algorithms satisfy any modern criterion of "definiteness." Take, for example, an Old Babylonian cuneiform tablet, a fragment of which is now held in Berlin, that shows how to calculate inverses of numbers.[20] (Fig. 4.2.) (Inverses played a key role in Babylonian division, which was conducted in two stages: first calculate the inverse of the divisor and then multiply it by the dividend.) Here is historian of mathematics Otto Neugebauer's translation and reconstruction (in brackets) of one of the five legible problems:

The number is 2;13;20. [What is its inverse?]
Proceed as follows.
Form [the in]verse of 3;20, [you will find] 18.
Multiply 18 by 2;10, [you will find] 3 [9].
add on 1, [you will find] 1;30.
Multiply 1;30 by 18, you will find 27.
The inverse is 27. [Such is the way to proceed.][21]

Very little about this translation-reconstruction is straightforward. Quite aside from the difficulties of deciphering Akkadian cuneiform script and filling in the parts that went missing in the intervening four thousand years, the Babylonian notation system is ambiguous: 2;13;20 could mean $(2 \times 3600) + (13 \times 60) + 20$, or it could mean $(2 \times 60) + 13 + 20/60$. All numbers are represented with a combination of two symbols, a vertical wedge and the so-called *Winkelhaken* (hook: imagine the letter *V* rotated 90 degrees clockwise), with place determining value (60^n, where $n = 1, 2, 3, \ldots$), with no place for units (60^0). The numbers effaced by time on the tablet must be reconstructed using the algorithm that is itself in question, with the obvious risks of circular reasoning. Even after these difficulties are surmounted, it is quite unclear what is going on in the step-by-step instructions. Historian of mathematics Abraham Sachs has suggested the following algebraic translation of the procedure,[22] where the initial number $c = 2;13;20$ and c^{-1} denotes its inverse; a and b are the parts into which c is decomposed:

$$c^{-1} = (a + b)^{-1} = a^{-1} \times (1 + ba^{-1})^{-1}$$

To the modern reader, this algebraic reformulation comes as a great relief, even after a translation in a modern language with modern notation has been supplied: finally, we have an inkling of the reasoning behind the otherwise inscrutable instructions.

But is this the way the Babylonian scribes understood the calculations? Almost certainly not. As historian of Mesopotamian mathematics Christine Proust notes, the algebraic version of the algorithm does not clarify the actual practices of calculation used by the Babylonian scribes and their pupils. Nor does it give any clue as to why these precise numbers—and not others—have been chosen in the example. And nor does it explain the format in which the steps are laid out on the tablet. As she shows, the numbers have not been selected at random but rather for convenience of calculation using the standard tables of inverse numbers available to the scribes. These computation tools may well have been supplemented by more ephemeral computation technologies, such as an abacus or some other counting device. Moreover, the decomposition of the initial number c into $a + b$ can be done in multiple ways, but the values chosen also correspond to those with inverses given by the tables.

Another Old Babylonian tablet, CBS 1215, provides numerical calculations that correspond to the same algorithm but without any verbal instructions and in a different spatial layout that clearly distinguishes the factors of the initial number (left) and those for its inverse (right), with the partial products in the center. These discrepancies even within Old Babylonian practice signal deliberate and functional choices on the part of the scribes who formulated the algorithms. Once again, it is crucial to keep in mind the diverse educational contexts in which these tablets were produced. Proust suggests that tablet VAT 6505 was a school exercise but that in CBS 1215, the same material "was developed, systematized and reorganized with different objectives than the construction of a set of exercises," possibly including "the functional verification of the algorithm" by reversing the sequence of steps.[23] The algebraic version of the algorithm, illuminating though its generality is to modern minds, by its very nature erases the specifics of format, choice of particular numbers, and repetition of certain modules or "subroutines" (such as factorization) that provide vital clues to how the Old Babylonian algorithm was actually used and interpreted.

Thin rules in the modern sense are ideally general rules. They are unencumbered by examples and exceptions; they do not traffic in specifics; they float above context. Thick rules, as we have seen in Chapter 3, shuttle back and forth between precept and practice, each refining and defining the other. Thin rules, in contrast, aspire to be self-sufficient and explicit. In principle, they wear their interpretations on their sleeves; they eschew commentary and have no need of hermeneutics. Nor must they enlist discretion to distinguish among cases and adjust to particular circumstances. Their generality presupposes that the class of cases to which they apply is unambiguous, that all cases in this class are identical, and that they will remain so for all eternity. Thin rules need not be concise—computer programs can go on for pages; ditto arithmetic calculations—but they cannot be vague. Algebra is their native tongue, at once general yet definite. It is no accident that champions of artificial, universal languages, from the German polymath Gottfried Wilhelm Leibniz in the seventeenth century to the French *philosophe* Étienne Bonnot de Condillac (1714–1780) in the eighteenth century to the Italian logician and mathematician

Giuseppe Peano (1858–1932) in the late nineteenth century, have held up algebra and arithmetic as their models of maximum generality and minimum ambiguity.[24] Modern algorithms, to paraphrase the Duchess of Windsor, cannot be too thin.

What are we then to make of the nubbly specificity of most pre-modern algorithms, which were almost always embedded, first, within a particular problem text; second, within a repertoire of computation techniques and tools; third, within a pedagogical setting that presumably made explicit what the text leaves only implicit; and fourth, within a broader category of step-by-step instructions that, depending on the culture, may include recipes, rituals, or how-to manuals? Can thin rules be pried out of these dense matrices, like metal extracted from ore, as the modern algebraic reformulations would suggest? Or are pre-modern algorithms really just thick rules in disguise, capable at most of the restricted generality of the rules of art described in Chapter 3? The answers to these questions depend on rethinking the idea of generality—but this time without the crutch of algebra.

Generality without Algebra

One of the most famous pre-modern algorithms about numbers makes no mention of numbers, either general or specific: the method given in Euclid's (c. 325–c. 270 BCE) *Elements* (c. 300 BCE) for determining whether any given magnitude can be used to measure another exactly, without a remainder, and, if it can, for finding the largest magnitude that can measure both.[25] In modern mathematical terms, Euclid's algorithm (a term first applied in the twentieth century) is a procedure for determining whether any two unequal numbers are mutually prime to one another, and, if not, for finding their greatest common divisor.[26] In the original text, however, continuous lines rather than discrete numbers represent the magnitudes, and the proof of the method (sometimes called *anthyphairesis*, "reciprocal subtraction") is geometric. Like Euclid's other proofs (for instance, that the sum of the angles of any triangle is equal to two right angles or that the alternate angles defined by any line intersecting parallel lines will be equal), this method is concrete (it applies to lines, not abstractions) but perfectly general within that domain. Just as the sum of the three angles of *any* triangle—equilateral, isosceles, scalene; tiny as a pinhead or as big as the earth—equals two right triangles, so the method of anthyphairesis, as demonstrated in Book VII of Euclid's *Elements*, applies to *any* two lines of unequal magnitude. Of course, the actual lines used in the diagrams that illustrate these propositions will be of a specific length that can be measured numerically.[27] But nothing in the demonstration (which proceeds by contradiction) depends on these specificities.

Generality comes in kinds and degrees. In the twentieth century, mathematicians recast Euclidean geometry in austerely formal terms. Some focused on Books VII–IX and rechristened them "the arithmetic books of Euclid."[28] Others speculated (especially in connection with Book II) about the implicit algebraic structures underlying the geometric demonstrations[29]—a view emphatically rejected by some historians as anachronistic, igniting a fierce controversy.[30] However debatable the historical accuracy of these reinterpretations of geometric demonstrations in terms of modern algebra and number theory (or as computer programs)[31] may have been, such reformulations did raise the level of generality of the propositions by greatly expanding the scope of the mathematical objects to which they applied. In his *Vorlesungen über neuere Geometrie* (Lectures on the new geometry, 1882), German mathematician Moritz Pasch (1843–1930) helped pave the way for these expansionist interpretations by his insistence that, in the name of ironclad deductive rigor, Euclidean geometry must free itself as completely as possible from the sense perceptions in which it had originated: "If geometry is to be really deductive, the process of inference must everywhere be independent of the *meaning* [*Sinn*] of the geometric concepts, just as [this process] must be independent of the figures."[32] Following Pasch, Hilbert pushed this generality to new heights in his *Grundlagen der Geometrie* (Foundations of geometry, 1899), insisting that whether geometry was about points, lines, and planes or a special case of group theory made no difference to the logical validity of the formal relationships deduced from the axioms.[33] Generalization had ended up in abstraction. From this mountaintop perspective, the objects of Euclidean propositions need not even be mathematical, much less geometrical.

Judged by these empyrean standards of generality, even the most general of pre-modern algorithms, such as Euclid's propositions VII.1–2, seem myopically specific. But formalization, whether by means of algebra or logic, is not the only means of achieving generality—and generality of mathematical objects is not the only kind of generality. The twentieth-century efforts to generalize Euclidean geometry by assimilating it to arithmetic, algebra, number theory, and logic aimed to safeguard the consistency and rigor of mathematics—not to solve problems, the original objective of most pre-modern (and many modern) algorithms, and most certainly not to train students in these practices, the context of most pre-modern texts about algorithms.[34] So the question concerning generality must be reframed: what standards of generality suit problem solving, especially in pedagogical and practical contexts?

Two striking features leap out from pre-modern algorithm texts, however diverse they may be in other respects: first, they are overwhelmingly about solving specific problems; and second, there are many problems involving the same algorithm. Recall the medieval French textbook on commercial arithmetic described in Chapter 3: although the Rule of Three is stated in general form, readers are expected to master it by working through problem after problem about converting currencies, pricing different lengths of cloth, dividing up profits among investors, and so on— and on and on and on. This format still dominates most elementary mathematical textbooks, to the point that the specific problems form their own genres: remember all the train and bathtub problems in your introductory algebra text that taught how to solve simultaneous equations in two unknowns? Or, for those who were schooled before the affordable pocket calculator, learning to extract square roots by actually doing so from many specific numbers, over and over again? There are general algebraic algorithms for all of these procedures; a computer can be programmed to perform all of them; even without algebra and computers, the general rules can be and were formulated verbally, as we saw in the case of the Rule of 3. Yet actual learning—including learning how to generalize from one specific problem to the next, equally but differently specific problem—occurs knee-deep in the weedy specifics, pencil (or stylus or abacus bead or counting rod) in hand. Although the process can and does yield more general rules, these are an afterthought, more a summary of what has been learned than a guide for how to learn the algorithm. What the students perform in solving problem after problem about the Rule of Three or the Rule of False Position[35] is a kind of induction: not an induction from particulars to a generalization but rather from particulars to particulars.

John Stuart Mill (1806–1873) contended that all induction proceeds from particulars to particulars, the premises of syllogisms (or mathematical axioms and postulates) being no more than the condensation of millions of particular observations made since time immemorial.[36] But for our purposes, there is no need to embrace Mill's sweeping generalization about all generalizations. It suffices to acknowledge that some sort of induction from particulars to particulars describes how beginners actually learn algorithms, from ancient Egypt to almost any elementary school classroom in the world right now. It does yield generalizations, but of a special kind, which are more akin to the classifications of natural history than to logical universals. After dutifully working through a dozen or so specific problems on converting currencies or dividing a certain number of loaves of bread among a different number of laborers or the arrival times of trains traveling at different speeds, the student will somehow recognize a new problem of this type—even if it has nothing to do with currencies or loaves of bread or trains. Just as the fledgling naturalist begins by painstakingly comparing each individual bird or plant with the image of the redheaded wood-pecker or foxglove in the guide but after much practice can iden-tify these species at a glance, undeterred by individual variations or diverse seasonal coloring, so the math tyro who has slogged through many individual examples of an algorithm can spot an-other example of the same species of problem, despite the entirely different specifics.

At least in some pre-modern algorithmic traditions, there exists a further parallel with natural history—and with the history of non-mathematical rules understood as models or paradigms, as described in Chapter 2. Since at least the sixteenth century, when first woodblock and then engraved illustrations proliferated in printed natural history treatises, naturalists have striven to repre-sent the essence of a botanical or zoological genus by a typical image, often a composite or idealization, that is at once specific and general: specific enough to be unmistakably this genus and not another, so that the image can be used for the purposes of identifying specimens; yet general enough not to include indi-vidual variations or incidental features (an unusual number of pet-als, for instance, or a gnawed leaf).[37] Chemla offers an analogous example from ancient Chinese mathematics in which a particular problem becomes a "paradigm" that probes the "extension" of the algorithm used to solve it: a way of bounding the category of op-erations that underlie the several versions of the problem enunci-ated in the text and commentary.[38] Paradigms function differently than induction from particulars to particulars; they epitomize a genus of problems and its solution algorithms in a single, still specific problem.

These lightning classifications, whether of birds or math prob-lems, do not achieve universals, only species and genera. Yet as in the case of taxonomy in natural history, prolonged and, especially, broad observation of many species and genera reveals structural affinities that lead to bundling species into genera, genera into families, families into orders, and onward and upward to ever more inclusive taxa. Deep immersion in textbook algorithms seems to produce an analogous impulse to expand and unify, as regularities emerge in the course of long practice. Proust detects such systematization at work in the calculations of the Old Babylonian tablet CBS 1215;[39] Chemla argues for similar generalization by "formal analogies" in Liu Hui's commentary (3rd c. CE) on the Chinese classic *Nine Chapters* (1st c. CE), in which general terms are coined to collect all specific examples of the same procedure (such as "to homogenize" for finding the common denominator of fractions).[40] Commenting on the absence of general rules in ancient Akkadian algorithmic texts, Ritter compares the form of reasoning to that of Anglo-American jurisprudence, in which lawyers link up precedents on the basis of analogy to the case at hand, describing it as "an alternative approach to the development and communication of mathematical practice, one that systematically covers the domain of the possible by a grill of typical examples. Generalization for instance is achieved not by creating englobing 'rules' or 'laws' but by interpolating any new problem in the mesh of existing known results."[41]

A crucial precondition for discerning such analogies is a well-stocked repertoire of techniques and examples. In the case of algorithms, the line between techniques and examples is often blurred. Almost all algorithms are built up from other algorithms, starting with the elementary operations of arithmetic and extending to more advanced techniques such as finding inverses, reducing fractions to a common denominator, or computing the area of a triangle. Although very few pre-modern mathematical texts (including most ancient Greek ones) constructed edifices from definitions, axioms, and postulates in the manner of Euclid's *Elements,* most are at least implicitly architectural.[42] First the foundations are laid in the form of the basic operations and equalities; thereafter each succeeding stage rests upon the ones below it. A surefire way of figuring out on what "floor" a textbook is located is to note what is *not* explained: what can the student be expected to know already? Chemla dubs this "uniformity in the level of detail chosen for writing down the algorithm" its "granularity," a rough-and-ready index of how many and which algorithms originally presented as examples have been internalized as techniques.[43] Examples from the "lower floors" of an algorithmic tower may also be cannibalized as "modules" or "sub-routines" in a more complicated algorithm from the "upper floors," just as composers may recycle motifs and excerpts from earlier music.

There is no repertoire without memorization, even in thoroughly literate and gadget-happy cultures. There is no escape from memorizing at least the multiplication tables, even with an electronic calculator in every pocket. Memorized equalities ($2 + 7 = 9$, $9 \times 9 = 81$), memorized methods (how to solve a quadratic equation), and memorized techniques (how to manipulate a counting board) stabilize into the bottom-most layer of the algorithmic tower, the foundation that supports everything else. Or to shift metaphors, memorized algorithms are the equivalent of the pianist's finger exercises or the weaver's basic patterns, the submerged competence that is first laboriously learned, then practiced until the skill becomes second nature, and finally assimilated into the subconscious realm of intuition.

The word *assimilated*, with its associations to how the body incorporates food, is chosen advisedly here. Since the eighteenth century, the prestige of the faculty of memory in cultures in which printed books are readily and plentifully available has plummeted among intellectual elites. For a scholar with a good library, Mnemosyne, the ancient Greek goddess of memory, was no longer mother of all the muses. Whereas a Renaissance humanist might still have learned thousands of Latin and Greek verses by heart and constructed "memory palaces" of the mind, an Enlightenment *philosophe* like Denis Diderot (1713–1784) could claim that having a comprehensive reference work such as his own *Encyclopédie* on one's bookshelf would preserve everything worth knowing in case of a cataclysm engulfing civilization, thereby rendering such feats of erudition superfluous.[44] The stars of analysis and critique waxed as that of memory waned; memorization was on its way to becoming "brute memorization." With this fall from favor and the predominance of print, images of how memory functioned also shifted. Enlightenment writers on mental faculties such as David Hartley (1705–1757) imagined memory as etching or impressing sensations upon a tabula rasa, much as the printer impressed wooden or metal type onto the blank page.[45] In contrast, medieval scribes likened memory, and especially memorization, to mastication, rumination, and digestion.[46] To memorize a text or a table of numbers was to make it one's own—in almost literal terms.

For the fortunes of memorization, the key transition was not between orality and literacy but between texts that were rare, costly, and therefore in the possession of a few, and those that were abundant and abundantly available at moderate prices. Historian of medieval music Anna Maria Busse Berger describes how assimilatory memory might actually have been reinforced rather than made redundant by the spread of musical notation in Latin Europe after the invention of the staff (c. 1030 CE). A written text could be pored over and absorbed down to the last detail of form as well as content—and also later consulted as to whether recall was exact or approximate. She cites Hugh of Saint Victor's advice to students on how to memorize psalters: they should be accumulating a lifelong treasury upon which to draw on as occasion demands. To this end, they should always use the same copy of the text to be memorized to remark both the verses and "at the same time the color, shape, position, and placement of the letters."[47] Analogously to medieval arithmetic and grammar instruction, young choristers would have memorized large chunks of plainsong by heart, just as other students were drilled on memorized Latin conjugations and declensions or multiplication tables into the seventeenth century and beyond.

In all these cases, the pedagogy of memorization and endless repetition produced textbooks that consisted mostly of specific problems to be solved, generating almost as many rules as problems. Overarching rules subsuming many specific problems were scarce, but a rich repertoire of memorized examples could be extended to novel situations by analogy. As in the case of natural history, classifications emerged: new terms were coined to pick out patterns and genres. This was a form of generality better suited to a world of problems to be solved rather than theorems to be proven—especially one in which the problems, like the world, were too unpredictable and particular for universal generalizations to gain much purchase.

What evidence survives points to a similar, if not even greater, emphasis on memorization in the education of elites throughout the pre-modern world. Historian of Old Babylonian mathematics Eleanor Robson observes that the thousands of cuneiform tablets containing multiplication tables that have survived (a fraction of the original numbers produced by scribal schools) were the "throwaway products of training in an essentially oral, memorized numerate culture," and historians of both medieval India and medieval Europe have interpreted the proliferation of versified texts (including mathematical texts) as evidence that they were meant to be memorized.[48] Chinese models of education in the classics (including mathematical classics) since the Han dynasty enshrined memorization as a first step toward mastery of the material.[49]

Modern pedagogy stigmatizes memorization and regularly opposes it to originality, analysis, understanding, and other virtues associated with independent thinking. Especially in fields like contemporary mathematics, which strive for unifying insights and abstract generalizations, memorization of long lists and tables of specific numerical values, much less of specific problem solutions, elicits contempt. Nowadays virtuoso mental calculators like the great eighteenth-century mathematician Leonhard Euler (1707–1783) would be more likely to be labeled idiot savants than brilliant mathematicians, the latter often making a point of emphasizing how hopeless they are at arithmetic. In the context of classroom learning, memorization is cordoned off from the exercise of truly human intelligence by the demeaning adjectives "rote" (mechanical repetition) or "brute" (animal imitation). Modern metaphors of memory, from the photographic plate to computer storage, highlight passivity and mechanical fidelity. Intellectual traditions that cultivate memorization seem at best curious, like the circus tricks of a card sharp, and at worst authoritarian. Small wonder that minds schooled in this catechism of pedagogical vices and virtues should balk at texts that teem with specifics to be committed to memory.

Yet even modern European languages preserve another, less pejorative metaphorical register for memorization: "to learn by heart," *auswendig lernen, apprendre par coeur.* Applied preferentially to memorization of music or poetry or canonical texts (the Declaration of Independence, soliloquies from Shakespeare, biblical psalms), learning by heart faintly echoes the associations of internalization, of taking full possession of the material. Even if the achievement remains ceremonial—trotting out an apposite passage for a festive speech, for instance—it stands as an achievement to be admired rather than scorned as mental servility. What accounts for the contrast between the perception of rote memorization and that of learning by heart, which after all both refer to the same cognitive practice? Whereas the mechanical tinge of rote memorization implies that the material is as inert as an unopened book gathering dust on a shelf, what is learned by heart has been taken to heart, metabolized as an integral part of the self. A sonata or sonnet learned by heart and rehearsed over and over again is deeply learned and therefore deeply *understood* in ways that the same piece played from notes or read from the page is not. Immersive understanding, like immersive observation, uncovers analogies and forges classifications: fugues in music, epics in poetry—and algorithms for finding the area of plane figures in mathematics.

Memorized repertoires, analogy, and classification work together to enable forms of generalization that do not fit the modern mathematical ideal of abstract universals rigorously deduced and formally expressed. Instead, the relevant model for pre-modern algorithm texts—primarily mathematical but also other step-by-step sequences of instructions designed to achieve a specific end, whether a recipe or a ritual—may once again be natural history. Observers steeped in the flora and fauna of a particular region discern affinities, common structures, and traits that underpin classification into species and genera. The broader their observational repertoires, the more ambitious their taxonomies. Early modern European botanists confronted with several thousand new domestic and exotic species began a wholesale revision of plant taxonomy; the Linnaean classificatory system depended on botanical gardens amply stocked with exotic plants from Far East and Far West and a network of Carl Linnaeus's (1707–1778) students dispatched on voyages throughout the world to send back descriptions and specimens to their teacher back in Uppsala.[50] Only the plunge into an ocean of specifics, minutely and comparatively observed, made the imposing generality of Linnaeus's *Systema naturae* (1758) possible.[51] Deep and broad immersion in a memorized repertoire of specific problems and algorithms proved similarly fertile in classificatory generalizations, even without the intrinsically general language of algebra.

Especially among modern mathematicians, natural history and indeed anything smacking of empiricism are in bad odor. As we have seen in the case of Pasch and Hilbert, suspicion of intuitions derived from experience (for example, intuitions about motion imported into geometry), coupled with the hope that formalization and axiomatization would guarantee rigor, led to a program of research and eventually pedagogy that elevated pure mathematics over applied, abstraction over concreteness, and generality over specificity, epitomized by the Bourbaki *Éléments de mathématique* series—from which algorithms are almost wholly absent.[52] The context of pre-modern algorithms, in contrast, was overwhelmingly applied. Even if the specific problems were sometimes contrived, they were intended first and foremost to teach students how to solve real problems in the real world. Moreover, the scribes, sages, and merchants who wielded these algorithms had to be able to find a bridge of analogy between old, familiar textbook problems and new applications, equally specific. They had to be able to recognize analogies between old and new problems at a glance, just as the seasoned naturalist recognizes that the whale is a mammal, not a fish: "Ah! This is basically a train problem—even though it has nothing to do with trains." General abstract rules are peculiarly unsuited for this purpose, useful as they are for others.[53] An algebraic expression is a powerful tool for revealing underlying, unified structures, but it offers no clue as to how those structures match up with applications. What is wanted is not an X-ray machine like algebra but a linked chain that can be indefinitely extended: induction from particulars to particulars. The two striking features of pre-modern algorithm texts noted at the outset of this section—specific problems and lots of them—now make sense. Saturation in specificity fosters its own brand of generality.

Historian of ancient mathematics Jens Høyrup has argued that modern mathematicians (and some historians in their thrall) have belittled pre-modern algorithms taught by "paradigmatic cases exemplifying rules," rather than by rigorous demonstration, because modern critics subscribe to a "mathematical Taylorism" that separates the work of mind and hand. Viewed through the lens of mathematical Taylorism, the "explicit or implicit rules" of pre-modern algorithm texts look like "mindless rote learning."[54] As we have seen, memorization need not imply "mindless rote learning"; a rosier cloud of associations is conjured by the phrase "learning by heart." Yet at some point in their very long history, algorithms—and the computations they made possible—did become mechanical, even before there were machines to execute them. This is the moment, sometime in the late eighteenth or early nineteenth century, when a form of mathematical Taylorism *avant la lettre*, a rigid and vigilantly policed division of labor, transformed computation into semi-skilled piecework for poorly paid assistants. This is the moment when algorithms became modern—and began to thin down.

Computing before Computers

On an August morning in 1838, seventeen-year-old Edwin Dunkin (1821–1898) and his brother began work as "computers" at the Royal Observatory in Greenwich under the directorship of Astronomer Royal George Biddell Airy (1835–1881):

> We were at our posts at 8 am to the moment. I had not been many minutes seated on a high chair before a roomy desk placed on a table in the centre of the Octagon Room, when a huge book was placed before me, very different indeed to what I had anticipated. This large folio book of printed forms, was specially arranged for the calculation of the tabular right ascension and north polar distance of the planet Mercury from Lindenau's Tables. . . . After very little instruction from Mr. Thomas, the principal computer in charge, I began to make my first entries with a slow and tremulous hand, doubting whether what I was doing was correct or not. But after a little quiet study of the examples given in the Tables, all this nervousness soon vanished, and before 8 pm came, when my day's work was over, some of the older computers complimented me on the successful progress I had made.[55]

Two boys sent out to support their widowed mother, the high chair and the huge ledger, the twelve hours of eye-straining, hand-cramping calculation (alleviated only by an hour's dinner break), the standardized printed forms that divided computation into steps like the manufacture of pins—it could be a vignette from Dickens, and both Airy and his predecessor in the office, John Pond (1767–1836), have been cast by contemporaries and historians alike in the roles of Bounderby in *Hard Times* or Scrooge in *A Christmas Carol*.[56]

But the reality of massive calculation of the sort that went on in astronomical observatories in parts of Asia since at least the medieval period and in Europe since the sixteenth century (and since the nineteenth century in insurance offices and government statistical offices) was considerably more varied—as varied as the nature of work itself in different historical and cultural contexts. The only constant was that calculations on the large scale needed to reduce astronomical observations, compute life expectancies, or tally statistics on everything from crime to trade was indeed work: the first Astronomer Royal, John Flamsteed (1646–1719), called it "labour harder than thrashing."[57] Before and even after the invention and diffusion of reliable calculating machines, the challenge to astronomers and other heavy-duty calculators was how to organize the work of deploying many algorithms, over and over again. These combined experiments in labor organization and algorithmic manipulation ultimately transformed both human labor and algorithms.

Let us return to young Edwin Dunkin perched on his high chair in the Octagon Room of the Royal Observatory at Greenwich. Edwin's father William Dunkin (1781–1838) had also been a "computer"—a word that until the mid-twentieth century referred primarily to human beings, not machines—and had worked for Airy's predecessors, Astronomers Royal Nevil Maskelyne (1732–1811) and John Pond calculating tables for the *Nautical Almanac*, a navigational tool for the globalized British navy and merchant marine that had been produced under the direction of the Astronomer Royal since 1767. Unable to supply the labor necessary to compute the *Almanac*'s numerous tables from the Greenwich Observatory's own resources, Maskelyne organized a network of paid computers throughout Britain to perform the thousands of calculations according to a set of "precepts" or algorithms, to be entered on preprinted forms that divided up calculations (with reference to fourteen different books of tables) into a step-by-step but by no means mechanical process.[58] This distributed piecework approach to computation was not new: already in the late seventeenth century Flamsteed had sent his assistant Abraham Sharp (1653–1742) parcels of computations to perform.[59] Nor were the pre-printed forms to guide astronomical calculation, which had been in use in China (where they were also adopted by Jesuit astronomers) since at least the Ming period, a groundbreaking innovation.[60] What is noteworthy about Maskelyne's operation (which involved a computer, an anti-computer, and a comparer to check each month's set of calculations) was its integration into an established system of piecework labor done in the home and often involving other family members. Each computer completed a whole month's worth of lunar position or tide prediction calculations according to algorithms bundled like the patterns sent to cottage weavers tasked with producing finished textile wares.

Just as the mid-eighteenth-century manufacturing system, in which many workers were gathered together under one roof and subjected to close managerial supervision, began to replace the family textile workshop long before the introduction of steam-driven looms,[61] so too did the development of heavy-duty computation trace a parallel arc a good half-century before algorithms were reliably calculated by machines. The careers of William and Edwin Dunkin, father and son computers in the service of the British Astronomers Royal, span the transition between piecework and manufacturing—but not yet mechanized—systems of labor organization. William, a former miner from Cornwall, spent most of his career as a computer in Maskelyne's network, working from his home in Truro. When the computational work of the *Nautical Almanac* was centralized in London under the direction of its own superintendent in 1831, William was the only member of the old computation network to be carried over into the new system, and he moved with his family to London. His son Edwin recalled the painful transition: "My father, however, never felt satisfied with the great change of life and habits which necessarily followed our removal from a home (his own property) that was endeared to us all by so many family associations. I have often heard him express a real regret at the loss of his semi-independent position at Truro, in exchange for the daily sedentary confinement to an office-desk for a stated number of hours in the company of colleagues all junior to himself in years and habits."[62]

Edwin Dunkin's experience as a computer began in a clerical setting like that from which his father had recoiled: all the computers gathered together in a single room; fixed hours (which were significantly shortened soon after he began work at the Greenwich Observatory); more supervision and hierarchy with differential pay for the various grades of computers and assistants; young personnel at the lowest ranks with a high turnover. But Airy's "system," as it was called, cannot be described as a factory of computation. Quite aside from the absence of any machines, the division of labor was loose and the possibilities for advancement significant. Young computers like Edwin were also expected to shoulder their share of night-time observing duties, and although William Dunkin was so unhappy with his prospects of social advancement as a computer that he discouraged his sons from following in his footsteps, Edwin eventually became a Fellow of the Royal Society and president of the Royal Astronomical Society.[63] A survey of Airy's Greenwich computers and assistants reveals a spectrum of livelihoods, from teenagers hired as computers at the lowest wages, many of whom did not last long, to assistants hired straight out of university (often with strong mathematical credentials) and salaries substantial enough to support a family in solid middle-class style.[64] Maskelyne's pre-printed forms and Airy's "precepts" structured the algorithms (and consultation of multiple tables) in a clear and rigid sequence adapted to contexts of domestic piece-work and supervised office work, respectively. But neither much resembled Adam Smith's (1723–1790) pin factory in the minute division of labor or endless repetition of the same task. Computation had not yet become "mechanical," in either the literal or figurative sense of the word.

Airy's "system" was in fact positioned between two extremes of organizing the labor of human computers in the nineteenth century. At one extreme was the American imitation of the *Nautical Almanac*, directed by Harvard mathematics professor Benjamin Peirce (1809–1880) in Cambridge, Massachusetts. Simon

Newcomb (1835–1909), who later became a prominent astronomer but who was largely self-educated in mathematics when he began work as a *Nautical Almanac* computer at age twenty-two, found working conditions decidedly casual: "The discipline of the public service was less rigid in the office [of the *Nautical Almanac*] than any government institution I ever heard of. In theory there was an understanding that each assistant was 'expected' to be in the office five hours a day. . . . As a matter of fact, however, the work was done pretty much where and when the assistant chose, all that was really necessary being to have it done on time." One of his fellow computers, the philosopher Chauncey Wright (1830–1875), concentrated a year's worth of computation into two or three months, staying up into the wee hours and "stimulating his strength with cigars."[65] No wonder Newcomb was so impressed by Airy's "Greenwich system" when he saw it in action on a visit to England. He credited it with producing results of "a value and an importance in its specialty that none done elsewhere can exceed."[66]

At the opposite extreme from the laissez-faire office of the American *Nautical Almanac* was the French project for calculating logarithms in base 10 initiated during the French Revolution to vaunt the advantages of the metric system. This was the moment when computation met modern manufacturing methods—though not yet machines—and could be reimagined as mechanical rather than as mental labor. It all began with one of the most famous scenes in the history of political economy: the pin factory.

The *Encyclopédie* article on pins opens with an evocation of vast variety in miniature: "The pin is of all mechanical works the tiniest, the most common, the least valuable, and yet one of those that requires perhaps the most combinations . . . for a pin undergoes eighteen operations before it enters commerce."[67] Step by step, the author of the article takes the reader from the arrival of coils of metal wire from Hamburg and Sweden to the sticking of the finished pins, a dozen at a time, into paper slips. A further, still more detailed article accompanies the painstakingly engraved plates illustrating the process: we learn exactly how the worker who cuts

FIGURE 4.3. Pin manufacture (*Encyclopédie, ou Dictionnaire raisonné des sciences, des arts et des métiers*, ed. Jean d'Alembert and Denis Diderot, *Recueil de planches, sur les sciences, les arts libéraux, et les arts méchaniques, avec leur explication* [Collection of plates on the sciences, the liberal arts, and the mechanical arts, with their explanation, supplement to the *Encyclopédie*], vol. 4, plate 1, 1765).

the heads must sit and hold his tools in order to achieve a rate of seventy heads per minute and how an experienced *bouteuse* (the woman who sticks the pins into paper) can reach a rate of up to forty-eight thousand pins a day. The wages of the workers responsible for each step in the process and costs of materials are laid out in a table alongside a calculation of profit margin.[68] (Fig. 4.3.)

In *The Wealth of Nations* (1776), Adam Smith, influenced by the *Encyclopédie* article among other sources, used pin manufacture to show how the division of labor increased the dexterity of the workers and the productivity of the workshop;[69] the French engineer Gaspard Riche de Prony (1755–1839), in turn, read Adam Smith's account of the division of labor and decided to "manufacture my logarithms as one manufactures pins";[70] the British mathematician Charles Babbage (1791–1871) personally inspected Prony's manuscript logarithm tables in Paris and concluded that not only logarithms but all mental operations might be mechanized.[71] At each stage in this chain of transmission of pin-factory fact and fantasy, from the *Encyclopédie* to Smith to Prony to Babbage, the meaning of the division of labor mutated in telling ways. For our purposes, it is the contrast between Prony and Babbage that is the most revealing for new thinking about machines, mechanicals, and rules.

As the director of the French *cadastre* (an official map and survey of land parcels for taxation purposes), Prony in 1791 had been charged with creating new logarithm tables based on the decimal metric system introduced by the French Revolutionary government.[72] Because the new tables were intended to advertise the superiority of the new French system of both rational measurement and rational governance, the project swelled to grandiose proportions: ten thousand sine values computed to twenty-five decimal places and some two hundred thousand logarithms to at least fourteen decimal places. The new tables would not only replace the older sexagesimal tables, many dating back to the seventeenth century; they would also, in Prony's words, stand forever as "the vastest and most imposing monument of calculation ever executed or even conceived"—a veritable Cheops' Great Pyramid of calculation.[73]

And it was indeed along the lines of a pyramid that Prony organized the division of labor for this massive feat of calculation. (Fig. 4.4.) Occupying the apex was a handful of highly proficient "mathematicians" who worked out the analytical formulas that would guide the whole operation; under them, a team of seven or eight "calculators" with knowledge of analysis who would translate the formulas into numbers; and, forming the broad base of the pyramid, seventy to eighty "workers" with no further mathematical skills beyond addition and subtraction who would carry out the actual calculations.[74] (Prony hinted that he had recruited his lowest-level calculators from among the former employees of aristocratic households, who were on the run from revolutionary zealots and found "in this sort of workshop, safeguard and asylum . . . thanks to the system of the division of labor, [that] they could, without being savants, live in safety under the aegis of science.") By methods

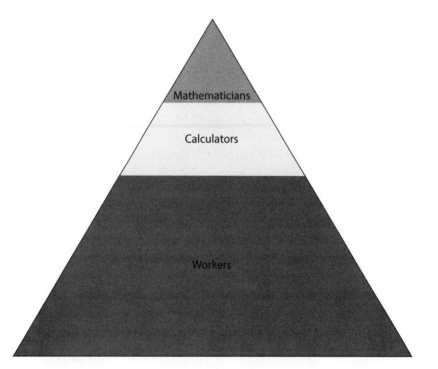

FIGURE 4.4. Pyramidical division of labor in Gaspard de Prony's logarithm workshop.

that Prony described as "purely mechanical," the workers performed about a thousand additions or subtractions a day in duplicate, in order to control for errors. In the midst of the political and economic tumult of the Terror during the 1790s, Prony's factory of logarithms managed to complete the task in a few years, filling seventeen folio volumes with manuscript tables—which are still preserved at the Observatoire de Paris.[75]

No machine more complicated than a quill pen was used in this herculean calculation project. What made it "mechanical," in the eyes of Prony and his contemporaries, was the nature of the labor at the bottom of the pyramid—or rather, the nature of the laborers. In a passage that Babbage was to repeat like a refrain, Prony marveled that the stupidest laborers made the fewest errors in their endless rows of additions and subtractions: "I noted that the sheets with the fewest errors came particularly from those who had the most limited intelligence, [who had] an automatic existence, so to speak."[76] This observation flew in the face of earlier accounts of the effects of the division of labor on the laborers. Neither the *Encyclopédie*'s nor Adam Smith's pin makers had been stupefied by their minutely divided tasks. On the contrary, Smith believed repetition of a narrowly defined task fostered ingenuity and dexterity as workers perfected skills and invented shortcuts.[77] Prony himself seemed surprised at this counter-intuitive finding: how could mindlessness improve the accuracy of mindful calculation? But for Babbage, steeped in the political economy of newly industrialized England, Prony's manufacture of logarithms proved that even the most sophisticated calculations could be literally mechanized. If mindless laborers could perform so reliably, why not replace them with mindless machines?[78]

Babbage's plans for his Analytical and Difference Engines took shape as he pondered Prony's tables and their lessons. The publication of the tables had been halted when the finances of the French government collapsed, and to this day they have yet to be published in their entirety.[79] In 1819 Babbage visited Paris, just as Lord Castlereagh (1769–1822) launched a British initiative to share the publication costs of the Prony tables with the French government. The publication plans came to naught, but Babbage was allowed to inspect the manuscript folio volumes at the Observatoire de Paris, a sneak preview from which he later profited in his own 1827 book of logarithm tables.[80] A few years later, in his treatise *On the Economy of Machinery and Manufactures* (1832), Babbage cited Prony's logarithm workshop as proof that the principle of the division of labor could also be applied to mental as well as bodily work. He repeated with emphasis Prony's observation that the less mathematical knowledge possessed by the calculator, the more correct the calculations. Whether the product was pins or logarithms, Babbage concluded, the division of labor widened the profit margin by stratifying skill levels, just as

Prony's pyramid had: "we avoid employing any part of the time of a man who can get eight or ten shillings a day by his skill in tempering needles, in turning a wheel, which can be done for sixpence a day; and we equally avoid the loss arising from the employment of an accomplished mathematician in performing the lowest processes of arithmetic."[81]

Prony's manufactured logarithms and the method of differences that made them possible were not the only inspirations for Babbage's Analytical and Difference Engines. The card system invented by Joseph-Marie Jacquard (1752–1834) that partly automated the weaving of elaborate patterns and that was fully operational by 1818 also greatly impressed Babbage, who cherished a portrait of Jacquard himself woven on a loom fitted with Jacquard cards.[82] (Fig. 4.5.) But although the Jacquard cards automated part (but by no means all) of the weaving process once installed, they did not replace the designer who invented the pattern, the transcriber who translated it onto a series of hundreds of cards, and the weaver who strung the loom with threads of the right fabrics and colors.[83] Nor of course did calculating machines dispense with human operators, whether Charles Xavier Thomas de Colmar's (1785–1870) workable Arithmometer or Babbage's unworkable Analytical Engine or even IBM's punch cards. Well into the twentieth century, the word *computer* referred to poorly paid workers, by the 1920s mostly women, who calculated, with or without mechanical aids, in astronomical observatories, census bureaus, and military undertakings such as the Manhattan Project during World War II.[84]

This elision between human and mechanical calculators dates back to Prony's manufacture of logarithms—or rather, to Babbage's interpretation of Prony's project. Mechanizing calculation first became thinkable not because machines could reliably calculate at that time but because mechanical workers could. Until the early nineteenth century, *mechanical* had referred to the lowest class of manual labor, conceived as all hands and no head. Machines existed to assist and perhaps replace mechanicals. In contrast, calculation, however wearisome, counted as headwork, and

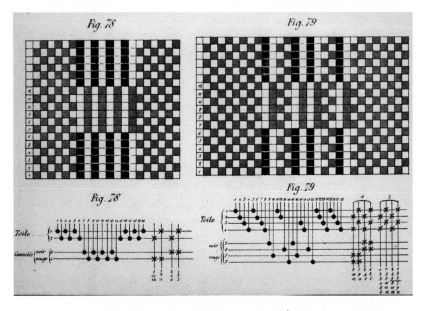

FIGURE 4.5. Textile pattern transcribed in Jacquard card (Constant Grimonprez, *Atlas tissage analysé* [Analytical textile atlas, 1878], fig. 178).

even after Babbage had built his first prototype of the Difference Engine, the idea that it might be possible to substitute "mechanical performance for an intellectual process" and thereby gain a degree of "celerity and exactness unattainable in ordinary methods" astonished contemporaries.[85] In some quarters, skepticism about the results obtained both by Prony's mechanicals and Babbage's machines persisted for decades. As late as the 1870s, the Scottish author of a hand-computed and -checked table of logarithms heaped scorn upon both Prony's tables and the up-and-coming Arithmometer in the name of mindful calculation: "we must fall back upon the wholesome truth that we cannot delegate our intellectual functions, and say to a machine, to a formula, to a rule, or to a dogma, I am too lazy to think; do, please, think for me."[86] But once calculation could be performed by mindless mechanicals, it seemed a small step, at least to fertile minds like Babbage's, to mindless machines and the rigid rules materialized in their whirring wheels and cogs.

Conclusion: Thin Rules

Algorithms became mechanical when it became possible to imagine their flawless execution by machines. The word *imagine* is used here advisedly. Babbage's never-realized Analytical Engine was a fantasy until the late twentieth century, a machine to think with, not to work with. (Fig. 4.6.) Real machines creaked and jammed; their wheels failed to turn and their gears to mesh. The prototype calculating machines devised by Pascal and Leibniz in the seventeenth century were too unreliable to be anything more than curiosities;[87] Babbage's calculating engines also never got beyond the prototype stage, a toy to amuse party guests.[88] Like the thick rules of pre-modern texts, machines required adjustment and judgment—if only to ascertain when a machine was malfunctioning, spewing out crooked pins or faulty sums. But fantasy machines defy friction and wear; no dust or moisture perturbs their inner workings; they never break down. An essential part of the story of the newfound rigidity of rules is how such fantasies first became imaginable, even if their realization lagged far behind.

The phrase "rigid rule" in eighteenth-century English usage applied most often to moral injunctions, for example the "rigid rules of honor" or of "strict propriety" or of "honesty and integrity." These rules were rigid because violations were intolerable, offenses that weakened the moral order. In contrast, "mechanical rules" usually referred to the manual or craft aspect of an undertaking, the operations of actual machines or the laws of nature (in association with "mechanical philosophy"), or, more pejoratively, to any attempt to reduce literary composition to rules: Alexander Pope (1688–1744), for example, mocked those French authors who would dictate "mechanical rules" for epic poetry.[89] Disdain for "mechanical rules" was at its most intense when the precepts of handiwork were transferred to headwork, implying *déclassement*

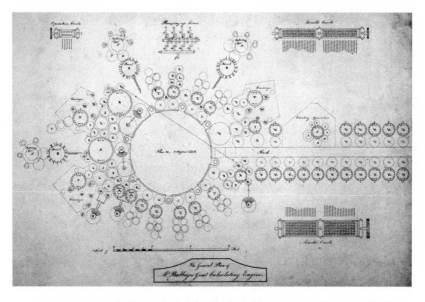

FIGURE 4.6. Joseph Clement's plans for Charles Babbage's never-realized Analytical Engine (1840). Science Museum, London / Science and Society Picture Library.

as well as de-skilling. "Mechanical" referred not simply to machines but to any kind of labor perceived as mindless, repetitive, and banausic—and to the people who performed such tasks, like Shakespeare's bumptious "rude mechanicals" in *A Midsummer Night's Dream* (III.ii).

Until the turn of the nineteenth century, the manipulation of algorithms counted as headwork. The status of such work depended on cultural context, the sophistication of the algorithms, and the sheer volume and standardization of the calculations to be performed. Even in scribal cultures of the ancient world, schoolboy calculations and schoolmasters' texts and commentaries on algorithms occupied very different rungs on the ladder of prestige. Yet even eminent astronomers and mathematicians occupied themselves with calculations in the eighteenth century. The French mathematician and liberal revolutionary Marie Jean Antoine Nicolas de Caritat, Marquis de Condorcet (1743–1794) went so far as to claim that the citizens of the new French republic might be inoculated against the deceits of priests and politicians by learning arithmetic.[90] The numbers from one to ten must never be memorized but instead taught "by intelligence and by reason; nothing is abandoned to routine." Far from being mindless, Condorcet insisted, calculation was the foundation of "the three intellectual operations of which our mind is capable; *the formation of ideas, judgment, reasoning.*"[91]

It was when calculations for state administration, mathematical and nautical tables, and the reduction of astronomical observations reached mountainous proportions, already by the mid-seventeenth century, that headworkers like Flamsteed balked. The most calculation-intensive seventeenth-century professions were astronomy (including navigation) and administration (Pascal invented his calculating machine in order to help his father, who was the intendant of Rouen), and there is much groaning testimony from these quarters that calculation was regarded as drudgery. John Napier's (1550–1617) work on logarithms and calculating rods ("Napier's bones") also emerged in response to the increasing burden of calculation.[92] However, it took the better part of a century to develop the standardization of procedures and the labor organization that made it possible to divide the crushing labor that calculation had become. Although Babbage fixated on the lowest level of Prony's pyramid of logarithm manufacture, the labor of the two upper levels was absolutely essential to getting the job done— as essential as Maskelyne's "precepts" and Airy's forms were to parceling out the computations needed by the Greenwich Observatory and the *Nautical Almanac.* The mathematicians and astronomers had to devise more than formulas; they had to do more than translate multiple complex algorithms into step-by-step numerical procedures. They had to imagine the whole process in terms of a division of labor so minute that semi-skilled computers could reliably execute the bulk of the calculations. In other words, they reimagined mathematics as a kind of pin factory, complete with its graduated scale of status and wages.

The poorly paid computers at the bottom of the scale, whether schoolboys, unemployed artisans, or (later) women, differed from the students who learned algorithms in the pre-modern world in at least one important respect: they no longer needed to exercise the faculty of analogical reasoning that bridged old and new applications. They received their problems and the methods to solve them pre-packaged, thanks to the labor of Maskelyne, Airy, Prony, and others who had divided and standardized procedures. There was no need for the induction from particulars to particulars so characteristic of pre-modern algorithm textbooks, and there was no scope for the classificatory generalization of algorithms practiced by earlier mathematicians. The problems had been pre-classified and the procedures specified to the last detail. No computer needed to ask what species of problem this was or what algorithms were needed to solve it. Nor were computers likely to encounter a wide variety of kinds of problems and algorithms. Their experience of algorithms contrasted sharply with that of pre-modern calculators. Their rules were genuinely thin.

They were thin not because they were independent of context but rather because their context had been carefully fixed. The element of unpredictability and variability so characteristic of thick rules, including even pre-modern algorithms with open-ended applications, had largely been eliminated by the efforts of Prony, Airy, and the other designers of computing "systems." Analogously to the way in which meticulously controlled laboratory conditions are required to produce effects impossible to achieve under messy real-world conditions, the impressively efficient systems of human computers presupposed a remarkable effort of analysis and organization. In both cases, perturbing factors had been diagnosed and eliminated. Reimagining how to calculate in the observatories of Greenwich and Paris made that small pocket of the world safe for thin rules to function—and supplied cheap labor to execute them.

The rules were also thin because they had been sliced into the smallest possible steps—just addition and subtraction in the case of Prony's logarithm project. This was an achievement in both mathematics and political economy: the division of a complex problem into analytic equations, numerical versions, and finally actual calculations; and the parallel division of the labor of solving the problem into three classes of workers of greatly differing levels of mathematical skill. Only the work of the lowest class of computers was ever called "mechanical." It was the division of labor, not the machines, that made the algorithms mechanical—and made the actual mechanization of algorithms on a grand scale thinkable.

5

Algorithmic Intelligence in the Age of Calculating Machines

Mechanical Rule-Following: Babbage versus Wittgenstein

In one of the most famous and enigmatic passages of twentieth-century philosophy, Ludwig Wittgenstein used a mathematical example to argue that even the rules of calculation cannot be followed mechanically. A teacher asks a student to continue the series of numbers starting with 0, 2, 4, 6, 8, . . . that has already been carried through by adding increments of two up to 1000. The student writes: 1000, 1004, 1008, 1012. The teacher thinks the student has misunderstood and made a mistake, but Wittgenstein disagrees: "In such a case we might say, perhaps: It comes naturally to this person to understand our order with our explanations as *we* should understand the order: 'Add 2 up to 1000, 4 up to 2000, 6 up to 3000, and so on.'" Suspicious that even a machine operated with mechanical precision—"do we forget the possibility of their [the machine's parts] bending, breaking off, melting, and so on?"—Wittgenstein concluded that to obey a rigid rule of calculation was more like following a custom than executing a mechanical motion.[1]

Wittgenstein's example of how even an apparently self-evident continuation of a mathematical series might yield surprises was not original, but he gave it a subversive spin. Over a century earlier, the British mathematician, inventor, and political economist Charles Babbage, whom we have already met in Chapter 4, had anticipated Wittgenstein's unruly series and even executed it with a real machine. In 1832 Babbage ordered a miniature version (approximately a cube of two feet in height, width, and breadth made of bronze and steel) of his Difference Engine to be made by the engineer Joseph Clement (1779–1844) for demonstration purposes. (Fig. 5.1.) Babbage regularly hosted soirées at his London home for the glitterati, where the likes of political economist Nassau Senior (1790–1864) rubbed shoulders with astronomer John Herschel (1792–1871) and distinguished foreign visitors such as Alexis de Tocqueville (1805–1859). Amidst the canapés and the madeira and in between bouts of dancing in the ballroom, guests would be entertained with demonstrations of the latest scientific curiosities, from electric batteries to some of the first photographs. As pièce de résistance, the Difference Engine climaxed these edifying amusements with what Babbage described as a kind of calculating miracle.[2]

The Difference Engine could be programmed to calculate an algebraic function, for example $2 + x = n$, as x was allowed to take on the values of the natural numbers starting with zero. However, it could further be programmed with a different equation to take effect at some point in the sequence—say, at $x = 1000$—after which the function becomes $4 + x = n$. The sequence produced by the Difference Engine would look like this:

2, 4, 6, 8, 10, 12, . . . 994, 996, 998, 1000, *1004*, 1008, . . .

In *The Ninth Bridgewater Treatise* (1837), his one foray into theology, Babbage boldly likened such pre-programmed surprises in the calculations of the Difference Engine to divine miracles. Just as bigger, better versions of the table-top engine might be programmed to generate an unbroken series of square numbers over millennia and at one crucial moment interrupt the sequence with

FIGURE 5.1. Charles Babbage's Difference Engine No. 1 (1824–1832).
Science Museum, London / Science and Society Picture Library.

a cube without contradicting the "full expression of the law by
which the machine acts," so the deity could have foreseen and ordained all apparent exceptions to natural laws from the moment
of creation.[3]

Of course, Wittgenstein's point was the very opposite of Babbage's. Whereas Babbage used his calculating machine to show

that even apparent anomalies did not violate the rule and that the rule could be mechanically obeyed, Wittgenstein argued that not even machines could perform a rule mechanically.[4] It is unclear whether Wittgenstein had ever read Babbage; if he had, it wouldn't be the first time that he turned a striking Victorian example inside out and upside down. British polymath Francis Galton (1822–1911) used his technique of making composite photographs to reveal human prototypes—for example the prototypical criminal—as the visual essence of a category. Wittgenstein used the composite photograph to undermine the very idea of essences with his concept of family resemblances.[5] However, even if Wittgenstein had never encountered Babbage and his Difference Engine, he lived in a world that Babbage had envisioned: one in which real machines were in daily operation wherever heavy-duty calculations were done—in astronomical observatories, government census bureaus, accounting offices—the sites of Big Calculation. Babbage did not create this world of arithmometers, comptometers, and tabulating machines; his Difference and Analytical Engines never got past the design stage. But taking his cue from Prony's logarithm project, Babbage did more than anyone else to reimagine calculation as mechanical, the first mental activity to be performed by mindless machines.

Since we now live at a moment when artificial intelligence, smartphones, and algorithms-for-anything-and-anyone foster dreams (and nightmares) of computers capable of mimicking and surpassing all human intelligence, Babbage's transfer of calculation from mind to machine seems prescient to us. We can even imagine the human mind itself as a kind of machine, which is the model underlying much contemporary cognitive science. Worse, we can imagine the machines developing minds of their own, and not very nice ones, either: we remember the computer HAL in the film *2001: A Space Odyssey* (1968). But in between Babbage's idea that mindless machines could calculate and our anxieties about being replaced by mechanical minds lies almost a century of calculating machines working in tandem with humans, from about

1870 to 1970. It was humans who figured out how to divide the labor of complex calculations so that machines with little or no programming capacity could perform them, and it was humans who operated the machines. This was the reality of calculation that Wittgenstein would have encountered firsthand when he was a student of engineering at the Technische Hochschule in Berlin and the University of Manchester, and perhaps that experience lies behind his doubts about the autonomy of such machines: "If calculating looks to us like the action of a machine, it is *the human being* doing the calculation that is the machine."[6]

During the decades when Big Calculation was done by humans and machines together, calculation straddled the line between mind and machine. This was not because calculating machines were viewed as intelligent but rather because calculation had become a mechanical mental activity, as we saw in Chapter 4. Yet human mindfulness remained essential to effective and accurate calculation by machines. Between the human intelligence that had laboriously worked through whole volumes of calculation by hand, as the astronomer Johannes Kepler (1571–1630) had for the orbit of the planet Mars in the early seventeenth century, and the artificial intelligence of the computers that could be programmed to execute such calculations in a trice in the late twentieth century, there is the hybrid intelligence of humans and machines working together.

This hybrid intelligence was doubly algorithmic. As we saw in Chapter 4, the term *algorithm* has had both a narrow and broad meaning. Narrowly and originally, *algorithm* referred to arithmetic calculations carried out with Indian numerals: addition, subtraction, multiplication, and division performed with the numerals 0,1,2,3,4, and so on. More broadly, most modern definitions of algorithm include any step-by-step procedure used in calculation or problem-solving. Both broad and narrow definitions are at stake in the history of algorithmic intelligence. The subject matter was algorithmic in the narrow sense, namely numerical calculation. But the ways in which the calculations were turned into procedures and workflows were also algorithmic in the broad sense of dividing up a complex task into a finite, definite sequence of small steps with precisely defined inputs and outputs. Cookbook recipes, IKEA assembly instructions, and any other procedure spelled out step-by-step resemble algorithms in this extended sense of the term, even if no calculations are involved. The broader sense of algorithmic could as easily apply to pin-making as to calculating logarithms—or for that matter, to the second step of Descartes' famous method: "to divide each of the difficulties that I examined into as many parts as possible and would be required to solve them satisfactorily."[7] It is analysis in the root sense of word, to unloose or take apart.

The introduction and widespread use of calculating machines in the late nineteenth and early twentieth centuries changed both narrow and broad algorithms: those used to calculate and those used to organize calculation. Machines also altered the meaning of calculation and the identity of calculators. But machines did not fundamentally transform the mental burden of calculation that they had been designed to relieve. Instead, they shifted it to other shoulders—or rather, to other minds. The labor of massive calculation, a cause for complaint among astronomers, surveyors, administrators, and navigators since the sixteenth century, remained as monotonous and tedious as ever—so much so that it inspired whole new psychophysical inquiries into mental fatigue and flagging attention. At least in its first century of widespread application, mechanical calculation never entirely succeeded in exorcising the ghost in the machine—and a very weary ghost it was, too.

"First Organize, Then Mechanize": The Human-Machine Workflow

If calculations were essentially mechanical, as Prony and Babbage claimed, why did it take so long for machines actually to perform them—especially since there was desperate demand among calculation-intensive enterprises like the *Nautical Almanac*? Any number of ingenious calculating machines had been invented and fabricated, at least in prototype version, since the French mathematician Blaise Pascal tried to sell his arithmetic machine in the 1640s, without notable success. Throughout the seventeenth, eighteenth, and nineteenth centuries inventors experimented with diverse designs and materials, but their machines remained difficult to construct, expensive to purchase, and unreliable to use, items to adorn a princely cabinet of curiosities rather than workaday tools.[8] Far more useful for lengthy, complex calculations were the logarithms invented by the Scottish mathematician John Napier, whose Latin description and instructions on how to compute tables appeared in 1614, went through at least seven editions until 1899, and inspired the computation of numerous tables, including by Babbage himself.[9] Such logarithm tables would have been in almost constant use by the human computers like Edwin Dunkin, whom we met in Chapter 4, throughout the nineteenth century, each calculation involving multiple consultations of tables.[10] Calculating devices such as the counting rods used in ancient China, the abacus, Napier's bones (calculating rods inscribed with multiplication tables), tokens, Genaille rods, and many others were ubiquitous in commercial contexts but were ill suited to the long, laborious calculations required for astronomical and navigational purposes, since they were limited to the manipulation of relatively few digits.[11] Neither calculating machines nor calculating devices are so much as mentioned in one of the most compendious eighteenth-century treatises on mathematical instruments, an indication that they were of little use to practitioners.[12]

The first calculating machine robust and reliable enough to be successfully manufactured and marketed was the Arithmometer, patented by the French businessman Thomas de Colmar in 1820, but not in widespread usage until the 1870s. (Fig. 5.2.) Even then, the insurance firms that were its primary purchasers complained that the Arithmometer broke down often and required considerable dexterity to operate.[13] By the second decade of the twentieth century, however, calculating machines manufactured in France, Britain,

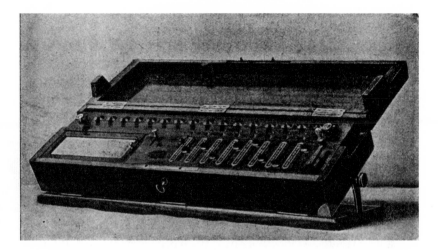

FIGURE 5.2. Thomas Arithmometer (Maurice d'Ocagne, *Le Calcul simplifié par les procédés mécaniques et graphiques* [Calculation simplified by mechanical and graphical procedures], 2nd ed., 1905).

Germany, and the United States were fixtures in insurance offices, banks, government census bureaus, and railway administrations. But a comprehensive 1933 survey of calculating machines then available admitted that for scientific purposes, "mental calculation aided by writing and numerical tables" still predominated.[14]

This was more or less exactly the moment when the British *Nautical Almanac* began to introduce mechanical calculating machines into its operations.[15] As one of the oldest and most regularly published navigational guides based on heavy-duty astronomical calculation and among the first to introduce calculating machines into its operations, the *Nautical Almanac* serves as a particularly illuminating example of how such calculations were organized both before and after numbers began to be crunched by humans and machines working together. Moreover, although the calculations carried out for the *Nautical Almanac* were of the positions of heavenly bodies, their goal was down-to-earth: to guide the world's most powerful navy and merchant marine safely and swiftly throughout the British Empire. The annual numbers of the

Nautical Almanac therefore had to be produced on a strict schedule, under time pressures more like those of a commercial undertaking than an astronomical observatory. The *Nautical Almanac* therefore sought to combine the high standards of accuracy expected of scientific calculation with the demands of efficiency expected of commercial calculations. It was Big Calculation with a deadline.

Recall the young Edwin Dunkin, seated on his high chair in the Octagon Room of the Royal Greenwich Observatory, with Airy's pre-printed forms before him and surrounded by books of tables in which to look up values at the proper step in his assigned calculations. Airy's system of calculation depended heavily on the division of labor and tables but not at all on machines. The transition from the silence of the Octagon Room, broken only by the scratching of pens and the turning of pages as junior computers and more senior assistants calculated and looked up tables, to the deafening clatter of adding machines in a crowded office at the Naval College in Greenwich must have been jarring. In an urgent plea to the Admiralty for larger quarters in 1930, Superintendent Leslie Comrie (1893–1950) described the scene: "We have a large Burroughs [Adding] Machine in continual use which is so noisy that no degree of concentration is possible in the room where it is working. It is essential, for the sake of the other workers, that the machine should have a room to itself."

And why was the office so crowded? Because use of the machines dictated that work previously parceled out to "outside workers"—retired staff members and their relatives, clergymen and teachers seeking to pad modest incomes—should now be assigned to "ordinary junior market labour with calculating machines" instead of to "the old-time highly-paid computers who knew nothing but logarithms and who often worked in their own houses." Such lower-paid workers needed "closer supervision," and the expensive machines could not leave the office.[16] And who were these cheap workers who operated the new machines under the gimlet eye of their supervisor? No longer boys fresh from school as in Edwin

Dunkin's day but rather a half-dozen unmarried women (at the time, British Civil Service regulations prohibited hiring married women) who had passed a competitive examination in "English, Arithmetic, General Knowledge and Mathematics."[17]

Paradoxically, the machines introduced with the intention of cutting costs, saving labor, speeding up production, and, above all, alleviating mental effort had at least the initial effect of more workers hired, more money spent, production disrupted, and mental effort increased—especially for the supervisors charged with reorganizing how calculations were done in order to integrate human and mechanical calculators into a smooth, efficient, and error-free sequence. Take the case of the Hollerith tabulating machine that Superintendent Comrie was keen to lease for at least six months to make an ephemeris of the Moon (i.e., the Moon's calculated positions over a specified period). In addition to the circa £264 for the rental itself, there would be the additional expense of £100 for 10,000 punch cards, plus the extra "wages of four girls for six months, and two girls for an additional six months" to punch in the numbers and operate the machine, amounting to another £234—and did I mention the extra £9 added to the electricity bill? That's a grand total of £607, compared to £500 per year for the same calculations using the old methods. Instead of calculating 10,000 sums of figures taken from seven different tables, it would now be necessary to punch twelve million figures onto three hundred thousand cards in order to run them through the Hollerith machine. (Fig. 5.3.) The superintendent must have anticipated some raised eyebrows at the penny-pinching Admiralty when he sent in these figures, for he hastened to acknowledge that "a heavy initial cost" would be justified by subsequent increases in "speed and accuracy and saving of mental fatigue obtained by using the tabulating machines."[18]

"A true calculating machine," ran one definition circa 1930, is one that "suppresses in its operation all that could genuinely demand a mental effort."[19] But like the return of the repressed, mental effort and fatigue tended to return through the back door.

FIGURE 5.3. Hollerith punch card operator at the U.S. Census Bureau (c. 1925).
National Archives, U.S.A.

Quite apart from the fatigue endured by the women who punched
the cards, a point to which I'll return, there was the effort of rethinking the division of labor in the millions of calculations necessary to produce the *Nautical Almanac*. As we have seen, observatory directors and almanac superintendents had been analyzing
the work of calculation into multiple steps and matching steps to
degrees of mathematical skill, from schoolboys to Cambridge
Wranglers (the students who received the highest marks on the
mathematics examination), since at least the eighteenth century.
Nor did efforts to rationalize work end with Airy's system in the
mid-nineteenth century. By the early twentieth century, in an attempt to save money on wages, the *Nautical Almanac* was experimenting with a smaller permanent staff supplemented by temporary computers to whom packets of calculation were farmed out
on an ad hoc basis and who, like women employees, could generally be paid less than the "inside" workers.[20]

But with the influx of new "inside" workers to operate the calculating machines in the 1930s, the superintendent and deputy superintendent found themselves confronted with a supervisory crisis: how could the new staff and new machines be meshed with the old staff and their tried-and-true methods? There were the difficult but invaluable Daniels brothers, who were the only staff members trusted to proofread tables but who were also deemed "temperamentally unfitted to supervise subordinate staff" and "too stereotyped in their habits to adapt themselves to the use of machines." Miss Stocks and Miss Burroughs, who were charged to transform heliocentric into geocentric coordinates using Brunsviga calculating machines, required three months *each* of private tuition in computing from the superintendent.[21] Trying to justify why, despite the sizable investments in new machines and personnel, the *Nautical Almanac* was still twelve months behind schedule, Superintendent Comrie explained to his bosses at the Admiralty that the supervisor's preparation of the work for the machines and their operators now constituted "20 or 30 per cent of the whole [calculation]." Whereas previously computing the ephemeris of the Moon at transit consisted of simply telling one W. F. Doaken, MA, to "'do the Moon Transit,' and four or five months later the printer's copy would be handed over," now the work had been divided up among "six or seven people, to whom perhaps 100 to 120 different sets of instructions are given."

But the bottom line was the bottom line: the new methods were at least 20 percent cheaper than the old—eventually. If the *Nautical Almanac* was not going to revert back to the luxurious staffing scheme of their German counterparts, who employed eleven PhD's, cheaper staff (i.e., women), machines, and, most important, constant and creative supervision would be necessary. New algorithms disrupted old methods of calculation on at least two levels. First, the machines rarely calculated in the way that humans had been taught to or even in the way indicated by theoretical mathematical solutions. For example, the Seguin machine multiplied not by iterating additions but rather by treating numbers as polynomials of powers of ten.[22] The best rules for mental calculation were not those for mechanical calculation—and different machines used different algorithms. Orchestrating calculations using a machine could mean rethinking the algorithms of arithmetic. Second, meshing the mental, mechanical, and manual aspects of calculation required supervisors to invent new procedural algorithms that divided a problem like the lunar transit into small, explicit steps. When Comrie complained,[23] as no doubt all superintendents before and after him did, about how much of his time was nibbled away by administrative duties, it was not scientific work to which he longed to return, although he had earned a doctorate in astronomy from Cambridge: "My mind should be free from administrative worries, so that I can exploit methods, devise improved arrangements of computations, and collate and supervise the work of individual members of the Staff."[24] Here was analytical intelligence concentrated to its doubly algorithmic essence: calculation and the division of labor simultaneously rethought to accommodate machines and the allegedly mechanical workers who operated them—all in the name of cost cutting.

Pressure to trim costs in order to justify the purchase of expensive machines and the hiring of more staff to operate them was even more intense in calculation-heavy industries like the railroads. At the same time as the Nautical Almanac in Greenwich was experimenting with the Hollerith and other calculating machines to streamline astronomical calculations, the French Chemins de Fer de Paris-Lyon-Méditerranée (C.F.P.L.M.) was introducing them to keep track of freight shipments and moving stock. In a 1929 article, Georges Bolle (1868–1955), head of accounting at the C.F.P.L.M. and graduate of the École Polytechnique, France's elite engineering school, explained that the economic advantages of the new machines were "really incalculable"—presupposing that every single detail of the workflow had been meticulously thought out in advance, from how to maximize the use of all forty-five columns of a Hollerith punch-card to devising icons for the kind of freight most frequently transported to speed up the coding of the information by the machine operators. No detail of the process was too small to escape the supervisor's scrutiny, not even the numbering of freight categories: "Every detail must be meticulously examined, discussed, weighed in work of this kind." As in the case of the *Nautical Almanac*, the use of machines entailed centralizing the workplace (in Paris, of course) and hiring the cheapest labor consistent with the qualifications of "much orderliness, care, concentration, and good will" (women, of course). The economic advantages of a cheap workforce were so great that Bolle concluded that all the difficulties involved in abandoning the old methods—not least the cost of the machines themselves— paled by comparison. But these gains could only be achieved by a vast effort of organization: "The study of every problem to be solved by machines requires painstaking mental labor, a considerable amount of reflection, observations, and discussions to mount the projected organization and make sure that all works well."[25] Or, in his lapidary motto: "First organize, then mechanize."[26]

Mechanical Mindfulness

However different in their design, materials, power, and reliability, all calculating machines, from the seventeenth century to the midtwentieth century, promised to relieve human intelligence, not replace it.[27] The inference drawn from the capacity of machines to calculate was not that machines were intelligent but rather that at least some intelligence was mechanical, in the sense of being mindless. But it was a peculiar sort of mindlessness, one that required the utmost efforts of attention and memory. This was most dramatically displayed by a wave of psychological studies devoted to calculating prodigies on the one hand and to the operators of calculating machines on the other. These two groups might once have been viewed as opposite ends of a spectrum: number geniuses versus number dunces. But the spread of calculating machines had simultaneously devalued the mental activity of calculation without eliminating the monotonous effort of concentration traditionally associated with it. As a result, the psychological profiles of the virtuosi of mental arithmetic and the operators of calculating machines converged in strange ways.

The history of eighteenth- and early nineteenth-century mathematics boasts several calculating prodigies who later became celebrated mathematicians, including Leonhard Euler, Carl Friedrich Gauss (1777–1855), and André-Marie Ampère (1775–1836).[28] Anecdotes circulated about their precocious feats of mental arithmetic as early signs of mathematical genius. But by the late nineteenth and early twentieth centuries, psychologists and mathematicians had come to believe that such cases were anomalous. Great mathematicians were rarely calculating virtuosi, and calculating virtuosi were even more rarely great mathematicians. It is significant that these arguments featured prominently in treatises on calculating machines. If calculating was a mechanical activity, then minds that excelled at it might seem perforce mechanical: "For it is a true heresy, albeit a widespread one, to take great calculating abilities as an index of superior mathematical disposition.... To confuse these two things is to commit a serious error of judgment, like that of confusing exceptional manual dexterity at the piano as an index of a remarkable gift for musical composition."[29] Given that the latest calculating machines featured keyboards with which operators entered numbers simultaneously, frequently likened to playing chords on a piano, the analogy is suggestive.[30] (Fig. 5.4.) Lightning calculation, whether performed mentally or mechanically, was now more akin to dexterity than to creativity.

Alfred Binet (1857–1911), professor of psychology at the Sorbonne and pioneer of experimental investigations of intelligence, in the 1890s subjected two calculating prodigies making the rounds of Paris vaudeville shows, the Italian Jacques Inaudi and the Greek Pericles Diamandi, to a long series of tests in his laboratory. (Fig. 5.5.) He concluded on the basis of his results and a review of the historical literature on such virtuosi of mental arithmetic that despite much individual diversity they constituted a "natural family": they were sports of nature, born into families with no previous

Cie Réal. Cliché « La Photoscopie ».

FIGURE 5.4. Operator using a Wahl machine (Louis Couffignal,
Les Machines à calculer [Calculating Machines], 1933).

history of such prodigies; grew up in impoverished circumstances;
exhibited their talents at an early age but were otherwise unre-
markable, even backward, in their intellectual development; and
even as adults resembled "children who did not age." In contrast,
mathematicians like Gauss who had dazzled parents and teachers
with feats of mental arithmetic at a young age allegedly lost these
abilities as their mathematical genius matured. Binet went so far
as to query whether the accomplishments of the calculating prodigies were remarkable even as mere "number specialists." In a competition with four cashiers from the department store Bon Marché,
who were used to toting up prices in their heads, one of Binet's
calculating prodigies lost to the best of the Bon Marché clerks
when it came to multiplication by small numbers, although he
surpassed them all in solving problems involving more digits.
Binet concluded that what was truly prodigious about calculating
prodigies were their powers of memory and "force of attention,"
at least as applied to numbers.[31]

FIGURE 5.5. Poster for the Théâtre Robert-Houdin, featuring calculating prodigy Jacques Inaudi (c. 1890). Musée de la Ville de Paris, Musee Carnavalet, Paris, France © Archives Charmet / Bridgeman Images.

It was exactly this focused attention, at once monotonous and monothematic, that the operators of calculating machines were expected to sustain for hours on end. The unbearable strain of attention required of human calculators had long been a bone of contention between them and their employers. Despite his zealous efforts to increase calculating productivity, Airy had in 1838 reduced the working day of the computers from eleven hours to eight. Attempts to add an hour of overtime in 1837 in order to complete calculations for Halley's Comet provoked a rebellion on the part of the computers, who protested that even the regular nine-to-five hours were "more than sufficient for the oppressive and tedious application of the mind to continued calculation."[32] In 1930, outgoing *Nautical Almanac* superintendent Philip Cowell (1870–1949) wrote his successor Comrie that "anyone who worked really hard for five hours could not possibly do more," adding parenthetically, "it may be different with your machines."[33]

It was indeed different with machines, but even the efficiency-obsessed Bolle at the French railways thought that a working day of six-and-a-half hours of punching three hundred cards, each with forty-five columns, was the maximum that could be expected from Hollerith machine operators, and then for only fourteen consecutive days per month.[34] As a 1931 psychological study devoted to the performance of French railway operators on Elliot-Fischer calculating machines observed, bodily gestures could become automatic with practice, but "attention to the work must be continuous and concentrated. The operator is obliged to check her machine incessantly, to verify the names on the pieces of paper, to make sure that the elements of the calculation are correct." Each calculation involved sixteen separate steps, from inserting the paper into the machine to clearing all the numbers before the next calculation. In the view of the psychologists who tested the operators, it was impossible to sustain such intense levels of attention for a long period "without rest."[35] (Fig. 5.6.) Commenting in 1823 on the advantages of Babbage's Difference Engine for computing mathematical and astronomical tables, English astronomer Francis Baily (1774–1844) had envisioned how the "unvarying action of machinery" would solve the problem of "confining the attention of the computers to the dull and tedious repetition of many thousand consecutive additions and subtractions."[36] Over a century later, in 1933, calculating machines were still being defined in terms of the suppression of mental effort.[37] Yet the calculating machines that had held out the promise of relieving the mental effort of attention had in the end exacerbated it.

In the teeth of its declared aims, mechanical calculation had become intensely mindful, at least by the standards of the day. Psychologists at the turn of the twentieth century were unanimous that the ability to muster voluntary attention for tedious but necessary tasks was the essence of the conscious act of will—and therefore the highest expression of consciousness.[38] Théodule-Armand Ribot (1839–1916), professor of comparative and experimental psychology at the Collège de France, speculated that it was the ability to sustain attention for boring work that distinguished civilized from savage peoples and respectable citizens from "vagabonds, professional thieves, [and] prostitutes." Like the psychologists who had tested the calculating machine operators, Ribot emphasized that the exercise of voluntary attention was always accompanied by a sense of effort, an abnormal state that "produced rapid exhaustion of the organism."[39] Calculation was therefore a routine task given to experimental subjects by psychologists in order to test the strength of voluntary attention and resistance to mental fatigue.[40] Results suggested wild fluctuations in attention as subjects became fatigued, their minds wandered, and errors literally added up. In the context of the classroom or the laboratory, the dread of the tedious task was observed to grow with fatigue, allegedly sometimes to the point of "milder forms of insanity."[41] In the context of mechanical calculation, the operators' fatigue also caused fluctuations in attention and an alarming propensity to error. But there was no getting rid of the operator, as a 1933 treatise on the latest calculating machines emphasized: "In the comparative study of modern machines, it is impossible not to take into account the manner in

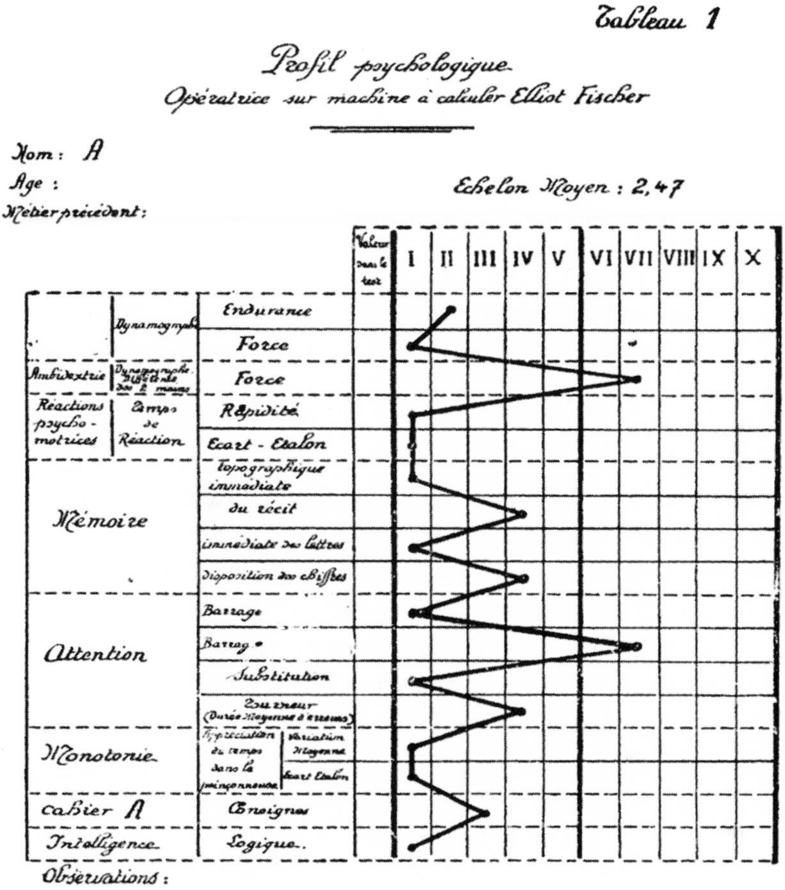

Tableau 1

Profil psychologique.
Opératrice sur machine à calculer Elliot Fischer

Nom : A
Âge :
Métier précédent :

Échelon Moyen : 2,47

		Valeur dans le test	I	II	III	IV	V	VI	VII	VIII	IX	X
Dynamographe		Endurance											
		Force											
Ambidextrie	Dynamographe suite de 2 mains	Force											
Réactions psycho-motrices	Temps de Réaction	Rapidité											
		Écart - Étalon											
Mémoire		Topographique immédiate											
		du récit											
		immédiate des lettres											
		Disposition des chiffres											
Attention		Barrage											
		Barrage											
		Substitution											
Monotonie		2u erreur (Durée moyenne à erreurs)											
		Appréciation du temps sans la mesure	Variation Moyenne leurs Étalon											
Cahier A		Enseignes											
Intelligence		Logique.											

Observations :

FIGURE 5.6. Test results of the best operators using an Elliott-Fischer calculating machine, showing wide variations in force and attention (J.-M. Lahy and S. Korngold, "Séléction des operatrices de machines comptables [Selection of calculating machine operators]," *Année psychologique* 32 (1931): 131–49).

which the operator intervenes [in the calculation]."[42] All that could be done was to organize the work of calculation so as to minimize the discretion of the operator—but at the same time to maximize her unflagging attention to her monotonous task: mechanical calculation made mindful.

Algorithms and Intelligence

This chapter began with a pointed contrast between how Babbage and Wittgenstein used the same example of continuing a mathematical series to opposite ends. Babbage argued that when the Difference Engine spewed out an apparently anomalous term, it was in fact faithfully and mechanically following the rule inscribed in its gearwork—just as apparent miracles had been inscribed in the machinery of nature by the divine engineer since the beginning of time. There were no exceptions to the rules, and that is why machines could execute them. In Wittgenstein's version, the teacher takes the anomalous term supplied by the student to be a mistake, not a miracle, but Wittgenstein was as skeptical as Babbage about whether the apparent anomaly really violates the rule. For Wittgenstein, however, the example shows the impossibility of mechanical rule-following because the rule cannot be unequivocally specified. The only way to cut off an infinite regress of interpretations of the rule is to understand the rule as a custom or institution, not as an algorithm. Not only did Wittgenstein cast doubt on whether humans followed rules mechanically; he also wondered whether even machines did so.

But what kinds of machines are at issue in these two parables about mechanical rule-following? Or are there any machines at all? As we have seen in the case of the Prony logarithm project in Chapter 4, "mechanical" could refer to calculation without machines. The use of that catch-all (and usually derogatory) phrase erases the differences among machines constructed out of different materials (wood, ivory, steel, silicon), with different parts (gears, levers, keyboards, weights, brakes), using different algorithms (multiplication by polynomials versus repetitive addition, finding differences versus calculating each value anew), and performing different operations (from simple addition and subtraction to the forty-five-column tabulations of the Hollerith machine). These differences were consequential: machines that jammed or slipped could not be trusted, and the most brilliant design could not be realized in practice without skillful craftsmen and suitable materials. Despite colossal government subsidies, neither Babbage's Difference nor his Analytical Engine got past the drawing board until precision machining techniques made it possible to build them in the latter half of the twentieth century.[43]

Neither Babbage nor Wittgenstein lived to see computers of the Difference and Analytical Engine sort in widespread use. The most successful realization of a calculating machine on the Difference Engine model was built by the Swede Georg Scheutz (1785–1873) and his son Edvard (1821–1881) in 1853 but was never mass-produced.[44] A 1905 survey of calculating machines relegated Babbage's vision of an Analytical Engine to "fairyland."[45] There is no straight-line path that connects Babbage's genial designs to the computers of the latter half of the twentieth century. In between these two points lies nearly a century of mechanical calculation accomplished by different means. For a history of rules, this point matters because the dream of unambiguous rules flawlessly followed has always fed upon the special case of calculation, the thinnest rules of all. Even before "mechanical calculation" involved actual machines, it referred to this dream, conjured by Babbage and Wittgenstein in contrasting fashion, of a rule with no wiggle room: explicit and unambiguous in its articulation and automatic and flawless in its execution. As we saw in Chapter 4, algorithms, even calculating algorithms, need not aspire to such wafer thinness. The problem-centered algorithms of many mathematical traditions more closely resemble the thick rules of the mechanical arts, which also emerged from examples. It was only in the nineteenth and twentieth centuries that calculation became the paradigm of the kind of rule that needed no paradigm, the algorithm that needed no model to imitate, no mind to interpret or adapt it. What gives the category of mechanical calculation its deceptive semblance of coherence is not the uniformity of the machines employed but rather the category to which it was opposed: mindful calculation.

For reasons at once material, conceptual, and economic, the first era of widespread mechanical calculation was one that

FIGURE 5.7. Women computers at the Jet Propulsion Laboratory, Pasadena, California (c. 1955). Courtesy NASA/JPL-Caltech.

meshed the intelligence of humans and machines. Increasingly, the human computers who operated the machines were women, actively recruited by observatories in Greenwich, Paris, and Cambridge (Massachusetts) already in the 1890s, and ubiquitous for decades thereafter wherever heavy-duty calculation took place, from observatories to weapons projects.[46] (Fig. 5.7.) Although some of these institutions, such as the Harvard College Observatory, took advantage of the women's advanced training in astronomy and mathematics, the chief attraction of female labor was that it was cheap: even women with college degrees were paid significantly less than their male counterparts.[47] Indeed, the principal motivation for introducing calculating machines in the first place was usually to cut costs, as we have seen in the scientific context of the British *Nautical Almanac* office and the industrial context of the French railway. Babbage the political economist would surely have approved.[48]

But would Babbage the prophet of automated intelligence have been as impressed? Certainly, the boundary between "mechanical" and "mental" work had been blurred, but this had already occurred in Prony's logarithm project, before any actual machines had been used in massive calculation projects. Yet the impact of calculating machines on the daily work of observatories and insurance offices seems not to have made the machines seem more intelligent—artificial intelligence in the modern sense—but rather to make the human calculators appear more mechanical. Emblematic of this shift was the plunging prestige of calculating prodigies: by the late nineteenth century, such talents were no longer premonitions of mathematical genius but the stuff of vaudeville acts. Calculating prowess was no longer correlated with human intelligence; nor did it endow calculating machines with anything like artificial intelligence.

Calculating machines did not eliminate human intelligence in massive calculating projects. On the contrary, human intelligence was doubly challenged to think algorithmically in new ways. At the level of the calculating algorithms built into the gears and levers of the machines, the operations of arithmetic had to be reconceived in ways that corresponded neither to mental arithmetic nor to mathematical theory. What was optimal for human minds was not optimal for machines, and as the machines became more complex in terms of moving parts, the divergences became more pronounced. At the level of the procedures required to mesh humans and machines in long sequences of calculation, whether in the offices of the *Nautical Almanac* or the French railways, tasks previously conceived holistically and executed by one calculator had to be analyzed into their smallest component parts, rigidly sequenced, and apportioned to the human or mechanical calculator able to execute that step most efficiently—where "efficiently" meant not better or even faster but cheaper. In one sense, the analytical intelligence demanded by human-machine production lines for calculations was no different than the adaptations required by any mechanized manufacture: mechanical weaving looms did not operate the way human weavers did; the sequencing of human and mechanical labor in a textile factory also required breaking down tasks in new and counter-intuitive ways. In another sense, however, the analytical intelligence applied to making human-machine cooperation in calculation work was a rehearsal for an activity that would become known first as operations research and later computer programming.[49]

The interaction of human and mechanical calculators also modified intelligence in more subtle ways. In whatever way calculation had been understood, as intellectual accomplishment or drudgework, and by whomever performed, whether Astronomer Royal or schoolboy computer, it had been intensely, even tediously mindful. Calculators from Kepler to Babbage complained of the strain imposed by the calculation of astronomical tables; inventors of calculating devices and machines since Napier and Pascal had promised a respite from labor that was at once monotonous but unremittingly attentive. Practice speeded up the rate of calculation, but it could not be allowed to become automatic and almost unconscious (as repetitive bodily gestures could) without increasing the risk of error. So strong was the link between mindfulness and accurate calculation that Prony professed surprise that the least intelligent, the most "automatic" of his calculators made the fewest mistakes, and later critics of the Prony tables refused to believe that such unconscientious workers did not in fact increase the number of errors.[50] But the spread of more reliable calculating machines not only downgraded the intellectual status of calculation; it also severed the connection between mindfulness and accuracy. By the early twentieth century, automation had become the guarantee of—no longer the obstacle to—error-free calculation. Reversing a centuries-long history of erratic calculating machines, the results of which often had to be checked by hand, improvements in design, materials, and construction had by the 1920s made automatic calculation and accurate calculation one and the same.[51]

Yet a ghost lingered in the machine: the human operator. As even enthusiasts for the new generation of calculating machines admitted, the efficiency and accuracy of the results depended crucially on the dexterity and attentiveness of the humans who entered the numbers, pulled the levers, punched the cards, and cleared the tally, all in precisely the correct, rhythmic order. The operators may no longer have performed the actual calculations, but the vigilant attention demanded by their task was every bit as wearisome as the mental labor that had motivated the invention of calculating machines in the first place. Mental fatigue among operators was evidently so great that their working hours were shortened, in defiance of the iron rule of economy that had originally justified the introduction of calculating machines. In contrast to other forms of repetitive factory or clerical work that subjected human operators to the tempo of machines, the gestures involved in the use of calculating machines could not be mastered to the point of becoming unconscious, fingers playing automatically over the typewriter keyboard as the mind wandered. It was just this unusual combination of routine and unwavering concentration that made calculation, with or without machines, so exhausting. Calculating machines, even reliable ones, did not banish mindfulness and monotonous attention from Big Calculation. They simply displaced those mental exertions to other tasks and other people.

Conclusion: From Mechanical to Artificial Intelligence

Calculating machines placed new demands on human intelligence, but did they pave the way for artificial intelligence? They did arguably expand the domain of algorithms, by forcing a rethinking of how to optimize Big Calculation at every level, from the innards of the machines to the organization of workflow to the attentive interaction with the machines. But making calculation even more algorithmic, in the sense of following standardized, step-by-step procedures, is a long way from making intelligence algorithmic. For that to happen, the reduction of intelligence to a form of calculation had to seem both possible and desirable. Although there are historical precedents for such visions, which made calculation and combinatorics the template for all intellectual activity, calculating machines did not advance their cause.[52] On the contrary, the effect of making calculation mechanical was to disqualify it as an intelligent activity. It would require a complete reconceptualization of both calculation and intelligence in order to make Artificial or Machine Intelligence something other than an oxymoron. This is the path that led through mathematical logic, from George Boole (1815–1864) to Alan Turing (1912–1954) via Gottlob Frege (1848–1925), David Hilbert, Bertrand Russell (1872–1970), Alfred North Whitehead (1861–1947), and Kurt Gödel (1906–1978), and is connected to efforts to secure the logical foundations of mathematics, not the daily routines of large-scale office calculation.[53]

However, the intelligence fostered by the era of calculating machines went beyond the reconceptualization of calculation per se—the narrow sense of algorithm. Algorithmic intelligence also cultivated the ability to analyze complex tasks and problems into step-by-step sequences—the broader, procedural sense of algorithms. The imprint of this second side of the doubly algorithmic intelligence of the era of calculating machines can be clearly discerned in the early history of artificial intelligence. In a seminal 1956 paper, Allen Newell (1927–1992) and Herbert Simon (1916–2001) developed a computer model to prove logical theorems, noting that their system, "in contrast to the systematic algorithms that are ordinarily employed in computation, relies heavily on heuristic methods similar to those that have been observed in human problem solving activity."[54] Newell and Simon's first model of the Logic Theorist program recalls the division of labor at centers of Big Calculation ever since Prony's logarithm project: index cards were distributed to Simon's wife, children, and various graduate students so that "each person became, in effect, a component of the L[ogic] T[heorist] computer program" to prove most of the first sixty theorems in the second chapter of Bertrand Russell and Alfred North Whitehead's *Principia Mathematica* (vol. 1,

1910).[55] This was the moment of transition between sequences of human beings to programs for computers. Decades later, Simon maintained that although there existed "no powerful factory method—no assembly line for the manufacture of scientific truth," he was confident that the same analytical methods that applied to the division of labor more generally—decomposing complex problems into simpler ones—could be used to model key episodes of scientific discovery with a computer program.[56] Computer subroutines were originally just an extension of the economic principle of the division of labor—and the intellectual de-skilling that went with it.[57]

Babbage did not foresee that even scientific discovery might someday be demoted from mindful to mechanical labor, and probably not even Simon foresaw the algorithmic exploitation of Big Data in current attempts to create "theory-free science."[58] These developments depend on computers that differ both in kind (flexibly and lengthily programmable) and degree (huge gains in speed and memory), as well as in design and materials, from those that defined the era of calculating machines. Perhaps equally important to making artificial intelligence more than an oxymoron was the black-boxing of both the narrow and broad algorithms in the inaccessible code of computer programs. In contrast to the production lines of mechanical calculation, visible in the spatial array of operators and machines arranged at rows of desks in open-plan offices, the program that divided a complex task into minute steps was hidden to most users of computers. The processes that produced the final results became as opaque as human mental processes—and therefore more plausible candidates for intelligence equal to or even surpassing human intelligence. Only in the context of these innovations and the vastly more powerful computation they enabled does the shift from mindless machines to machine minds make sense.

The era of calculating machines did not disappear without a trace. For the first time, humans worked together with machines to solve problems that had to be adapted both to the algorithms used by humans to calculate and those used by the machines. The subjection of humans to the inexorable rhythms of machines, to the point that the humans become machine-like, is one of the most enduring themes among critics of industrialization, from Thomas Carlyle (1795–1881) to Henri Bergson (1859–1941) to Charlie Chaplin's (1889–1977) film *Modern Times* (1936). In contrast, calculating machines disciplined human operators by demanding unflagging attention, not routinized habit. Even digital natives still rehearse this distinction every time they confront a computer screen: fingers may text or type as effortlessly and as unconsciously as legs walk, but attention is riveted by the demands of the algorithms—one false click and you have sent that confidential email to your entire list of contacts, or purchased the item next to the one you wanted, or invalidated the online tax form.

Absentmindedness takes its toll even in computer calculations: enter the wrong numbers or units of measurement and that $125 million Mars Climate Orbiter goes spinning off into space.[59] Most algorithms with which we interact are as unknown and as unbending to us as those incorporated into the innards of calculating machines were to their human operators, and now as then, it takes mental vigilance to be able to follow even the thinnest of rules without understanding them.

6

Rules and Regulations

Laws, Rules, and Regulations

A fluid but consequential division of labor governs the relationships between laws, rules, and regulations. During roughly the period 1500–1800, the distinctions among these three genres of prescriptions sharpened into a hierarchy of scope, specificity, and stability. At the pinnacle were laws, general in formulation, broad in jurisdiction, and august in their authority. In the seventeenth and eighteenth centuries, the most universal and majestic of all laws were the laws of nature such as those formulated by the natural philosopher Isaac Newton in his *Philosophiae naturalis principia mathematica* in the late seventeenth century and the natural laws codified by jurists such as Hugo Grotius (1583–1645) and Samuel Pufendorf (1632–1694) in search of internationally valid norms for human conduct in an age of global expansion. Both laws of nature and natural laws allegedly derived their ultimate authority from God or at least from the constants of human nature. Absolutist monarchs increasingly aspired to universality and uniformity in issuing laws for their territories.[1] Next came the rules of both the natural and human realms: for example, the weather rule that summer days are generally warmer than winter ones or the legal rules that dictated how inheritances were to be divided among heirs in the absence of a will. Rules were both more specific and more restricted in their jurisdiction than laws.[2] At the bottom of the pyramid were regulations, which were still more circumscribed, far more numerous, and fiendishly detailed. Chapter 7 will address the most universal laws of all, laws of nature and natural laws; this chapter deals with the other end of the spectrum, local regulations.

If laws show the most dignified and elevated face of rules (as in the phrase "the rule of law"), then regulations are rules with sleeves rolled up, the ones that get things done on the ground. Laws are rules with a telescope, far-seeing and aiming for the stars; regulations are rules with a microscope, myopic and focused on detail. Ideally, laws are relatively few and seldom altered; regulations are many and constantly in need of updating. Laws aspire to universality; regulations are fixated on particulars. The meaning of rules is defined by both. But if laws dominate in terms of prestige, regulations preponderate in terms of everyday experience in modern societies. The average citizen rarely collides with a law; we bark our shins against regulations almost every day.

Because governments of complex societies, especially in modern cities, are charged with ordering everything from traffic to lighting to food and water supplies, regulations have proliferated—to the point that libertarian critics equate all of government not with security or infrastructure, much less with the rule of law, but with regulations as numerous and bothersome as a swarm of mosquitoes. They want the whole kit and kaboodle done away with. The sheer density of regulations in daily life has therefore shifted the meaning of rules toward the regulations pole of the laws-regulations spectrum of rules. In the course of the last five hundred years, the most familiar rules have become more like the injunction "stop at a red light" than "thou shalt not kill."

This shift mirrors economic, demographic, technological, and political transformations in how people live together, especially under the high-density conditions of big cities. This chapter singles out three such transformations that have fattened the registers of regulations from the High Middle Ages to the present. First, quickening trade swelled purses and kindled new desires. When a city became a node in far-flung trade networks, as cities such as Genoa, Florence, and Venice had by the fourteenth century, newly made fortunes begged to be spent on newly imported luxuries: silks, satins, velvets, gold and silver braid and buttons. The temptations of fashion and the social status it signaled threatened to impoverish patrician families and turn the social order upside down. Uppity merchants outshone dukes; fights erupted between apprentice artisans and foppish students over whose hat was the more stylish.

Second, burgeoning urban populations strained old infrastructures of streets and sanitation. There were step-differences between the complexity of a city with a population of circa 30,000 (a respectable-sized city in 1600, e.g., Vienna or Bordeaux), 50,000 (a metropolis, e.g., Genoa or Madrid), and 250,000 (a megalopolis, e.g., Istanbul or London).[3] Once a city crossed the 500,000 threshold, as London and Paris had by the first half of the eighteenth century, even pedestrian traffic could snarl in narrow streets; add horses, carriages, and mule-driven carts to the mix and mayhem broke out. Jean-Jacques Rousseau (1712–1778) was only one of the thousands of Parisian pedestrians run down by carriages being driven hell-for-leather down public thoroughfares.[4] In the largest European cities of the late seventeenth and eighteenth centuries, municipal authorities struggled to convert spaghetti tangles of medieval lanes into broad boulevards, drive market stalls and pedestrians from the streets to make way for carriages, and reduce the stench of human and animal waste that was, not inaccurately, associated with the spread of disease.

Third, the political consolidation of nation states from the seventeenth century to the present day enforced uniformity on what were previously disparate territories, not only legally but culturally. Schools taught a national language alongside or to the exclusion of local dialects; uniformity of speech and script symbolized the unity of the nation. How citizens spell, once an informal and idiosyncratic practice that could vary not only from person to person but for the same person on the same page, became a patriotic cause. An astonishing amount of energy and vitriol has consequently been expended to regulate spelling, from the rise of European vernaculars in the sixteenth century right down to right now.

Each of the three case studies that make up this chapter picks out an episode in which an explosion of regulation signals one of these transformations: the sumptuary laws that responded to the economic boom, fueled mostly by luxury textiles, in European cities from circa 1300 to 1800; the traffic and sanitation regulations designed to cope with Paris's enormously expanded population, circa 1650 to 1800; and the spelling reforms that expressed a dawning vernacular patriotism from Elizabethan England to Enlightenment France to newly unified Germany in the late nineteenth century to the here and now. Each of these examples shows how rules-as-regulations tried, with varying degrees of success, to bridge the chasm between the universal ideal of good order and the most minute particulars in real life. The universal: expenditure should be prudent and excess avoided. The particular: don't spend the money needed for your son's education and your daughter's dowry on that modish velvet trim that will in any case be out of fashion next year. The universal: city streets should be clean and traffic free-flowing. The particular: stop throwing the contents of your chamber pot out the window and playing ball games in the middle of the street. The universal: citizens of a nation should be able to communicate with each other freely and intelligibly, united by a common tongue. The particular: spell *Schifffahrt* (ship voyage) with three *f*s, not two. Regulations are rules in action.

But action, even concerted, sustained action, is not always enough to make regulations work. These three case studies have also been chosen to illustrate how rules succeed—and fail—in practice. Like most rules, regulations are uttered in the imperative mood of do's and don't's. But unlike many rules and a fortiori many laws, they do not aspire to high generality. Regulations do not lay claim to the moral high ground of principle, whatever their preambles may say. Instead, they wallow in the weediest details. The default stance of regulations is adversarial: like the tax auditor, the regulations assume that almost everyone wants to game the rules and that every loophole must be anticipated and closed. Laws may conjure up a vision of an ideal polity to be brought into being; regulations are in contrast always reactive, issued in response to glaring abuses. The imperative of laws is timeless and addressed to all; that of regulations anchored in the present moment and addressed to you there—yes, you, the one who's splurging on velvet trim, emptying your chamber pot out the window, or still spelling like a Bavarian.

Even if rigorously enforced, these scowling imperatives don't always bring about the desired results. European sumptuary regulations are a case of five hundred years of abject rule failure; traffic and sanitation regulations achieve eventual if partial success; thanks to universal public schooling, spelling conventions have entrenched themselves even among those, like advertisers, who slyly undermine them. Regulations, the most explicit, detailed, and unnatural of rules, paradoxically succeed only once they become internalized as implicit norms, conventions that have become second nature. The proof that some regulations do indeed succeed in becoming genuine norms is the indignation unleashed by proposed reforms, as we'll see in the case of spelling. Just how regulations—rules that are local, particular, and conventional and almost by definition unpopular—do or do not metamorphose into taken-for-granted norms is the question that threads through all three case studies.

Five Hundred Years of Rule Failure:
The War on Fashion

In the menagerie of odd rules, none now seem odder than sumptuary regulations: rules that attempt to bridle tendencies toward expense (in Latin, *sumptus*) in all the domains in which the temptation to outdo one's neighbors is strongest, the cost be damned. In an astonishing number of cultures, from ancient Greece and

Rome to medieval Europe to Tokugawa Japan to contemporary Sudan, governments have attempted to restrain people from extravagant displays at funerals, weddings, and feasts and to curb their consumption of costly clothing, jewelry, carriages, and other status symbols—whether in the name of modesty, frugality, piety, hierarchy, patriotism, or plain old good taste.[5] The oddity of these rules is twofold: first, their maniacal specificity; and second, their stubborn longevity in the face of acknowledged and repeated failure. Never have rules stipulated do's and (mostly) don't's in more detail; never have rules proved themselves to be so utterly ineffective in fulfilling their declared aims. Yet for just those reasons, their ubiquity and longevity cry out for explanation.

Sumptuary regulations, which usually took the form of easily updated regulations or edicts rather than longer-lasting laws, furnish the historian of rules with an extreme case of rule failure. In the case of medieval and early modern Europe, over a period of over five hundred years (c. 1200–1800), these regulations not only failed to stamp out excess (or what now might be called conspicuous consumption), they arguably exacerbated the very ills they were meant to remedy. The minute specificity with which the regulations described the latest forbidden fashion and luxury fabric, be it gold lace, short doublets, or velvet trim, inadvertently triggered an arms race, as designers rushed to invent new, still more extravagant frippery that was not yet expressly banned.[6] Officials scrambled in vain to keep up with fashion, issuing and reissuing updated rules that were always at least a season behind the latest styles. This was why sumptuary rules took the form of revisable regulations rather than stable laws. As the English Parliament remarked apropos of the 1363 ordinances specifying who could wear cloth of gold and silver, ordinances that "they might amend at their pleasure" were preferable to more enduring statutes for such matters.[7] Although the officials kept at their hopeless task for centuries, a moan of exhaustion is all but audible in the later regulations: was there no end to the crazy Saint Vitus's dance of novelty in dress? The sumptuary ordinances published by the German kingdom of Saxony in 1695 complained that the breathless tempo of fashion was an evil in itself and pleaded with its own officials and their families to stick to their current mode of dress "in the future without noticeable changes, once and for all."[8] The book of favorite outfits kept by Matthäus Schwarz (1497–c. 1574), accountant to the wealthy Fugger bankers of Augsburg and a dedicated dandy, gives some idea of just how quickly (and extravagantly) fashion could change.[9] (Fig. 6.1.)

Worse, regulations designed to cement the social order by ordaining who could wear what and on which occasions could perversely also supply social-climbers with a detailed instruction manual on how to ape their betters.[10] If, for example, the 1294 French "Ordinance against Luxury" prohibited all bourgeois subjects from wearing sable, the socially ambitious could take careful note.[11] No wonder the prevailing tone of the preambles of these regulations, many issued multiple times to no avail, was one of exasperation bordering on hysteria. In 1450 King Charles VII of France (1403–1461, r. 1422–1461), looking back at the by-then long series of sumptuary laws issued by his predecessors and flaunted by their subjects, lamented that "of all the nations of the habitable earth, there are none so deformed, variable, outrageous, excessive, or inconstant in their clothing and costumes as the French nation."[12]

Indeed, sumptuary regulations flew in the face of all experience, as anyone, whether teacher or pupil, who has ever dealt with a high school dress code knows. The authorities had only to outlaw sable trim (Genoa, 1157), slashed sleeves (Ferrara, 1467), or "beaked" shoes with points longer than one finger's width (Landshut, 1470) for the ingenious to redefine the offending item ("Not slashed, officer—it's just the lining poking through") or for the next season's fashions to render last year's prohibitions irrelevant ("Beaked shoes are *so* 1470"). (Fig. 6.2.)

Why then did these ineffectual regulations endure so long? For economic historians, the mystery only deepens: why would municipal authorities want to throttle the sources of prosperity by

·17·

Im zener iç 13. auff tiengartt
maics horckzeit mit der degerstein
mein bas, dz roams roas attlas
Cünst mit all dingen wie da 2c

Dz angesicht ist rechr Contrafatt

16. Jar minđ 4 i. tag

FIGURE 6.1. Augsburg fashion plate Matthäus Schwarz shows off his new outfit with slashed sleeves and fur trim. *Das Trachtenbuch des Matthäus Schwarz aus Augsburg* [The costume book of Matthäus Schwarz of Augsburg, 1520–1560]. Leibniz Bibliothek Hannover, c. 1513).

FIGURE 6.2. Beaked shoes (*The Translator Presents the Book to Charles the Bold. Quintus Curtius, Fais d'Alexandre le Grant* [Deeds of Alexander the Great, 1470], Paris, Bibliothèque nationale de France, MS fr. 22547, fol. 2). *Source:* gallica.bnf.fr / BnF.

discouraging consumption? This is a particularly vexing question for cities that owed their wealth to luxury trades, especially in textiles such as silk and velvet. (Because goods and wealth were concentrated in cities, sumptuary regulations were almost exclusively urban phenomena.) These historians have largely thrown up their hands in dismay at such apparently irrational legislation and invoked the stifling influence of religion. But dissenting voices have pointed out that the situation is more complicated. Luxury per se was rarely forbidden; officials in Florence or Genoa were not about to kill the goose that laid the golden eggs and had nothing against golden eggs per se.[13] Moreover, fines paid by scofflaws may in some cases have padded city budgets, providing as steady a stream of extra income as traffic fines or vice taxes do in modern cities.[14] Social and cultural historians have had an easier time of it, since at least some sumptuary legislation was clearly intended to stabilize social hierarchy and enshrine symbols of social difference—between men and women, maid and mistress, burgher and peasant, student and artisan. But once again, a closer and broader look qualifies this explanation. By no means all sumptuary regulations were organized by social categories, and even those that were may well have been occasions to re-order rather than to consolidate existing hierarchies.[15]

The sheer variability of the declared motives behind sumptuary regulations, as well as the diversity of the particular form of excess they sought to restrain, baffles easy generalization. In different times and places, regulations forbade over-indulgence at table, like the 1327 English law drawing the line at two courses per meal for all ranks,[16] or unseemly displays of grief at funerals, like the 1276 Bologna ban on women mourners shredding their clothes and tearing their hair,[17] or decadent ostentation, like the 1563 French royal edict threatening tailors who made puffy pantaloons still puffier by stuffing them with wool or cotton with a smarting fine of 200 livres,[18] or imports that competed with local wares, like the 1712 Württemberg ordinance that controlled cotton chintz made in Switzerland.[19] The stated motives for regulations were just as diverse: fear of God's wrath (especially after recent military defeats and outbreaks of plague), saving good families from impoverishing themselves by trying to keep up with the Joneses, indignation at social *arrivistes* who usurped the honor and dignity of higher ranks, enforcing gender roles (cross-dressing was almost the only infraction of sumptuary regulations that risked corporal punishment),[20] upholding standards of modesty for both men and women, checking luxury and frivolity, or economic protectionism. Often, religious, social, and economic justifications were heaped up in the same text, as in the everything-but-the-kitchen-sink style of the 1695 Saxon ordinance, which never gave one reason where two or three would do: semi-transparent shawls worn by women were impious, immodest, impractical—and unhealthy to boot.[21] Sometimes the very same item was banned in one ordinance for one reason but later for an entirely different one. The French royal edict of 1563 banned gold buttons "with or without enamel" as yet another extravagant new fad, but a 1689 edict prohibited the same items because fashionistas were depleting the currency store by melting down coins to make them.[22]

Yet from the standpoint of the historian of rules, two aspects of these protean regulations do remain relatively constant amidst all of this pied variety: first, the combination of exacting detail in their formulation but considerable elasticity in their enforcement; and second, the refusal of the rule-makers to give up in the face of centuries of failure. Sumptuary regulations may be examples of rules that failed, over and over again, but the reasons for their failure are rich in lessons about the sub-category of rules known as regulations.

Tracked over decades and centuries, there is an unmistakable trend toward ever greater specificity in the sumptuary regulations. No *Vogue* editor ever covered the catwalk in more precise detail than sumptuary regulations did at their zenith, which, for European cities, usually coincided with the rise of luxury trades and increased commercial contact with other entrepôts as far away as India and China. The earliest laws were relatively short and unspecific. For example, a 1279 French ordinance issued by Philip III (1245–1285, r. 1270–1285) set the limit of dishes per meal at three, which were to be "very simple," but allowed dessert, as long as the latter was restricted to "fruit and cheese" and did not include "tartes and flans";[23] the 1294 ordinance regulating clothing was lengthier but still generic in its approach, limiting the annual number of new robes for noblemen possessing an income of less than 6,000 livres to "four and no more."[24] By the seventeenth century, however, not only had the list of prohibited luxuries lengthened to include items such as gold buttons, imported lace, and carriages, all regulated in minute detail; so had the list of previous royal ordinances, all roundly ignored. Louis XIV's (1638–1715, r. 1643–1715) edict of 1670 begins with a doleful list of previous sumptuary edicts just from his own reign: the edicts of 25 October 1656, 27 November 1660, 27 May 1661, 18 June 1663, 20 December 1667, 28 June 1668, 13 April 1669.[25] Each was longer, more detailed, and more ineffectual than the previous one, as the preambles freely admitted.

The growing proliferation and prolixity of sumptuary regulations in municipalities from Genoa to Augsburg to Paris in medieval and early modern Europe serve as a rough barometer of economic growth. The more luxury items to buy, the more temptations to splurge—and the more *nouveau riche* merchant families threatened to eclipse older aristocratic families in splendor. New textiles as well as new fashions came into the crosshairs of sumptuary rules: the 1463 Leipzig ordinances regulated only silk and velvet, but by 1506 twelve more items had been added to the list, including damask and taffeta, a tribute to Leipzig's growing wealth and will to spend it.[26] Both the backbone of long-distance trade and the most enticing luxuries on offer, silks, velvets, satin, brocades, cloth of gold, and other rich fabrics made fortunes and fashion. They also reoriented sumptuary regulations. Dating back to ancient Greek and Roman restrictions on extravagant feasting and mourning rites, sumptuary rules sought to curb excess and luxury wherever they cropped up, originally in funeral, wedding, and baptismal ceremonies. Although these occasions continued to be regulated, by the twelfth century, starting in northern Italy, personal attire had become the focus of sumptuary prohibitions. Just whose clothing and ornaments came under scrutiny varied by locale. The majority of sumptuary laws promulgated by Italian city-states between 1200 and 1500 regulated women's clothing; French laws appear to have been more concerned with the uppity male nobility; the Bavarians had their eye on everyone and everything.[27] The motivations behind the legislation were equally varied, but in almost all cases upholding the visible signs of social hierarchy and discouraging unnecessary expenditure featured prominently in official justifications.

These rules differed from those of coeval how-to books discussed in Chapter 3 in at least three significant respects. First, they were not how-to but how-not-to rules, spelling out exactly which shoes or bonnets or ornaments were forbidden to whom and under what circumstances. Second, they were statutes that could be and often were enforced with sanctions, not voluntary guides to self-improvement. Third, they sought to narrow the margin of discretion to a sliver. Sumptuary laws overflowed with specifics, but they were not thick rules. The legislators who framed them hoped to slam the door on all interpretation, special cases, and discretion, at least on the side of the offenders, if not the enforcers. Nor were they thin rules like the calculating algorithms we encountered in Chapter 5. A great deal of background knowledge about local context was required to understand and follow them. Historians of fashion have filled whole dictionaries with the abstruse terminology for this or that short-lived but must-have article of clothing.[28] But sumptuary regulations did resemble both thick and thin rules in one respect, indeed the same respect: their teeming detail. Like the thick rules of Chapter 3, they wallowed in concrete particulars; like the thin rules of Chapter 5, they were intended to be obeyed to the letter, with minimal discretion, as laid out in those same concrete particulars about ruffs and sleeve lengths and velvet trim.

Rule-makers and rule-breakers were locked in an endless cycle of prohibition, evasion, innovation, and revised prohibition—otherwise known as fashion. If long, pointy shoes were banned by this year's edict, next year's style, equally extreme and expensive, would feature high heels and buckles. By the time the authorities had caught up with the latest style, the tailors, cobblers, and their customers had all moved on. It is quite possible that an unintended consequence of the waves of ever more detailed prohibitions was to accelerate the tempo of fashion, as suppliers created and customers embraced novelties to stay one step ahead of the authorities.[29] The result was not unlike a tax code repeatedly amended to plug loopholes opened up by clever accountants who exploit every ambiguity and possibility not yet expressly prohibited: a mare's nest of detail so complicated that it becomes even more ambiguous and difficult to enforce in practice. Questions from subjects directed to French officials who had offered to clarify the sumptuary prohibitions of 1549 give some idea of the hermeneutics of velvet bonnets and social rank: "Whether velvet hats and caps are included among [banned] 'velvet bonnets'? (they are); "whether the word 'mechanicals' applies to retail merchants, goldsmiths, apothecaries, and the other principal crafts of Paris, and whether the wives of mechanicals may wear silk borders and other trim?" (yes, they're all mechanicals, but their wives may wear silk trim and sleeves).[30] In a sterling example of the law of unintended consequences, the more officials attempted to limit discretion by heaping up specific details, the more they inadvertently encouraged innovation and interpretation.

As a result, sumptuary rules were difficult to enforce, although there is strong evidence that the officials tried to do so by every means at their disposal, at least sporadically. As early as 1286 Bologna seems to have instituted a special magistracy to deal with infringements of sumptuary rules; many cities offered informants up to half of the fines levied for offenses as a reward; and a Venetian law of 1465 promised freedom to slaves who denounced their profligate masters and mistresses.[31] But officials encountered stiff resistance. Quite apart from the social risks of denouncing employers and close acquaintances, who often came from influential and wealthy families, the offenders could be counted upon to put up a fight. They balked at the fines and sometimes insulted or even assaulted officials, who were hard to recruit and were themselves subject to fines for shirking their duties.[32] Even if they escaped insult and injury, the officials could reckon with a torrent of protests and excuses: "What, this old thing? I've had it for ages, long before those rules were issued." "Silk? No, no, it's only a wool imitation." "But I *am* entitled to wear ribbons on my robes: I have a doctorate in theology."[33] The 1695 Saxon code warned magistrates against all manner of "misinterpretation and deceptive excuses" from those who had run afoul of its twenty-six pages of detailed regulations concerning who could wear what when.[34] The very specificity of the sumptuary rules invited haggling over details and interpretations.

Matters were not made easier by the increasing number of distinctions and exceptions made by the rules themselves. Although some cities, such as Padua, applied sumptuary proscriptions to all residents, regardless of rank, many others drew exceedingly fine distinctions among both forbidden ornaments and the ranks of those who could and could not wear them.[35] The French edict of 1661 dictated that women could wear lace (domestic manufacture only) and other trim of no more than two inches width "around the bottom and front of dresses and skirts, and on the middle of sleeves," and gave men even more detailed instructions;[36] the Strasbourg ordinance of 1660 distinguished among 256 ranks of residents and specified in acribic detail what each was and was not allowed to wear.[37] Enforcing such distinctions must have been a nightmare: what if the lace trim was 2.2 inches wide, or on the wrong part of the sleeve, and who had the authority to decide whether that woman wearing fox fur trim on her cloak belonged to social rank 135 or 136? Then there were the exceptions introduced in the regulations themselves. A 1459 Venetian edict gave women a temporary dispensation from sumptuary rules in order to impress a visiting foreign dignitary with the splendor of the city;[38] a 1543 French ordinance offered a three-month grace period before enforcement began so that subjects could get some wear out of newly purchased finery;[39] Bologna, Padua, and Leipzig all granted exemptions to foreign students attending their universities.[40]

Unsurprisingly, the net effect of swarming detail, fine distinctions, frequent revisions, numerous exceptions, and, above all, unrelenting public resistance was to make enforcement devilishly difficult. The same combination of factors led to the exercise of considerable latitude on the part of the responsible officials in individual cases. In medieval and early modern Italy, where the extant evidence of enforcement has been especially well researched, offenders seem rarely to have paid the full amount of the fine, and magistrates often relaxed the rules in order "to design a supple, flexible instrument, suited to extant circumstances, which had to be administered with care and discretion."[41] Despite or rather because of its detailed specifications, the 1695 Saxon sumptuary rules elevated the discretion of the officials to a principle, to be exercised in the name of both vigilance and clemency. On the one hand, magistrates should be on the lookout for new fashion excesses "not expressly forbidden in the current ordinance . . . because one cannot cover everything or anticipate future new inventions"; on the other hand, anyone who offended not out of "arrogance and cockiness but rather with the view that this [item of clothing] was not unsuited to his rank" should be treated with indulgence.[42] Although formulated in formidable detail in order to eliminate any latitude for interpretation and special pleading on the part of offenders, the sumptuary rules, like the rules of the mechanical arts we encountered in Chapter 3, required discretion on the part of officials in order to be applied in practice to particular cases. In contrast to the thick rules of Chapter 3, however, discretion was entirely one-sided. As in the case of the *Rule of Saint Benedict* discussed in Chapter 2, discretion was the prerogative of the powerful: the officials, not the offenders, decided whether to bend or suspend a rule in an individual case.

Sumptuary rules in Europe (though not necessarily in the European colonies)[43] were on the wane by the eighteenth century, as old ones were no longer being enforced and no new ones were being promulgated. Historians of sumptuary legislation point to the watershed moment in 1793 when the French Revolution proclaimed dressing as one pleased to be a right. Even this edict contained restrictions, however: clothing must conform to the citizen's sex, and the wearing of the tricolor cockade was mandatory.[44] Nor have sumptuary rules disappeared from the contemporary world, and a preponderance of them still regulate what women may and may not wear, whether in the name of religion and modesty, as in the case of the regulations repealed in Sudan after the revolution of November 2019 or in the name of a secular liberal polity, as in the case of France's 2004 law banning the wearing of any conspicuous religious symbol in public, a response to a decades-long debate over whether Muslim girls and women may wear a head-scarf in schools.[45] Pockets of explicitly regulated dress survive in schools, the military, hospitals, and of course academic ceremonies with their color-coded regalia of caps, gowns, and hoods.

But the realm of implicit regulation of who may wear what on which occasion remains vast. If you're skeptical, just try wearing a bathing suit to a job interview or a tuxedo to a barbecue. As countless protests and debates about the place of women in public space, whether in the streets or on the internet, make painfully clear, sanctions, sometimes violent ones, still menace those perceived to transgress implicit rules of dress. Modern societies may pride themselves on uninhibited consumption and unrestrained freedom to wear whatever one likes, whenever and wherever one likes. But the right to dress has never been unconditional; nor has it ever been equally enjoyed by all, even when not restricted by regulations on the book.

What does the long, strange history of sumptuary regulations teach us about the nature of these most niggling of rules? First, detail and specificity can never eliminate ambiguity and interpretation—quite the contrary. This is especially the case when there is motive and opportunity for evasion, as medieval munici-palities discovered when they tried to regulate dress and modern governments learn when they try to perfect tax codes. Second, fail-ure, even abysmal, acknowledged failure for centuries on end, is not in itself sufficient reason for giving up on regulation. Do not expect governments to surrender to tax evaders anytime soon. Nor are sumptuary regulations dead and buried, once and for all. All it takes to revive them is a hotly politicized connection between, say, fur and cruelty to animals or cotton and sustainability or cheap cloth-ing and sweatshop conditions. The resulting bans may not be as sweeping as those proclaimed in early modern European cities, but they will be no easier to enforce, even if there is widespread public agreement on the reasons to abridge the right to dress. Almost everyone in medieval and early modern Europe would have agreed that excessive luxury was immoral and wasteful, but they disagreed strenuously as to whether in their own case wearing puffy panta-loons or gold braid was excessive. Third and finally, just because of the obstacles to enforcement, implicit norms work far better than explicit regulations in achieving the desired results. Only newcom-ers need to be told about the unwritten dress code for most social occasions, and violations are both rare and deliberate (for example, Marlene Dietrich's calculated appropriation of male evening dress for dramatic effect in the 1930 film *Morocco*).

The quandary posed by the case of the sumptuary regulations for the historian of rules is why, hobbled by their own maniacal detail and rubbery revisability, they never achieved the status of implicit norms. They could never take the form of the rules-as-models of Chapter 2 or the thick rules of Chapter 3 (or even the pre-modern algorithms of Chapter 4): what good was a model or example that was already out of date in a matter of months? And what good were lots of specific details if they could not, as in the case of the examples that composed thick rules, be generalized by analogy? If the promul-gators of sumptuary regulations could have stopped the fashion clock, as some religious communities managed to do, explicit rules might have hardened into implicit norms. But such victories usually come at the cost of iron discipline and separation from the rest of society, as in the case of the Amish, and are consequently infrequent and fragile. In contrast, traffic regulations eventually did take hold, though their progress was slow and fitful and their hold always precarious, as all city-dwellers know to their peril.

Rules for an Unruly City: Policing the Streets of Enlightenment Paris

"The rule proper concerns those things one must do; and the regulation, the manner in which one must do them."[46] So the author of the entry "Rule, Regulation" in the great *Encyclopédie* of the eighteenth-century European Enlightenment attempted to distill the essence of an elusive distinction. Neither the timing nor the location of this effort to pin down the difference between rules and regulations was accidental: mid-eighteenth-century Paris was the site of Europe's most admired and reviled attempt to control urban chaos through unparalleled police powers and an avalanche of regulations. Here are a few examples plucked from the thousands issued between 1667 and the eve of the Revolution in 1789.

> *Paris, police ordinance, 22 June 1732*: In defiance of the ordinance of 1729, carriages are still being rented to drivers under the age of seventeen and mules and horses intended as beasts of burden are being ridden through the streets, injuring pedestrians.[47]

> *Paris, police ordinance, 28 November 1750*: In defiance of the edicts of 1663, 1666, and 1744, Parisians are still not sweeping their stoops at 7:00 a.m., are still emptying the contents of their chamber pots onto the street, still blocking the streets with manure and bricks, and generally "not at all conforming to the edicts, ordinances, and prohibitions" repeatedly issued by the authorities.[48]

> *Paris, police ordinance, 3 September 1754*: In defiance of the edicts of 1667, 1672, 1700, 1703, 1705, 1722, 1724, 1732, 1746, and 1748,

FIGURE 6.3. Tumult in the streets of Paris (Étienne Jeaurat, *Le Carnaval des rues de Paris* [The carnival of the streets of Paris], 1757, Musée de Carnavalet, Paris.) bpk / RMN—Grand Palais / Agence Bulloz.

Parisians are still playing games in the street and endangering passers-by and breaking street lanterns. The culprits, "shop boys, artisans, liveried servants, and other young people," are hereby enjoined to cease and desist or pay a stiff fine of 200 livres.[49]

These rules are typical of the thousands of police regulations issued between 1667, when the office of the Lieutenant de police of Paris was created, in the words of the royal decree, to "assure peace of mind to the public and individuals, to purge the city of all that could cause disorder, to procure abundance, and to make each live according to his condition and estate,"[50] and the outbreak of the French Revolution in 1789. Catching and punishing criminals ranked rather low among police priorities; far more important were the sorts of topics covered by the never-ending stream of regulations that sought to govern every detail of urban life from firefighting to street cleaning to traffic to lighting.[51] No unruliness was too small to escape police attention: fishmongers who blocked the rue Saint-Paul, rowdies who hissed during performances at the Comédie-Française, carriage-drivers who swore at pedestrians. Unprecedented in their number, scope, detail, and ambition, these rules aimed to control everyone and everything within the city limits and to turn famously unruly Paris into a place where everyone always obeyed all the rules. Never before had the Parisian vision of what rules could accomplish been so all-encompassing and so unbending.

And in such ludicrous contrast to the lived reality of the city. If there was one thing that Parisians and visitors alike agreed upon, it was that Enlightenment Paris was a squalid, stinking, crowded chaos where, then as now, one took one's life in one's hands just to cross the street. (Fig. 6.3.) A mid-eighteenth-century German visitor complained of the "incessant din of carriages, fiacres, and street vendors . . . the dirty streets, the horrid, multifarious steam and unhealthy stink."[52] Describing Paris a decade or so later in his *Tableau de Paris* (1782–88), Paris native Louis-Sébastien Mercier (1740–1814) described harrowing scenes of panicked pedestrians fleeing carriages driven at breakneck speeds down narrow lanes and condemned the "barbaric luxury" of such vehicles.[53] In his utopian novel *L'An 2440: Rêve s'il en fut jamais* (The year 2440. A dream if ever there were one, 1771), Mercier imagined the Paris of the future as a place where, to the astonishment of the time-traveler, Parisians are polite and hard-working and have abandoned high fashion for sturdy, plain clothing. The streets are broad, well-lit, and safe for pedestrians (including the king, who has abandoned his state carriage).[54] It is worthy of note that he thought it would take Paris on the order of 650 years to make these improvements to urban life. The prolific, prolix, and relentlessly re-issued rules of the Lieutenant de police seemed wildly inadequate to the task of taming Enlightenment Paris.

Yet the rules kept coming, thousands of them, each more un-yielding than the previous in its expectation of being obeyed to the letter, backed up by fines or worse. Only the dour recital of the long list of previous, obviously inefficacious edicts and the exas-perated tone of the preambles betray any sign that all had not gone exactly according to plan. The obduracy and repetitive rigidity of rule-making in the face of rule-failure is striking. In contrast, even the sumptuary regulations made desperate attempts to keep up with the times, amended as often as clothes were altered to catch up with the latest styles. The rule-mania of Enlightenment Paris represents the advent of a new kind of rule that contrasted starkly with the thick rules of the fifteenth and sixteenth centuries that we encountered in Chapter 3. The latter were almost always formu-lated with an eye toward adjustments necessary in practice, and rule-makers anticipated exceptions from the outset. These earlier rules were as supple in their formulation as the later Parisian ordi-nances were rigid. Nor were such regulations formulated as if con-text could be held permanently constant, as in the case of the thin rules of calculation at the Greenwich Observatory in Chapter 4 or the British *Nautical Almanac* in Chapter 5. Eighteenth-century Paris was a percolating place, full of novelty, enterprise, and people on the make. What made the Parisian authorities so confident that their rules could be formulated as if particulars always conformed to universals, as if Parisians always did as they were told—in the teeth of such abundant experience to the contrary? The answer lies in a seductive fantasy of order that held the Parisian police in its thrall.

This image (Fig. 6.4), from a 1749 manuscript submitted by an officer of the Paris police to Louis XV (1710–1774, r. 1715–1774) and exquisitely illustrated by artist Gabriel Saint-Aubin (1724–1780), shows the invention of license plates. Its author, François-Jacques Guillote (1697–1766), officer of the constabulary, resident in Paris, and friend of *Encyclopédie* editor Denis Diderot,[55] proposed in the same treatise the numbering of Paris houses, indeed the number-ing of the stairways within each house and the lettering of each

FIGURE 6.4. Plan for numbered fiacres and horses in Paris (François-Jacques Guillote, *Mémoire sur la réformation de la police de France* [Memoir on the Reformation of the French Police, manuscript presented to Louis XV, 1749]), reproduced from *Mémoire sur la réformation de la police de France. Soumis au Roi en 1749*, ed. Jean Seznec (Paris: Hermann, 1974).

apartment of every floor. He recommended a kind of identity card that would allow the police to trace the comings and goings of every single one of Paris's circa 500,000 residents. He imagined a gigantic paper-shuffling machine that would allow the police to find the right file among millions of documents with the spin of a wheel. (Fig. 6.5.) He wanted to weave a finely meshed net of policing that would "leave [everyone] the freedom to do good but make doing evil extremely difficult."[56] He was obsessed with the regulation of the booming, expanding, and notoriously unruly city of Paris circa 1750. No wonder philosopher of surveillance Michel

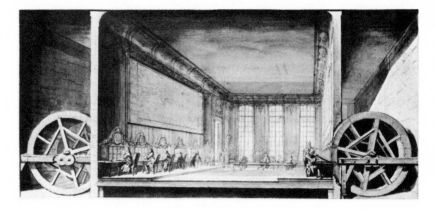

FIGURE 6.5. Plan for a machine to retrieve police dossiers (François-Jacques
Guillote, *Mémoire sur la réformation de la police de France* [Memoir on the
Reformation of the French Police, manuscript presented to Louis XV, 1749]),
reproduced from *Mémoire sur la réformation de la police de France.
Soumis au Roi en 1749*, ed. Jean Seznec (Paris: Hermann, 1974).

Foucault was morbidly fascinated by the centralized police of
eighteenth-century Paris. Guillote's treatise is a phantasmagoria of
the surveillance and control of every aspect of urban life, from
traffic to trash collection.[57]

It was of course a complete fantasy, as one look at the actual
efforts of the police to keep even a semblance of order in
eighteenth-century Paris confirms. Contemporaries testified to
the squalor, stink, and congestion of the streets, as carts, carriages,
horses, mules, pedestrians, and market stands competed for space
in the muddy lanes heaped with garbage and usually divided in the
middle by a filthy stream meant to carry at least some of the refuse
into the Seine.[58] Sidewalks were a rarity[59]—as the names *trottoir*
and *montoir* suggest, the original purpose of such raised walkways
was to give riders a leg up in mounting their horses[60]—and pedestrians milling the streets lived in terror of being run over by a
speeding carriage or perhaps a pack mule cantering home unbur-
dened from its load. From the late sixteenth century to the mid-
nineteenth century, the Parisian police and municipal administra-

FIGURE 6.6. Traffic jam on the Pont-Neuf, Paris (Nicolas Guérard, *L'Embarras de Paris* (Pont-Neuf) [Paris Congestion, c. 1715]), Musée du Louvre.

tion saw their chief task as the conquest of public space, which often boiled down to keeping the streets clean and clear of obstacles to traffic. (Fig. 6.6.)

But how? Paris, like many early modern European cities, was freed from its constraining medieval walls in the late seventeenth century, at the same time that its population and commercial activity were sky-rocketing. Rising revenues from North Atlantic trade triggered a building boom: by 1779, Paris was estimated to have 50,000 houses, 17 public squares, 12 bridges, 975 streets ranging in width from about 2 to 20 meters wide, and a population of circa 650,000.[61] A city that had had 8 carriages in 1594 had about 300 in 1660 and somewhere between 14,000 and 20,000 in 1722.[62] Aside from a few newly created broad boulevards on the city's repurposed ramparts, most of the streets were crooked and narrow. Houses were arranged higgledy-piggledy, each façade oriented in a different direction and all encroaching upon what little space separated them.[63] Guillote toyed with the idea of just razing the city to the ground and starting all over again.[64]

It was the Parisian police who were charged with ordering this chaos. From the late seventeenth century on, the Parisian police were responsible for almost all aspects of urban administration and for assuring not only the safety but also the comfort and convenience of its citizens. Amsterdam was often held up by observers at the time as the paragon of effective early modern policing, in the broad sense of assuring welfare and order as well as security. Praised for its cleanliness, handsome and uniform street façades, efficient sewage system, spacious public squares, night-time illumination by oil lamps, strictly regulated traffic, and workhouses to keep beggars out of the public eye, Amsterdam set a standard that Paris and London fell well short of.[65] (Fig. 6.7.) By the late seventeenth century, Western Europe's metropolises were in competition with each other to straighten, illuminate, sanitize, broaden, and above all order their thoroughfares and granted the police enormous power to effect these improvements. After the creation of the office of the Paris Lieutenant de police in 1667, to whom approximately fifty *commissaires* stationed in the city's neighborhoods reported on a daily basis and collected thousands of dossiers filed chronologically and alphabetically, the police became the vanguard of the French absolutist bureaucracy, admired and feared throughout Europe.[66] Political economist and Paris police archivist Jacques Peuchet (1758–1830) described the Paris Lieutenant de police as the center of "the immense machine of the police; all the spokes from the circumference converge on him, only he sets them in motion."[67] It was no accident that Guillote's fantasies about not only surveillance but also paperwork centered on the Parisian police.

A good deal of that mass of paperwork was generated by regulations,[68] which stipulated everything from who may have a home laboratory (apothecaries and professors of chemistry only), the minimum age for driving a hired carriage (eighteen), permissible celebrations of a royal birth (candles in the window yes, firing

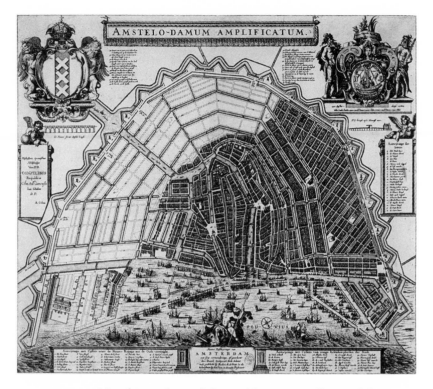

FIGURE 6.7. Map of Amsterdam, with design of the symmetrically expanded city
(Daniel Stalpaert, 1657), Rijksmuseum, Amsterdam.

guns into the air no), the maximum number of horses or mules
that may be yoked together (two), how gold and silver should be
used (for coins only, with the occasional exception of a cross for
an archbishop), the spacing of trees planted along main thoroughfares (at least eighteen feet apart), and innumerable prohibitions
against blocking the streets—with trash, snow, carts, animals,
bricks, stalls, or ball games.[69] Reading through all of these ordinances decade by decade, one occasionally catches a glimpse of
the events that Enlightenment historians habitually use as land-
marks of the era: the closing of the Saint-Médard cemetery in the
wake of alleged miraculous cures in 1732 or the suppression of the
Encyclopédie in 1752. But these are the merest drops in the ocean

of regulations that occupied the Parisian police day in, day out. The scope and detail of these regulations is staggering: a heroic effort to anticipate, counter, and regulate every possible affront to public safety and good order. As Charles de Secondat, Baron de Montesquieu (1689–1755) said of the police: "[They] are perpetually concerned with details; . . . with regulations rather than laws."[70]

But apparently all of this bureaucratic foresight, surveillance, and record-keeping was largely in vain. All infringements carried fines and some even prison sentences, and those daily reports from neighborhood commissioners on infractions provide evidence of vigilance and enforcement, even for minor offenses. Every Tuesday and Friday the Lieutenant de police heard cases at the Grand Châtelet, handing down, for example, a hefty fine of 300 livres[71] to one "demoiselle Truque, resident in the rue de Harlay" who was spotted wearing a dress of contraband *coton indien* (i.e., chintz) printed with red roses, or a lighter fine of 100 sous to the widow Girard who had emptied the contents of her chamber pot onto the street below at 9:00 p.m. on a January evening.[72] (It was not considered exculpatory first to yell "Garre-l'eau!" ["Watch out below!"] as a warning to passers-by.) More serious offenses, such as riding faster than a trot, and cases of recidivism were fined more heavily, and, because the commissioners usually cashiered a cut of the fines, there was every motive to find and prosecute culprits.

Yet the sheer number of times that the ordinances were reissued, often word-for-word identical to the earlier ones (but for the weary prologue bemoaning the necessity of repeating the regulations yet again) is damning evidence of their ineffectiveness. Recall the examples I began with: The police ordinance of 28 November 1750 on street cleaning repeated the edicts of 1663, 1666, and 1744 verbatim (Parisians were still not waking up at 7:00 a.m. to sweep their stoops).[73] Edicts banning games from Paris streets were re-issued seventeen times between 1667 and 1754.[74] As a 1644 royal decree prohibiting (yet again) imported lace despaired: "Experience has shown that heretofore all regulations made by the kings our predecessors and by ourselves have been futile and not executed, having served only to display defiance to their authority, the weakness of the magistrates, and the corruption of the manners of this century."[75]

In the face of such humiliating failure to get Parisians to shovel snow, foreswear lace, stop playing ball in the streets, or place their trash in the appointed containers at the appointed hour, the response of the police bureaucracy was to issue yet more regulations, even more detailed, and to redouble surveillance and reporting. Guillote's treatise for Louis XV recommended more police inspectors, more reports, more registration and observation of everyone and everything. What in retrospect looks like a glaring example of rule-failure was interpreted at the time as a call for rule repair: if the existing rules had encountered resistance and exceptions, the solution was to weave an even tighter mesh of rules, darning the loopholes and catching the scofflaws. This bureaucratic reflex is so familiar to us that we hardly query its oddity. Why should the response to failed rules be to repeat the old ones and make new ones? What delusion of order, what vision of rules, had so bewitched the famously worldly Lieutenant of the Parisian police, a man who had seen everything and who knew everyone's secrets, that no amount of countervailing evidence could dislodge it? The Lieutenants of the Parisian police, arguably France's and perhaps Europe's foremost bureaucrats, refused to give in to the recalcitrance of the Parisians.

What accounts for obstinacy in the face of failure, time and time again? Why were so many ordinances neither scrapped nor amended but simply re-issued verbatim except for an ill-tempered preamble, despite the evident refusal of most Parisians to pay them any heed? The explanations for this lamentable state of affairs found in the preambles range from the conciliatory (perhaps, ran one 1735 preamble of re-issued fire regulations, people had simply forgotten previous ordinances)[76] to the indignant (it was intolerable that people were melting down gold and silver coins to make buttons to flatter their vanity).[77] Historians of Paris document the resistance of the Parisians and the inadequacy of the regulations to bring chaos under control but rarely remark upon the puzzling obstinacy and inflexibility of the regulations themselves.[78]

The rule-mania of the fifteenth and sixteenth centuries had been just as prolific in rules, just as confident that the right rules would solve all problems, from learning to swim to arriving at self-evident truths. But the earlier rules had been thick with examples and supple in the face of exceptions. Sumptuary regulations rarely succeeded, but their failure could not be ascribed to rigidity in the face of resistance. If anything, sumptuary regulations were *too* responsive to changing circumstances and too flexible (and sporadic) in their enforcement to gain traction. In contrast, police regulations seeking to bring order to Enlightenment Paris were rigid in their formulation and, if the archives of the police magistrates at Châtelet are to be believed, consistently enforced.[79] It was as if the Parisian police suffered from some kind of obsessive-compulsive neurosis, doomed to repeat the same futile rules year after year, decade after decade, unable or unwilling to adjust to circumstances.

A clue to the causes of their obstinacy lies in the competition among European metropolises that began in the late seventeenth century and gathered momentum throughout the eighteenth century: Amsterdam, Paris, and London were not only in competition with each other; they were emulating each other, implicitly establishing new standards for what a first-rank city should look, sound, and smell like. Travelers and also official delegates reported home about the new fire pumps and street lantern systems in Amsterdam, which were duly copied in London and Paris.[80] Parisian displays of luxury goods in vitrines on the rue Saint-Honoré found their way back to London's fashionable shopping districts. Rival cities vied with each other for the most free-flowing traffic, the most splendid parks and promenades, and the cleanest, best-lit streets.[81] When in 1649 Queen Christina of Sweden (1626–1689, r. 1632–1654) issued an edict to upgrade Stockholm's streets, she noted that such amenities belonged to the "graces and utilities of wealthy towns."[82] Although the stated goal of all these improvements was the comfort, safety, and convenience of the city's residents, the authorities were acutely conscious of the judgment of foreigners. When, for example, the Parisian police banned merchants' stalls from the Pont-Neuf for the umpteenth time, they justified the regulations not just by pointing to the traffic congestion the stalls caused but also by noting that they blocked "the most magnificent view and the one most worthy of the admiration of foreigners."[83]

It is tempting to bundle all of these measures to control traffic, fight fires, clean streets, and beautify views together as attempts at "modernization," and that is indeed the way urban historians have described the late seventeenth- and eighteenth-century transition from medieval walled cities to sprawling commercial metropolises in Europe's most populous cities. But it would be more accurate to say that this competition among cities was inventing the first version of modernity, a modernity that had as yet very little to do with science and technology (the nineteenth-century version of modernity) and everything to do with orderliness, predictability, and, yes, rules. When Mercier imagined the Paris of the future, he did not foresee technological marvels of transportation and communication. Parisians in the year 2440 would still be getting around in horse-drawn carriages and on foot, but they would be doing so in an orderly manner. Rather than striving to realize a vision of modernity that did not yet exist (and certainly not under that name), Enlightenment Paris and its rivals were aiming at a vision already glimpsed in the uniform façades, efficient sewage, free-flowing traffic, and night streets blazing with lanterns in Amsterdam. Here was a city in which the radius of predictability in everyday life had been impressively extended, at least within the city limits. It was no accident that the Dutch also pioneered mathematically based annuities, lotteries, and insurance schemes during the same period to rein in the role of chance in human affairs.

In his justly celebrated book *The Passions and the Interests: Political Arguments for Capitalism before Its Triumph* (1977), political economist Albert O. Hirschman described how the vices of greed and pursuit of self-interest were morally rehabilitated by Enlightenment thinkers such as Bernard Mandeville (1670–1733) and Adam Smith. These thinkers argued that even if self-interest did not make people virtuous, it did make them calculable, and that was the great advantage of the interests over the volatile passions of ambition, anger, and lust. The interests began as "calm passions," well suited to bridling the tempestuous ones, and ended up as demi-virtues because they lubricated commerce and stabilized social life.[84] What Hirschman does not explain is *why* the doctrine of the benign interests—which, as his subtitle announces, antedates rather than rationalizes the triumph of capitalism—emerges where and when it does. The passions had, after all, been excoriated by philosophers and moralists as the enemies of reason and virtue since antiquity. Moreover, why should the argument that the calmer interests could subdue the notoriously wild passions have been persuasive? Finally, why was it better to be predictable than to be truly good?

In the answer to these questions about the rising stock of the interests lies at least part of the answer to the question about why the Parisian police so stubbornly issued and re-issued their thousands of rules without adjustments, much less concessions of defeat. In both cases, partial success, however fragmentary and fragile, fueled hopes that total success was possible. Rather than bow to immediate experience, as the thick rules had, the municipal authorities banked on experience eventually bowing to the rules. In some places, few in number but populous and much publicized in both word and image, what was by early modern European standards an astonishing degree of orderliness and predictability had in fact been achieved. Amsterdam played a starring role in these visions and revisions of ideals of the possible in urban improvement. But even in chaotic Paris and London, microcosms of regularity brought about by regulation, whether imposed from above or below, were emerging. Even the simplest traffic conventions were hailed as marvelous innovations. Mercier's time-traveler observed that traffic in the Paris of 2440 kept to the right: "This simple method of avoiding obstruction has been lately discovered; so true it is, that all useful inventions are produced by time."[85] By 1786 London visitors were being advised that if they kept the walls of buildings to their right while walking the city's crowded streets, "you will have no interruption, everyone will give way."[86] And in 1831, fifty years after Mercier's book was published but a good six hundred years before he thought Parisians would finally discover this simple expedient, the Paris police issued an ordinance directing traffic to keep to the right.[87] Change came slowly, but not as slowly as a well-informed observer of eighteenth-century Parisian traffic chaos had predicted.

In Paris, the broad boulevards created on the city's former ramparts between 1668 and 1705 from the Porte Saint-Antoine to the Porte Saint-Honoré became one of these microcosms of order. (Fig. 6.8.) They were much remarked upon by visitors and residents alike throughout the eighteenth century, and Mercier was still admiring them in the 1780s. Divided into lanes by trees planted at precise intervals, the rampart boulevards segregated horse, carriage, and pedestrian traffic for the first time in Paris's history. In dry seasons the dusty paths were watered down; in wet times they were strewn with sand; at all times they enjoyed great popularity with a broad cross-section of the public as a spacious, safe promenade. A 1751 ordinance began with a proud declaration of how pleasant the rampart boulevards were and an assertion of the police's intention to "remove all obstacles to the appeal and comfort to which the public has come to expect" and to insure their continued "ease and complete cleanliness, which contribute a great deal to the satisfaction of the people who go along the ramparts, whether in carriages or on foot."[88] On the rampart boulevards an oasis of good order had been created and sustained by rules, a small success as measured against the disorder that reigned in much of the rest of Paris, but a success that nurtured ambitions that the oasis of order could be expanded.

The new rampart boulevards are emblematic of another aspect of why seventeenth- and eighteenth-century municipal authorities

FIGURE 6.8. The Boulevard Basse-du-Rempart, later the Boulevard des
Capucines, on a repurposed city rampart (Jean-Baptiste Lallemand, *Boulevard
Basse-du-Rempart*, mid-18th c.). Source: gallica.bnf.fr / BnF.

were obsessed with order and predictability. Once the medieval
city walls had been rendered obsolete by new siege warfare techniques in the latter half of the seventeenth century, cities like Paris,
London, and Amsterdam could expand beyond their old boundaries, and expand they did, at a breathtaking rate. Amsterdam had
a population of circa 50,000 in 1600 and 235,000 in 1700; in the
same period Paris swelled from 210,000 to 515,000 inhabitants. On
the eve of the French Revolution, as many as 630,000 people were
living in the city. London's growth curve was even steeper. These
were cities bursting at the seams, and neither physical infrastructure nor social customs could absorb so many newcomers without
buckling under the strain. Eighteenth-century almanacs of professions show that as population and prosperity waxed, trades became
ever more specialized and interdependent.[89] Between two and four
times as many people were jostling each other in the narrow streets,
throwing their waste out the windows, crowding both official and

unofficial markets, blocking thoroughfares with bricks to build new dwellings, driving their carriages through crowds, and generally interacting with more people in more ways than ever before. Under these circumstances of high-density mobility and sociability, it is understandable that a premium was placed upon predictability: the great virtue of those demi-virtues, Hirschman's interests.

Once achieved, even within a narrow compass, predictability can become addictive, as our own epoch of self-avowed control freaks hardly needs to be told. Small successes feed vaunting ambitions. Slowly, at least some of the oft re-issued regulations deepened into habits and even norms of behavior. Such shifts admittedly proceeded at a glacial pace. The first ordinance requiring Parisian householders to build latrines to stop residents from throwing excrement out onto the streets was issued in 1534; like so many other regulations, it was reiterated to no avail, right down to 1734, and violators were being regularly fined well into the 1760s.[90] Yet neo-Hippocratic ideas associating contagion with corrupt air and, conversely, the agreeable experience of broad streets like the rampart boulevards that permitted the free and therefore salubrious circulation of air seem to have gradually taken root in the population at large. Police regulations were thereby fortified with sentiments of disgust, fear of infection, and shame, on the one hand, and a desire for fresh air and open spaces on the other.[91] Even those without a smattering of medical theory could be expected to understand the language of a 1758 royal edict that instructed residents to pile up garbage and "fecal matter" in places far away from the residential faubourgs, where such depots might "corrupt the air and cause disease."[92]

Already in the early eighteenth century, especially in the context of booming cities like London, Amsterdam, and Paris, aspirations were on the rise: a well-policed city was not simply a safe city; it was an orderly city, in which the streets were broad and straight, houses were numbered and all faced the same way, the night blazed with thousands of lanterns, a fire department arrived in time with pumps that worked, carriages were licensed and carriage drivers didn't menace pedestrians, and residents disposed of their garbage at the appointed time and place. Success was always fitful and partial. It took almost two hundred years for Parisians to internalize this vision of urban order—to turn regulations into norms—and the norms were always fragile, as the repeated street uprisings and perpetual traffic snarls testify. Every new form of transportation—the carriage, the bicycle, the tram, the automobile, the metro—upended established traffic regulations and conventions and called new ones into existence. The registers of ordinances thickened: the 1897 police ordinance for Paris traffic ran to 424 articles and more than two hundred pages.[93] New paving and hydraulic technologies as complex as the modern sewer system and as simple as the standardization of the trash receptacle (by an 1883 edict by Prefect of the Seine Eugène Poubelle, whose name became thereafter synonymous with the trash can)[94] all played their part. What is important for my purposes is that partial success nourished hopes of complete success. It was the *relative* orderliness of early eighteenth-century Paris with its first straight, broad boulevards as opposed to the rabbit's warren of medieval lanes that encouraged Guillote and his fellow police officers to press for more regulation of more aspects of urban life and to persevere in the face of resistance.

The history of early modern cities like Amsterdam, London, and Paris offers insights concerning the circumstances under which regulations gradually gain acceptance and eventually, if selectively, become internalized as norms. Disasters like the Amsterdam fire of 1521 and the London fire of 1666 created opportunities for new building and new regulations, for example those that called for replacing wood and thatch with less flammable brick and tiles. French absolutist monarchs from Henri IV (1553–1610, r. 1589–1610) to Louis XIV aggrandized themselves through the grandeur of Paris, favoring broad boulevards, imposing squares, and stately gardens like the Luxembourg or the Tuileries.

But the most effective way to accelerate lasting change in urban behavior through regulation seems to have been a municipal government that was at once republican and authoritarian. The Amsterdam municipal authorities enacted measures far more drastic than the almighty Lieutenant of the Paris police or absolutist monarchs dared contemplate, and yet their regulations won compliance. The Amsterdam authorities demolished whole neighborhoods to make way for new canals and streets, banished carriages from the city altogether, required households to install lead pipes to dispose of waste, and rid the streets of beggars, sometimes by draconian measures that shocked foreign visitors.[95] Why did Amsterdammers comply with these stern regulations while Parisians resisted milder and more moderate ones? Urban historians cite the long history of the Dutch uniting to fight their common and perpetual enemy, the sea, thereby consolidating "a wider outlook that placed the communal good above the welfare of the individual citizen."[96] Yet a similarly authoritarian republican regime achieved similar compliance in revolutionary Paris without the threat of inundation. It was, for example, the revolutionary and later the imperial authorities who pushed through the regulations Guillote had envisioned decades before concerning the uniform dimensions and orientation of building façades and the numbering of houses.[97]

One can only speculate as to why the authoritarian approaches of republican regimes enjoyed somewhat greater success in getting citizens to obey regulations. Perhaps a republican regime enjoyed greater legitimacy among citizens and therefore exacted more compliance—or perhaps its belief in its own legitimacy served as a justification for harsher enforcement. Whatever the reason, even their successes were halting and partial. No one has yet succeeded in taming Paris traffic. Contrast Mercier's vision of Paris in the year 2440 with another fantasy about the future of Paris written ninety years later, Jules Verne's (1828–1905) *Paris au XXe siècle* (Paris in the 20th century, composed c. 1863). Verne's leap of the imagination took him only a century forward in time, to the Paris of 1960, but the face of the city has been altered more than in Mercier's 650 years. Gone are Mercier's horse-drawn carriages and happy pedestrians. Silent, speedy electromagnetic trains crisscross the city; gas-powered automobiles have completely replaced horse-drawn vehicles; correspondence is sent by the "photographic tele-graph" (a kind of fax machine); shops and streets are dazzlingly illuminated by electric lighting. Gone too are Mercier's morally reformed citizens. Paris in 1960 has been transformed by techno-logical marvels, but human nature has remained the same, dulled by complacency and driven by greed: "the people of 1960 no lon-ger wondered at these marvels; they enjoyed them calmly, without being any happier, for in their urgent expression, in their hectic pace, in their American rush, one sensed that the demon of money pushed them forward relentlessly and mercilessly."[98] Mercier's vi-sion of the Paris of the future is a utopia; Verne's, a dystopia. All that unites them—and all Parisians to this day—is an obsession with how to bring order to Paris's traffic chaos.

Rules That Succeed Too Well: How and How Not to Spell

In 1996 Germany was in an uproar. Special meetings of the minister-presidents of the German states were convened; the press ran front-page articles and up-in-arms editorials; public indigna-tion boiled over in letters to the editor, protests, and daily acts of resistance to the new rules. The brouhaha had nothing to do with politics, the economy, or even the perennial debate over whether there should be a speed limit on the Autobahn. What had sent the national blood pressure soaring were proposed spelling reforms that affected not even 1 percent of the words in the German lan-guage: for example, should the word *Balletttänzerin* (ballerina) be spelled with two t's or three?[99] Ultimately, the matter was brought to the German Constitutional Court in 1998 by a group of over five hundred professors who issued a legal challenge to the new rules as a violation of their constitutional rights.[100]

Nor was the obsession with spelling rules peculiar to the Ger-mans. A 2008 proposal that British university instructors overlook common spelling errors in student papers (for example, "super-seed" or "supercede" instead of "supersede") in awarding grades triggered a furious response: "THREE words. World. Hell. Hand-cart. It's not often I despair of civilisation as we know it. . . . But when a university lecturer proposes an amnesty on students' 20 most common spelling mistakes, I fear things may have taken a turn for the apocalyptic."[101] The spelling reforms proposed by the French government in 1990 unleashed *"la guerre du nénufar"* ("war of the water lily," previously spelled *nénuphar*), which eventually forced the Académie française to retreat from its initial unanimous endorsement of the proposed changes.[102] In 2019, a French femi-nist suggestion to change the rule dictating that the gender of pro-nouns referring to a mixed group is automatically masculine (for example, *tous les femmes et hommes*, "all the women and men") aroused ire even on the left: describing himself as "irrevocably feminist," Sorbonne professor emeritus of linguistics Danièle Ma-nesse nonetheless avowed that he was also irrevocably opposed to the proposed new rule.[103]

Spelling reformers are just as vehement in their convictions as spelling conservatives. Since at least the nineteenth century, socie-ties for simplified spelling, especially in anglophone countries, have enlisted the sympathies and funding of the great and the good. Anglo-Irish playwright George Bernard Shaw (1856–1950), who opined that Shakespeare might have had time to write a couple more plays if he had spelled his name with seven letters rather than eleven, left a handsome bequest in his will to the win-ner of a competition to devise a new Shavian alphabet that would finally allow English speakers to spell words effortlessly and eco-nomically. In a similar spirit, protestors dressed as bees and sport-ing mottoes like "Enuff is enuff, but enough is too much" and "I laff at laugh" demonstrated in 2010 outside the U.S. National Scripps Spelling Bee, which has been fetishizing correct spelling since 1925.[104]

Spelling rules are the rules that succeeded all too well. Although at some level everyone knows that the orthography enshrined in dictionaries is the most conventional of conventions, the haphazard result of history and habit, any attempt to rid English of its welter of silent letters (*night*, not to mention *knight*), German of its arcane capitalization rules (not just nouns but also pronouns in certain contexts), and French of its antique circumflexes provokes an intensity of outrage usually reserved for the massacre of innocents. This is not just a modern phenomenon. Since the advent of printing and the rise of national vernaculars in the sixteenth and seventeenth centuries, linguistic reformers in Spanish, Italian, French, English, German, and other languages have attempted to rationalize orthography in the name of purity, reason, consistency, patriotism, and simple kindness to schoolchildren and foreigners struggling to master reading and writing. Resistance to such reforms was as ferocious in the sixteenth century as it is in the twenty-first. In contrast to regulations governing dress and traffic, spelling rules have been so fully internalized as norms that violations can undermine social status, credibility, and careers. Running a red light is certainly more dangerous to public safety than not knowing the difference between "its" and "it's," but it's a toss-up as to which will trigger more indignation in some circles. How did spelling rules become norms, and why?

For most modern European languages, the debate over spelling began in the early modern period and was (and remains) inextricably intertwined with printing, the rising status of vernaculars over the learned languages of ancient Greek and Latin, expanding access to elementary education, and linguistic nationalism. Printing enabled the mass production of dictionaries, and dictionaries in turn raised questions of authority: who had the power to prescribe spelling rules, pronunciations, and definitions, and how were they to be enforced? Then as now, vernaculars were diversified by dialect and accent; spelling both reflected and amplified these differences. Moreover, the very practices of sorting and setting type in an early modern print shop could encourage inventive spelling in order to fill up a line. It is not unusual to see the same word spelled inconsistently in sixteenth-century books—including books of spelling rules. Yet both practical and ideological pressures pushed toward greater uniformity. At the practical level, pedagogy and perhaps an interest in greater efficiency in printing militated in favor of clear, easily remembered rules followed by all. At the ideological level, uniformity in the written language, like the uniformity of laws, became the symbol and substance of polities attempting to assert their sovereignty over new territorial acquisitions in an age of conquest and imperialism. For regions that achieved nationhood by rebellion, as in the case of the United States in 1776, or belatedly and convulsively, as in the case of Germany in 1871, unity of spelling served as a patriotic counterweight to the disunity of history, geography, dialect, and religion. The American motto *E pluribus unum* ("out of many, one") was first achieved by Webster's dictionary, not federal legislation.

In the case of English and French, the first salvos in the spelling wars (still ongoing) were fired in the sixteenth century. Spanish and Italian humanists of the late fifteenth and early sixteenth centuries had already published grammars and dictionaries that sought to stabilize and "purify" at least the written forms of certain dialects of their vernaculars, for example in Antoni de Nebrija's (1441–1522) *Gramática Castellana* (1492) or the Florentine Accademia della Crusca's *Vocabulario degli Accademici della Crusca* (1612) of Tuscan Italian.[105] In 1569 John Hart (c. 1501–1574), Chester Herald of the College of Arms in London, published *Orthographie, conteyning the due order and reason, howe to write or paint thimage of mannes voice, most like to the life or nature*, a scathing critique of the chaos of English spelling and a proposal to radically reform its irrationalities and inconsistencies by reorganizing the alphabet (for example, by disambiguating the letters *u* and *v*, then used interchangeably, by using the one as a vowel and the other as a consonant) and thereby making spelling rigorously phonetic. Hart took the analogy between portraiture and spelling in his subtitle seriously: just as the artist should depict the sitter as faithfully as possible, writing should mirror speech. "And what writer doth nearest and most iustly decerne the divers voices of the speech, he is best able to describe and paint the same with his pen."[106] Rightly anticipating stiff resistance—his preface is addressed "To the doubtfull"—Hart likened spelling traditionalists to painters who ignored their sitters' actual features and apparel, wrote parents' names on sitters' foreheads (symbolizing excessive respect for etymology), transposed eyes and ears, and doubled the size of the head. When the sitter objects and demands an explanation for these distortions, the painter, speaking for the traditionalists, replies: "Because the Painters of this countrie, for time out of minde, have used the like, and we continue therein, and bicause it is so commonly receyved as it is, no man needeth to correct it."[107]

I have quoted Hart at length to give the reader not only the flavor of his arguments in favor of phonetic spelling, destined to be repeated many times in many languages by reformers right down to the present, but also a sense of conventional sixteenth-century orthography, quaint but still intelligible, even when printed in Gothic font. But now look at a page printed in Hart's proposed new alphabet and spelling. With Hart's phonetic alphabet in hand (the sixteenth-century reader would have either have had to memorize it or leaf back and forth between pages), the modern reader can laboriously sound out words, and no doubt practice would eventually have made perfect. But the first impression—and the second—is of a foreign tongue, as remote from modern as from Elizabethan English. (Fig. 6.9.) However rational the proposed reforms and however trenchant Hart's arguments against tradition for tradition's sake, the shock of the first encounter with the new, alien spelling was—and still is—the highest hurdle Hart and his reforming successors had to clear. He was well aware of the effect his new alphabet and spelling rules would have on readers, for he included, alongside the usual prefatory Latin ode praising author and work, an endorsement in English verse from the compositor who set the book's type to the reader. "You may be incouraged by me/ Until you haue read all this booke, / Loth I was the workman to bee, / Which yet at length in hand I

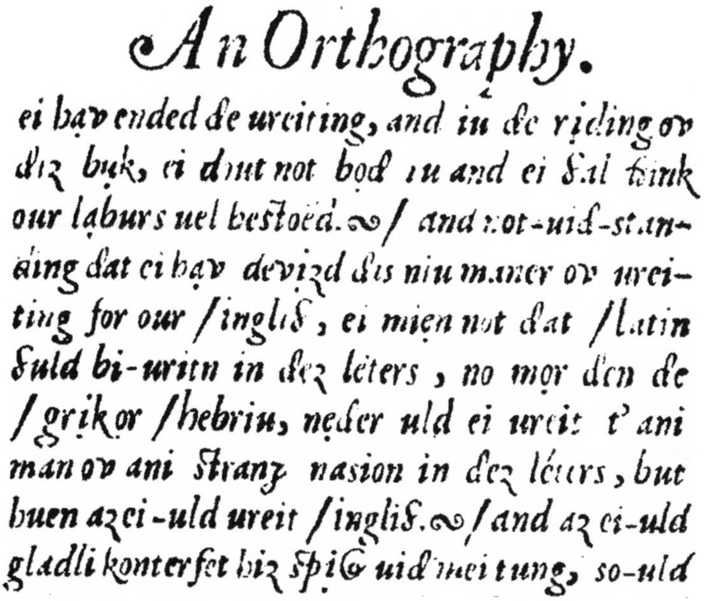

An Orthography.

ei hav ended de wreiting, and in de riding or
diz buk, ei dout not bod iu and ei Sal tink
our laburs uel bestoed. / and not-uid-stan-
ding dat ei hav devizd dis niu maner or wrei-
ting for our /ingliS, ei mien not dat /latin
Suld bi-writn in dez leters , no mor den de
/grik or /hebriu, neder uld ei wreit t' ani
man or ani Stranz nasion in dez leters , but
huen az ei-uld wreit /ingliS. / and az ei-uld
gladli konterfet hiz SpiG uid'mei tung, so-uld

FIGURE 6.9. A page printed in John Hart's rationalized English alphabet and
spelling (*Orthographie*, 1569).

tooke." By the end of the job, however, the initially reluctant
printer is won over. "That my senses were wholy bent, / To use and
keepe the new intent"—though the observant reader will have
noticed that the compositor still hadn't learned to use *u* as a vowel
and *v* as a consonant.[108]

The compositor's appeal to the senses is doubly apt. First, Hart
was arguing for the supremacy of the spoken over the written language, for the ear over the eye. Spelling rules, like mimetic portraiture, should aim for an eidetic (or echoic) likeness, barely distin-
guishable from the original—i.e., speech. In an age in which the
number of readers was steadily increasing, especially in Protestant
regions where the ability of the faithful to read scripture for themselves was a rallying cry, the experience of reading even in silent
solitude was imagined as a chorus of inner voices. By purging

churches of images and statues, more iconoclastic sects of the reformed religion in Huldrych Zwingli's (1484–1531) Zurich or Jean Calvin's (1509–1564) Geneva effectively sanctified the speaking voice of the minister. To use an anachronistic analogy, reformers like Hart conceived of spelling rules as a technique more like tape recording than stenography. Away with silent letters; down with superfluous double consonants; eliminate sound-alike duplicates *c* and *k*: *game* becomes *gam*; *bille* becomes *bil*; *crabbe* becomes *krab*. The new rules would above all benefit beginner readers. Hart promised that any native English speaker could learn to read with his phonetic system in a quarter of the time any other method of instruction took and that foreigners would finally figure out proper English pronunciation.[109] *Whose* pronunciation was a thorny matter, as we'll see.

Yet reading was ultimately about sight rather than sound, and as printed material proliferated in the sixteenth and seventeenth centuries, the association between spelling and seeing intensified. Hart waited until almost two-thirds of the way into his book before daring to show readers what his reformed orthography would actually look like, well knowing that it would be "right lathsome unto them [the readers] and grieve them to look thereon."[110] Richard Mulcaster (1531–1611), headmaster of Merchant Taylors' School in London and author of a more moderate 1582 treatise on English spelling reform, firmly anchored writing to reading, not speaking: "For can reading be right before writing be righted, seing we read nothing else, but what we se written?"[111] (Note not only the repetition of forms of the verb "to see" but also Mulcaster's elimination of the second, arguably superfluous *e*.) The very gestures used to sort and set type in print shops may have sharpened the compositor's eye for words recognized holistically, rather than letter by letter, leading to memorized, standardized spellings, at least within the same shop.[112] Three centuries later in 1878, the seventh edition of the *Dictionnaire de l'Académie française*, final court of appeal in matters of French spelling, underscored the "physiognomic" character of orthography that linked words to their origins by family lineages and concluded that all radical spelling reforms were doomed to fail. For who had the authority to overturn "the habits of those who read and write?"[113] The battle of the eye and ear in spelling matters pitted the already literate, who recognized words as they recognized faces, holistically and at a glance, against the learners, who sounded out the letters and syllables one by one as they tried to match spoken words with their unfaithful written portraits.

In the almost five-hundred-year history of attempts to reform the spelling rules of European languages, it is remarkable how little has changed, both in the arguments pro and contra and in the paltry results. Victories for reformers advocating simplification and rationalization have been few and far between, and what changes have occurred over the centuries have proceeded glacially. Ironically, it was one of the earliest reforms, without even local official authority, much less national reach, and unreinforced by compulsory schooling, that proved to be the most radical and enduring. The private Accademia della Crusca (Academy of the Bran, perhaps on the association of separating wheat from chaff), founded in 1583 in Florence to purify and codify the Tuscan dialect of Italian, succeeded in elevating Tuscan to the status it still enjoys at the pinnacle of Italian regional dialects. It also created the closest approximation to phonetic spelling of any European language, with the possible exception of Finnish. Its classically trained humanist members, who made sure to include Greek and Latin cognates for entries in their 1612 dictionary, nonetheless sacrificed even the ancient Greek orthographical pedigree of the "ph" (the transliteration of the letter Φ in the Greek alphabet) to phonetic consistency in words like *filosofia*.[114] Not even the German reformers in their most optimistic moment of nationalist fervor in 1876 were so audacious. Although other early modern reformers cited the Accademia della Crusca's efforts with approval, and some, like the Académie française (established 1635), modeled themselves closely on its mission, few embraced its ruthless consistency, and none achieved anything like its success. Kindred radical spirits such as Hart in England and Louis Meigret (c. 1510– c. 1558) in France attracted more ridicule than adherents. It took Meigret five years to persuade a printer to take on his *Tretté de la grammaire françoese* (1550), and we have already seen how loath Hart's compositor was to tackle the job.[115]

More typical and ultimately more successful were moderate reformers like Mulcaster, who attempted to balance the conflicting demands of what he called "Prince Sound" and his counselors, Reason and Custom. In Mulcaster's extended allegory, headstrong Prince Sound, who "is passionat, in autoritie tyrannous," wants to govern all spelling according to his fickle dictates. But he is reined in by Reason, who formulates "generall law in the province of writing" and defends the prerogatives of regularities and consistency, and by Custom, who upholds actual usage, "not that which men do or speak commonlie or most, but onelie that, which is grounded at the first, vpon the best and fittest reason." Sound, Mulcaster argues, is too dynamic and variable to serve as the ultimate basis of stable spelling. Which regional accent will triumph in the contest to determine correct pronunciation, and who can hold back the tide of phonetic changes observable even within a decade or two in a city like London, where booming foreign trade had enlarged and modified the language? Reason alone can never purge language of inconsistencies, exceptions, and novelties and must take Custom as its raw material. The resulting three-way compromise is an "Art, which gathering al these roming rules, that *custom* had beaten out, into one bodie, disposed them so in writing, as everie one knew his own limits, *reason* his, *custom* his, *sound* his."[116]

Mulcaster's rules of the "Art" of spelling closely resemble the rules of the mechanical arts described in Chapter 3: a back-and-forth between universals and particulars, mediated by examples and amended by exceptions. Because of the dynamism of sound and the inertia of custom, reason, the advocate of rules must occasionally relax its strictures, just as the rules of the mechanical arts must adjust to the vicissitudes of experience and the recalcitrance of matter. Although language, especially in its written form, is patently a human creation, Mulcaster endows it with a "soulish substance" that causes it to change in an almost organic fashion.[117] His successors would invoke the "genius" of a language that granted it life, in contrast to the dead languages of ancient Greek and Latin, and also imprinted it with a characteristic form.[118] The seventh edition (1878) of the *Dictionnaire de l'Académie française*, while more welcoming toward neologisms from philosophy, industry, and politics than its predecessors had been, "ruthlessly excluded those [new words] that seemed badly composed, contrary to analogy and the genius of the language"—ironically choosing *actualité* ("current events," now a perfectly acceptable French word) as its prime example of a rightly rejected novelty inconsistent with the *génie* of the French language.[119]

By treating language as ensouled, animated by some "quikining spirit," moderate reformers like Mulcaster wed mysticism to pragmatism. Accusing radical reformers like Hart of dogmatism, Mulcaster claimed that the "secret misterie" of every living language could thwart "all their rules, be theie neuer so generall, be theie never so certain." Mulcaster's own spelling rules were therefore riddled with exceptions. The rule dictated that consonants should not be doubled—except in some instances of "ff" and "ll." The rule specified that all foreign words should be pronounced according to English phonetics—except in the case of learned speakers who wished to show off their polyglot accents. The rule of consistency would spell "mere" as "mear," on the analogy of "hear, fear, dear, gear," but the Latin root *merus* made for a "privat exception" to the "generall precept." Spelling was an art, not a science, and although art could discern what was "fittest to be made a pattern for others to follow," no art could force all particulars into a rigid framework.[120] What experience had been to the mechanical arts, ensouled language was to the art of spelling: the source of both rules and exceptions.

All subsequent attempts to regularize spelling in living languages have had to bow to Mulcaster's "quikining spirit," which threw up exceptions to every rule. The first edition (1694) of the

Dictionnaire de l'Académie française championed historical spelling because it revealed the origins of French words and stalwartly resisted the efforts of "certain individuals, and especially printers" to introduce new letters or eliminate old ones, for example the silent "p" in *temps* (time) or *corps* (body), both vestiges of Latin etymologies (*tempus, corpus*). But all rules admitted of exceptions: the silent "b" in *devoir* (duty, debt) disappeared, despite its Latin lineage (from *debitum*). Even the mighty Académie française, established to govern the French language like an absolute monarch, admitted that "one must recognize usage as the Master of Orthography," and, no doubt with radical reformers like Meigret and Louis de L'Esclache (c. 1600–1671) in mind,[121] predicted the failure of all who proclaimed "rules that no one wanted to observe."[122] German, perhaps the modern European language most often and most consistently reformed since the late nineteenth century, still hasn't managed to purge its capitalization rules of exceptions.[123] The familiar English spelling rule "*i* before *e*, except after *c*, or when sounded as *a*, as in *neighbor* and *weigh*" applies to only 11 out of the 10,000 most common English words and is contradicted by familiar words such as *weird* and *seize*.[124] The last of Mulcaster's eight "Generell Rules" of English spelling, which he likened to the axioms of geometry, proclaimed the limits of all rules of art: "That no rule of Art can deall so, but it must leave manie particularities to dailie practis."[125] The rule that every spelling rule had its exceptions became the watchword of spelling moderates like British writer and lexicographer Samuel Johnson (1709–1784) ever after: "Every language has its anomalies, which, though inconvenient, and in themselves once unnecessary, must be tolerated among the imperfections of human things."[126]

As in the case of other arts, practice derived from experience could be supplemented with well-chosen examples. The lasting influence of Mulcaster's book on English spelling probably owed less to his rules than to the list of eight thousand frequently used words he appended for those who couldn't understand "the reason of a rule." Mulcaster intended his examples to confirm his rules, although they sometimes contradicted them (for example, "though" is spelled throughout the book as "tho," deliberately suppressing the silent letters, but appears in the list as "though"—the printer's revenge?).[127] As early modern spelling reformers recognized, dictionaries were the most effective means of enforcing spelling rules. Modern dictionary users may consult them first and foremost for definitions and secondarily for etymologies, but starting with the landmark mid-sixteenth-century Latin and Latin-French dictionaries of the French humanist printer Robert Estienne (1503–1559), such reference works also served to fix and standardize spelling. Mulcaster referred approvingly to the efforts of the Italians, French, and Spanish in this line and explicitly invoked Estienne's *Thesaurus linguae latinae* (final edition 1543) as a model for future English dictionaries;[128] the first edition of the *Dictionnaire de l'Académie française* (1694) also took Estienne's *Dictionaire françoislatin* (1540) as its model for French orthography.[129]

But who endowed the dictionaries with their authority? Very few dictionaries enjoyed official backing. Even those that did, most famously that of the Académie française, established in 1635 in order to "give rules to our language and . . . make it pure, eloquent, and capable of treating the arts and sciences" and in 1674 granted a royal monopoly for its dictionary, could not override usage or stamp out competition.[130] Spelling conservatives elsewhere greatly exaggerated the Académie's real power to stabilize written language. In 1712 Jonathan Swift (1667–1745), who feared that changes in English would disrupt the continuity of the literary tradition and render his own works unintelligible to future readers, addressed an open plea to the Earl of Oxford, Lord High Treasurer of Great Britain (1661–1724), to follow France's good example and establish a body to purify English, including its spelling, and then devise a method for "fixing our Language for ever after such Alterations are made in it as shall be thought requisite."[131] But the Académie française itself was under no such illusions about its ability to stem the tide of change or even buck the currents of usage. When the first edition of its dictionary finally appeared in 1694, after sixty years of gestation, it was already confronting competition from the dictionary of French grammarian César-Pierre Richelet (1626–1698), published in Geneva in 1680, which used semi-reformed French spelling. Although the Académie française clung to older spellings that reflected etymologies, following the example of Estienne's *Dictionaire françoislatin*, it otherwise took "the common language, such as it is [found] in the ordinary commerce of *honnestes gens*."[132]

And who were these *honnestes gens* (note that the old-style "s" in *honneste* was eventually replaced by the semi-reformed orthography of the circumflex, *honnête*)? They were cultivated, polished men and women of the world, not necessarily learned but at home in court circles, well informed about noble activities like swordsmanship and horsemanship if not of noble birth. Swift despaired of using the British court as his linguistic standard, claiming that in the decadent reign of Charles II (1630–1685, r. 1660–1685) it had lost its status as the model of "Propriety and Correctness of Speech," but he too looked to the educated nobility, including women, to guide both speech (no swallowing of vowels) and spelling.[133] Swift hoped to fix the best usage by the best people at a moment in time—his time—in rules, preserved forever thereafter like a fly in amber. In contrast, the Académie française yoked itself to the shifting habits of its chosen elite, which in turn altered with the spelling practices of the printers whose books they read. As a result, no French spelling rule was forever, and all rules were riddled with exceptions: for example, the 1740 edition finally shed many silent letters—but kept the *h* in *méchanique*.[134] By the third edition of 1740 the Académie française, the greatest linguistic authority in eighteenth-century Europe, had abandoned all hope of "a systematic orthography with rules based on invariable principles, remaining always the same. In matters of language, usage is stronger than reason [and] would have soon transgressed the laws."[135]

The question of *whose* usage would be declared authoritative in spelling matters was in fact a question of whose usage when and where and why. Even before major printing houses began to cluster in commercial centers such as Venice, Frankfurt, Leipzig, Lyon, Amsterdam, and Paris, cities that had served as the seats of princely residences, chancelleries, universities, and dioceses of high ecclesiastical officials exerted out-sized influence on spelling because they were centers of writing of all kinds—academic, bureaucratic, legal, and religious. As a result, court and urban usage dictated national spelling. Among languages with significant diversity in regional dialects, such as German and Italian, but lacking a central political authority to codify standard usage by a royally anointed dictionary, as in France, or by elite metropolitan example, as in Britain, literary fame could establish a title to supremacy in vocabulary, pronunciation, and spelling. The Tuscan dialect could boast of being the language of Dante (c. 1265–1321); the Luther Bible of 1534 served as a model for spelling among many German dialects centuries before the first state-sponsored spelling reform conferences in 1876.

When and why to systematize usage was just as tendentious a question as whose usage, where, would set the standard. All of the early modern attempts to reform or standardize spelling argued that the vernacular language had reached a state of sufficient polish and perfection that justified basing rules on usage at just this moment. Just as the Greek of Demosthenes (384–322 BCE) and the Latin of Cicero (106–43 BCE) represented the zenith of those ancient languages, Mulcaster thought that the English of his own time, enriched by new terms introduced in foreign trade, "cañot proue fairer, then it is at this daie"—and fully expected that any change would portend decline.[136] The first edition of the *Dictionnaire de l'Académie française* proudly proclaimed that the French of the seventeenth century was French at its most flourishing, even surpassing Ciceronian Latin because its syntax corresponded more faithfully to "the natural order of thought," the latter a belief still cherished in some French circles.[137] Vernacular patriotism about sixteenth-century English or seventeenth-century French was not necessarily identical to modern nationalism. Pride in language might not correspond to the territorial boundaries of a polity and often applied only to a particular moment in time. Indeed, the vigor of a vernacular could track its imperialistic reach well beyond the homeland, as in the case of early modern Spanish and French.[138] Mulcaster's vernacular patriotism was more local—"I honor *Latin*, but I worship *English*"—and for that reason he favored English pronunciations of foreign words while welcoming such imports, in contrast to the more nationalist stance of the Académie française today toward anglicisms.[139] Swift was already convinced in the early eighteenth-century that the English language—but not necessarily the British nation—was in decline.

By the early nineteenth century, however, language, including spelling, had become intertwined with nationalist fervor. Noah Webster (1758–1843) proclaimed his patriotic intentions in his *American Spelling Book* (1786 and many later editions), from which generations of American children learned to read and write: "To diffuse an uniformity and purity of language in America—to destroy the provincial prejudices that originate in the trifling differences of dialect and produce reciprocal ridicule—to promote the interest of literature and harmony of the United States, is the most ardent wish of the author; and it is his highest ambition to deserve the approbation and encouragement of his countrymen."[140] Although Webster generally followed the model of British lexicographers like Samuel Johnson, in later editions of his *Dictionary* and spelling guide he did not hesitate to change spellings on phonetic grounds (for example, *colour* and *labour* became *color* and *labor*) and was adamant that American place names like "Niagra" and "Narraganset" were going to be pronounced and spelled in the American way.[141]

Nationalist spelling reforms reached fever pitch in the late nineteenth century, when Prussia, leading the newly unified German nation, convened a congress to unify German spelling in 1876, a project that turned out to be almost as controversial as unifying the German states. Even more than other modern European vernaculars, the German language was fragmented into many regional dialects spoken throughout central Europe in a mosaic of principalities, duchies, kingdoms, and imperial cities. Although key works like Luther's Bible and the practice of printers helped partially to stabilize what became High German orthography by the late seventeenth century, controversies between phonetic reformers and etymological conservatives raged throughout the eighteenth century along the lines already defined by French and English polemics in the sixteenth and seventeenth centuries.[142] The political unification of much of the northern Germanophone world (excluding Austria and parts of Switzerland) in 1871 was almost immediately followed by efforts to unify the German school system, especially the way spelling was taught. Representatives of all the German lands along with fourteen linguists met in Berlin in January 1876 at the invitation of the Prussian minister of education to lay down the law to schoolmasters throughout the German empire as to whether the letter *c* should be eliminated and other weighty matters.[143] Despite the fact that the proposed reforms were quite modest, for example omitting the silent *h* in words like *Sohn* (son), they triggered such a furious storm of protest in the press that individual German lands such as Bavaria, Saxony, and Prussia each published its own spelling textbook with its own regional rules in the chaotic aftermath of the Berlin conference. To make matters still worse, Chancellor Otto von Bismarck (1815–1898) forbade Prussian and imperial officials from using the slightly reformed spelling set forth in the 1880 Prussian spelling textbook, so that Prussian bureaucrats had to unlearn the spelling they had been taught in Prussian schools.[144]

In the end the school textbooks won, reinforced by the printers and above all by lexicographer Konrad Duden's (1829–1911) enormously successful *Vollständiges Orthographisches Wörterbuch der deutschen Sprache* (Complete orthographic dictionary of the German language), which went through six printings between 1880 and 1900 and quickly established itself as the definitive reference work in the German-speaking world, although it was backed by no official authority.[145] When a second orthographic conference convened in Berlin in June 1901 after Bismarck's death in 1898, the combined influence of especially the Prussian school textbook and Duden's dictionary consolidated the much-yearned-for unification of German spelling, a quarter of a century after the unification of the German nation: *c* was mostly replaced by *z* and *k*; *Brennnessel* ("burning nettle") kept its triple consonant. Although Kaiser Wilhelm II (1859–1941, r. 1888–1918) at first refused to read any letter written in the new spelling, even he finally gave up in 1911. Far more consequential than the results of the conference was the all-but-official coronation of the *Duden* (as the reference work is still reverently known) as the final authority in matters orthographic throughout the German-speaking world and symbol of its linguistic if not political unity. Even after the division of Germany into two ideologically polarized states after World War II, both East and West Germans clung to *Duden* as their spelling standard.[146]

The wars over spelling rules that began in the sixteenth century are far from over. In German, reformers clamor to collapse the gendered pronouns *der*, *die*, and *das* into a single definite article on the analogy of the English *the*. In French, the Académie française is manning (*le mot juste* in this context) the battlements against proposed changes to the rules for writing collective pronouns like *tous/toutes*. In English, teachers and schoolchildren tear their hair out over spellings that diverge wildly from pronunciations. Everywhere, blood pressures and decibel levels sky-rocket as opposing sides battle it out in the press, on television, online, and even in street demonstrations. Why do we care so much about spelling rules? Those who have invested time and effort in mastering them understandably grumble about having to learn new ones, but these latter usually affect fewer than 5 percent of the words in a language. Learning a new word-processing program is more time-consuming, but few people complain about it in the-end-of-civilization-as-we-know-it rhetoric. Nor is social capital at stake, although the press delights in ridiculing misspellings by prominent public figures. Especially in English, accuracy in spelling is an unreliable proxy for social class or level of education: Oxford students join the ranks of those who cannot figure out whether it's *embarrass* or *embarass* or, for that matter, whether it should be *it's* or *its*.[147] Besides, won't the computer spellchecker feature relieve us of having to think about spelling rules ever again, just as the calculator function has made knowing the rules of arithmetic all but superfluous? Yet many people still respond as wrathfully to proposals to change the entirely conventional, historically mutable, and exception-ridden rules of spelling as if they were defending the Ten Commandments from revisionists.

Perhaps a clue to this puzzle of rule outrage lies in another puzzling phenomenon: highly literate writers, even professional ones, sometimes spell erratically in their manuscripts and private correspondence. Swift, that stickler for regulating English spelling once and for all, peppered his letters with variant spellings, as did Samuel Johnson, high priest of eighteenth-century English lexicography. Long after English spelling had effectively been standardized by dictionaries, school instruction, and printers in the mid-nineteenth century, the letters of the likes of Charles Dickens (1812–1870) and Charles Darwin (1809–1882) were strewn with spelling mistakes that they would have blushed to have spotted in their published works. Historical linguist Simon Horobin plausibly suggests that these divergences between private and public spelling were "a marker of relative formality" and that authors left corrections of their manuscripts to the compositors in printshops.[148]

Extending Horobin's insight about the sociability of spelling, we might conceive of letters dashed off to intimates as inner conversations, converting correspondents into mind's-ear interlocutors. "Mind's ear" should be taken as more than metaphorical in this context: many people sub-vocalize as they write or type, especially at top speed, as the striking frequency of homonym mistakes (for example, typing *there* for *their*) testifies. Perhaps even proficient spellers revert back to phonetics with correspondents whom they know well and can count upon not to interpret errors as ignorance. But even if the reader of a misspelled missive doesn't write off the sender as illiterate, the recipients of such dashed-off notes may reproach writers with carelessness. In so doing, they respond as readers, i.e., primarily with their eyes rather than their ears. Once the line between speaking and seeing is crossed, a different kind of spelling sociability takes over, one that recognizes whole words as if they were individual faces. Cognitive psychologist Stanislas Dehaene argues that learning to read colonizes parts of the brain originally devoted to facial recognition.[149] The common experience of registering a word as misspelled before being able to pinpoint precisely where the error lies also suggests that practiced readers see words holistically, just as all but sufferers from prosopagnosia see faces holistically, not as a composite of this kind of eyebrow and that kind of nose. If this analogy holds, reading misspelled words might be as unsettling as seeing familiar faces distorted—perhaps unsettling enough to explain a measure of the vitriol vented in the spelling wars.

The analogy also suggests that the bellowing ferocity of opposition to any proposed change to spelling rules isn't just about social distinction, the link between present and past literature, the history of words, or the sunk costs of having sweated to learn the old rules, though it is also about these things. It may not be about rules at all. The sheer number of spelling rules in most European languages—169 of them in German alone, even after multiple twentieth-century reforms[150]—not to mention the even larger number of exceptions to each of them, would discourage anyone from learning and using them on a daily basis. It is the models given by the dictionary, not the rules, that we consult when in doubt. The spelling rules to which opponents of reform rally with such passion are rules in the pre-modern sense: the many, many models stored in the visual memories of lifelong readers, as familiar and reassuring as the faces of friends and family or the landscapes of childhood. These were the emotionally saturated associations that allowed an infuriated German opponent of the spelling reforms proposed in 1988 to write that "the mother tongue is like the landscape into which one is born, a legacy, a homeland, from which no one may be expelled."[151] Homeland [Heimat], legacy [etwas Angestammtes], and forced expulsion [*vertrieben werden*] are all words heavily freighted in twentieth-century German history, evocative of loss, rupture, and exile. However melodramatic, this vocabulary bears witness to the improbable success of spelling rules in becoming deeply felt norms.

Conclusion: From Rules to Norms

Regulations are rules at their nitty-grittiest. On the spectrum from the majestic natural laws that order the universe to pinpoint rules applied to pinpoint domains, regulations tilt toward the latter. Just how far depends on the domain: rules of capitalization can apply to an entire language; rules stipulating the maximum length of beaked shoes apply only to beaked shoes. There are global regulations governing, for example, trade and diplomacy, but most regulations are local, where particulars matter. And even global regulations must inevitably be adjusted to local circumstances, if only because enforcement is always ultimately local.

Regulations are therefore a case of *multum in parvo*: much compressed within a small compass. The scales within which the regulations examined in this chapter operate range from the small city to the metropolis to a linguistic community, and in all three cases regulations pack a multitude of detail into the bounded realms they govern. What is characteristic of times and places where there is an upsurge of regulations is not just size but also complexity and density. More far-flung and tightly woven trade networks created the wealth and wares that drove sumptuary regulations in commercial cities; exploding population and demands on fragile infrastructure drove traffic and sanitation regulations in Enlightenment metropolises; increased literacy and the printing press drove efforts to regularize spelling. Wherever human interactions expanded and intensified at an accelerated pace, regulations cropped up to order the perceived disorder of many people doing many different things in many different ways in the same space, whether at a Bolognese wedding, in a Paris street, or on the pages of a printed book.

At this point, the libertarian in all of us will protest: what's wrong with wearing beaked shoes (or ripped jeans), letting carriages (or cars) go as fast as they like, and spelling *fox* as *focks* or *phawx* or all of the above on the same page? (There are probably fewer libertarians in favor of emptying the contents of chamber pots onto the heads of unsuspecting passers-by.) Aren't all of these regulations at root an authoritarian effort to stamp out variety and individuality? It is undeniable that the prologues of many of these rules and regulations often exude a prim and tidy aesthetic: the Saxon authorities who begged fashion to halt, the Parisian authorities who dreamt of uniform house façades all facing the same direction, the German authorities who howled in horror over the "lawlessness" of spelling textbooks. One can easily imagine a counter-aesthetic of wardrobe miscellany, mismatched street fronts, and devil-may-care orthographic inconsistency. But beyond aesthetic preferences, hard realities also motivated many regulations: the reality of family fortunes dissipated on frippery, of trying to find one's way in a labyrinth of unnumbered, turned-around houses, and of deciphering the words that strange configurations of letters on the page spell out. Not all realities are equally hard. Co-ordinating traffic and sorting out *its* versus *it's* are orders of magnitude apart in terms of their consequences. Yet the latter probably stirs more passions than the former.

This brings us back to the central problem posed by this chapter: when do regulations succeed and fail, and why? We are now in a position at least to discard a few plausible hypotheses. Repeated failure, even over centuries, does not necessarily eliminate regulations. Hard-headed functionalism is at best an uncertain guide as to which regulations stick and which don't. Regulations imposed by absolutist monarchies may be less sweeping and authoritarian than those imposed by more republican governments. If there is a positive finding, it is that enforcement alone cannot entrench regulations. Without swift, strict, and sustained enforcement, almost no regulation can take hold, for there would be no need for regulations if the forbidden objects or conduct were not beckoning temptations. Yet constant, ubiquitous enforcement is impossible even in the most tyrannical police state.

The most effective regulations must be anchored in norms and habits. Norms and habits are best instilled early, and the power of the nation-state to legislate universal schooling for children to teach reading and writing means that spelling rules are regulated as a matter of national unity and patriotic pride. Becoming a virtuoso speller in English can become a badge of full citizenship for the children of immigrants and marginalized minorities. When the very first U.S. spelling bee was held in Cleveland, Ohio, in 1908, a crowd of four thousand cheered the winner, a fourteen-year-old African-American schoolgirl named Marie Bolden. Today's Scripps National Bee, staged annually in Washington, D.C., before large audiences, is regularly won by the children of immigrants to the United States.[152] Also, spelling rules are learned at an age when almost all rules are hallowed. Developmental psychologists have documented how young children treat even the most obviously conventional rules (for example, of games) taught in kindergarten and primary school as sacred writ.[153] Perhaps this is why few regulations are so passionately upheld as the humble trivia of spelling rules.

All rules aspire to be prophetic. If obeyed, the desired results or order will be realized. A cookbook recipe followed to the letter should produce a picture-perfect cake; traffic rules followed to the letter should bring about safe, orderly streets. These predictions carry conviction because they codify past experience with cakes and traffic. But the regulations examined in this chapter had greater ambitions. Their framers envisioned an order that did not yet exist and perhaps never would: a fashion for unchanging simplicity and restraint in dress; a city where the houses were all neatly numbered and it was safe to cross the street; a nation united by a language spoken and spelled by all citizens in the same way. There was a utopian element in these hard-headed regulations that assumed both the best and worst of human nature in their formulation. The worst, in that many of the specifics anticipated all manner of ruses and subterfuges to get around the rules; the best, in that the very persistence with which the rules were issued and re-issued implied a faith in progress. Ultimately, the regulations were a wager on human perfectibility. Draconian enforcement and nudging infrastructure like sidewalks could only do so much to achieve compliance; the rules would have to solidify into norms if the wager was to be won. The framers of the sumptuary regulations lost their bet; the Parisian police partially won theirs; the spelling reformers succeeded beyond their wildest dreams. But all of them were in it for the long haul. The transmutation of rules into norms could take centuries.

Regulations were too keyed to their ever-changing contexts to qualify as context-insensitive thin rules. But they could be described as aspirational thin rules, both because of the rigidity with which they were promulgated and their ambition to bring into being a new, improved order that could then be frozen forever. Utopias, by definition, do not change, and their rules can therefore be as thin as algorithms and just as rigidly executed.

The sheer particularity of regulations drives their proliferation. There are always more specifics to specify, more loopholes to close, more exceptions and evasions to head off at the pass. In principle, regulations were rigid rules that brooked no ifs, ands, or buts. But in practice, no amount of specificity could forestall exceptions or obviate the need for discretion—albeit one-sided discretion, reserved for the rule-enforcers, not the rule-followers. More and more detailed regulations were often self-defeating. Sumptuary regulations lost the race with nimble fashion, time and time again: no amount of detail could keep pace with the latest frills and flourishes. Traffic regulations that attempted to foresee and forbid every possible obstacle to free-flowing circulation collapsed under their own weight. Similarly, attempts to codify and rationalize all the spelling quirks of a natural language that is constantly evolving end up with almost as many rules as there are words. Too many regulations are almost as unenforceable as none at all. A regulation that pinpoints an abuse requires analogy and interpretation to extend its radius beyond the pinpoint. In the next chapter we will turn to the opposite extreme: rules with a radius as long as that of the whole world and even the universe, natural laws and laws of nature.

7

Natural Laws and Laws of Nature

The Grandest Rules of All

Imagine two scenes, both visible only to the imagination. The first is a God's-eye view of the cosmos, of galaxies and solar systems, of innumerable worlds barren and fertile, of planets circling suns inexorably in their orbits and of the tiniest dust particles tracing their equally inexorable paths through the intergalactic void. This is the vision of laws of nature, the most universal, uniform, and inescapable laws of all. The second scene shrinks to some tiny patch of the earth, only a cave or forest glade, inhabited by the smallest human society, perhaps just a single family, in conditions of near total isolation and autarchy. Encounters with other human beings are few and fleeting; politics, economy, priests, and princes have yet to be invented. Whether envisioned as an Edenic paradise or as the war of all against all, this imaginary ground-zero of humanity is also ruled by laws, natural laws, as uniform and immutable as laws of nature, albeit far more restricted in their jurisdiction. Together, laws of nature and natural laws occupy the opposite extreme of the spectrum of rules from the regulations examined in Chapter 6, as universal, uniform, and enduring as regulations are local, variable, and changeable.

Both scenes are thought experiments. No one has encompassed the universe at a glance, though the dream of taking a cosmic vantage point is as old as the ancient Stoics and as new as the image of the black hole reconstructed from radio telescope data.[1] No one has ever glimpsed human beings living before human societies, though travelers and anthropologists have claimed to have discovered close approximations of the state of nature.[2] Yet however fantastical, both visions have exerted vast influence over ideas of what it means to be rule-governed in science, philosophy, theology, political theory, and jurisprudence. From Newtonian gravitation to the field equations of General Relativity Theory, from the American Declaration of Independence to the imperatives of the United Nations Declaration of Human Rights, the ideal of rules that know no boundaries, no amendments, no variations, no exceptions still exalts the imagination. These are rules that purport to hold everywhere and always, guarantors of ultimate justice and ultimate order.

Both versions of this ideal, the natural laws that govern human (and even animal) relationships and the laws of nature that govern the cosmos, are strange hybrids of the natural and the human. Laws are promulgated by legislators and obeyed by subjects who must understand them in order to comply; all laws can be violated, or else there would be no need for them in the first place. Why then speak of "laws" to describe the regularities of nature, which can be neither understood nor transgressed by the mostly inanimate objects they constrain? As even its most fervent proponents admitted, the concept "laws of nature" must be taken as a metaphor, and an awkward one at that. The concept of natural laws is equally perplexing. What is the "nature" that dictates such laws? And if it is human nature, uniform throughout the species, why is natural law always supplemented (and sometimes contradicted) by highly variable positive law? What is the authority of nature to legislate, especially when compliance with its laws seems at best partial when it comes to human conduct and cultures? That slide between the physical necessity of the laws of nature and the moral authority of natural law highlights a further strain between the components of both hybrids: "law" and "nature" tug in different directions. The ambiguity is neatly captured by a poster showing an admonishing policeman and captioned: "Gravity. It's not just a good idea. It's the law."

The history of these extreme rules, natural laws and laws of nature, presents two puzzles. First, how did the mismatched components of each hybrid become fused together so tightly that they have endured despite oft-remarked internal incoherence? And second, how did these two hybrids, which existed for centuries apart in the writings of jurists and astronomers, theologians, and philosophers, come together in a powerful symbiosis in early modern Europe—only to come apart again by the end of the eighteenth century? The answers to these questions are intertwined. At the precise moment in the seventeenth century when the incoherence of law/nature hybrids became most glaring, the resonances between the hitherto distinct traditions of natural law and laws of nature were loudest. This was the moment when new conceptions of the human and natural orders emerged in counterpoint with each other—sometimes in the writings of one and the same person, such as Francis Bacon and Gottfried Wilhelm Leibniz, both trained as lawyers and both intent on establishing natural philosophy as well as legal codes on new foundations. In their work, as well as in that of natural law theorists Hugo Grotius, Thomas Hobbes (1588–1679), Samuel Pufendorf, and Christian Thomasius (1655–1728) and natural philosophers such as René Descartes, Robert Boyle, and Isaac Newton, a new vision of universal legality took shape: rules that reach around the globe and to the remotest stars, rules that are permanently inscribed in the human heart and in the order of things, rules that hold regardless of place and time and admit of neither change nor exception— the grandest rules of all.

Natural Law

In the ancient Greek play by Sophocles (c. 496–c. 406 BCE), the title figure Antigone faces a stark choice: either she obeys the decree of her uncle Creon, king of Thebes, to leave her dishonored brother Polyneices unburied, or she observes "God's ordinances, unwritten and secure" and performs the rites due to the dead.[3] Although Antigone invokes the gods, not nature, to defend the burial of her brother, Aristotle and later commentators made her decision to defy Creon's edict a paradigmatic case of upholding natural over merely human law. Quoting Antigone's words in the play, Aristotle interpreted them as an appeal to universal law, "just and unjust in accordance with nature" and common to all peoples, as opposed to the "particular law" of a given community.[4] Even after medieval Christian thinkers such as Thomas Aquinas assimilated Aristotelian notions of universal law to the eternal law of God, the idea that universal law was somehow derived from or warranted by nature persisted.

But what exactly was nature, and what were its dictates? Two starkly contrasting answers shaped the natural law tradition from Roman antiquity through the eighteenth century and beyond. On the one side, nature was the expression of reason, both of human beings and the cosmos as a whole. The Roman politician and Stoic philosopher Cicero crystallized this view in his treatise *De re publica* (c. 44 BCE): "True reason is right reason in agreement with nature; it is of universal application, unchanging and everlasting; it summons to duty by its commands, and averts from wrongdoing by its prohibitions."[5] Like Antigone's duty to her dead brother, this was a law divinely decreed, binding on all people in all places and neither in need of interpreters nor at the mercy of fickle legislators. Human reason alone sufficed to know and to obey it. On the other side, nature was the expression of instinct, what humans had in common with other animals. In the systematic compendium of Roman law made at the behest of the

Christian Emperor Justinian in the sixth century CE, natural law (*jus naturale,* sometimes *lex naturae* or *lex naturalis*)[6] was defined by the jurist Ulpian (c. 170–c. 228 CE) as that which "nature teaches all animals, whether born on air, sea, or land," including the sexual union of male and female to procreate and the care of offspring.[7] Whereas Cicero's version of natural law expressed the highest human faculties, Ulpian's was grounded in the lowest, those that weren't even distinctively human.

These two contrasting views of the human nature from which natural law derived remained uncomfortably entwined in the corpus of Roman law for millennia. Roman law in turn profoundly shaped all Western legal traditions, even those following common law.[8] Almost the only features shared by the two views were first, that natural laws were universal laws, in contrast to the laws of a particular polity or historical period (civil law, *jus civile*); and second, natural laws were not products of human agreement, in contrast to both civil law and the law of nations (*jus gentium*). Whether natural laws originated in divine decree, the order of the universe, reason, instinct, or some other facet of human nature, such as sociability or physical frailty, remained an open and often contentious question. Later Christian authors found the Stoic view of natural law sympathetic, identifying Cicero's *lex naturae* with God's eternal law, as promulgated by revelation (divine positive law set down in scripture) and recognized by human reason (natural law, equated with the "law written on the human heart" of Saint Paul, Romans 2:15).[9] In the influential thirteenth-century formulation of Thomas Aquinas, natural law was nothing less than the participation of human reason in the eternal law (*lex aeterna*) of God and contained within it all the moral precepts of the Decalogue.[10] But medieval jurists and theologians also upheld the natural law of animal instinct, enacting ever more savage laws to punish "crimes against nature," a category that extended to almost any form of non-procreative sexual acts (all lumped together under the rubric "sodomy"), incest, or infanticide (especially by women trying to abort or hide an illicit pregnancy). Once such "unnatural" acts came to be associated with both religious heresy and divine retribution in the form of natural catastrophes (by analogy to the biblical story of the destruction of Sodom and Gomorrah, Genesis 19:24), prosecutions intensified, especially in cities prone to floods and earthquakes, such as Venice.[11]

Depending on which view had the upper hand, natural law had more or less clout than local custom or civil law. For example, the *Digest* of Justinian made it clear that according to natural law, all men are born free and equal.[12] But slavery was a widespread and perfectly acceptable institution within the Roman Empire, legitimated and regulated by civil law. In this case, universal natural law did not trump Roman civil law: why should the state that humans shared with animals be elevated over the laws of a civilized society?[13] On this conception, natural law was not fundamental but primitive, however universal and unchanging. If, however, natural law represented the dictates of human reason, or even divine edicts, it transcended all civil law. As Cicero asserted, "Justice is one; it binds all human society, and is based on the Law, which is right reason [*recta ratio*] applied to command and prohibition."[14] In Sophocles' play, Creon's obstinacy in upholding his own decrees over Antigone's appeal to a higher law leads to his family's destruction. Not even the king could flout these natural laws with impunity.

Roman authors saddled with both natural law traditions managed to smooth over their contradictions either by elevating the natural law of animal instinct to a divine decree or by attributing violations of instinct such as infanticide to the loss of reason. In an instance of the first strategy, Saint Augustine of Hippo (354–430 CE) in his *Confessions* (c. 400 CE) made an exception to the time-honored Roman imperial maxim of following local customs—"When in Rome, do as the Romans do"—for sodomy, an "unnatural" act because it was non-procreative, though accepted in many parts of the ancient Mediterranean world. Augustine writes: "But when God commands anything to be done, either against the customs and constitutions of any people whatsoever, though the like

FIGURE 7.1. Dame Nature taking her orders from God as she hammers out the animal species on her anvil (*Roman de la rose*, c. 1405, MS Ludwig XV 7, fol. 124v, Paul Getty Museum, Malibu). Digital image courtesy of the Getty's Open Content Program.

were never done heretofore, yet it is to be done now; . . . and if it were never made a law before, it is to be made one now."[15] Echoes of this argument have reverberated for centuries in Christian theology, from Aquinas's claim that bestiality was worse than adultery because the former crossed a species line drawn by "the Author of nature" to recent versions of the catechism of the Catholic church on the subject of homosexuality.[16] The reverse strategy was to connect acts counter to animal instinct with a failure of reason and even of the cosmic order. In his reworking of Euripides's (c. 480–c. 406 BCE) tragedy about the Colchian princess Medea, who murders her two sons to avenge herself on her unfaithful husband Jason, Seneca (c. 4 BCE–65 CE) not only portrays Medea as possessed by a "mad rage" as she contemplates infanticide but also has her recall how her magic has overturned "heaven's law" by changing the cycle of the seasons and reversing the ocean tides.[17] Like Cicero a Stoic, Seneca coupled the overthrow of reason with the subversion of cosmic order—and in the figure of Medea, he linked both to the betrayal of animal instinct.

These cross-cutting ties between the two versions of natural law, however loose and analogical, were strongly reinforced by medieval Christian theological and legal traditions that made God the creator of both cosmic nature and human nature and thereby ensured a harmony between them. As the supreme monarch of the universe, God's jurisdiction was infinite, eternal, immutable, and superior to that of any earthly authority. Nature, variously personified as God's viceroy or his handmaiden, worked tirelessly to keep the stars in their orbs, the seasons in their proper order, and all the created animal species perpetuated by procreation. In the rich allegorical and iconographical traditions of the High Middle Ages, Dame Nature appears busily at work replenishing the species (sometimes hammering them out at the blacksmith's forge), occasionally complaining about how sodomy was thwarting her efforts, as in the French allegorical poem *De planctu naturae* (The complaint of nature, c. 1165).[18] (Fig. 7.1.)

Just as Augustine's God reigned as "Lord Paramount" over the princes of the earth who in turn ruled their subjects, as "the greater authority is set above the lesser," medieval theologians constructed interlocking hierarchies of laws: divine, natural, and positive.[19] As the intermediate term in this pyramid, natural law enjoyed both divine authority and human jurisdiction, a precarious position between the necessity of God's decrees and the vagaries of human free will. Similarly, nature mediated between divine omnipotence and human frailty. Dame Nature was mighty but not almighty— otherwise, she would have never had cause for complaint about human violations of her edicts.

This tissue of analogies and personifications, delegation and mediation veiled the most gaping contradictions within the rival natural law traditions rooted in low and lofty human nature as well as those within the very idea of natural law. The latter could be stark. In one prominent strand of ancient Greek philosophy, Sophists opposed law (*nomos*) and nature (*physis*): they pointed out that funeral customs may vary widely among peoples, some burying, some burning, some preserving their dead, but that fire burns everywhere.[20] Impressed by travelers' tales of exotic cultures from Herodotus (c. 484–c. 425 BCE) to Marco Polo (1254–1324) to Sir Walter Raleigh (c. 1552–1618), philosophers in this lineage, from the Sophist Protagoras (c. 490–c. 420 BCE) to the skeptic Michel de Montaigne (1533–1592), contrasted the constancy of nature with the diversity of law. Seen from this perspective, a compound like "natural law" made about as much sense as "a chilly heat" or "a bright shadow." Only by subordinating both nature (human and cosmic) and law (divine and natural) to God's will could medieval natural law traditions paper over these cracks.

European natural law theorists of the sixteenth and seventeenth centuries confronted novel challenges that forced a radical re-examination of their doctrines. Voyages of commerce and exploration to Asia and the Americas brought Europeans into direct and prolonged contact with cultures that shared none of their legal and religious premises. Jesuits attempting to make converts in Ming dynasty China found that even logic could get lost in translation;[21] Spanish Dominicans debated whether the indigenous inhabitants of the Americas could be dispossessed of their land on the grounds that they more resembled children or beasts than rational human beings.[22] Skeptics also called into question the distinction between barbarous and civilized nations. After he had interviewed indigenous Brazilians about their customs in 1563, Montaigne concluded, "I find (from what has been told me) that there is nothing savage or barbarous about these peoples, but that every man calls barbarous anything he is not accustomed to."[23] Closer to home, religious schism, commercial and imperial rivalries, and an almost constant state of war, both among the Christian states of Europe and between them and Ottoman forces, splintered consensus on how polities could regulate international relations in the absence of shared precepts. Globe-spanning ambitions of trade and empire revived the rhetoric of universality, and the geographically more circumscribed ambitions of absolute monarchs to consolidate their territories elevated the value of uniformity.

But how could such universal, uniform laws be justified without parochial appeal either to the divinized nature of the Stoics or the lawgiver God of medieval Christian theologians?[24] This was the quandary facing early modern natural law theorists such as Hugo Grotius in the Netherlands, Thomas Hobbes in England, Samuel Pufendorf and Christian Thomasius in Germany—all notably Protestants keen to deprive Catholic polemicists of a weapon with which to attack Reformation schismatics for defying God's eternal law.[25] These thinkers differed greatly in terms of what they thought natural law prescribed and proscribed (were slavery, polygamy, and sodomy licit or illicit?), how it could be ascertained (solely from a priori principles or also by empirical inquiry into norms upheld by all human cultures?), its relationship to both divine and human positive law (did it trump scripture?), and even whether it was properly law at all (is there such a thing as a law that is not enforced by sanctions?). Nonetheless, they were foursquare agreed that first, natural law derived not only from human nature but human nature in a mythical state of nature, and second, that natural law held for human beings everywhere and always, despite the bewildering diversity of local laws and customs.

Neither of these claims was self-evident. What exactly was human nature in the wild? Which aspects were relevant for natural law? Even if the thought experiment of human nature in a state of nature was accepted for argument's sake, why should the state of humans *prior* to society dictate laws for humans *in* society? The seventeenth-century natural law theorists differed among themselves on all these points. Grotius conceded that humans were animals, "but animals of a superior kind," capable by dint of their intelligence of acting in accord with general principles and of restraining the impulse to pursue immediate pleasure: "Whatever is clearly at variance with such judgment is understood to be contrary also to the law of nature, that is to the nature of man." So much would be true, Grotius argued, even if God did not exist.[26] Whereas Grotius anchored natural law in superior human intelligence, Hobbes took a more jaundiced view: the chief concern of humans in a state of nature was self-preservation, most especially from the depredations of other humans driven by a relentless desire for power. The law of nature was "a Precept, or generall Rule, found out by Reason, by which a man is forbidden to do, that, which is destructive of his life, or taketh away the means of preserving the same; and to omit, that, by which he thinketh it may be preserved."[27] Pufendorf conceded the sovereignty of self-preservation among all animals, including humans, but softened Hobbes's harsh depiction of life in the state of nature as the war of all against all by further positing that for humans, born helpless and without claws or fangs or other means of protection, self-preservation entailed sociability. Therefore, the "fundamental Law of Nature" was "that EVERY MAN OUGHT, AS MUCH AS IN HIM LIES, TO PRESERVE AND PROMOTE SOCIETY: That is, the *Welfare of Mankind*."[28]

However much these prominent natural law theorists differed among themselves as to the nature of human nature and what laws derived from it, they converged on two points: natural law compelled by reason, not necessity, and what reason dictated was to escape the state of nature by any means possible. Even if reason did not preponderate in human nature, contrary to Grotius's optimistic assertion, it was nonetheless reason that revealed what must be done to survive. Although animals seemed to know how to preserve themselves by instinct and were moreover outfitted with the means to do so, humans were born naked and without weapons, endowed with reason (and caring parents) instead of fur or talons. This was a bare-bones reason of rational self-interest: if you wish to survive, then you must make common cause with other human beings. The safety of society might come at great cost—according to Hobbes, the sacrifice of natural rights and liberties; according to Thomasius, of natural equality[29]—but anything was preferable to the state of nature, variously imagined as perpetual war with other humans, vulnerability to animal predators and the inhospitable elements, or the complete absence of amenities like books (as Thomasius reminded bookworms who might have craved asocial solitude in order to read undisturbed).[30] In short, the essence of *human* nature, and therefore of natural law, was headlong flight from the *state* of nature.

By rethinking both elements of ancient natural law jurisprudence—natural law as reason and natural law as what nature teaches all animals—early modern jurists shifted its foundations from divine law to human reason (and a narrow version of reason at that) and from procreation and care of progeny to survival in a mythical state of nature. Rationality and animality were still fused in early modern natural law, but both terms had been redefined and their relationship to each other reconfigured. This was natural law fit for purpose in a world of war and empire, a world of inquisitive, acquisitive, and often violent cultural encounters in which almost nothing in the way of shared assumptions could be taken for granted. Natural law became an exercise in deducing maximal consequences from minimal principles, formulated to be as allegedly self-evident and as universally valid as the axioms of geometry.[31]

Beyond these two compact cornerstones, namely reason boiled down to discerning the best means to the end of self-preservation and self-preservation boiled down to trading the state of nature for society, the early modern natural law theorists debated endlessly among themselves. Was natural law now identical to the law of nations, since it applied to all humans and only to humans? Could natural law be established purely by appeal to self-evident first principles, or would the empirical evidence of laws and customs common to many peoples in many times and places suffice? Did natural law ordain that a wife should obey or even remain faithful to her husband? Was sodomy really a crime "against nature"? Did natural law supplement, complement, supersede, or concede precedence to positive law? All of these questions and many more were furiously debated throughout the seventeenth and eighteenth centuries. What was *not* up for debate was that natural law was universal, uniform, and inalterable for all human beings, whether in ancient or modern times, in Mexico or China, among the religiously orthodox or heterodox, for the subjects of a monarchy or the citizens of a republic, for prince or pauper.

At the very same historical moment that the origins and jurisdiction of natural laws shrank to the realm of the human, a new category that embraced the entire universe was taking shape in astronomy, mechanics, and natural philosophy: laws of nature. In contrast to the theorists of early modern natural law, who pared down their principles to the point that even the bare existence of God became a superfluous assumption, the theorists of the laws of nature leaned heavily on theology, making the nature of God the guarantor of the order of nature. Although uncomfortably aware that the expression "laws of nature" could only metaphorically describe natural regularities such as the collisions of elastic bodies in mechanics, proponents of this new way of thinking about nature as law-governed often recurred to analogies between natural laws and laws of nature. Nature had its local customs as well as its universal laws; God was a legislator who decreed the laws of nature just as princes decreed the laws of the realm; exceptions to laws of nature were rare acts of divine dispensation just as princely pardons were rare acts of royal grace; natural laws and laws of nature could both ideally be derived from self-evident principles. Most important, natural laws and laws of nature transcended all other rules and regularities in their universality, uniformity, and immutability.

Laws of Nature

In 1644 the French mathematician, natural philosopher, and sometime soldier of fortune René Descartes published a Latin treatise of metaphysics and physics that set forth a radical new vision of how to think about the order of nature. All the blooming, buzzing confusion of the world, from stars to starfish, from the color red to the texture of velvet, could be reduced to matter in motion. Matter could be further reduced to geometric space, and motion to three compact principles: first, a body in motion or at rest continues in that state "as far as is in its power"; second, all motion "is, of itself, along straight lines"; and third, when bodies collide the product of their speed and volume is conserved overall.[32] Descartes called these three principles "laws" to underscore their fundamental status, in contrast to mere "rules," a term he had used in earlier works to list an indefinite number of precepts on how to think.[33] By reserving the term *laws* for the most general underlying principles of his mechanical philosophy, the fundamental principles from which all other phenomena could allegedly be derived, Descartes launched a powerful and puzzling metaphor that has dominated scientific thinking ever since: laws of nature.

The power of laws of nature lay in their generality, simplicity, and fertility. Like natural laws, laws of nature were universal in scope—but universal in the root sense of the word, applying to the universe in its entirety, not just the tiny province of the human realm. And like natural laws, laws of nature were general in the sense of uniformity, holding everywhere and always. Just as natural law theorists such as Grotius and Pufendorf had contrasted

universal laws with local customs or positive law, both famously
diverse and variable, natural philosophers such as Francis Bacon
and Robert Boyle contrasted the laws of nature with nature's "customs" or "municipal laws"—lower-level regularities that held only
some of the time or under particular local conditions.[34] Laws of
nature and natural laws were both simple in the sense of being few
in number, concisely formulated, and, most importantly, fundamental. In theory, both natural laws and laws of nature supplied
the bedrock upon which the whole edifice of, respectively, jurisprudence and natural philosophy could be erected. Solid as gran-
ite because self-evident and prodigiously fertile in derived consequences, these foundations guaranteed the stability and scope of
the disciplines they grounded. In practice, deriving unequivocal
consequences proved much trickier than anticipated. Natural law
theorists debated over whether natural law did or did not justify
slavery or polygamy;[35] Descartes himself admitted that experiments would be necessary to decide among the several possible
world systems deduced from his laws of nature.[36] To continue the
architectural conceit, the same foundations could support either
a baroque palace or a Bauhaus apartment block. In the case of both
natural laws and laws of nature, general, simple laws could turn out
to be *too* fertile in possible consequences.

The puzzle lay in the very idea of nature obeying laws. The
problem was particularly acute for proponents of the mechanical
philosophy, who insisted that all matter was, as the phrase went,
brute, passive, and stupid: incapable of motion or change, much
less thought, unless acted upon by intelligent minds, whether divine or human. Mechanical philosophers such as Descartes and
Boyle attacked personifications of nature as goddess and insisted
that God had no need of an assistant. According to Boyle, to
"imagine, as we commonly do, that God has appointed an intelligent and powerful Being, called nature, to be, as his vicegerent,
continually watchful for the good of the universe" showed disre-
spect for divine providence and flirted with idolatry. Nature was
nothing more than matter in motion, an elaborate engine crafted

by God. Boyle followed Descartes in using the terminology of "laws of nature," although he conceded its awkwardness: "But I cannot conceive, how a body devoid of understanding and sense, truly so called, can moderate and determine its own motions, as to make them conformable to laws, that it has no knowledge or apprehension of."[37] Boyle nonetheless held onto the ill-fitting metaphor of laws of nature, which by the end of the seventeenth century had become entrenched as *the* way of describing nature's most regular regularities and has remained so ever since.

Why the law metaphor succeeded despite its disadvantages is something of a puzzle. It was not as if alternatives were unavailable. Natural order can be conceived in several different ways, and we still shift effortlessly among these diverse orders in everyday conversation. The most ancient and still most prevalent colloquial sense of nature, the original meaning of both the ancient Greek word *physis* and the Latin *natura*, is specific nature: that which makes something unmistakably what it is, and not something else. It is the nature of water to seek its own level, the nature of cranes to migrate, and the nature of crocuses to bloom in spring. This is the sense of nature invoked by the natural law theorists when they appealed to human nature: shared characteristics that imprint a natural kind with predictable properties. Specific natures make classification of both the animate and inanimate world possible, whether in the form of the periodic table of elements or Linnaean taxonomy. Almost as ancient are local natures, the configuration of flora and fauna, geography and topography, weather and climate that create distinctive landscapes and biotopes. Observed by Hippocratic physicians in ancient Greece and mathematically modeled by modern ecologists, local natures are tightly intertwined with the local customs and regimens of the people who inhabit them. Ways of life on the arctic tundra or on the shores of tropical seas are exquisitely attuned to ambient landscapes and life forms. The orders of both specific and local natures account for stable regularities that are at least as pervasive and consequential as laws of nature like those of Descartes.[38]

However, neither specific nor local natures achieve anything like the generality, simplicity, or immutability of laws of nature. The plethora of specific natures creates the dazzling diversity of animals, vegetables, and minerals on Earth, not to mention the worlds and galaxies beyond. No overstuffed museum or compendious encyclopedia could ever do justice to their infinite variety. Just as specific natures cannot be simplified, local natures, as the name suggests, cannot be generalized. A patchwork quilt made up of tropical rainforests, craggy mountains, broad steppes, verdant pastures, and heather-covered heaths covers the planet, as depicted in the maps of the nineteenth-century Prussian naturalist Alexander von Humboldt (1769–1859). (Fig. 7.2.) Nor are specific and local natures immutable: although both guarantee an order that can be relied upon most of the time, both can be occasionally disrupted by exceptions. Every now and then the swallows may not return in spring or wind-driven water may run uphill; the monsoon rains may fail or Siberian temperatures soar. In contrast to the universal and inviolable laws of nature, specific and local natures resembled what Bacon and Boyle called "the customs of nature"— what happens most of the time under restricted conditions.[39]

Nature's order conceived in terms of laws was not entirely absent in ancient and medieval natural philosophy, particularly in astronomy, optics, and the other mathematical sciences. Seneca, for example, called for a "law" of cometary motion in his *Natural Questions* (c. 65 CE) and Epicurean philosopher Lucretius (94–55 BCE) in his poem *On the Nature of Things* (1st c. BCE) described how nature has insured the uniformity of species through "covenants" (*foedera naturae*).[40] In medieval and Renaissance Latin sources, the metaphor of "law" (*lex*) to describe regularities that occurred in astronomy and optics (and occasionally grammar), but a slew of alternative terms—including "axioms," "principles," "rules," and "causes"—also mapped much of the same semantic territory.[41] Bacon, who served as attorney general and later Lord Chancellor of England, had flirted with the language of laws to describe the basic alphabet (another of his metaphors) of simple

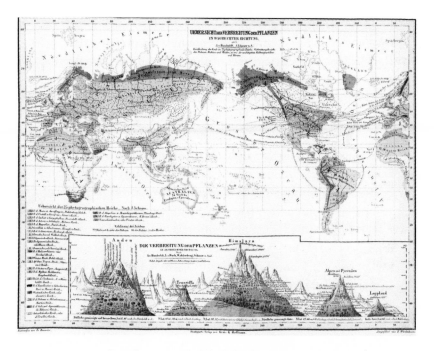

FIGURE 7.2. Alexander von Humboldt's global distribution of plant kinds (*Atlas zu Alexander von Humboldts Kosmos* [Atlas of Alexander von Humboldt's *Cosmos*], ed. Traugott Bromme, 1851, Table 31).

natures such as whiteness or heat but ultimately repurposed the older Aristotelian term "forms."[42] Until Descartes's 1644 laws of matter in motion, the use of the metaphor "law of nature [*lex naturalis*]" to describe natural regularities was rare outside of astronomy (Nicolaus Copernicus [1473–1543] and Johannes Kepler both used the term selectively).[43] Other terms with connotations that would later become part of the concept of laws of nature, such as "generality," "certainty," "necessity," and "foundations," were plentiful. Nature was conceived as orderly, but neither uniformly nor unexceptionably so; specific and local natures rather than systems of universal laws or rules guaranteed stability.[44]

Descartes's laws thus mark a turning point; thereafter the metaphor of "laws of nature," despite its obvious unsuitability, became irresistible. Subsequent uses of the term in mid- and late-seventeenth-century natural philosophy often bore the stamp of the Cartesian prototype even if they diverged from Cartesian formulations. In the 1660s the Royal Society of London called on natural philosophers to improve on "the Lawes of Motion given by Des Cartes," and Isaac Newton famously titled his three fundamental anti-Cartesian principles "Axioms, or Laws of Motion [*Axiomata, sive Leges Motu*]" in his epoch-making *Principia mathematica philosophiae naturalis*.[45] Mechanics, like astronomy and optics, had been one of the "mixed mathematical" sciences in which "law" terminology had occasionally appeared prior to Descartes, but even Galileo, arguably the most important figure in the science of mechanics prior to Newton, had hardly ever used that metaphor; nor had mathematician Blaise Pascal in his work on pneumatics and hydrostatics.[46] But after circa 1660, "laws of nature" became a way of talking about all kinds of natural regularities, not just in the traditionally mathematical sciences, and it crowded out competing terms such as "rule," "theorem," or "principle" in the space of just a few decades.[47] Why?

There is a mountain range of historical literature on this question. Views diverge on the relative importance of metaphysics, mathematics, theology, technology, and political theory.[48] However, the champions of laws of nature—Descartes, Boyle, Newton, Leibniz—bear witness in their writings to the centrality of debates over God's power versus his wisdom. Their claims about natural laws were invariably framed in theological terms that by the mid-seventeenth century already had a long and disputatious history.[49] Is even God bound by logic, or can his will defy even the principle of non-contradiction? Are divinely ordained laws of nature contingent on God's unfathomable purposes or necessary and therefore accessible to human reason? Do miracles really violate the laws of nature or had God foreseen and planned all eventualities from the beginning of time? Was divine providence the solicitous care of each and every one of God's creatures—not a sparrow falls but that God attends—or did God prefer "catholic laws, and higher ends, before subordinations, and uniformity in his conduct before making changes in it according to every sort of particular emergencies," as Boyle believed?[50] At just the moment many natural law jurists were distancing themselves from such theological conundrums and grounding their theories in human nature, their counterparts among the natural philosophers plunged head-first into debates about God's nature.

The most famous of all of these debates over God and the laws of nature among the natural philosophers took place in a correspondence between the German mathematician, philosopher, and jurist Gottfried Wilhelm Leibniz and the Anglican clergyman and scientific translator Samuel Clarke (1675–1729), who represented Newtonian views—and was probably advised by Newton in his replies to Leibniz—in 1716–1717. Newton and Leibniz were scientific rivals who had already dueled publicly in a bitter priority dispute over the calculus,[51] and both would have been aware of the political as well as theological and scientific stakes of the correspondence, which began when Leibniz wrote to Caroline of Ansbach (1683–1737), Princess of Wales, on the allegedly damaging consequences of Newtonian natural philosophy for orthodox religion.[52] Writing for Caroline's discerning eyes as well as for each other, Leibniz and Clarke turned their disagreements about God, gravitation, the existence of a vacuum, miracles, and space into a showdown over just how law-governed nature was.

In his opening volley, Leibniz accused Newton of casting God as an incompetent craftsman, whose clockwork universe had to be cleaned and mended from time to time, as opposed to a perfect machine that ran perpetually and "agreeably to the laws of nature, and the beautiful and established order." The reference was to Query 31 of Newton's Opticks (1704), in which Newton had argued that the whole universe would eventually grind to a halt without the intervention of "certain active principles" like gravitation and fermentation and further speculated that God might "vary the laws of nature" to create other kinds of worlds elsewhere in the universe.[53] Clarke countered that Leibniz's vision of a machine that ticked along forever all by itself was incompatible with God's providence and sovereignty: a king whose kingdom never required "his government or interposition" was a king only in name. Back and forth the correspondents went on this issue, Leibniz insisting that God's wisdom entailed foresight and precluded the need for any tinkering with the world-machine once set in motion by the divine engineer and Clarke retorting that God's power expressed itself in his constant sustenance of the universe. Leibniz's laws of nature were eternal, self-sustaining, and "the best among things possible"; Clarke's were edicts that depended entirely on God's will and might be altered at any moment. For Leibniz, this amounted to reducing divine will to the caprices of chance; for Clarke, an inviolable order of nature was indistinguishable from fatalism. Leibniz minimized the role of miracles and emphasized that they served the ends of grace, not the maintenance of nature. Clarke countered that the only distinction between natural and supernatural events was that the latter were simply unusual, for nothing happened without the immediate action of God. The "course of nature" or even "nature" *tout court* were just circumlocutions for God's busy maintenance of every detail of his creation.[54] At the heart of these many-sided disagreements lay incompatible ideals of good governance, Leibniz's far-sighted legislator versus Clarke's (and Newton's) interventionist monarch.

Whereas Newton's science prevailed on the issues of gravitation and the vacuum (though not on the conservation of momentum), it was Leibniz's divine engineer who eventually won out over Newton's imperious "Universal Ruler" (though not when it came to the rational necessity of actual laws of nature).[55] By the mid-eighteenth century, enlightened opinion conceived of nature as a system of universal, eternal, and immutable laws. As Montesquieu summarized this worldview in 1748, God had created and conserved the world in accordance with laws consistent with his power and wisdom; the motions of matter must follow these "invariable laws; and if one could imagine another world than this one, it [too] would have its constant rules, or be destroyed."[56] As

Montesquieu hinted in his gesture toward other worlds, *which* constant rules applied was a matter of divine discretion. On this point Leibniz's uniquely rational laws had lost out to Newton's vehement voluntarism. Laws of nature like gravitation came to be seen as God's positive law, universal and inexorable but arbitrary.[57] Leibniz was, however, the clear victor on the larger issue of God's interventions in nature. Even the devout abandoned Newton's meddlesome God in favor of a universe that required neither miracles nor maintenance and were moreover prepared to countenance the occasional earthquake or injustice as the price of generality, simplicity, and uniformity. Like Boyle, the French Oratorian priest Nicolas Malebranche (1638–1715) shrugged off monstrous births and other mishaps as the inevitable consequence of God's having chosen to work by the simplest means possible.[58] Although only a few radical philosophers in the tradition of Baruch Spinoza (1632–1677) categorically denied the in-principle possibility of miracles, in practice even the orthodox clergy, both Catholic and Protestant, minimized their number and significance.[59] David Hume's (1711–1776) essay "Of Miracles" (1748), which argued that even the most copious and unimpeachable testimony concerning miracles could never outweigh the overwhelming evidence of inviolable laws of nature, was simply the endpoint of a long intellectual trajectory.[60]

Conclusion: Universal Legality

Throughout the early modern period, European thinking about natural law and laws of nature had evolved in parallel. There were obvious contrasts: natural law held only for human nature and compelled by reason rather than physical necessity; laws of nature could be called such only metaphorically and had to be discovered by empirical inquiry rather than thought experiments about a hypothetical primordial state. Yet their commonalities dwarfed these differences. Both embraced a foundational model in which vast and varied consequences could be derived from a few simple, general laws; both contrasted the universality, uniformity, and immutability of these laws with the mosaic of local customs and local natures. There is a striking analogy between Bacon and Leibniz's efforts as jurists to simplify, respectively, the common and civil law into "one competent and uniform corps of law" and their advocacy of simple, uniform laws of nature.[61] Both traditions imagined universal laws in interaction with local positive or municipal laws, in which the latter supplemented, limited, and sometimes modified the former as specific circumstances required.[62] Boyle invoked such "particular and subordinate (or as it were municipal) laws" of nature to explain apparent local deviations from the "general laws whereby things corporeal are guided," such as monsters and other anomalies.[63] Unsurprisingly, Leibniz was as adamant about excluding exceptions from natural law as he had been in the case of laws of nature.[64] Natural law and laws of nature were connected by more than just a punning similarity of names.

A common vision of good governance as rule of law, as inexorable as it was universal and uniform, animated both traditions. On this model, divine dispensations of the sort God had granted in the Bible to favored persons and peoples were no longer acts of grace; instead, they resembled the whims of tyrants. Whether the dispensations transgressed a natural law (for example, God commanding Abraham to kill his son Isaac) or a law of nature (God parting the Red Sea for the Israelites), they were an embarrassment for thinkers who considered inconsistency and inconstancy as flaws. The law, not the law-maker, was almighty. Medieval commentators on these problematic passages had concluded that whatever God ordained, even in defiance of his own commandments, was *ipso facto* mete and right, and early modern voluntarists such as Newton had asserted that the laws of nature held only as long as God willed them. In contrast, eighteenth-century proponents of natural law in jurisprudence and laws of nature in natural philosophy equated human justice and natural order with unflinching adherence to fundamental laws.[65] Even the monarch—even God—bowed before the law. The article on

"Law" (1765) in the great Enlightenment *Encyclopédie* cited an edict by Louis XII (1462–1515, r. 1498–1515) with approval: "The law is always to be obeyed, despite orders contrary to the law that might be wrest from an importunate monarch."[66]

By no means everyone subscribed to this vision of unbending universal legality. Naturalists who tracked the vicissitudes of variable phenomena like the weather discerned at best local "rules," never stable laws.[67] In the human realm, where universal predictability all too often diverged from justice in particular cases, protests abounded. The seventeenth-century French jurist Jean Domat (1625–1696), whose 1689 treatise on the civil law arranged in "natural order" went through over sixty editions, acknowledged the existence of immutable natural laws but gave many examples in which they were limited by the arbitrary laws of a particular place and time. Such exceptions to the general laws were too numerous to be memorized; judges must instead respect "the spirit of the laws to be applied, in order not to injure the exceptions by extending the general rules too far."[68] Montesquieu, magistrate of the parliament of Bordeaux, also rang the changes on the Pauline opposition between the letter and spirit of the law in his 1748 treatise of that title, in which he argued forcefully against universal laws. Each people required laws appropriate to its climate, soil, way of life, religion, wealth, morals, and manners. In the context of efforts by centralizing powers all over Europe to subordinate regional to royal law, for example in the French crown's late-seventeenth-century compilation of royal ordinances applicable to the entire kingdom, to champion local custom over universal law was freighted with concrete political as well as abstract theoretical implications.[69] Local nature and local customs, twinned since antiquity, here vigorously reasserted themselves in defiance of both universal human nature and uniform physical nature.

Montesquieu understood that his defense of local custom rooted in local nature wrenched apart the alliance between natural law and laws of nature, grounded in a shared vision of universal legality. He explained that although the world of intelligent beings had its own invariable laws, it "did not follow them as constantly as the physical world followed its [laws]."[70] Endowed with both free will and a tendency to err, human beings strayed from the primitive laws of the state of nature once they entered into society. Montesquieu here highlighted the critical disanalogy between natural laws and laws of nature: the latter compelled obedience by physical necessity, the former only by the assent of reason. Some eighteenth-century thinkers, such as the physician and economist François Quesnay (1694–1774), tried to fuse physical compulsion and rational compliance by arguing that if governments did not follow the laws of nature that caused agriculture to succeed or fail, they would then also violate the natural law that entitled all to enjoy the fruits of the earth.[71] But such efforts were few and largely ignored. The gap between the natural and human realms widened in the course of the eighteenth century, straining the analogy between natural law and laws of nature.

Yet even the figure who did most to split the two realms apart clung to that analogy. Immanuel Kant drove a metaphysical and moral wedge between what he called the "kingdom of ends," composed of rational beings free to choose their own laws, and the "kingdom of causes," in which everything in nature is determined by ironclad laws of nature. Human beings inhabit both and therefore view everything in double perspective: "first, as belonging to the world of sense under laws of nature (heteronomy), and second, as belonging to the intelligible world under laws which, independent of nature, are not empirical but founded in reason [autonomy]." *Pace* the natural law theorists, the latter had nothing to do with human nature, only with reason, which Kant was careful not to qualify as human reason: a believer in the possibility of intelligent life on other planets, his kingdom of ends and its laws embraced all rational beings everywhere in the universe. *Pace* the theorists of the laws of nature, the former were not the edicts of God but the cognitive precondition for understanding nature as an order at all. Kant thereby radically reconceptualized both natural law and the laws of nature and severed almost all the ties that had once bound them together. But he nonetheless retained the metaphor of universal legality that had illuminated both visions of the grandest rules of all. Kant's categorical imperative, the ultimate law of practical reason, exhorts all rational beings: "Act as though the maxim of your action were by your will to become a universal law of nature."[72]

8

Bending and Breaking Rules

At the Limit

What happens when even the most ironclad rule confronts an exception? Consider the following three celebrated examples of rules bending and breaking under the strain.

Thou shalt not kill (Exodus 20:13). But it is God himself who orders Abraham, "Take your son, your only son Isaac, whom you love, and go to the land Moriah, and offer him there as a burnt offering upon one of the mountains of which I shall tell you" (Genesis 22:1). Has God violated his own law? Thomas Aquinas, greatest of Catholic theologians, contended that there could be no dispensation from the commandments of the Decalogue, which express "the very intention of the lawgiver, who is God." But in the case of Abraham and Isaac, he invoked secondary principles that "in some particular cases of rare occurrence" might suspend the "first principles" even of eternal divine law.[1]

Theft is forbidden by both natural and positive law. But the poor man is cold, hungry, and homeless; there is no honest work to be had. The rich man's table overflows with delicacies, but he will spare not even a crust of bread for charity. Is the poor man justified in stealing necessities from the rich man that the latter will not even notice are missing? Seventeenth-century German natural law jurist Samuel Pufendorf pleaded mitigating circumstances: "And tho' regularly what depends upon *Courtesie* [i.e., giving alms to the poor] ought by no means to be extorted by *Force*, yet the *Extreme Necessity* alters the Case, and makes these Things as *claimable*, as if they were absolutely *due* by a formal Obligation."[2]

The rule of law preserves citizens from executive orders not subject to checks and balances. But an emergency has erupted—a devastating flood, an epidemic, a surprise attack—and the executive takes command without consulting either legislature or judiciary. Philosopher John Locke, the most eloquent seventeenth-century defender of the right of a free people not to be subject to the arbitrary power of even the most benevolent ruler, nonetheless endorsed the exercise of executive prerogative to "provide for the public good in such cases, which depending on unforeseen and uncertain occurrences, certain and unalterable laws could not safely direct."[3]

When does bending the rule break it? These three cases taken from the realms of moral theology, law, and political theory pose the question in starkest terms: must law, even divine law, or the rule of law itself sometimes bend like Aristotle's pliable ruler of Lesbos, which curved to measure rounded surfaces, or break altogether? When does rigidity become injustice and flexibility mere capricious whim? These are questions that have exercised interpreters of the law since ancient times. In *The Statesman*, Plato recognized that no fixed system of laws could possibly render justice in all cases, "for the differences of men and of actions and the fact that nothing, I may say, in human life is ever at rest, forbid any science [*technê*] whatsoever to promulgate any simple rule for everything and for all time."[4] Constitutional lawyers and judges today wrestle over whether the letter or the spirit of the law should take precedence. Advocates for hewing to the letter of the law argue for fidelity to the original intentions of past legislators and for predictability to guide future decisions; their opponents point to the need to recognize the variability of circumstances, including historical changes in public opinion.[5] Plato would probably have been astonished by the content of cases currently being tried before the United States Supreme Court, but he would have been perfectly at home with the terms in which originalists and progressivists frame their arguments.

Nor are moralists and jurists the only people who must decide whether, when, and how much to adjust universal rules to particular cases. Every physician confronted with a familiar disease manifesting itself in an unfamiliar fashion in an individual patient must weigh the pros and cons of following the standard treatment protocol in this particular case. The very idea of the case as an epistemic genre (historian of medicine Gianna Pomata's felicitous term) is most at home in medicine and the law, in Chinese as well as in European traditions.[6] But case-based reasoning is also a prominent complement to rule-based analyses in the human and life sciences, which must also deal with diverse particulars.[7] Historical change can destabilize rules originally formulated for a different context. Thomas Jefferson (1743–1826) was acutely aware— and glad—of this fact when he drafted the procedural rules of the U.S. Senate, which "those who come after me will successively correct and fill up, till a code of rules shall be formed for the use of the Senate, the effects of which may be accuracy of business, economy of time, order, uniformity, and impartiality."[8] In any domain in which there is high and consequential variability or in which significant changes occur over time, rules will have to be bent and sometimes broken.

The need for discretion and judgment in applying general rules to particular cases is therefore enduring and widespread— perhaps as permanent and universal as the rules themselves aspire to be. But from the historical perspective of this book, another question arises: when and why does rule-bending and rule-breaking come to be perceived as problematic, as opposed to just the way the world works? In earlier chapters, we have seen how rules were elasticized from the outset, in anticipation of the challenge of recalcitrant and unpredictable particulars. Rules conceived as models could guide practice by imitation and improvisation, much as works within a literary genre such as the epic build upon but do not identically copy each other: Virgil's (70–19 BCE) *Aeneid* in relation to Homer's (8th c. BCE) *Iliad* and John Milton's (1608–1674) *Paradise Lost* in relation to both.[9] Examples, exceptions, and experience were all enlisted in the formulation of thick rules, even the apparently unequivocal rules of games and arithmetic, in order to render them supple enough to withstand the test of practice.

Yet starting in the seventeenth century, we have also witnessed the rise of more ambitious and less accommodating rules. More ambitious, because they aimed to regulate either in greater detail (the micro-managing municipal regulations of Chapter 6) or to broaden their jurisdiction across space and time (the universal natural laws of Chapter 7). Less accommodating, because either more explicit (the spelled-out procedures in cookbook recipes in Chapter 3) or less open to discretion (the calculation workflows of Chapter 5). Increasingly, rules come shorn of the woolly coat of examples, exceptions, and appeals to experience that had cushioned earlier rules (like those of the mechanical arts of Chapter 3 and even the algorithms of Chapter 4) against collision with unforeseen circumstances. Their tone becomes peremptory rather than expansive. In principle, these rules were expected to be obeyed to the letter; in practice, letter and spirit inevitably clashed in application to hard cases. Even the deliberately rigid regulations described in Chapter 6 required some adjustment on the part of the rule-enforcers when applied to circumstances unforeseen by even the most detailed rule.

Judgment and discretion did not become obsolete. But they did become deeply controversial. Specific decisions that stretched the rules had always encountered resistance, especially in the legal sphere. What was new in the seventeenth and eighteenth centuries were principled challenges to *any* rule-stretching, whether in cases of religious conscience, legal adjudication, or political sovereignty. In this chapter I will examine the ways in which early modern debates over casuistry in moral theology, equity in law, and sovereign prerogative in politics tested the firmness of rules—not just this or that rule but rules in general.

Casuistry: Hard Cases and Tender Consciences

Paris, 1630: The Jesuit Étienne Bauny (1564–1649) counsels French Catholics, especially the merchants among them, on how to reconcile sharp dealings with their religious duties. Is a lender justified in charging interest to a merchant about to undertake a perilous but potentially lucrative voyage—and if so, how much? Canon law would ordinarily prohibit any interest charged on a loan as usury. But Father Bauny, speaking for the maritime insurers who had been conducting business in every European port city since at least the fourteenth century, defends the practice, provided that the amount of interest is in proportion to the expected profit and the risks of the voyage. In effect, the interest is not really interest but the "price of perils" that threaten to deprive the lender of any repayment of the loan. Fine-tuning of costs to case does not stop there. Bauny also enjoins merchants to take account of the relative financial situations of the parties to such a contract. If one becomes rich but the other is impoverished by the deal, "said contract is null and void."[10] In prose dense with subtle distinctions and Latin references to theological authorities, Bauny attempts to guide tender consciences and their perplexed confessors through the thicket of vexed moral decisions faced by (as his subtitle advertises) "all conditions and qualities" in society.

Bauny's moral counsel did not meet with universal approval. Although he was spiritual director to the powerful Cardinal François de la Rochefoucauld (1558–1645), his book was condemned as too permissive by both the Pope and the theologians of the Sorbonne. But the book nonetheless clearly met a felt need: it was re-issued even after having been in 1640 put on the *Index librorum prohibitorum*, the list of books officially censored by the Catholic Church. Early modern Europe was a period of tumultuous change: religious reformation and persecution affected tens of thousands of people; new commercial opportunities opened up via trade routes to Asia, Africa, and the Americas; the spread of both literacy and printed books and broadsides catalyzed intellectual and political ferment; ingenious financial instruments like joint stock companies and bills of exchange made and lost vast fortunes; and fratricidal wars raged all over the continent for almost two hundred years. As we have seen in Chapter 6, during this period new riches upended old social orders as bankers out-spent nobles, city infrastructures buckled with the arrival of inhabitants attracted by new opportunities, and the recently literate struggled to master reading and writing. These economic, social, religious, and political transformations threw up new kinds of moral dilemmas of the sort Bauny's in-demand manual addressed.

Although many of the moral quandaries treated by Bauny may have been novel, the genre of moral reasoning that he and many other theologians, both Catholic and Protestant, plied during this period had time-honored tradition behind it. Indeed, casuistry meant bringing the full weight of tradition to bear on a knotty specific case. Casuistry originally referred to the interpretation of biblical and patristic teachings, canon law, and learned opinion as applied to particular cases, mostly for pastoral use, and had since the thirteenth century been practiced by confessors throughout the Catholic Church. Just as Anglo-American common law requires trained experts to interpret the bearing of centuries of statute law, precedents, and legal opinion on any given case, or medicine demands that doctors be well versed in the latest relevant scientific literature as well as in historical observations of similar cases, the casuist was steeped in the voluminous theological and moral literature that had accumulated over centuries. The analogy between casuistry and the practice of common law or medicine was frequently drawn: common law lawyers were called the casuists of law; confessors, the surgeons of souls.[11] All reasoned first and foremost from the case itself, not from some more general rule or principle to the specific case in question.

Or rather, they reasoned from case to case, from particulars to particulars. As historian and philosopher of science John Forrester noted, case-based reasoning differs from induction over particulars in not aiming at an over-arching generalization.[12] Casuist reasoning is anti-statistical in that it refuses to generalize over homogenized cases; yet it is nonetheless profoundly empirical. Characteristic of all case-based reasoning are collections of cases, sometimes loosely classified in thematic groups but open to cross-hatched analogies that cut across such provisional taxonomies. Just as early modern European doctors and jurists published collections of annotated cases to guide practical reasoning in their fields, theologians gathered learned opinion on a vast array of moral conundrums into fat compendia, such as Spanish Jesuit Antonio Escobar y Mendoza's (1589–1669) encyclopedic *Summula casuum conscientiae* (Compendium of cases of conscience, 1627) and *Liber theologiae moralis* (Treatise on moral theology, 1644).[13] Nor were such collections of cases an exclusively European genre: Chinese jurists also boasted a centuries-long tradition of such compilations.[14]

The kind of empiricism that such collections of cases represent differs from other forms of empiricism—for example, the observation, the experiment, the statistical survey—in that ascent from the particular case to the universal rule is not its goal. In contrast, a single observation is a mere anecdote; an experiment seeks causes that operate everywhere, not just in this laboratory; a statistical survey deliberately erases individual differences so that mass regularities emerge. But case-based empiricism remains rooted in particulars. Collections of cases, especially well-chosen cases, highlight telling similarities and differences and serve as a repository to understand the present case at hand in light of past experience. However, which cases—which legal precedents, which medical histories, which moral decisions—will turn out to be the most relevant, the ones resoluble by appeal to similar principles, is not a matter of abstraction or generalization. Nor is the case solved when it is tidily subordinated to its proper general principle, unlike an example subordinated to the rule it illustrates. Rather, as literary scholar André Jolles observed, cases pit rival rules and principles against each other, "norm weighed against norm."[15] If anything, the rule is subordinated to the case. Rhetorician John Arthos remarks apropos of casuistry that the case "does not simply fall under, but somehow actually changes the law."[16] To describe reasoning by cases as analogical is at best only a half-truth. The gauntlet thrown down by the case is to discern *which* analogy, out of an indefinite number of possibilities, weighs most heavily—not exclusively—in this particular case, without ever losing sight of the rival analogies that would have favored alternative governing principles. Cases are good to think with because the thinking never stops.

Let us now return to the Reverend Father Bauny and his advice to confessors on how to deal with merchant parishioners anxious about the welfare of both their investments and their souls. The heaping up of contextual detail (Are there reports of pirates and other perils en route? How valuable is the cargo? What are the relative financial circumstances of lender and borrower?) that would be a distraction if the fair pricing of interest on the loan were simply a mathematical problem are of the essence in a moral conundrum. Casuists of all stripes, Protestant or Catholic, legal or medical, were as avid for such particulars as mathematicians were averse to them. Asked whether it was permissible to lie to a thief, Bauny's English Puritan counterpart William Perkins (1558–1602) rang all the circumstantial changes—Was the lie made under oath? Would respecting the oath harm the commonwealth? In how much danger was the victim? Would other lives be put in jeopardy?—and in the end refused to come down on one side or the other: "the most and best Divines" might absolve the liar, but "for my part I leave it in suspense."[17] Amidst the swarm of particulars and rival principles, casuists could hope only to achieve plausible judgments, not definitive ones. As the particulars of a case proliferated, so did the potentially applicable rules. In the end, some rules were chosen as more salient than others, but only after a contest among them. Casuistry tests rules before it bends them.

This kind of reasoning might have been specially designed to drive mathematicians and rigorists of all persuasions fairly mad, and Bauny and his fellow Jesuit casuists fell famously afoul of French mathematician and religious rigorist Blaise Pascal. As a

Jansenist, an austere Catholic sect under fire from more orthodox theologians, Pascal had religious and political motives to attack the Jesuits.[18] But the theological content of his phenomenally successful polemic *Les Provinciales* (The provincial letters, 1657) was almost entirely eclipsed by his withering satire on Jesuit casuists like Bauny (whom Pascal mentions by name).[19] Adopting the persona of one Louis de Montalte, who writes letters to a friend in the provinces about the latest goings-on in Paris, Pascal skewered what he presented as the all-too-obliging, all-too-flexible morality of the Jesuit casuists. By quoting the casuists' own texts (selectively excerpted from Escobar, often out of context) against them, Pascal insinuated that there was no moral failing so grave, no sin so heinous that it could not be absolved by the accommodating Jesuit confessors. Strait-laced Montalte is increasingly scandalized as a genial Jesuit explains to him that because only a few people are capable of adhering strictly to the dictates of scripture and the church fathers, confessors would risk losing the majority of their flock if they showed no leniency when it came to specific cases of moral scruples. Moreover, times had changed, and casuists had to pronounce upon actual cases in their here-and-now contexts. "The [Church] Fathers were good for the morality of their time," Montalte quotes, "but they are too remote from that of our own." Availing himself of the doctrine of probabilism, which allowed the confessor to follow the most convenient opinion of a learned authority even if less well supported than contrary views, the affable Jesuit manages to acquit priests and nuns who violate Lenten dietary restrictions, nobles who shed blood in duels of honor, and Jesuits who suppressed Christ's crucifixion so as not to shock their Chinese converts. "How useful these probabilities are!" exclaims Montalte with bitter irony.[20]

Casuistry (and the Jesuits) never recovered from Pascal's parody of its rubbery on-the-one-hand-on-the-other-hand (and often on-the-third-and -fourth-hand) style of reasoning. *Les Provinciales* is the only seventeenth-century French polemic to survive its epoch, and even Pascal's Jesuit adversaries acknowledged the brilliance of his style.[21] Largely due to the influence of *Les Provinciales*, which was quickly and widely translated, the words *Jesuistical* and (in French) *escobarie* became synonymous with overly subtle, sophistical, and slippery arguments. Jesuit casuistry was condemned for laxism even by popes in the course of the seventeenth century.[22] Especially but not only in Protestant countries, casuistry permanently lost its status as a serious form of moral reasoning, despite some efforts in our own time on the part of philosophers to restore its respectability.[23] Pascal, as unbending in religion as he was in mathematics, had championed the cause of steely principles over squishy particulars—and, perhaps not coincidentally, offered a general mathematical solution to the problem of finding the fair price for an uncertain outcome that Bauny had tackled with the particularistic tools of casuistry.[24]

In the course of the eighteenth century, the very meaning of conscience shifted from a learned tradition that embraced every theological statute and precept as well as individual circumstances and intentions to an internal faculty that reached its judgments as much by feeling as by reasoning. In the work of Jean-Jacques Rousseau, Immanuel Kant, and other Enlightenment moral philosophers, conscience explicitly replaced casuistry. Conscience dictated rather than dithered; its conclusions were as swift as they were definitive.[25] Kant briskly dismissed the need to guide conscience by casuistry or probabilism: moral judgments must be principled and certain: "Conscience does not judge the action as a case, which is subordinate to the law; . . . rather, here reason judges itself, whether it has really undertaken the evaluation of the actions (whether they are right or wrong) with all due care." Instead of casuistry, "a kind of dialectic of conscience," Kant displaced the back-and-forth between countervailing rules and principles to a second-order internal dialectic: reason sitting in judgment of itself.[26] The "Casuistical Questions" in Kant's *Die Metaphysik der Sitten* (Metaphysics of morals, 1797) preserved the subtle questions that were always the meat and drink of casuistry (for example, would the self-esteem every rational person should feel lead to arrogance?), but reason always supplied Kant with a final answer (true humility has nothing to do with bowing and scraping to authority).[27] Gone is the external director of conscience; gone is the heaping up of particulars; gone is the provisional tone of all casuistical judgments. But the dialectic so characteristic of casuistical reasoning, pitting rival rules against each other, lingered.

As did casuistry, by any other name, and not just in the sacrament of confession. Hospitals in many countries have installed medical ethics committees to deliberate on the moral dilemmas that arise in the treatment of patients in their care.[28] Major newspapers run regular advice columns to which readers submit hard cases for adjudication. Recent dilemmas submitted to the *New York Times* "The Ethicist" column include "Should I Accept Free Covid Testing I Don't Really Need?" "I Used a Sperm Donor. Should I Introduce My Daughter to Her Half-Siblings?" and other thoroughly modern conundrums, as up-to-date for our time as Bauny's cases were for his.[29] Casuistry is always exquisitely sensitive to context, quick to adjust to the way we live now. As the Puritan casuist Perkins insisted, "[w]ee must give place to the sway of the times, wherein we live."[30] The Ethicist's petitioners are as sincerely perplexed as Bauny's parishioners were. *Pace* Kant (and Pascal), their consciences had not swiftly and unequivocally determined which moral rule to follow in their various cases. All of these hard cases bristle with particulars; in all, two or more competing ethical principles are in play; in all, the door is left open to further considerations. There is always more thinking to be done, more shuttling back and forth between particulars and principles. A true case is never closed.

Equity: When the Law Commits Injustice

Paris, 1862: A poor man on the brink of starvation steals a loaf of bread and is condemned to five years of hard labor. So begins the tangled tale of Jean Valjean in Victor Hugo's (1802–1885) great

novel of legal injustice, *Les Misérables* (1862). In the adventures
that follow, Valjean is often on the wrong side of the law but almost
never on the wrong side of justice. Equity is the concept that spans
law and justice when the two diverge and the practice that bends
law in the name of justice.

The Latin word *aequitas*, meaning evenness, equality, and fairness, derives its legal significance from Roman law. As we saw in
Chapter 2, Aristotle had invoked the Greek word *epieikeia*, meaning kindness, lenience, and suitability, to temper the rigidity of
laws that occasionally encountered cases unforeseen by legislators
and in which the strict application of the law would result in injustice. Roman magistrates known as *praetors* had by the second
century BCE institutionalized the practice of correcting and supplementing the law on an ad hoc basis.[31] Medieval commentators
on Roman law extended ideas of equity from principles of fairness
to a holistic view informed not just by the relevant statute but by
the entire *Corpus iuris civile*.[32] Early modern European notions of
equity were further enriched by new translations not only of classical sources like Aristotle but also of the Hebrew Bible, layering
the associations of the Greek and Latin cognates with those of the
Hebrew word *mesarim* (straightness, rectitude, justice), also often
translated into English as *equity*.[33] Finally, although all European
law recognized some doctrine of equity, English jurists had by the
fourteenth century developed a full-blown dualistic system of
common law courts and the court of Chancery, the former pre-
sided over by the king's judges and the latter by the king himself
(later by the Lord Chancellor), with a rough division of labor between statute law and equity, between strict rule-following and
discreet rule-bending.[34]

These multiple sources endowed the early modern concept of
equity with considerable breadth and flexibility, depending on
which etymology and nuance an author chose to highlight. Evok-
ing the mild and indulgent associations of the Greek *epieikeia* in
his 1604 treatise of that title, Perkins allied the legal practice of
equity with Christian charity, natural law, and human fallibility.

His leading example of necessary mitigation was a "young boy pinched with hunger, cold, and povertie, [who] steales meat": to punish the culprit with death, as the law required, would violate equity, "as the moderation [of the sentence] is then the equitie of the lawe, and the extremitie is more iniustice."[35] Francis Bacon, who himself served as Lord Chancellor and was all too accustomed to clashes between the courts of common law and Chancery, defended equity in more procedural terms, as the final word when laws "encounter and cross one another" or are simply silent concerning the case at hand. But he also insisted that the discretionary judgments "afterwards be set down with their expositions and limitations" as rules to guide future cases.[36] French jurist Jean Domat, although a friend of Pascal and a fellow Jansenist, defended supple equity over rigid laws. Equity, Domat asserted, upheld natural law and was indeed the supreme principle of all law, natural and positive, "the universal spirit of justice . . . that is the primary foundation of the use and specific interpretation of all the rules."[37]

Both casuistry and equity dealt with outliers, extraordinary cases that stretched the ordinary resources of rules, whether moral principles or statute laws, to their limit and beyond. But whereas casuistry tested rules and principles against each other, there was rarely any doubt when equity was invoked as to which law applied. The hungry poor who stole food (the paradigmatic case that lived on in Hugo's novel) had unequivocally transgressed a law. Nor in most cases was the law itself on trial: few commentators queried the need for a law against theft that carried severe sanctions. What equity tested was whether applying the rigor of the law to this particular case served the higher cause of justice. Either implicitly or explicitly, arguments from equity established a hierarchy of rules and asserted the precedence of the top tier over the bottom. This schema had many variants. A Christian moralist like Perkins might elevate New Testament precepts of forgiveness and moderation over the rigor of the law against theft; a natural law jurist like Grotius might invoke universal over local law in the same case; Domat and many others honored what they called the spirit over the letter of the law. Whatever the justification, the law survived intact, if somewhat diminished in scope and stature. Equity bent but did not break the rule.

But a rule bent too far and too frequently could break. Even the champions of equity were uneasily aware that equity exercised in excess could undermine all rules. Aristotle favored laws that "define the issue of all cases as far as possible, and leave as little as possible to the discretion of the judges," and all subsequent writers on equity have fretted about the thin line between discretion and arbitrariness, mercy and indulgence.[38] The English historian and jurist John Selden (1584–1654) ridiculed the law of equity as practiced by Chancery as an arbitrary standard, "larger or narrower" as the conscience of whoever happened to occupy the office of Lord Chancellor.[39] Although Perkins pleaded for equity in the name of Christian charity, he condemned too much mercy as "a weakenes of witt, and an effeminateness of minde," as dangerous as the opposite extreme of cruelest rigor.[40] In Shakespeare's roughly contemporary play *The Merchant of Venice* (1600), these anxieties about excesses of both kinds were finely balanced. Portia pleads for mercy on behalf of Antonio, who has rashly promised to deliver up a pound of flesh on a defaulted loan, but she ultimately wins her case by insisting that the law be obeyed to the absurd letter: Antonio's creditor may take his pound of flesh—but not one drop of blood.

In the long history of equity as an essential corrective to imperfect laws, only Plato seems to have advocated the untrammeled exercise of discretion by a wise ruler so skilled in the art of governance as to render law superfluous. Like a seasoned ship's captain adapting to every shift in wind and weather, a master of the arts of navigation, such a ruler would be justified in overriding written law and tradition to decide in each specific situation what best served the common weal.[41] But even Plato admitted that such rulers were rarer than rubies. The majority of polities would have to settle for the second-best alternative of written laws, which would always be inadequate to the endless shuffle of situations and circumstances in human affairs.

At the heart of equity lay a Platonic pessimism about the intrinsic imperfection of human laws. Whatever their aspirations to universality and permanence, laws would always be ambushed by unexpected particulars and unpredictable changes in circumstances. By their very nature, laws projected the will of the legislator into the future, binding not only the present generation but generations to come. An element of hubris was intrinsic to laws, a denial of mortality and change. From this perspective, the more all-encompassing and enduring the law—for example, fundamental or constitutional law—the more necessary the remedy of equity to correct its failure to foresee all future eventualities. Whether such course corrections (to return to Plato's metaphor of the sea captain) are justified as upholding underlying principles over specific rules, the spirit over the letter of the law, or present over past public values, they raise the question of the bare possibility of permanent law under conditions of permanent uncertainty. In this scheme of things, equity expressed not so much basic humanity as human-all-too-human fallibility.

Seventeenth-century writers on equity contrasted the "vniversall righteousness" of God's laws, everywhere and always "of the same equitie in all cases; and therefore to be executed without dispensation, relaxation, or any mitigation," with imperfect human laws that "doe not hold the same equitie, and therefore must needes be executed with a discreet and wise moderation."[42] Divine law had been linked to natural law since at least the thirteenth century by Aquinas and others, but only with the rise of natural law in the seventeenth and eighteenth centuries as the basis for the actual codification and administration of justice, taught at universities and invoked in legal opinions, was it possible to conceive of human law approximating the universality and permanence of divine law. As we have seen in Chapter 7, natural law jurisprudence (and the metaphysics of laws of nature) went hand in hand with a reluctance to admit exceptions of any kind, for whatever reason.

The result was not to abolish equity but to rein in its workings and to shift its theoretical foundations.

We have already heard Bacon qua Lord Chancellor attempting to regularize singular acts of equity into rules, a program extended by his successors in Chancery throughout the eighteenth century. From the late seventeenth century onward, Chancellors fortified their decisions with reasoned justifications that emphasized consistency and stable procedures.[43] These developments coincided with a rise of Ciceronian over Aristotelian notions of equity, i.e., of equity understood as conformity to the universal rules of natural law over equity construed as an exception to the rules.[44] When David Hume claimed in 1751 that even robbers and pirates "could not maintain their pernicious confederacy did they not establish a new distributive justice among themselves and recall those laws of equity which they have violated with the rest of mankind," he was endorsing the Ciceronian sense of equity as itself a rule, not an exception.[45]

Hugo's tale of Jean Valjean measures the distance between equity as institutionalized exception versus equity as natural law. The case of a poor man absolved for stealing the necessities of life if there was no alternative had been a touchstone for theorists of equity since at least the thirteenth century, and the weight of learned opinion had consistently swung the scales of justice in favor of moderating equity over strict enforcement of the law. Even Grotius, who viewed the prohibition against theft as part of natural law, sided with the poor against the rich. But the Kantian argument against theft, which enjoined those inclined to make an exception in a special case simultaneously to will that this become a general law of human conduct, registered an end to such lenience as an official moral and legal doctrine. By the late eighteenth century, natural law had been pulled into the orbit of laws of nature, suspended no longer by mercy but only by a miracle—or executive pardon. Under the Napoleonic Penal Code of 1810, no considerations of equity mitigated Jean Valjean's mandatory sentence of five years of hard labor; only a pardon from on high could rescue him.

As in the case of casuistry, equity in its ancient Aristotelian sense as an unavoidable exception to even the best-laid laws did not disappear, however much the meanings of the word itself might have evolved. In current controversies over whether sentencing for drug-related offenses should be mandatory or discretionary or whether self-defense can be invoked by victims of domestic violence who kill their abusers or whether children or the mentally ill who commit crimes should be shielded from the full severity of the law, the same considerations that exercised early modern jurists and moralists are once again rehearsed by the opposing sides. Yet the word *exception* is rarely used by those who plead mitigating circumstances in this or that case. In the course of the seventeenth and eighteenth centuries new political and philosophical visions opposing the rule of law to the whims of the ruler and exalting equality before the law reinforced tendencies to prefer overall consistency and uniformity to case-by-case adjustments, even if the latter better serve the cause of justice. Some contemporary legal theorists go so far as to argue that these values trump those of justice and fairness in cases of conflict:

> It is not the law's purpose, of course, to be unfair for the sake of being unfair. But there is an important group of values— predictability of results, uniformity of treatment (treating like cases alike), and fear of granting unfettered discretion to individual decision-makers even if they happen to be wearing black robes—that the legal system, especially, thinks it valuable to preserve. These values often go by the name of the Rule of Law, and many of the virtues of the Rule of Law are ones that are accomplished by taking rules seriously as rules.[46]

The hallowed status of the Rule of Law (note the majestic majuscules) not only in jurisprudence but, as we saw in Chapter 7, also in theology and natural philosophy, had its counterpart in the political philosophy of seventeenth and eighteenth century.[47] Just as casuistry fell into disrepute in moral theology and equity shed its meaning as an exception to the law, sovereign prerogative, whether human or divine, came to be branded as arbitrary caprice rather than wise intervention.

Prerogative and States of Exception:
Rulers and the Rule of Law

London, 1617: Sir Francis Bacon, in his capacity as Lord Keeper of the Seal, instructs Sir John Denham on his duties as newly appointed Baron of the Exchequer: "First, therefore, above all you ought to maintain the King's prerogative, and to set down to yourself that the King's prerogative and the law are not two things; but the King's prerogative is law, and the principal part of law, the first-born or 'pars prima' of the law; and therefore in conserving or maintaining that, you conserve and maintain the law."[48] Here Bacon, who occupied almost every high legal office in England during the reigns of Elizabeth I (1533–1603, r. 1558–1603) and James I (1566–1625, r. 1603–1625), takes a clear stand in what was already a fraught political debate in England over the rights of Parliament versus those of the monarch. By the 1640s this controversy would erupt into civil war, and only in the Bill of Rights of 1689 would the King's "power of dispensing with and suspending of laws and the execution of laws without consent of Parliament" finally be declared to be "utterly and directly contrary to the known laws and statutes and freedom of this realm."[49] But in 1617, Bacon could still assert that royal prerogative, the power of the monarch to override statute law, was not only consistent with the law; it *was* the law.

The twentieth-century German political theorist Carl Schmitt (1888–1985) famously defined sovereignty as the power to decide on the exception. Schmitt was adamant that the exception, which arises in times of "extreme peril," cannot "be codified in the existing legal order." Unlike casuistry, which tests one rule against another, or equity, which bends the letter of the law to conform to its spirit, the state of exception proclaimed by the sovereign breaks with rules altogether.[50] In Schmitt's modern totalitarian version, the sovereign wields "unlimited authority," which was never the case for even the most sweeping pre-modern doctrines of prerogative. Even absolutist monarchs were held to be answerable to natural law and to God, who sanctified their rule.[51] Nonetheless, Schmitt's twentieth-century state of exception and Bacon's seventeenth-century royal prerogative both defined themselves against a legal order purged of all exceptions and arbitrariness. Schmitt, writing from a modern perspective, identified this serene vision of universal legality with Enlightenment natural law. But early modern writers on the question of sovereignty looked back to the republicanism of ancient Rome in search of an alternative ideal of law and freedom. For them, the poles that staked out the range of positions were, at one extreme, the Roman imperial doctrine of *legibus solutus* (the emperor is not bound by law) revived in sixteenth-century defenses of absolutism and, at the other extreme, the Roman republican doctrine that to be subject to the arbitrary decisions of a ruler, no matter how benevolent, amounted to slavery.[52] However defined, the power to declare an exception lies at the heart of modern political theory: who can break, not just bend the rules?

This question was not merely of academic interest for early modern European thinkers such as Bacon, Jean Bodin (1530–1596), Thomas Hobbes, Locke, and Robert Filmer (1588–1653), not to mention the monarchs who ruled them. Contesting the legitimacy of particular kings and queens, often on the battlefield, was hardly a novelty in the sixteenth and seventeenth centuries. What was new was a sustained challenge to the legitimacy of monarchy itself, especially to its prerogative powers to abrogate law and custom. Treatises and pamphlets, sermons and speeches debated these questions fiercely and consequentially: these were ideas that ignited civil wars, reformed constitutions, triggered repression, and ultimately brought into existence modern political ideals that narrowed once sweeping prerogative powers—the Rule of Law that Schmitt so detested.

FIGURE 8.1. *The Father in the Circle of His Family, Represented as the Possessor of Patriarchal Power* (c. 1599), from Hans Fehr, *Das Recht im Bilde* [Law in images, 1923], fig. 195.

Sovereignty flowed from three mutually reinforcing sources in the political traditions inherited by early modern Europe: divine authority, the patriarchal power of the male head of household over his wife and children, and the power of the conqueror over the vanquished in war. In his treatise *Patriarcha, or the Natural Power of Kings* (comp. 1620–42, publ. 1680), arch-royalist Filmer traced a continuous line from God's grant of dominion over the earth to Adam down to the reigning monarchs all over the world. As the title of the work indicates, divine right mirrored paternal authority: the "subjection of Children being the Fountain of all Regal Authority, by the Ordination of God himself," which Filmer interpreted as a direct refutation to the claim that the form of government derived from "the Choice of the people," who no more chose their governments than children did their parents.[53] (Fig. 8.1.) Bodin, professor of law at Toulouse and member of the parliament of Paris, also emphasized the origins of kingship in patriarchy, including wife as well as children among those subject to absolute paternal will. Indeed, Bodin asserted that the ultimate source of all authority in human institutions was the subjection of wife to husband, ratified by "all laws divine and human" and by nature itself, because the *pater familias* was "the true image of the great sovereign God, universal father of all things."[54] These tight links between paternal and royal prerogative allowed Bacon to argue that submission to a king as "a father, or chief of a family" was "more natural and simple" than submission to laws.[55] Both Bodin and Filmer upheld the King's power of prerogative to suspend the law as intrinsic to the very definition of sovereignty, unlimited in "either power, or charge, or time" (Bodin), and justified "upon Causes only known to him" (Filmer).[56] When King James I, whom Bacon served, asserted to a fractious English Parliament in 1610 that kings were "God's lieutenants upon earth," "*parens patriae*, the politic father of his people," and therefore empowered to "make and unmake their subjects," he was ringing the changes on familiar themes.[57]

Notably absent from the works of Bodin and Filmer and even the haughty speeches of James I was the third and most ancient source of legitimation of unrestricted royal prerogative by right of conquest, although its contemporary relevance remained undiminished. Early modern monarchs exercised sovereignty in its name both in the Old and New Worlds to an unprecedented degree, whether over the Spanish Netherlands under the Habsburgs or Mexico under the conquistadors. Moreover, the absolute power of the conqueror was increasingly invoked to defend slavery during this period, especially in New World colonies. As secretary of the Proprietors of Carolina and author of the Constitution of Carolina, Locke explicitly countenanced the institution of slavery and also defended it in his *Second Treatise on Government* (1690) as a more merciful way of dealing with "captives taken in a just and lawful war" than killing them outright.[58] Yet it was precisely this dangerous proximity to slavery that contaminated the argument from conquest as a justification for royal prerogative to break with law and custom. Because Locke was the strongest voice on *both* sides of this argument, invoking the right of conquest to defend the despotical rule of master over slave but opposing the same power of king over subject as tyrannical, he is a telling witness to shifting early modern attitudes toward the power of exception.

At the heart of Locke's position on both slavery and royal prerogative was an ideal of freedom ultimately derived from Roman republicanism but greatly invigorated by debates among early modern political philosophers.[59] Centered on the ancient Roman distinction between freemen and slaves, the republican ideal of freedom was essentially negative: not a freedom to do something but a freedom *from* something—or rather someone. Whether exercised by master or monarch, despotical power was "an absolute arbitrary power one man has over another, to take away his life, whenever he pleases." As historian Quentin Skinner has emphasized, the key word in Locke's definition is not the power over life and death but "arbitrary." Even if the master is the very model of benevolence and the probability that the slave will be killed or maltreated negligible, the mere fact of being subject to the whims of another person is unbearable. Bound by no rules, there is nothing to prevent the master suddenly turning cruel or just capricious. The slave cannot know if or when kindness might curdle into brutality. It is the freedom from this very specific form of psychological uncertainty that Locke and other republican thinkers enshrined: not freedom from uncertainty per se—freeman and slave alike were at the mercy of the vicissitudes of disease, foul weather, and other natural misfortunes—but freedom from the uncertainty of the human will, its weathercock whims and caprices. So fundamental is this "*freedom* from absolute, arbitrary power" that no one can by "his own consent, enslave himself to anyone, nor put himself under the absolute, arbitrary power of another, to take away his life, when he pleases." No freeman is free to renounce his own freedom voluntarily. As the similarity of wording testifies, only a hair's breadth separated illegitimate tyranny from legitimate slavery, and that fine distinction rested for Locke on the right of conquest, carefully hedged in by qualifications concerning just wars, the sacrosanct status of property, and protection of the children of slaves.[60]

It is against this background that seventeenth-century polemics concerning the sovereign power to declare an exception to all rules must be understood. In contrast to Schmitt, who took aim at the liberal Enlightenment natural law tradition as the enemy of sovereign prerogative, Bodin, Filmer, and other early modern absolutists were battling republican and social contract theories of restricted royal rule. Their opponents, unlike Schmitt's, were often contradicting rather than affirming one or another tenet of natural law. On the side of wide-reaching sovereign prerogative, Bodin and Filmer saw no contradiction in appealing to natural law (what could be more natural than the family, they queried). Schmitt for his part had no truck whatsoever with the biblical and patriarchal defenses of sovereignty so favored by Bodin and Filmer. On the side of narrowed prerogative, Locke and other republicans exalted freedom from the arbitrary will of a despot, whereas natural law theorists like Pufendorf and Leibniz argued that it ill-befitted the dignity and wisdom of the monarch to disturb the constant order of the kingdom.

To return to the seventeenth-century debates over laws of nature discussed in Chapter 7, the early modern republicans emphasized the ruler's power and its abuses; the natural law theorists emphasized wisdom and its dictates. There were, in short, mismatches between early modern and modern positions on all fronts, even though the conclusions of Schmitt on the sovereign power of exception might resemble those of Bodin and Filmer, just as the countervailing conclusions of Locke might resemble those of Leibniz and Pufendorf. The justifications for these positions, however, diverged widely. The one point at which both early modern and modern debates in political theory converged was the crucial question of whether anyone should have the power to declare an exception not just to this or that law but to suspend the rule of law altogether.

The protracted and bitter disputes between Crown and Parliament over royal prerogative in the first half of the seventeenth century, ultimately exploding into civil war and the temporary abolition of the monarchy, turned England into the arena for the sharpest clashes over the question of exception. Conflicts over royal power to levy taxes unilaterally under James I and imprisonment without charge under Charles I (1600–1649, r. 1625–1649) pitted those who held royal prerogative to be "too high to come under the roof of the *Law*" against those who feared that subjects would be "exposed to an unbounded *Arbitrary power*, so that they never know an end of their own obeying." Sir Edward Coke (1552–1634), who as Chief Justice had already crossed swords with the crown over the precedence of Chancery over the courts of common law, opined that though "Prerogative is highly tendered and respected of the Law, yet it hath bounds set unto it by the Laws of England"—in this case, the right of habeas corpus guaranteed by the Magna Carta.[61] Royalists retorted that "the King be onely and immediately dependent from God, and independent from the Body of the People."[62]

Framed by these debates, Locke's mature position on royal prerogative curiously complemented his stance on the slave master's despotical power. Whereas *subjective* uncertainty made the condition of the slave intolerable, *objective* uncertainty rationalized the exercise of prerogative. Royal prerogative was "nothing but power, in the hands of the prince, to provide for the public good, in such cases, which depending upon unforeseen and uncertain occurrences, certain and unalterable laws could not safely direct." When overtaken "by the uncertainty and variableness of human affairs," the sovereign was rightly empowered to put the public good before the law.[63] Locke's rationale was the familiar one offered by philosophers since Plato and Aristotle: no rule, no law, was proof against the vicissitudes of particulars.

No legislator could foresee all future eventualities; therefore all laws ran up against exceptions. Viewed from this perspective, executive prerogative became the extreme version of equity. (Fig. 8.2.)

FIGURE 8.2. Justice armed with a sword against malefactors and a scale
tipped in favor of equity over iniquity (Samuel de Rameru, *Justitia*, 1652).
© Musée d'art et d'histoire, Ville de Genève, photograph: Yves Siza.

Just as equity intervened in unusual cases to save the courts from
committing injustice, prerogative intervened in a general emergency to save the polity from disaster. In both cases, circumstances
unforeseen by the rule required action that bent or broke the rule.
In the absence of rules or even the rule of law, Locke believed that
the principle of *salus populi lex suprema* ("the welfare of the people
is the highest law") still checked royal prerogative from degenerat-
ing into tyranny—but only in principle. Locke insisted that prerogative must serve public, not private, good but implicitly left it
up to royal discretion to decide in practice when to declare a state
of exception and decide wherein the public good lay. No rules
could be given to oversee when and how rules could be legiti-
mately broken without an infinite regress of rules, meta-rules,
meta-meta-rules, and so on. At some point, executive discretion
must put an end to the series, and that point cannot be foreseen.

The same uncertainty that made the exercise of absolute power incompatible with freedom when exercised by master over slave gave the monarch unfettered royal prerogative when events capsized all reasonable expectations. No rule escaped its exceptions.

In the limiting case, at least for seventeenth-century theorists of prerogative, the parallel lines of the uncertainty of events and that of royal discretion converged in the unfathomable will of God, which dictated the one and authorized the other. Historians of political thought, including Schmitt, have remarked upon how closely debates over God's freedom and wisdom, such as the exchange between Samuel Clarke and Gottfried Wilhelm Leibniz described in Chapter 7, tracked coeval debates over royal prerogative and the rule of law waged by Locke, Filmer, and others.[64] What a miracle was to nature, governed by laws of nature, prerogative became to the polity, governed by natural law: an intolerable exception to rules that held everywhere and always. For Schmitt, this vision of universal legality was the metaphysical foundation of the liberal constitutionalism he so detested, and for that reason he excoriated what he called the "political theology" of Leibniz and Nicolas Malebranche. Yet his own position owed more than he admitted to the background assumptions of universal legality, which in principle eliminated the uncertainty around which early modern debates over sovereignty revolved. By the early twentieth century, Schmitt no longer needed to appeal to uncertainty to ground the state of exception; instead, he framed exception in terms of "unlimited authority, which means the suspension of the entire existing order."[65] But authority is meaningless without efficacy, which in turn implies an order of command and execution nearly as reliable as that of cause and effect in nature. Schmitt rejected this Leibnizian analogy between the divine machine of natural law and the machinery of the state, but in the end, his dictator, all impassioned will and agency, was impotent without the rational bureaucracy of rules Schmitt so loathed—as Schmitt, a member of the Nazi Party, witnessed when Adolf Hitler mobilized the efficient German bureaucracy to his own totalitarian ends after 1933.

It is precisely such rational bureaucracies that in modern times have gradually nibbled away at the power of exception. In Great Britain, the sovereign's prerogative to dissolve Parliament, already merely ceremonial by the nineteenth century, was officially abrogated by the Fixed Term Parliaments Act of 2011; the power of granting pardons is now exercised by the Secretary of State of Justice with no direct involvement of the monarch. The one remaining shred of what were once vast powers of prerogative is the sovereign's full discretion to grant certain honors, such as membership in the Order of the Garter.[66] Similarly in the United States, the power of presidential pardon for federal crimes, the one prerogative power granted by the Constitution and explicitly modeled on royal prerogative, has since 1865 been largely in the hands of the Pardon Clerk (after 1891, Pardon Attorney) within the office of the Attorney General.[67] Even in the absence of explicit rules, institutions and procedures have for the most part replaced the exercise of executive discretion to make exceptions, whether in the name of mercy or survival.

For the most part. Exceptions cannot be entirely banned, even by the routinized modern state, for reasons Locke and his interlocutors would have recognized all too well. Politics may have become predictable enough to fix a rule for when to assemble and dissolve Parliament—for Locke, the prototypical example of why royal prerogative was needed because of the "uncertainty and variableness of human affairs"—and to delegate decisions concerning clemency to experienced lawyers guided by precedent and consistency. Yet new emergencies, whether in the form of terrorist attacks or pandemics, have widened executive discretion and state powers to suspend laws; recent pardons in both the Clinton and Trump administrations have been granted purely on grounds of presidential preferences, in defiance of precedent and procedure.[68] Despite the enormous gains in stability and predictability achieved by at least some modern polities, not least through regulations and the rule of law, the uncertainties of circumstance and caprice still overwhelm the rules from time to time, and no system of rules, no matter how circumspect and far-sighted, has ever been able to do without exceptions.

Conclusion: Which Came First, the Rule or the Exception?

Historian Carlo Ginzburg, reflecting on Schmitt's definition of the state of exception, summarizes its premise: "Exceptions include the norms, not the other way around."[69] This is true enough of the rules that began to emerge in the late seventeenth and eighteenth centuries: explicit, rigid rules enunciated without equivocation or extenuation. An exception to such a rule defines a sharp boundary and therefore contains the rule as a property line contains the land it circumscribes. Not all rigid rules are thin rules, as we saw in Chapter 6, but both thin and rigid rules presume such boundaries to mark out their domains of application. For both, a fixed, stable context is the *sine qua non* of their validity. To recognize an exception as such is ipso facto to recognize the rule it contradicts—and, implicitly, also the *kind* of rule that can be so clearly bounded by its exceptions.

As the foregoing chapters in this book have shown, not all rules fit this description. Rules conceived as models to imitate or guidelines to follow encompassed variability in their very formulation. Examples, experience, and exceptions thickened these rules in precept and rendered them supple in practice. In a world of large fluctuations and low predictability, exceptions were the rule, in every sense: they occurred so often that rules incorporated them. Improvisation, adjustment, and adaptation to circumstances were taken for granted. The art of making rules consisted in building in enough give to accommodate every circumstance that could be foreseen and quite a few that couldn't. Rules for governing monastic communities or teaching musical composition or perfecting the mechanical arts anticipated their own incompleteness. These thick, expansive rules included their exceptions, not the other way around.

This book has traced a historical arc that partially justifies the distinction between pre-modern and modern rules, but only partially. The chronological terms *pre-modern* and *modern* distract from the underlying preconditions of stability and standardization that are more domain- than period-specific. Wherever pockets of predictability and uniformity emerge, thick rules can be slimmed down into thin rules; flexible rules (as all thick rules must be) can stiffen into rigid ones. As we have seen in previous chapters and especially in this one, no rule is so thin or rigid to eliminate the need for discretion altogether, not even computer algorithms. But in an artificially stabilized world, the margin of discretion can be and has been significantly narrowed. Enormous efforts of technical know-how, political will, and cultural imagination must be invested to create and sustain such islands of ruliness. The lazy abbreviation "modernity" embraces a vast array of globe-spanning projects that have standardized everything from weights to time zones, clothing sizes to airport designs. International bureaus and regulatory bodies, their headquarters often discreetly located in the cities of small, neutral countries, oversee the largely invisible machinery that delivers the post or monitors epidemics or inspects nuclear reactors worldwide. They enforce the background rules that make thin rules possible.

But this machinery is neither perfect nor invulnerable nor even truly global. It reaches only as far as human will and foresight extend. Miscalculation and misfortune—in the form of an epidemic, a nuclear reactor accident, a wildfire—can still wreak havoc in the world's most thoroughly modern cities. When the background conditions for thin, rigid rules suddenly collapse, thick, flexible rules return, no matter what the epoch. Even in calmer times, thick rules persist wherever variability is either inevitable or desirable—for example, in individualized medicine or in teaching. While it is true that thin rules have proliferated in many domains since the eighteenth century, many thick rules have crept in through the back door, dragging discretion along with them. Bureaucratic rules followed to the letter are so cumbersome as to amount to a form of strike: "work to rule." Legions of lawyers and accountants have sprung up to interpret the cut-and-dried rules of the tax code. Computer algorithms, the thinnest rules of all, require an anonymous army of human monitors to correct their oversights and excesses on social media platforms. Behind every thin rule is a thick rule cleaning up after it.

EPILOGUE

More Honored in the Breach

"We have no rule book." As I write these words at the end of 2020 in the midst of a worldwide pandemic, I have lost count of the number of times doctors, nurses, public health officials, scientists, politicians, and the rest of us have intoned this sentence like a dirge. It is not that we are living in a rule vacuum. On the contrary, we are pelted with rules, new and different ones every week: rules about keeping our distance and just how much distance, when and where to wear masks, whether and for what reason to leave the house, who should and should not go to school or work, whom we may greet in person and whom only in the pallid medium of video conferencing, under what circumstances it is permissible to gather, indoors or outdoors. Almost everyone acknowledges that we need rules in order to deal with the current emergency; indeed, we long for them, those sturdy guard rails that keep our lives on track. But in a state of uncertainty, in which knowledge and circumstances mutate even faster than the virus, the rules change so quickly as to undermine all rules. We are living in the breach.

When Hamlet remarked that the Danish custom of making a racket to applaud the king's drunken toasts was "more honoured in the breach than in the observance" (*Hamlet*, I.4), he was expressing contempt for the custom. But resonant phrases, especially Shakespearean ones, have a way of taking on a life of their own, and this one has come to mean that a rule can be even more emphatically affirmed by its exceptions than by its observance. Both the long history of rules traced in this book and the current experience of living without a rulebook suggest that the 180-degree turn of Hamlet's phrase is not an accident. The exception does prove the rule, in the double sense of both testing and confirming it. Rules don't simply have exceptions; they define and are defined by their exceptions, as right defines left and as fence defines breach.

Context choreographs the *pas de deux* between rules and their exceptions. Rules formulated to guide practice in situations in which the unexpected is the expected, whether in running a monastery or besieging a city, build in examples and exceptions, as we saw in Chapters 2 and 3. These thick rules are prepared to deal with any and all eventualities. Rules formulated for more stable, standardized circumstances, whether applying an algorithm to a routine calculation or setting speed limits for city streets, barely mention exceptions. Such would-be thin rules flourish in the same settings that averages do: where what happened in the past is a reliable guide to what will happen in the present and future. As we saw in Chapters 4, 5, and 6, an immense amount of infrastructure, both human and material, goes into making the world safe for thin rules. Workflows for calculations; sidewalks and broad, straight streets for city traffic; schooling and sanctions for everyone. Even under the most propitious circumstances, in which rules are so effectively drilled into schoolchildren that a slight change can provoke a national wave of protest, as in the case of orthography, rules must be constantly shored up by the editor's red pencil and the demon spellchecker. The court of equity in English law (Chapter 8) or the dictionary of the Académie française (Chapter 6), both venerable institutions established to adjudicate between rules and their exceptions, offer eloquent testimony to the fact that exceptions we shall always have with us.

There is, however, a vast difference between exceptions, boon companions of all rules, and states of exception, the suspension of rules altogether. States of exception substitute the prerogative of the ruler for the rule, whether in the form of the divine miracle that violates natural law (Chapter 7) or the head of state who waives the rule of law in an emergency or in a pardon (Chapter 8). In such situations, discretion soars to a maximum; predictability correspondingly plunges to a minimum. Unlimited discretion has stirred uneasiness since at least Aristotle, but thick rules depended on this faculty. One historical arc traced by this book is how the evolution from thicker to thinner rules has in part been driven by growing distrust of discretion, variously impugned as arbitrary, capricious, inconsistent, unpredictable, unfair, opaque, self-serving, and even tyrannical. More precisely, low tolerance for discretion indexes rampant distrust in society: governments that don't trust their citizens to decide where it's safe to park or whether to report lottery winnings on their taxes; citizens who don't trust their governments to treat rich and poor alike or not to pocket bribes and fees. Under these circumstances, all exceptions become suspect, and states of exception most of all.

Yet dramatic breaches of natural and social order are not the only way to loosen the hold of rules. More effective in the long run is to change rules so frequently and so drastically that none can take hold in the first place: rule vertigo. Miracles and emergencies are by definition flashes in the pan. If the Red Sea had remained forever parted after the safe passage of the Israelites it would have become just another natural attraction; an emergency that stretches on for years becomes the way we live now. Yesterday's showy exceptions eventually become today's rules with the passage of time. In contrast, rule vertigo undermines the very idea of a rule if it persists too long. If yesterday's rule becomes tomorrow's exception, then no rule can harden into habit or solidify as norm. The galloping pace of fashion doomed the medieval and early modern sumptuary regulations that tried to discourage extravagance; conversely, it took well over a century of stubborn persistence on the part of the Parisian authorities, who issued and reissued the same sanitation regulations over and over again, to entrench rules in everyday conduct (Chapter 6). Rules succeed best when they make themselves superfluous, when stopping at a red light or queueing up to board a bus or plane becomes second nature, a long-term process. As politicians charged with containing a pandemic in dynamic circumstances have discovered, the faster rules change, the weaker the hold of any rule, no matter how urgently promulgated. Rules in general begin to decay, a graver threat to order than any short-lived state of exception.

How can rules cope with variability, instability, and change without losing their grip? Each of the three ancient meanings of rules as model, algorithm, or law (Chapter 1) points to a different strategy. Laws come in many shapes and sizes, from local regulations teeming with specifics to august natural laws proclaimed for all of humanity. But whether general or specific, the more closely laws themselves imitate the permanence and predictability they aim to create, the stronger their normative authority, even if enforcement is sporadic and sanctions are mild. Fundamental or constitutional law profits from this insight by ensuring that amendments are few and far between. Legislation too often altered sows uncertainty about what the rules are, much less how to follow them. When times change or laws conflict or exceptions crop up, formidable argumentative resources of equity, casuistry, analogy, precedent, and prerogative are mustered to stretch existing law to fit the unforeseen case (Chapters 6, 7, and 8).

Algorithms escape context by ignoring it. Mathematical problems contain only those details needed to solve them, no more and no less. Observatories, census bureaus, and banks standardized Big Calculation in the same way that factories standardized mass manufacturing in the nineteenth century: by making the work mechanical, with or without machines (Chapters 4 and 5). But context, with all of its disruptive details and special cases, inevitably creeps back in, as legions of behind-the-screens human workers who must repair the errors made and damage wrought by algorithms online know. Machine learning algorithms that work impressively well in development stages can be thwarted in practice by the most minute changes in input data. Making the world safe for algorithms turns out to mean freezing context: a world without anomalies or surprises.

And models? In the end, the one ancient meaning of rules that seemed to go extinct around 1800 may prove to be the most enduring. Rules-as-models are the most supple, nimble rules of all, as supple and nimble as human learning. Whether the model was the abbot of a monastery or the artwork by a master or even the paradigmatic problem in a mathematics textbook, it could be endlessly adapted as circumstances demanded (Chapters 2, 3, and 4). In an age of exact copies, whether churned out on the assembly line or spread online as viral images, imitation has come to mean mindless imitation. But wherever traditions or simply genres exist, whether in the sciences or the arts, whether the elegy or the still life, imitation-without-copying perpetuates the lineage without fossilizing it. Just as in the case of a living language, rules can be formulated for how to construct a grammatical sentence, write a play, compose a symphony, conduct a laboratory experiment. Yet following models remains a more efficient and flexible way to learn than following explicit rules—even for those activities that are the most rule-bound, like playing chess. Moreover, models as implicit rules pave the way for explicit rules, just as a grammatical paradigm of the conjugation of a specific verb paves the way for an explicit general rule of conjugation. A well-chosen model—a paradigm, to remain with grammar—is already halfway to a generalization. Models bridge the ancient philosophical opposition between universal and particulars, rules and cases. And they circumvent the modern philosophical problem of how to interpret rules unambiguously altogether: ambiguity in a model is a feature, not a bug.

Why then did rules-as-models not only disappear but become downright paradoxical by the mid-twentieth century? The implicit rules of models hardly ever existed apart from explicit rules; for the most part, they worked together to regularize and refine practice (Chapter 3). One way of rephrasing the question is, under what circumstances do explicit rules no longer need the support of implicit ones? One answer—Wittgenstein's answer—is, never: even the most apparently straightforward, unambiguous rules— algorithmic rules such as how to continue a numerical series—

cannot evade interpretation. Wittgenstein's solution was in essence to reinvent implicit rules: rules as customs or institutions—in other words, rules-as-models. But this philosophical response, however valid, begs the historical question: why did it ever come to *seem* that explicit rules could do without implicit ones? This book's answer has been that success—slow, fitful, fragile, partial but real—in creating islands of uniformity, stability, and predictability fostered the dream of rules without exceptions, without equivocations, without elasticity. Both the mechanical algorithms of Chapter 5 and the natural laws of Chapter 7 were versions of this dream of rules that followed themselves, everywhere, always. The models that mediated between rules and the unruly world could be kicked away like the scaffolding from a completed building.

These dream worlds have never been fully realized, but in some places, at some times they were approximated. From standardized cooking measurements to the rule of law, from street safety to reliable statistical projections, parts of the world have become rulier—easier to govern by rules because less unruly. So impressive were these partial successes that approximation was mistaken for perfection, the mistake that Wittgenstein's problem lays bare. But it is a problem that would not have occurred to Aristotle, or even Kant, both of whom wrestled with the more ancient philosophical problem about rules: how to square universals and particulars. It took a transformation in ideas about what rules could be—explicit, exacting, unqualified, and unequivocal—to generate the first new philosophical problem about rules in over two thousand years.

The two philosophical problems about rules, ancient and modern, are still very much our problems, as this book has tried to show. But the same historical circumstances that gave rise to the second, modern problem have greatly hampered solutions to both. Explicit rules not only pushed out rules-as-models; they also made the cognitive skills needed to follow rules-as-models—or almost any rules—suspect. Discretion, judgment, and reasoning by analogy, all faculties required to select which rule suits each case and to tailor the rule for a better fit, are in danger of slipping into the murky regions inhabited by intuition, instinct, and inspiration, all opaque to critical scrutiny. Worse, the faculties that save explicit rules from themselves can appear both unfair and irrational. Bureaucratic rules define fairness as treating everyone alike, regardless of circumstances. Their notorious rigidity stems from the fact that any deviation from uniform application counts as prima facie evidence of corruption, not wise discretion. Like modern ideals of fairness, rationality itself has become a matter of explicit rules, mechanically applied. The fact that the forms of reasoning needed to rescue explicit rules from exceptions and equivocations cannot themselves be spelled out as explicit rules renders them ipso facto irrational. Irrational, but also necessary: hardly a rule can be applied without discretion, judgment, and analogy.

Enemies of rules chafe against the restrictions that rules impose. Good sense seems thwarted at every turn; new and better ways of doing things are strangled by red tape; mechanical rules enforced by actual machines make no allowances for the natural diversity of persons and circumstances. Who has not cursed at an obdurate computer program or online algorithm, well knowing that we curse in vain? Yet every rule, no matter how rigid, no matter how cut-and-dried, is also an occasion for covert rule reasoning. Every time we seek to follow (or evade) a rule, we are honing the very faculties explicit rules banished: judgment, discretion, analogy. Which rule applies best to this case? Must it be tweaked to fit better? What exactly does the rule stipulate? Should the spirit or the letter of the rule take precedence? In normal times, our judgments about such matters are so swift and sure as to be invisible to us. But in abnormal times, when we are thrown into the breach without a rulebook, we once again become aware that there are no rules to help us reason about rules.

ACKNOWLEDGMENTS

This book began as the Lawrence Stone Lectures delivered in 2014 at Princeton University, under the auspices of the Shelby Cullom Davis Center. I am most grateful to all who extended their hospitality, both intellectual and creaturely, on that occasion and especially to the then–director of the Davis Center, Philip Nord. Brigitta van Rheinberg, then Editorial Director of the Humanities at Princeton University Press, gave welcome encouragement to expand the lectures into a book that would be learned but lucid, scholarly but not specialized, of interest to a wide range of disciplines but accessible to the general reader. Fulfilling that charge proved a lengthier undertaking than either I or Princeton University Press anticipated, and I thank all concerned for their patience as I galloped off into one province after another of the endless realm of rules.

As I struggled to rein in both the topic and my curiosity, many interlocutors came to my rescue with suggestions, comments, criticisms, and stern injunctions not to write the Universal Key to All Mythologies. I am grateful to all of those who listened so attentively to various versions of what became the chapters of this book. Colleagues at three institutions in particular suffered through presentations of draft after draft, year after year, and their responses improved almost every page: the Max Planck Institute for the History of Science (MPIWG), the University of Chicago, and the Wissenschaftskolleg zu Berlin. I owe a particular debt to the members of the MPIWG Cold War Rationality Working

Group, where the idea of a history of rules first germinated, and to the participants of an MPIWG workshop, co-organized with David Sepkoski, on "The Intelligence of Algorithms," for mind-stretching discussions.

Conversations with Anna Maria Busse Berger about memorization practices in medieval music and arithmetic, Karine Chemla about mathematical generalization without algebra, Angela Creager on the snares and pitfalls of government regulation, Wendy Doniger about *dharma*, Gerd Gigerenzer about artificial intelligence, Michael Gordin about formalism in logic and linguistics, Jens Høyrup about what makes a mathematical problem paradigmatic, Susan Nieman about Kant and casuistry, Katja Krause about Aquinas and discretion, and Gianna Pomata about cases and caprice reoriented my thinking on these topics, and I thank each of them most heartily. I am also indebted to three anonymous referees who offered valuable suggestions on the style and content of the penultimate version of the manuscript, to which I hope the final version does justice.

Without the gracious assistance of the librarians and archivists at the MPIWG, the University of Chicago, the Schlesinger Library at Harvard University, the Observatoire de Paris, the Archives de l'Académie des Sciences, and the Cambridge University Library, this book could not have been written. Marius Bunzel, Luise Römer, and Molly Ludlam-Steinke were resourceful research assistants; Josephine Fenger helped to secure image permissions and prepare the final manuscript with care and perseverance. Eric Crahan and his colleagues at Princeton University Press shepherded the book from gleam in the editor's eye to ink on the page with remarkable professionalism and good humor, even in the trying circumstances of the pandemic. Martin Schneider's sharp-eyed copyediting saved me from many an inconsistency and infelicity. My warmest thanks to all.

This book is dedicated to Wendy Doniger, scholar *extraordinaire* and great-souled friend, who urged me on when I faltered, shared my delight over a serendipitous find in the library or archive, chided me when I succumbed to the distraction of writing or lecturing on any other topic, supplied endless examples and counter-examples from her own vast stores of erudition in Sanskrit and B-movies, and gave the book's epilogue its title—which could also serve as her own motto.

NOTES

Unless otherwise noted, all translations are my own.

Chapter 1. Introduction: The Hidden History of Rules

1. Herodotus, *The History*, trans. David Grene (Chicago: University of Chicago Press, 1987), II.35, 145.

2. Ludwig Hoffmann, *Mathematisches Wörterbuch*, 7 vols. (Berlin: Wiegandt und Hempel, 1858–1867).

3. Matthew L. Jones, *Reckoning with Matter: Calculating Machines, Innovation, and Thinking about Thinking from Pascal to Babbage* (Chicago: University of Chicago Press, 2016), 13–40.

4. For overviews on various aspects of this history, see Ivor Grattan-Guiness, *The Search for Mathematical Roots, 1870–1940: Logic, Set Theory, and the Foundations of Mathematics from Cantor through Russell Russell to Gödel* (Princeton: Princeton University Press, 2000); Martin Campbell-Kelly, William Aspray, Nathan Ensmenger, and Jeffrey R. Yost, *Computer: A History of the Information Machine*, 3rd ed. (Boulder, Colo.: Westview Press, 2014); David Berlinski, *The Advent of the Algorithm: The 300-Year Journey from an Idea to the Computer* (New York: Harcourt, 2000).

5. I. Bernard Cohen, "Howard Aiken on the Number of Computers Needed for the Nation," *IEEE Annals of the History of Computing* 20 (1998): 27–32.

6. Jorge Luis Borges, "Pierre Menard, Author of the *Quixote*" (1941), in *Collected Fictions*, trans. Andrew Hurley (London: Penguin, 1998), 88–95.

7. Robert J. Richards and Lorraine Daston, "Introduction," in *Kuhn's "Structure of Scientific Revolutions" at Fifty: Reflections on a Scientific Classic*, ed. Robert J. Richards and Lorraine Daston (Chicago: University of Chicago Press, 2016), 1–11.

8. Margaret Masterman, "The Nature of a Paradigm, " in *Criticism and the Growth of Knowledge*, ed. Imré Lakatos and Alan Musgrave (Cambridge: Cambridge University Press, 1970), 59–89.

9. Thomas S. Kuhn, *The Structure of Scientific Revolutions* (1962), 4th ed. (Chicago: University of Chicago Press, 2012), 174, 191.

10. Ian Hacking, "Paradigms," in *Kuhn's "Structure of Scientific Revolutions"* ed. Richards and Daston, 99.

11. Ludwig Wittgenstein, *Philosophical Investigations* (1953), trans. G.E.M. Anscombe, 3rd ed. (Englewood Cliffs, N.J.: Prentice Hall, 1958), §199, 81.

12. Herbert Oppel, *KANΩN: Zur Bedeutungsgeschichte des Wortes und seiner lateinischen Entsprechungen (Regula-Norma)* (Leipzig: Dietrich'sche Verlagsbuchhandlung, 1937), 41.

13. Pliny the Elder, *Natural History*, trans. H. Rackham, Loeb Classical Library (Cambridge, Mass.: Harvard University Press, 1952), 34.55, 168–69.

14. Dionysius of Halicarnassus, *Commentaries on the Attic Orators*, Lys. 2; quoted in Oppel, *KANΩN*, 45.

15. [Chevalier de Jaucourt], "RÈGLE, MODÈLE (*Synon.*)," in *Encyclopédie, ou Dictionnaire raisonné des sciences, des arts et des métiers*, ed. Denis Diderot and Jean d'Alembert (Lausanne/Berne: Les sociétés typographiques, 1780), 28:116–17.

16. Claudius Galen, *De temperamentis libri III*, ed. Georg Helmreich (Leipzig: B. G. Teubner, 1904), I.9, 36; Sachiko Kusukawa, *Picturing the Book of Nature: Image, Text, and Argument in Sixteenth-Century Human Anatomy and Medical Body* (Chicago: University of Chicago Press, 2012), 213–18.

17. Oppel, *KANΩN*, 17–20, 32, 67. There is, however, at least one significant novelty in the usage of the Latin regula in connection with Roman law, in which the word was used by jurists of the first century CE to collect ancient legal decisions into a general precept or proverb, some two hundred of which were appended to the Justinian *Digest* under the rubric *De diversis regulis juris antiqui*. See Heinz Ohme, *Kanon ekklesiastikos: Die Bedeutung des altkirchlichen Kanonbegriffs* (Berlin: Walter De Gruyter, 1998), 51–55.

18. Immanuel Kant, *Erste Einleitung in die Kritik der Urteilskraft* (1790) ed. Gerhard Lehmann (Hamburg: Felix Meiner Verlag, 1990), 16.

19. Paul Erikson, Judy L. Klein, Lorraine Daston, Rebecca Lemov, Thomas Sturm, and Michael D. Gordin, *How Reason Almost Lost Its Mind: The Strange Career of Cold War Rationality* (Chicago: University of Chicago Press, 2013), 1–26. See also Edward F. McClennen, "The Rationality of Being Guided by Rules," in *The Oxford Handbook of Rationality*, ed. Alfred R. Mele and Piers Rawling (New York: Oxford University Press, 2004), 222–39.

20. Catherine Kovesi Killerby, *Sumptuary Law in Italy, 1200–1500* (Oxford: Clarendon Press, 2002), 120.

21. This long and still-ongoing debate is epitomized by the literature on modernization theory. For classic statements of the opposing views, see Walter W. Rostow, *The Stages of Economic Growth: A Non-Communist Manifesto* (Cambridge: Cambridge University Press, 1960); and James C. Scott, *Seeing Like a State: How Certain*

Schemes to Improve the Human Condition Have Failed (New Haven: Yale University Press, 1998).

22. Barry Bozeman, *Bureaucracy and Red Tape* (Upper Saddle River, N.J.: Prentice Hall, 2000), 185–86.

23. The work-to-rule slowdown (*Streik nach Vorschrift* in German, *grève du zèle* in French, *sciopero bianco* in Italian) is especially favored by public officials who are often forbidden to strike, as in the case of the West German postal workers who paralyzed the country in this fashion in 1962 or the French jurists who did so in 2010.

24. Gerd Gigerenzer, *How to Stay Smart in a Smart World* (London: Penguin, 2022), 58-66.

25. On the meanings of *historia*, see Gianna Pomata and Nancy G. Siraisi, "Introduction," in *Historia: Empiricism and Erudition in Early Modern Europe,* ed. Gianna Pomata and Nancy G. Siraisi (Cambridge, Mass.: MIT Press, 2005), 1–38.

Chapter 2. Ancient Rules: Straightedges, Models, and Laws

1. See for example the Hebrew Bible: "They lavish gold out of the bag, and weigh silver in the balance [*qaneh*], and hire a goldsmith; and he maketh it a god: they fall down, yea, they worship" (Isaiah 46:6).

2. Herbert Oppel, *KANΩN: Zur Bedeutungsgeschichte des Wortes und seiner lateinischen Entsprechungen (Regula-Norma)* (Leipzig: Dietrich'sche Verlagsbuchhandlung, 1937), 1–12, 76–78. Oppel's work still remains the definitive source for ancient Greek and Latin uses of *kanon* and *regula*, and I draw heavily on it in this section.

3. Aristophanes, *The Birds* (414 BCE), in *The Peace—The Birds—The Frogs,* trans. Benjamin Bickley Rogers, Loeb Classical Library (Cambridge, Mass.: Harvard University Press, 1996), 226–27, ll. 1001–1005, spoken by the astronomer Meton.

4. Andrew Barker, *Greek Musical Writings,* Vol. 2, *Harmonic and Acoustic Theory* (Cambridge: Cambridge University Press, 1989), 239–40. The word *canon* was not applied to rounds and other imitative songs for several voices (known in medieval Latin as *rota* or *fuga perpetua*) until the sixteenth or seventeenth century. See Otto Klauwell, *Der Canon in seiner geschichtlichen Entwicklung* (Leipzig: C. F. Kahnt, 1874), 9–10.

5. Claudius Galen, *De temperamentis libri III,* ed. Georg Helmreich (Leipzig: B. G. Teubner, 1904), I.9, 36. Galen's remarks have inspired several attempts to reconstruct the lost *Kanon.* See Richard Tobin, "The Canon of Polykleitos," *American Journal of Archaeology* 79 (1975): 307–21.

6. Anne Tihon, *Πτολεμαιου Προχειροι Κανονες: Les "Tables Faciles" de Ptolomée: 1a. Tables A1–A2. Introduction, édition critique,* Publications de l'Institut Orientaliste de Louvain 59a (Louvain-La-Neuve, Belgium: Université Catholique de Louvain/

Peeters, 2011); Raymond Mercier, Πτολεμαιου Προχειροι Κανονες: Ptolemy's *"Handy Tables": 1a. Tables A1–A2. Transcription and Commentary,* Publications de l'Institut Orientaliste de Louvain 59a (Louvain-La-Neuve, Belgium: Université Catholique de Louvain/Peeters, 2011).

7. Edward Kennedy, "A Survey of Islamic Astronomical Tables," *Transactions of the American Philosophical Society* 46, no. 2 (1956): 1–53. The word *kanon* came to be used more generally for other kinds of tables, such as the chronological tables of Bishop Eusebius of Caesarea (4th c. CE). See Oppel, *KANΩN,* 67.

8. See for example Francis Baily, *An Account of the Revd. John Flamsteed, the First Astronomer Royal* (London: n.p., 1835), 10.

9. Pliny the Elder, *Natural History,* trans. H. Rackham, Loeb Classical Library (Cambridge, Mass.: Harvard University Press, 1952), 34.55, 168–69.

10. Plutarch, "kanon tes aretes," quoted in Oppel, *KANΩN,* 42.

11. Aristotle, *Art of Rhetoric,* trans. John Henry Freese, Loeb Classical Library (Cambridge, Mass.: Harvard University Press, 1994), I.9, 1368a; 105.

12. Henner von Hesberg, "Greek and Roman Architects," in *The Oxford Handbook of Greek and Roman Art and Architecture,* ed. Clemente Marconi (Oxford: Oxford University Press, 2014), 142.

13. Plato, *Timaeus,* trans. R. G. Bury, Loeb Classical Library (Cambridge, Mass.: Harvard University Press, 1989), 48–51, 50–53, 112–13; 27d28a, 28c–29a, 48e–49a; Plato, *Republic Books VI–X,* trans. Chris Emlyn-Jones and William Freddy, Loeb Classical Library (Cambridge, Mass.: Harvard University Press), 388–89; 592b.

14. Immanuel Kant, *Critique of Judgment* (1790), trans. Werner S. Pluhar (Indianapolis: Hackett, 1987), I.46, Ak. 5.307–10, 174–75.

15. Oppel, *KANΩN,* 53–69.

16. Oppel, *KANΩN,* 69–70.

17. James A. Brundage, *Medieval Canon Law* (London and New York: Longman, 1995), 8–11; Gérard Fransen, *Canones et quaestiones: Évolution des doctrines et systèmes du droit canonique* (Goldbach, Germany: Keip Verlag, 2002), 597.

18. Heinz Ohme, *Kanon ekklesiastikos: Die Bedeutung des altkirchlichen Kanonbegriffs* (Berlin and New York: Walter de Gruyter, 1998), 1–3; 570–73.

19. Ohme, *Kanon ekklesiastikos,* 46–48. In Roman law, the Greek word *canon* was already a technical term for a regular economic payment by the 4th c. CE.

20. Oppel, *KANΩN,* 76–105.

21. Peter Stein, *Roman Law in European History* (Cambridge: Cambridge University Press, 1999), 47.

22. Ohme, *Kanon ekklesiastikos,* 51–55.

23. "Non ex regula ius sumatur, sed ex iure quod est regula fiat." Paulus, *On Plautius,* Book XVI. *Digest* L 17,1, available at www.thelatinlibrary.com/justinian/digest50 .shtml, accessed 21 August 2021.

24. On the history and distribution of Benedictine monasteries in the Middle Ages, see James G. Clark, *The Benedictines in the Middle Ages* (Woodbridge, Suffolk: Boydell, 2011).

25. A *hemina* was a Roman unit of measure, probably corresponding to about 10 fluid ounces.

26. D. Philibert Schmitz and Christina Mohrmann, eds., *Regula monachorum Sancti Benedicti*, 2nd ed. (Namur, Belgium: P. Blaimont, 1955), 70–72, 98–104, 86–87; chs. 9.1–11, 10.1–3, 38.1–12, 39.1–11, 40.1–9, 41.1–9, 23.1–5, 24.17, 25.1–6.

27. On the genealogy of the Rule of Saint Benedict, see Adalbert de Vogüé, *Les Règles monastiques anciennes (400–700)* (Turnhout, Belgium: Brepols, 1985), 12–34.

28. Charlemagne (c. 742–814) prepared a decree (enacted by his son, Louis the Pious [778–840]) enjoining all monks and nuns throughout the Holy Roman Empire to abide by the Rule of Saint Benedict. See Douglas J. McMillan and Kathryn Smith Fladenmuller, eds., *Regular Life: Monastic, Canonical, and Mendicant Rules* (Kalamazoo, Mich.: Medieval Institute, 1997), 7–8.

29. *Regula Sancti Benedicti*, 99–100, 103–4; chs. 39.6, 42.9–10.

30. Uwe Kai Jacobs, *Die Regula Benedicti als Rechtsbuch: Eine rechtshistorische und rechtstheologische Untersuchung* (Vienna: Böhlau Verlag, 1987), 14, 149–51.

31. "Discrete," *Oxford English Dictionary* Online, available at www.oed.com, accessed 28 July 2021.

32. Jean-Claude Schmitt, *Ghosts in The Middle Ages: The Living and Dead in Medieval Society* (1994), trans. Teresa L. Fagan (Chicago: University of Chicago Press, 1998), 156–59.

33. Roberto Busa S.J. and associates, eds., *Index Thomisticus*, web edition by Eduardo Bernot and Enrique Marcón, available at www.corpusthomisticum.org/it /index.age, accessed 28 July 2021. See also the entry "Discretio" in Roy J. Deferrari and Sister Mary M. Inviolata Barry, *A Lexicon of Saint Thomas Aquinas* (1948; repr. Fitzwilliam, New Hampshire: Loreto Publications, 2004), 317–18. I am grateful to Professor Katja Krause for these references.

34. "Discretio," in Rudolph Goclenius, *Lexicon philosophicum* (Frankfurt: Matthias Becker, 1613), 543.

35. "Discretion," *Oxford English Dictionary* Online, available at www.oed.com, accessed 28 July 2021; see also "Discret," *Le Robert Dictionnaire historique de la langue française*, ed. Alain Rey (Paris: Dictionnaires Le Robert, 2000), 1:1006–1007.

36. Frederick Schauer, *Thinking Like a Lawyer: A New Introduction to Legal Reasoning* (Cambridge, Mass.: Harvard University Press, 2009), 119–23.

37. *Regula Sancti Benedicti*, Prologue 47: "sed et si quid paululum restrictius, dictante aequitatis ratione, propter emendationem vitiorum vel conservationem caritatis processerit." Jacobs, *Die Regula Benedicti als Rechtsbuch*, 147.

38. Aristotle, *Nicomachean Ethics*, trans. H. Rackham, Loeb Classical Library (Cambridge, Mass.: Harvard University Press, 1934), V.10, 1137b, 24–33, 314–17.

39. Jack M. Balkin, *Living Originalism* (Cambridge, Mass.: Harvard University Press, 2011), 35–58.

40. *Regula Sancti Benedicti*, 2.2–3.

41. See for example the entries and examples for *Regula* in D. H. Howlett, *Dictionary of Medieval Latin from British Sources*, Fascicule XIII: PRO-REG (Oxford: Oxford University Press, 2010), 2727–28; J. F. Niermeyer and C. van de Kieft, *Mediae latinitatis lexicon minus: M–Z* (Darmstadt: Wissenschaftliche Buchgesellschaft, 2002), 1178.

42. See for example the entry and examples for *Regola* in *Vocabulario degli Accademici della Crusca*, 4th ed. (Florence: Domenico Maria Manni, 1729–38), 4: 96–97; for *Règle* in *Le Dictionnaire de l'Académie française*, 2nd ed. (Paris: Imprimerie royale, 1718); and for *Rule* in Samuel Johnson, *Dictionary of the English Language*, 1st ed. (London: W. Strahan, 1755).

43. See for example the entry *Rule* in Noah Webster, *American Dictionary of the English Language* (New Haven: B. L. Hamlen, 1841).

44. Aristotle, *Posterior Analytics*, trans. Hugh Tredennick, Loeb Classical Library (Cambridge, Mass.: Harvard University Press, 1939), I.2, 71b10–15, 30–31.

45. Aristotle, *Metaphysics*, trans. Hugh Tredennick, Loeb Classical Library (Cambridge, Mass.: Harvard University Press, 1989), VI.2, 1027a20, 302–303; II.3, 995a15–20, 94–95.

46. Aristotle, *Metaphysics*, I.1, 981a5–15, 4–5. Sometimes Aristotle seems to make so much of this point (and medical example) that he suggests that even *technê* does not deal with individual particulars. See also Aristotle, *Rhetoric*, I.2,1356b, 20–23.

47. Aristotle, *Metaphysics*, I.1, 981a30–b5, 6–7.

48. Pascal Dubourg Glatigny and Hélène Vérin, "La réduction en art, un phénomène culturel," in *Réduire en art: La technologie de la Renaissance aux Lumières*, ed. Pascal Dubourg Glatigny and Hélène Vérin (Paris: Éditions de la Maison des sciences de l'homme, 2008), 59–74. Engineers were prominent in this movement to systematize the knowledge of experience. See Pamela O. Long, "Multi-Tasking 'Pre-Professional' Architect/Engineers and Other Bricolage Practitioners as Key Figures in the Elision of Boundaries Between Practice and Learning in Sixteenth-Century Europe," in *The Structures of Practical Knowledge*, ed. Matteo Valleriani (Cham, Switzerland: Springer, 2017), 223–46.

49. Pamela Smith, *The Body of the Artisan: Art and Experience in the Scientific Revolution* (Chicago: University of Chicago Press, 2004); Christy Anderson, Anne Dunlop, and Pamela Smith, eds., *The Matter of Art: Materials, Practices, Cultural Logics, c. 1250–1750* (Manchester: Manchester University Press, 2014).

50. Jean d'Alembert, *Discours préliminaire* (1751), quoted in Hélène Vérin, "Rédiger et réduire en art: un projet de rationalisation des pratiques," in *Réduire en art*, ed. Glatigny and Vérin, 23.

51. Anne Balansard, *Techné dans les dialogues de Platon* (Sankt Augustin, Germany: Academia Verlag, 2001).

52. The seven liberal arts were allegorized in the late antique encyclopedic work of Martianus Capella; the category of the *artes mechanicae* emerges much later, during the Middle Ages, on the analogy of the *artes liberales*. See Capella, *De nuptiis Philologiae et Mercurii* (5th c. CE, *The Marriage of Philology and Mercury*) (Turnhout, Belgium: Brepols, 2010); Peter Sternagel, *Die artes mechanicae im Mittelalter: Begriffs- und Bedeutungsgeschichte bis zum Ende des 13. Jahrhunderts* (Kallmünz, Germany: Lassleben, 1966); R. Jansen-Sieben, ed., *Ars mechanicae en Europe médiévale* (Brussels: Archives et bibliothèques de Belgique, 1989).

53. William Eamon, *Science and the Secrets of Nature: Books of Secrets in Medieval and Early Modern Culture* (Princeton: Princeton University Press, 1994); Lissa Robert, Simon Schaffer, and Peter Dear, eds., *The Mindful Hand: Inquiry and Invention from the Late Renaissance to Early Industrialisation* (Chicago: University of Chicago Press, 2007); Pamela O. Long, *Artisan/Practitioners and the Rise of the New Science* (Corvallis: Oregon State University Press, 2011).

Chapter 3. The Rules of Art: Head and Hand United

1. Albrecht Dürer, *Unterweysung der Messung, mit dem Zirckel und Richtscheyt, in Linien, Ebenen und gantzen corporen* (Nuremberg: Hieronymus Andreae, 1525), Dedicatory Epistle, n.p.

2. Hélène Vérin, "Rédiger et réduire en art: un projet de rationalisation des pratiques," in *Réduire en art: la technologie de la Renaissance aux Lumières*, eds. Pascal Dubourg Glatigny and Hélène Vérin (Paris: Éditions de la Maison des sciences de l'homme, 2008), 17–58; Pamela H. Smith, "Making Things: Techniques and Books in Early Modern Europe," in *Things*, ed. Paula Findlen (London: Routledge, 2013), 173–203.

3. Martin Warnke, *The Court Artist: On the Ancestry of the Modern Artist* (1985), trans. David McLintock (Cambridge: Cambridge University Press, 1993).

4. Vérin, "Rédiger et réduire en art," 17–58, 27–28.

5. Dürer, *Unterweysung der Messung, mit dem Zirckel und Richtscheyt*, Dedicatory Epistle, n.p.

6. See for example Johann Heinrich Alsted, *Encyclopaedia* (1630), ed. Wilhelm Schmidt-Biggemann, 4 vols. (Stuttgart-Bad Cannstatt: Fromann-Holzboog, 1989), 3:1868–1956, for descriptions of what counted as mechanical arts by the early seventeenth century. The mechanical arts (*artes mechanicae*) refer here to the whole range of handicrafts, not only to practical mechanics, although the latter played a particularly important role in early modern natural philosophy. See Walter Roy Laird and Sophie Roux, eds., *Mechanics and Natural Philosophy before the Scientific Revolution* (Dordrecht: Springer, 2008).

7. The plates of the *Nova reperta* were designed by Jan van der Straet, engraved by Jan Collaert, and published by Philips Galle. The images may be seen at www .metmuseum.org/art/collection/search/659646, accessed 29 July 2021.

8. William Eamon, *Science and the Secrets of Nature: Books of Secrets in Medieval and Early Modern Culture* (Princeton: Princeton University Press, 1994), 134–67.

9. Matteo Valleriani, *Galileo Engineer* (Dordrecht: Springer, 2010); Pamela O. Long, *Artisan/Practitioners and the Rise of the New Sciences, 1400–1600* (Corvallis: Oregon State University Press, 2011).

10. Roberto Vergara, ed., *Il compasso geometrico e militare di Galileo Galilei* (Pisa: ETS, 1992); Ari Belenky, "Master of the Mint: How Much Money Did Isaac Newton Save Britain?" *Journal of the Royal Statistical Society: Series A* 176 (2013): 481–98; Andre Wakefield, "Leibniz and the Wind Machines," *Osiris* 25 (2010): 171–88; Kelly Devries, "Sites of Military Science and Technology," in *The Cambridge History of Early Modern Science*, ed. Katharine Park and Lorraine Daston (Cambridge: Cambridge University Press, 2006), 306–19.

11. Francis Bacon, *Novum organum* (1620), Aphorism I. 74, in *The Works of Francis Bacon*, ed. Basil Montagu (London: William Pickering, 1825–34), 9:225.

12. William Eamon, "Markets, Piazzas, and Villages," in *The Cambridge History of Early Modern Science*, ed. Park and Daston, 206–23.

13. René Descartes, *Regulae ad directionem igenii* (c. 1628), Regula X, in *Oeuvres de Descartes*, ed. Charles Adam and Paul Tannery (Paris: J. Vrin, 1964), 10:403–406; Neal Gilbert, *Concepts of Method in the Renaissance* (New York: Columbia University Press, 1960); Nelly Bruyère, *Méthode et dialectique dans l'oeuvre de La Ramée: Renaissance et Âge classique* (Paris: J. Vrin, 1984).

14. Sébastien Le Prestre de Vauban, *Traité de l'attaque des places* (comp. 1704), in *Les Oisivités de Monsieur de Vauban*, ed. Michèle Virol (Seyssel, France: Éditions Camp Vallon, 2007), 1212–13.

15. Leonard Digges, *A Boke Named Tectonion* (London: John Daye, 1556), sig. f.ii recto.

16. Charles Cotton, *The Compleate Gamester: Instructions How to Play at Billiards, Trucks, Bowls, and Chess* (London: Charles Brome, 1687), 147.

17. [Anonymous], *Traité de confiture, ou Le nouveau et parfait Confiturier* (Paris: Chez Thomas Guillain, 1689), sig. ãiiij recto.

18. The subtitle of Robert May, *The Accomplisht Cook, Or the Art and Mystery of Cookery*, 3rd ed. (London: J. Winter, 1671).

19. See for example Jean Baptiste Colbert, *Instruction generale donnée de l'ordre exprés du roy par Monsieur Colbert . . . pour l'execution des reglemens generaux des manufactures & teintures registrez en presence de Sa Majesté au Parlement de Paris le treiziéme aoust 1669* (Grenoble: Chez Alexandre Giroud, 1693) and other such "general instructions" issued during Colbert's ministry, reprinted in Jean Baptiste Colbert, *Lettres, instructions et mémoires de Colbert*, 7 vols. (Paris: Imprimerie impériale, 1861–1873).

20. The classic statement concerning the tacit quality of craft knowledge comes from Michael Polanyi, *Personal Knowledge: Towards a Post-Critical Philosophy* (1958; repr. London: Routledge, 2005), 65: "This is the usual process of trial and error by which *we feel our way* to success. . . . Hence the practical discovery of a wide range of not consciously known rules of skill and connoisseurship which comprise important technical processes that can rarely be completely specified, and even then only as a result of extensive scientific research." Emphasis in the original.

21. Quoted in Stéphane Lamassé, "Calculs et marchands (XIVe–XVe siècles)," in *La juste mesure: Quantifier, évaluer, mesurer entre Orient et Occident (VIIIe–XVIIIe siècles)*, ed. Laurence Moulinier, Line Sallmann, Catherine Verna, and Nicolas Weill-Parot (Saint-Denis, France: Presses Universitaires de Vincennes, 2005), 79–97, 86.

22. Digges, *A Boke Named Tectonicon*, Preface, n.p.

23. Digges, *A Boke Named Tectonicon*, n.p.

24. Elway Bevin, *Briefe and Short Instrvction of the Art of Mvsicke, to teach how to make Discant, of all proportions that are in vse* (London: R. Young, 1631), 45.

25. Cotton, *The Compleate Gamester*, 1, 5, 21, 154, 109, 57, 147.

26. Edmond Hoyle, *A Short Treatise on the Game of Whist, Containing the Laws of the Game: and also Some Rules, whereby a Beginner may, with due Attention to them, attain to the Playing it well* (London: Thomas Osborne, 1748), 17, 25.

27. Cotton, *The Compleate Gamester*, 49–50

28. Jean-Marie Lhôte, *Histoire des jeux de société* (Paris: Flammarion, 1994), 292–293.

29. Christy Anderson, Anne Dunlop, and Pamela H. Smith, eds., *The Matter of Art: Materials, Practices, Cultural Logics, c. 1250–1750* (Manchester: Manchester University Press, 2014).

30. Naomi Miller, *Mapping the City: The Language and Culture of Cartography in the Renaissance* (London: Continuum, 2003), 151–58, 179; Marion Hilliges, "Der Stadt-grundriss als Repräsentationsmedium in der Frühen Neuzeit," in *Aufsicht—Ansicht—Einsicht: Neue Perspektiven auf die Kartographie an der Schwelle zur Frühen Neuzeit*, ed. Tanja Michalsky, Felicitas Schmieder, and Gisela Engel (Berlin: trafo Verlagsgruppe, 2009), 355; Daniela Stroffolino, "Rilevamento topografico e processi construttivi delle 'vedute a volo d'ucello,'" in *L'Europa moderna: Catografia urbana e vedutismo*, ed. Cesare de Seta and Daniela Stroffolino (Naples: Electa Napoli, 2001), 57–67.

31. Reasons for the inaccuracy of the computed tables included nonstandardized weaponry and ammunition as well as "windage," i.e., the difference between the diameter of the cannon barrel and that of the ball, which allowed the latter to ricochet inside the cannon and lose momentum. George A. Rothrock, "Introduction," Sébastien Le Prestre de Vauban, *A Manual of Siegecraft and Fortification*, trans. George A. Rothrock (Ann Arbor: University of Michigan Press, 1968), 4–6. These problems persisted well into the eighteenth century, leading to altercations between mathematically trained military engineers and experienced gunners. Ken Alder, *Engineering the*

Revolution: Arms and Enlightenment in France, 1763–1815 (Princeton: Princeton University Press, 1997), 92–112.

32. Vauban, *Manual of Siegecraft and Fortification*, 21.

33. Blaise de Pagan, *Les Fortifications du comte de Pagan* (1689), quoted in Michèle Virol, "La conduite des sièges réduite en art. Deux textes de Vauban," in *Réduire en art*, eds. Glatigny and Vérin, 155.

34. Vauban, *Traité de l'attaque des places* (comp. 1704), 1213.

35. Vauban, *Traité de l'attaque des places*, 1321.

36. Vauban, *Manual of Siegecraft and Fortification*, 175.

37. Vauban, *Traité de l'attaque des places*, 1194.

38. Vauban, *Traité de la défense des places*, 1375.

39. "Ingenium," in Rudolph Goclenius the Elder, *Lexicon philosophicum* (Frankfurt: Matthias Becker, 1613), 241–42.

40. Aristotle, *Art of Rhetoric*, trans. John Henry Freese, Loeb Classical Library (Cambridge, Mass.: Harvard University Press, 1994), I.2, 1356b26–35, 23.

41. There are strong parallels here with the coeval genre of *observationes* addressed to jurists and physicians: Gianna Pomata, "Sharing Cases: The *Observationes* in Early modern Medicine," *Early Science and Medicine* 15 (2010): 193–236.

42. On early modern recipes generally, see Elaine Leong, *Recipes and Everyday Knowledge: Medicine, Science, and the Household in Early Modern England* (Chicago: University of Chicago Press, 2018).

43. By the latter half of the eighteenth century, wealthy French households might boast various "officiers de la bouche," including sommeliers, maîtres d'hôtel, and confectioners as well as cooks. Instruction manuals addressed to this group presumed supplementary experience: "On convient que pour s'y render parfaitement habile, ou pour concevoir plus facilement des choses, il est necessaire d'y travailler quelque temps sous les Maîtres. C'est-là que la pratique apprend d'un coup d'oeil, plusieurs preparations qu'on ne peut bien expliquer." François Massialot, *Nouvelles instructions pour les confitures, les liqueurs et les fruits*, 2nd ed. (Paris: Charles de Sercy, 1698), 1:sig. äiiij.

44. Robert May, *The Accomplisht Cook, Or The Art and Mystery of Cookery* (1660), 3rd ed. (London: J. Winter, 1671), Preface, n.p. The book went through at least five editions between 1660 and 1685.

45. Mary Kettilby, *A Collection of above Three Hundred Receipts in Cookery, Physick and Surgery* (1714), 6th ed. (London: W. Parker, 1746), vii. The book went through at least seven editions between 1714 and 1749.

46. May, *Accomplisht Cook*, 177

47. Kettilby, *Collection of above Three Hundred Receipts*, 61.

48. [Anonymous], *The Forme of Cury, A Roll of Ancient English Cookery, Compiled about A.D. 1390, by the Master-Cooks of King Richard II . . . By an Antiquary*. (London: J. Nichols, 1780), xvii.

49. Hannah Glasse, *Art of Cookery, Made Plain and Easy* (1747; repr. London: L. Wangford, c. 1790). The book went through at least five editions during Glasse's lifetime; the most recent edition was published in 1995.

50. Glasse, *Art of Cookery*, 102.

51. Polanyi, *Personal Knowledge*, 17.

52. Harry Collins, *Tacit and Explicit Knowledge* (Chicago: University of Chicago Press, 2010), 7.

53. Jutta Bacher, "Artes mechanicae," in *Erkenntnis Erfindung Konstruktion: Studien zur Bildgeschichte von Naturwissenschaften und Technik vom 16. bis zum 19. Jahrhundert*, ed. Hans Hollander (Berlin: Gebr. Mann, 2000), 35–50.

54. Francis Bacon, *New Atlantis* (1627), in *The Great Instauration and New Atlantis*, ed. J. Weinberger (Arlington Heights, Ill.: Harlan Davidson, 1989), 75.

55. See for example the entry "Mechanical" in the *Oxford English Dictionary*, which includes the now rare definition: "Belonging to or characteristic of people engaged in manual work, esp. regarded as a class, vulgar, coarse."; available at www.oed.com, accessed 17 August 2020.

56. Isaac Newton, "Preface," *The Mathematical Principles of Natural Philosophy* (1687), trans. Andrew Motte (London: Benjamin Motte, 1729), sig. a recto and verso.

57. Gerd Gigerenzer, *How to Stay Smart in a Smart World* (London: Penguin, 2022), 37–57.

Chapter 4. Algorithms before Mechanical Calculation

1. Parts of Chapters Four and Five were previously published in Lorraine Daston, "Calculation and the Division of Labor, 1750–1950," *Bulletin of the German Historical Institute* 62 (2018): 9–30. I am grateful to the editor of the journal for granting permission to reprint them here.

2. Professor Wendy Doniger points out that the standard English term for this numeral system, Hindu-Arabic numbers, is both incoherent and misleading: incoherent, because "Hindu" refers to a religion, "Arabic" to a language and/or culture; misleading, because Persian played as important a part in the transmission of these numerals as Arabic did. "Indian numerals" (as they are indeed called in German) would be more accurate, since the system did originate there; I use this term throughout. Doniger, personal communication.

3. Kurt Gödel, "Über formal unentscheidbare Sätze der *Principia Mathematica* und verwandter Systeme," *Monatsheft für Mathematik und Physik* 38 (1931): 179.

4. David Hilbert and Wilhelm Ackermann, *Grundzüge der theoretischen Logik* (Berlin: Springer, 1928), 77.

5. Charles Xavier Thomas de Colmar, who also founded several insurance companies, patented the first calculating machine to be manufactured and sold in large

numbers in 1820; it did not go into production until 1851. R. Mehmke, "Numerisches Rechnen," in *Enzyklopädie der Mathematischen Wissenschaften*, ed. Wilhelm Franz Meyer (Leipzig: B. Teubner, 1898–1934), vol. 1, part 2, 959–78. For a brief overview of office calculating machines in the late nineteenth and early twentieth centuries, see Mary Croarken, *Early Scientific Computing in Britain* (Oxford: Oxford University Press, 1990), 12–20.

6. Kurt Vogel, *Mohammed Ibn Musa Alchwarizmi's Algorismus: Das frühste Lehrbuch zum Rechnen mit indischen Ziffern: Nach der einzigen (lateinischen) Handschrift (Cambridge Un.Lib. Ms.Ii.6.5)* (Aalen, Germany: Otto Zeller Verlagsbuchhandlung, 1963), 42–44. On the medieval tradition of algebra in Arabic and Latin mathematics, see Victor J. Katz and Karen Hunger Parshall, *Taming the Unknown: A History of Algebra from Antiquity to the Early Twentieth Century* (Princeton: Princeton University Press, 2014), 132–213.

7. Menso Folkerts (with Paul Kunitzsch), eds., *Die älteste lateinische Schrift über das indische Rechnen nach al-Hwarizmi* (Munich: Verlag der Bayerischen Akademie der Wissenschaften, 1997), 7–11.

8. Donald Knuth, *The Art of Computer Programming, Vol. 1: Fundamental Algorithms*, 3rd ed. (Boston: Addison-Wesley, 1997), 4–6.; § 1.1.

9. Annette Imhausen, "Calculating the Daily Bread: Rations in Theory and Practice," *Historia Mathematica* 30 (2003): 7 (Problem 39 of the Rhind papyrus).

10. Lis Brack-Bernsen, "Methods for Understanding and Reconstructing Babylonian Predicting Rules," in *Writings of Early Scholars in the Ancient Near East, Egypt, Rome, and Greece*, ed. Annette Imhausen and Tanja Pommerening (Berlin and New York: De Gruyter, 2010), 285–87.

11. Karine Chemla, "De l'algorithme comme liste d'opérations," *Extrême-Orient-Extrême-Occident* 12 (1990): 80–82.

12. Agathe Keller, Koolakodlu Mahesh, and Clemency Montelle, "Numerical Tables in Sanskrit Sources," HAL archives-ouvertes, HAL ID: halshs-01006137 (submitted 13 June 2014), §2.1.3. https://halshs.archives-ouvertes.fr/halshs-01006137, Accessed 20 August 2021.

13. Jim Ritter, "Reading Strasbourg 368: A Thrice-Told Tale," in *History of Science, History of Text*, ed. Karine Chemla (Dordrecht: Springer, 2004), 196.

14. Keller, "Numerical Tables," §§ 2.1, 2.2.2.

15. Eleanor Robson, "Mathematics Education in an Old Babylonian Scribal School," in *The Oxford Handbook of the History of Mathematics*, ed. Eleanor Robson and Jacqueline Stedall (Oxford and New York: Oxford University Press 2009), 225.

16. Agathe Keller, "Ordering Operations in Square Root Extractions, Analyzing Some Early Medieval Sanskrit Mathematical Texts with the Help of Speech Act Theory," in *Texts, Textual Acts, and the History of Science*, ed. Karine Chemla and Jacques Virbel (Heidelberg: Springer, 2015), 189–90.

17. Karine Chemla, "Describing Texts for Algorithms: How They Prescribe Operations and Integrate Cases: Reflections Based on Ancient Chinese Mathematical Sources," in *Texts,* ed. Chemla and Virbel, 322, 327.

18. J. W. Stigler, "Mental Abacus: The Effect of Abacus Training on Chinese Children's Mental Calculations," *Cognitive Psychology* 16 (1986): 145–76; Mary Gauvain, *The Social Context of Cognitive Development* (New York: Guilford Press, 2001), 49–51.

19. Vogel, *Mohammed Ibn Musa Alchwarizmi's Algorismus,* 45–49.

20. The inverse of any number n is n^{-1}, such that $n \times n^{-1} = 1$. For example: the inverse of 2 is $1/2$. Because the Old Babylonian numeration system was a hybrid of decimal (the numbers 1 through 59, with no zero) and sexigesimal (60 and all numbers thereafter) notation, inverses of numbers with finite sexigesimal forms (i.e., numbers with the prime factors 2, 3, and 5, of the form $2^x 3^y 5^z$, where x, y, and z are integers) played an important role in computation, and many cuneiform tables of such inverses survive. Jean-Luc Chabert, ed., *A History of Algorithms: From the Pebble to the Microchip* (Berlin: Springer, 1999), 11.

21. Otto Neugebauer, *Mathematische Keilschriften* (Berlin: Verlag von Julius Springer, 1935–37), 1:270, II: plate 14,43. See also the somewhat more literal translation in Abraham J. Sachs, "Babylonian Mathematical Texts, I," *Journal of Cuneiform Studies* 1 (1947): 226.

22. Sachs, "Babylonian Mathematical Texts, I," 227.

23. Christine Proust, "Interpretation of Reverse Algorithms in Several Mesopotamian Texts," in *The History of Mathematical Proof,* ed. Karine Chemla (Cambridge: Cambridge University Press, 2012), 410.

24. Gottfried Wilhelm Leibniz, "Towards a Universal Characteristic" (1677), in *Leibniz Selections,* ed. Philip P. Wiener (New York: Charles Scribner's Sons, 1951), 17–25; Étienne Bonnot de Condillac, *La Langue des calculs* (Paris: Charles Houel, 1798), 7–9; Giuseppe Peano, *Notations de logique mathématique* (Turin: Charles Guadagnigi, 1894). On Peano's involvement in universal language schemes, see Michael D. Gordin, *Scientific Babel: How Science Was Done Before and After Global English* (Chicago: University of Chicago Press, 2015), 111–13, 137.

25. T. L. Heath, *The Thirteen Books of Euclid's Elements,* 2nd ed., 3 vols. (New York: Dover, 1956), Book VII, Propositions 1–2, 296–300.

26. A search of the term "Euclid's algorithm" for the Google Ngram corpus of English books from 1800 to 2000 suggests that the term was not used before the twentieth century, with a steeply rising trend only after 1940. This corresponds roughly to the usage of the term "algorithm" itself, which is flat until about 1950 and then rises sharply and steadily.

27. No ancient mathematical diagrams survive, but on the evidence for their existence and central role in ancient Greek mathematics, see Reviel Netz, *The Shaping*

of Deduction in Greek Mathematics: A Study in Cognitive History (Cambridge: Cambridge University Press, 1999), 12–67.

28. Jean Itard, *Les Livres arithmétiques d'Euclide* (Paris: Hermann, 1961).

29. Jacob Klein, *Greek Mathematical Thought and the Origin of Algebra* (1934), trans. Eva Brann (Cambridge, Mass.: MIT Press, 1968); B. L. van der Waerden, *Science Awakening*, trans. Arnold Dresden (New York: Oxford University Press, 1961).

30. Sabetai Unguru, "On the Need to Rewrite the History of Greek Mathematics," *Archive for the History of Exact Sciences* 15 (1975): 67–114; B. L. van der Waerden, "Defense of a 'Shocking' Point of View," *Archive for History of Exact Sciences* 15 (1976): 199–210; Hans Freudenthal, "What Is Algebra and What has Been Its History?" *Archive for History of Exact Sciences* 16 (1977): 189–200; André Weil, "Who Betrayed Euclid?" *Archive for History of Exact Sciences* 19 (1978): 91–93.

31. Jean-Luc Chabert, ed., *A History of Algorithms: From the Pebble to the Microchip* (Berlin: Springer, 1999), 116.

32. Moritz Pasch, *Vorlesungen über neuere Geometrie* (Leipzig: B. G. Teubner, 1882), 98. Emphasis in the original.

33. David Hilbert, *Grundlagen der Geometrie* (1899), 8th ed., with revisions by Paul Bernays (Stuttgart: Teubner, 1956), 121.

34. Efforts in the 1960s to introduce these modern mathematical approaches in secondary schools (known as the "new math" in the United States), a movement that was especially strong in France because of the influence of the Bourbaki group, were not notable successes. Hélène Gispert and Gert Schubring, "Societal Structure and Conceptual Changes in Mathematics Teaching: Reform Processes in France and Germany over the Twentieth Century and the International Dynamics," *Science in Context* 24 (2011): 73–106.

35. In algebraic terms, the Rule of False Position is a method for solving n equations in $n + 1$ unknowns through estimation using false but plausible values. Many mathematical traditions used some version of this algorithm, albeit under different names ("operating with a trial number" in Sanskrit, "rule of too much and not enough" in classical Chinese, "calculation of two errors" in Arabic, "rule of the false" in Latin), couched in different metaphors, applied to different problems, and formulated in different steps. Chabert, ed., *A History of Algorithms*, 85–99.

36. John Stuart Mill, *A System of Logic Ratiocinative and Inductive* (1843), ed. J. M. Robson (London: Routledge, 1996), 186–95; Book II.3, §3–4.

37. Lorraine Daston, "Epistemic Images," in *Vision and Its Instruments: Art, Science, and Technology in Early Modern Europe*, ed. Alina Payne (College Station: Pennsylvania State University Press, 2015), 13–35.

38. Karine Chemla, "Le paradigme et le général: Réflexions inspirées par les textes mathématiques de la Chine ancienne," in *Penser par cas*, ed. Jean-Claude Passeron and Jacques Revel (Paris: Éditions de l'École des Hautes Études en Sciences Sociales, 2005), 88–89.

39. Christine Proust, "Interpretation of Reverse Algorithms in Several Mesopotamian Texts," in *History of Mathematical Proof*, ed. Chemla, 410.

40. Karine Chemla, "Résonances entre démonstrations et procédure: Remarque sur le commentaire de Liu Hui (IIIe siècle) au *Neuf Chapitres sur les Procédures Mathématiques* (Ier siècle)," *Extrême-Orient, Extrême-Occident* 14 (1992): 99–106. See Chemla, "Describing Texts for Algorithms," 317–84.

41. Ritter, "Reading Strasbourg 368," 194.

42. G.E.R. Lloyd, "What Was Mathematics in the Ancient World?" in *Oxford Handbook of the History of Mathematics*, ed. Robson and Stedall, 12.

43. Chemla, "Describing Texts for Algorithms," 323.

44. Frances Yates, *The Art of Memory* (Chicago: University of Chicago Press, 1966); Denis Diderot, "Encyclopédie," in *Encyclopédie, ou Dictionnaire raisonné des arts, des sciences et des métiers*, ed. Jean d'Alembert and Denis Diderot (Paris: Briasson, David, Le Breton, and Durand, 1755), 5:635–48.

45. David Hartley, *Observations on Man, His Frame, His Duty, and His Expectations* (1749), ed. Theodore L. Huguelet (Gainesville, Fla.: Scholars' Facsimile Reprints, 1966), 1:374–77.

46. Mary J. Carruthers, *The Book of Memory: A Study of Memory in Medieval Culture*, 2nd ed. (Cambridge: Cambridge University Press, 2008), 164–69.

47. Anna Maria Busse Berger, *Medieval Music and the Art of Memory* (Berkeley: University of California Press, 2005), 52, 117.

48. Eleanor Robson, "Mathematics Education in an Old Babylonian Scribal School," 225; Berger, *Medieval Music and the Art of Memory*, 180; Hartmut Scharfe, *Education in Ancient India* (Boston: Brill, 2002), 30–37, 229, 240–51.

49. Nancy Pine and Zhenyou Yu, "Early Literacy Education in China: A Historical Overview," in *Perspectives on Teaching and Learning Chinese Literacy in China*, ed. Cynthia Leung and Jiening Ruan (Dordrecht: Springer, 2012), 83–86.

50. Brian W. Ogilvie, *The Science of Describing: Natural History in Renaissance Europe* (Chicago: University of Chicago Press, 2006); Staffan Müller-Wille, *Botanik und weltweiter Handel: Zur Begründung eines natürlichen Systems der Pflanzen durch Carl von Linné (1707–78)* (Berlin: VWB-Verlag für Wissenschaft und Bildung, 1999).

51. All biological systematics still count the publication of the *Systema naturae* as the Big Bang moment of the discipline, the reference point for all subsequent classifications. Charlie Jarvis, *Order Out of Chaos: Linnaean Plant Names and Their Types* (London: Linnean Society of London, 2007).

52. Nicolas Bourbaki, *Éléments de mathématique*, 38 vols. (Paris: Hermann, 1939–75). On the Bourbaki (a collective pseudonym adopted by a group of mostly French mathematicians), see Maurice Mashaal, *Bourbaki: Une société secrète de mathématiciens* (Paris: Pour la science, 2000).

53. Economist and historian Roy Weintraub attributes mathematicians' initial indifference to applications in general and computer science in particular to Bourbaki

schooling: "Mathematicians today, looking back to the period of the 1960s, shudder gently at much of what we were expected to believe. For we were America's first fully Bourbakist generation of mathematics students, thoroughly inculcated with the ideals of Bourbaki mathematics, in love with structure, avoidant of applications. [. . .] In the period of time in which the computer was making its entrance, the mathematics department [at the University of Pennsylvania] ignored computation. Computers were for electrical engineers, or maybe statisticians, and statisticians and engineers were intellectually lower class." E. Roy Weintraub, *How Economics Became a Mathematical Science* (Durham, N.C.: Duke University Press, 2002), 252–53.

54. Jens Høyrup, "Mathematical Justification as Non-conceptualized Practice," in *History of Mathematical Proof*, ed. Chemla, 382.

55. Edwin Dunkin, *A Far-Off Vision: A Cornishman at Greenwich Observatory*, ed. P. D. Hingley and T. C. Daniel (Cornwall: Royal Institution of Cornwall, 1999), 72–73.

56. Simon Schaffer, "Astronomers Mark Time: Discipline and the Personal Equation," *Science in Context* 2 (1988): 115–45. Charles Pritchard, Savilian Professor of Astronomy at Oxford, wrote to Admiral Ernest Mouchez, director of the Paris Observatory, on the occasion of Airy's funeral: "Airy was buried quietly in the country: his funeral attended solely by H. Turner the Chief Assistant at Greenwich. I ought not to say it, but A. was a semi–brute: he '*sat on*' Adams, Challis & myself among other young men." C. Pritchard to E. Mouchez, 28 March 1892, Bibliothèque de l'Observatoire de Paris, 1060-V-A-2, Boite 30, Folder Oxford (Angleterre). Emphasis in the original.

57. William J. Ashworth, "'Labour Harder Than Thrashing': John Flamsteed, Property, and Intellectual Labour in Nineteenth-Century England," in *Flamsteed's Stars*, ed. Frances Willmoth (Rochester: Boydell Press, 1997), 199–216.

58. Mary Croarken, "Human Computers in Eighteenth- and Nineteenth-Century Britain," in *Oxford Handbook of the History of Mathematics*, ed. Robson and Stedall, 375–403.

59. See for example Flamsteed's letter to Sharp, 9 October 1705, explaining his system of using two calculators working independently of each other. John Flamsteed, *The Correspondence of John Flamsteed, the First Astronomer Royal*, ed. Eric G. Forbes, Lesley Murdin, and Frances Willmoth (Bristol: Institute of Physics, 1995–2002), 3:224–25.

60. Li Liang, "Template Tables and Computational Practices in Early Modern Chinese Calendrical Astronomy," *Centaurus* 58 (2016): 26–45.

61. See Georges Friedmann, "L'*Encyclopédie* et le travail humain," *Annales: Économies, Sociétés, Civilisations* 8 (1953): 53–61 on the degree to which such "grandes manufactures" were dissociated from both machines and the division of labor in the views of mid-eighteenth-century French thinkers.

62. Dunkin, *Far-Off Vision*, 45.

63. Dunkin, *Far-Off Vision*, 70–97.

64. On the careers and wages of Airy's computers and assistants, see Allan Chapman, "Airy's Greenwich Staff," *Antiquarian Astronomer* 6 (2012): 4–18.

65. Simon Newcomb, *The Reminiscences of an Astronomer* (Boston and New York: Houghton, Mifflin, and Company, 1903), 71, 74. Like Edwin Dunkin, Newcomb in retrospect regarded his job as a computer as the first rung on the ladder of a distinguished scientific career, "my birth into the world of sweetness and light," 1.

66. Newcomb, *Reminiscences*, 288.

67. [Alexandre Deleyre], "Epingle," *Encyclopédie, ou Dictionnaire*, ed. d'Alembert and Diderot, 5:804–7; [Jean-Rodolphe Perronet], "Epinglier," Supplément Planches (1765), 4:1–8.

68. On the complicated genesis and relationship between these two articles, see Jean-Louis Peaucelle, *Adam Smith et la division du travail: Naissance d'une idée fausse* (Paris: L'Harmattan, 2007).

69. Adam Smith, *The Wealth of Nations* (1776), ed. Edwin Cannan (Chicago: University of Chicago Press, 1976), 11–14. On Smith's French sources, see Jean-Louis Peaucelle and Cameron Guthrie, "How Adam Smith Found Inspiration in French Texts on Pin Making in the Eighteenth Century," *History of Economic Ideas* 19 (2011): 41–67.

70. Gaspard de Prony, *Notices sur les grandes tables logarithmiques et trigonometriques, adaptées au nouveau système décimal* (Paris: Firmin Didot, 1824), 5.

71. Charles Babbage, *On the Economy of Machinery and Manufactures* (London: C. Knight, 1832), 153.

72. The metric system was initiated by the Constitutional Assembly of 1791 but instituted into French law only on 4 July 1837. Adrien Favre, *Les Origines du système métrique* (Paris: Presses universitaires de France, 1931), 191–207.

73. Gaspard de Prony, *Notices sur les grandes tables logarithmiques et trigonometriques, adaptées au nouveau système décimal* (Paris: Firmin Didot, 1824), 4. On the monumental character of the Prony tables, see Lorraine Daston, "Enlightenment Calculations," *Critical Inquiry* 21 (1994): 182–202.

74. For the formulas employed and other details concerning the project, see Ivor Grattan-Guiness, "Work for the Hairdressers: The Production of Prony's Logarithmic and Trigonometric Tables," *Annals of the History of Computing* 12 (1990): 177–85.

75. De Prony, *Notices*, 7.

76. De Prony, *Notices*, 7.

77. Smith, *Wealth of Nations*, 13.

78. Simon Schaffer has written brilliantly about the conceptions of intelligence implicit in Babbage's project, as well as the prolonged and acrimonious strife between Babbage and the engineer Joseph Clement, whom Babbage employed to build the engines. Schaffer, "Babbage's Intelligence: Calculating Engines and the Factory System," *Critical Inquiry* 21 (1994): 203–27.

79. The French publisher Firmin-Didot had originally been commissioned to publish the tables (originally for a sum of 139,800 francs), but the money ran out halfway through the printing. MS "Note sur les tables" (Paris, 2 March 1819), Dossier Gaspard de Prony, Archives de l'Académie des Sciences, Paris. On the abortive British-French initiative, see [Gaspard de Prony], *Note sur la publication proposé par le gouvernement anglais des grandes tables logarithmiques et trigonométriques de M. de Prony* (Paris: Firmin-Didot, n.d.). The French government eventually printed excerpts in *Service géographique de l'armée: Tables des logarithmes à huit decimals* (Paris: Imprimerie Nationale, 1891).

80. Charles Babbage, *Table of the Logarithms of Natural Numbers, from 1 to 108,000*, stereotyped 2nd ed. (London: B. Fellowes, 1831), vii.

81. Charles Babbage, *On the Economy of Machinery and Manufactures*, 4th ed. (London: Charles Knight, 1835), 201.

82. James Essinger, *Jacquard's Web: How a Hand-Loom Led to the Birth of the Information Age* (Oxford: Oxford University Press, 2004), 4–5.

83. Jacquard looms were profitable only if the same patterns stayed in fashion long enough and/or orders were large enough to repay the investment in both loom and cards (it took two extra adult workers just to tie the cards). Natalie Rothstein, "Silk: The Industrial Revolution and After," in *The Cambridge History of Western Textiles*, ed. David Jenkins (Cambridge: Cambridge University Press, 2003), 2:793–96.

84. David Alan Grier, *When Computers Were Human* (Princeton: Princeton University Press, 2006).

85. Henry Thomas Colebrooke, "Address on Presenting the Gold Medal of the Astronomical Society to Charles Babbage," *Memoirs of the Astronomical Society* 1 (1825): 509–12.

86. Edward Sang, 1871 lecture to the Actuarial Society of Edinburgh, quoted in "CALCULATING MACHINES," in *The Insurance Cyclopaedia*, ed. Cornelius Walford, 6 vols. (London: C. and E. Layton, 1871–78), 1:425. See also Edward Sang, "Remarks on the Great Logarithmic and Trigonometrical Tables Computed in the Bureau de Cadastre under the Direction of M. Prony," *Proceedings of the Royal Society of Edinburgh* (1874–75), 1–15.

87. Blaise Pascal, "Lettre dédicatoire à Monseigneur le Chancelier [Séguier] sur le sujet machine nouvellement inventée par le Sieur B.P. pour faire toutes sortes d'opération d'arithmétique par un mouvement réglé sans plume ni jetons," (1645), in *Oeuvres complètes de Pascal*, ed. Louis Lafuma (Paris: Éditions du Seuil, 1963), 190.

On Leibniz's first attempts to construct a calculating machine in the 1670s, see Maria Rosa Antognazza, *Leibniz: An Intellectual Biography* (Cambridge: Cambridge University Press, 2009), 143, 148–49, 159. On the early history of calculating machines more generally, see Jean Marguin, *Histoire des instruments à calculer. Trois siècles de mécanique pensante 1642–1942* (Paris: Hermann, 1994); and Matthew L.

Jones, *Reckoning with Matter: Calculating Machines, Innovation, and Thinking about Thinking from Pascal to Babbage* (Chicago: University of Chicago Press, 2016).

88. Laura Snyder, *The Philosophical Breakfast Club: Four Remarkable Friends Who Transformed Science and Changed the World* (New York: Broadway Books, 2011), 191–194.

89. Alexander Pope, *The Guardian*, no. 78 (10 June 1713): 467.

90. M.J.A.N. Condorcet, *Élémens d'arithmétique et de géométrie* (1804), reprinted in *Enfance* 42 (1989), 44.

91. M.J.A.N. Condorcet, *Moyens d'apprendre à compter surement et avec facilité* [Paris, Moutardier, 1804], reprinted in *Enfance* 42 (1989), 61–62.

92. John Napier, *Rabdology* (1617), trans. William F. Richardson (Cambridge, Mass.: MIT Press, 1990).

Chapter 5. Algorithmic Intelligence in the Age of Calculating Machines

1. Ludwig Wittgenstein, *Philosophical Investigations* (posthumous 1953), trans. G.E.M. Anscombe, 3rd ed. (Englewood Cliffs, N.J.: Prentice Hall, 1958) §§ 185, 193, 194, 199; 74, 77–81.

2. Laura Snyder, *The Philosophical Breakfast Club: Four Remarkable Friends Who Transformed Science and Changed the World* (New York: Broadway Books, 2011), 191–94.

3. Charles Babbage, *The Ninth Bridgewater Treatise: A Fragment* (London: John Murray, 1837), 93–99.

4. On Wittgenstein's use of calculating machines as examples with which to criticize Turing Machines, see Stuart Shanker, *Wittgenstein's Remarks on the Foundations of AI* (London: Routledge, 1998), 1–33.

5. Francis Galton, "Composite Portraits," *Nature* 18 (1878): 97–100; Carlo Ginzburg, "Family Resemblances and Family Trees: Two Cognitive Metaphors," *Critical Inquiry* 30 (2004): 537–56.

6. Ludwig Wittgenstein, *Bemerkungen über die Grundlagen der Mathematik*, ed. G.E.M. Anscombe, Rush Rhees, and G. H. von Wright (Berlin: Suhrkamp Verlag, 2015), IV.20, 234; emphasis in the original.

7. René Descartes, *Discours de la méthode pour bien conduire sa raison et chercher la vérité dans les sciences* (1637) in *Oeuvres de Descartes*, ed. Charles Adam and Paul Tannery (Paris: J. Vrin, 1964), 6:18.

8. Blaise Pascal, "Lettre dédicatoire à Monsieur le Chancelier Séguier sur le sujet de la machine nouvellement inventée par le Sieur B.P. pour faire toutes sortes d'opérations d'arithmétique par un mouvement réglé sans plume ni jetons," in Blaise Pascal, *Oeuvres complètes*, ed. Louis Lafuma (Paris: Éditions du Seuil, 1963), 187–91. On the long and difficult history of constructing and marketing such machines, see

Matthew L. Jones, *Reckoning with Matter: Calculating Machines, Innovation, and Thinking about Thinking from Pascal to Babbage* (Chicago: University of Chicago Press, 2016).

9. John Napier, *Mirifici logarithmorum canonis descriptio* (Edinburgh: A. Hart, 1614); Julian Havil, *John Napier: Life, Logarithms, and Legacy* (Princeton: Princeton University Press, 2014), 65–135; Herschel E. Filipowski, *A Table of Anti-Logarithms*, 2nd ed. (London: George Bell, 1851), i–ix; Charles Naux, *Histoire des logarithmes de Neper [sic] à Euler* (Paris: Blanchard, 1966).

10. For example, a computer using Maskelyne's "precepts" or algorithms for calculation might have had up to a dozen table look-ups per entry. Mary Croarken, "Human Computers in Eighteenth- and Nineteenth-Century Britain," in *The Oxford Handbook of the History of Mathematics*, eds. Eleanor Robson and Jacqueline Stedall (Oxford: Oxford University Press), 378.

11. Maurice d'Ocagne, *Le Calcul simplifié par les procédés mécaniques et graphiques*, 2nd ed. (Paris: Gauthier-Villars, 1905), 7–23.

12. Nicolas Bion, *Traité de la construction et des principaux usages des instruments de mathématique*, 4th ed. (Paris: Chez C. A. Jombret, 1752).

13. D'Ocagne, *Le Calcul simplifié*, 44–53; Martin Campbell-Kelly, "Large-Scale Data Processing in the Prudential, 1850–1930," *Accounting, Business, and Financial History* 2 (1992): 117–40. Between 1821 and 1865, only five hundred Arithmometers were sold, but by 1910, circa eighteen thousand Arithmometers were in use worldwide. Delphine Gardey, *Écrire, calculer, classer: Comment une revolution de papier a transformés les sociétés contemporaines (1800–1840)* (Paris: Éditions la découverte, 2008), 206–12.

14. Louis Couffignal, *Les Machines à calculer* (Paris: Gauthier-Villars, 1933), 2.

15. Croarken, "Human Computers," 386–87. On 10 December 1928, the Admiralty approved the purchase of new Burroughs Adding Machine (Class 111700) and the lease of a Hollerith machine. Secretary of the Admiralty to Superintendent of the Nautical Almanac, 10 December 1928, RGO 16/Box 17, Manuscript Room, Cambridge University Library.

16. Superintendent of the *Nautical Almanac* to the Secretary of the Navy, 28 October 1930, RGO 16/Box 17, Manuscript Room, Cambridge University Library.

17. Secretary of the Admiralty to the Superintendent of the Nautical Almanac, 23 November 1933. In a letter from the Superintendent to the Secretary of the Admiralty, 14 April 1931, the Superintendent sees no reason why women could not also be employed at the higher-level post of assistant but recommended that the positions of Superintendent and Deputy Superintendent "be reserved for men, especially in view of the fact that the greater part of the calculation is now performed by mechanical means." RGO 16/Box 17, Manuscript Room, Cambridge University Library.

18. Superintendent of the *Nautical Almanac* to the Secretary of the Admiralty, 4 May 1928, RGO 16/Box 17, Manuscript Room, Cambridge University Library.

19. Couffignal, *Les Machines*, 7.

20. Superintendent of *Nautical Almanac* (Philip H. Cowell) to Secretary of the Admiralty, 17 August 1929, RGO 16/Box 17, Manuscript Room, Cambridge University Library. According to the pay schedule set by the Admiralty in 1933, the starting wages for both men and women hired as a Junior Assistant Lower Grade was £80 p.a., but the maximum salary for men was £250; for women, £180: Committee on *Nautical Almanac* Office Report, 26 August 1933, RGO 16/Box 17, Manuscript Room, Cambridge University Library.

21. Superintendent of the *Nautical Almanac* (L. Comrie) to the Secretary of the Admiralty, 9 February 1937, RGO 16/Box 17, Manuscript Room, Cambridge University Library.

22. Couffignal, *Les Machines*, 41, 78.

23. On Comrie's scientific career, see Harrie Stewart Wilson Massey, "Leslie John Comrie (1893–1950)," *Obituary Notices of the Fellows of the Royal Society* 8 (1952): 97–105. After resigning from the Nautical Almanac in 1936 after repeated clashes with the Admiralty over his reforms, Comrie founded the very successful Scientific Computing Service, which offered advice on how to mechanize a wide range of scientific calculations.

24. Superintendent of the *Nautical Almanac* (L. Comrie) to the Secretary of the Admiralty, 14 October 1931, 25 January 1933, 30 September 1933, RGO 16/Box 17, Manuscript Room, Cambridge University Library.

25. Georges Bolle, "Note sur l'utilisation rationelle des machines à statistique," *Revue générale des chemins de fer* 48 (1929): 175, 176, 179, 190.

26. Quoted in Coffignal, *Les Machines*, 79.

27. As Matthew Jones notes, calculating machines, in contrast to automata, rarely inspired visions of machine intelligence in the eighteenth century, despite the fascination of materialist philosophers like La Mettrie with thinking matter. Jones, *Reckoning with Matter*, 215–18; Lorraine Daston, "Enlightenment Calculations," *Critical Inquiry* 21 (1994): 193.

28. Edward Wheeler Scripture, "Arithmetical Prodigies," *American Journal of Psychology* 4 (1891): 1–59, offers a historical overview of the phenomenon.

29. D'Ocagne, *Le Calcul simplifié*, 5.

30. Couffignal, *Les Machines*, 21.

31. Alfred Binet, *Psychologie des grands calculateurs et joueurs d'échecs* (Paris: Librairie Hachette, 1894), 91–109. The two calculating prodigies studied by Binet, Jacques Inaudi and Pericles Diamandi, were both the subjects of a commission of the Académie des Sciences that included Gaston Darboux, Henri Poincaré, and François-Félix Tisserand, who recruited the help of Binet's teacher Jean-Martin Charcot at the Salpêtrière, who in turn recruited Binet.

32. Wesley Woodhouse to the Lords Commissioners of the Admiralty, 10 April 1837, RGO 16/Box 1, Manuscript Room, Cambridge University Library.

33. P. H. Cowell to L. Comrie, 13 September 1930, RGO 16/Box 1, Manuscript Room, Cambridge University Library.

34. Bolle, "Note sur l'utilisation rationelle," 178.

35. J.-M. Lahy and S. Korngold, "Séléction des operatrices de machines comptables," *Année psychologique* 32 (1931): 136–37.

36. Francis Baily, "On Mr. Babbage's New Machine for Calculating and Printing Mathematical and Astronomical Tables," *Astronomische Nachrichten* 46 (1823): cols. 409–22; reprinted in Charles Babbage, *The Works of Charles Babbage*, ed. Martin Campbell-Kelly (London: Pickering & Chatto, 1989), 2:45.

37. Couffignal, *Les Machines*, 21.

38. For an overview of early twentieth-century psychological research on attention, see Hans Henning, *Die Aufmerksamkeit* (Berlin: Urban & Schwarzenberg, 1925), esp. 190–201.

39. Théodule Ribot, *Psychologie de l'attention* (Paris: Félix Alcan, 1889), 62, 95, 105.

40. Alfred Binet and Victor Henri, *La Fatigue intellectuelle* (Paris: Schleicher Frères, 1898), 26–27.

41. John Perham Hylan, "The Fluctuation of Attention," *Psychological Review* 2 (1898): 77.

42. Louis, *Les Machines*, 67, 72.

43. These points are brilliantly made in Jones, *Reckoning with Matter*; on the eventual realization of Babbage's machines, see 208–9.

44. Michael Lindgren, *Glory and Failure: The Difference Engines of Johann Müller, Charles Babbage, and Georg and Edvard Scheutz* (Cambridge, Mass.: MIT Press, 1990).

45. D'Ocagne, *Le Calcul simplifié*, 88.

46. David Alan Grier, *When Computers Were Human* (Princeton: Princeton University Press, 2006); Christine von Oertzen, "Machineries of Data Power: Manual versus Mechanical Census Compilation in Nineteenth-Century Europe," *Osiris* 32 (2017): 129–50.

47. Dava Sobel, *The Glass Archive: How the Ladies of the Harvard Observatory Took the Measure of the Stars* (New York: Viking, 2016), 96–97; Allan Chapman, "Airy's Greenwich Staff," *Antiquarian Astronomer* 6 (2012): 16.

48. Charles Babbage, *On the Economy of Machinery and Manufactures* (1832), 4th ed. (London: Charles Knight, 1835), 201.

49. Paul Erikson, Judy L. Klein, Lorraine Daston, Rebecca Lemov, Thomas Sturm, and Michael D. Gordin, *How Reason Almost Lost Its Mind: The Strange Career of Cold War Rationality* (Chicago: University of Chicago Press, 2013), 77–79.

50. [Gaspard Riche de Prony], *Note sur la publication, proposé par le gouvernement anglais des grandes Tables logarithmiques et trigonométriques de M. de Prony* (Paris: Firmin-Didot, n.d.), 8; Edward Sang, "Remarks on the Great Logarithmic and Trigonometrical Tables computed in the Bureau du Cadastre under the direction of M. Prony," *Proceedings of the Royal Society of Edinburgh* (21 December 1874), 10–11.

51. Jones, *Reckoning with Matter*, 244–45; Couffignal, *Les Machines*, 47.

52. On the visions of Leibniz, Stanhope, Condillac, and others, see Jones, *Reckoning with Matter*, 4–5, 197–99, 215–25; Daston, "Enlightenment Calculations," 190–93.

53. Martin Davis, *The Universal Computer: The Road from Leibniz to Turing* (New York: W.W. Norton, 2000) tells the story in this fashion, as does (in a more anecdotal vein) David Berlinski, *The Advent of the Algorithm: The 300-Year Journey from an Idea to the Computer* (New York: Harcourt, 2000). Hilbert's *Entscheidungsproblem* and the attempts of Turing, Alonzo Church, and Stephen Kleene to solve it played a crucial role in connecting mathematical logic to algorithms and ultimately to computers. See David Hilbert and Wilhelm Ackermann, *Grundzüge der theoretischen Logik* (Berlin: Springer, 1928), 77, and the papers reprinted in Martin Davis, ed., *The Undecidable: Basic Papers on Undecidable Propositions, Unsolvable Problems, and Computable Functions* (Hewlett, N.Y.: Raven Press, 1965).

54. Allen Newell and Herbert A. Simon, "The Logic Theory Machine: A Complex Information Processing System," *IRE Transactions on Information Theory* 1 (1956): 61.

55. Herbert A. Simon, *Models of My Life* (New York: Basic Books, 1991), 207.

56. Herbert A. Simon, Patrick W. Langley, and Gary L. Bradshaw, "Scientific Discovery as Problem Solving," *Synthèse* 47 (1981): 2, 4. The use of heuristics in both the Logic Theory and BACON programs are good examples of Simon's adroit use of heuristics to attain the same ends by more parsimonious means than either logical proof or scientific discovery, respectively. These constraints still shape computer algorithms, despite great strides in computer speed and memory. Matthew L. Jones, "Querying the Archive: Data Mining from Apriori to Page Rank," in *Science in the Archives: Pasts, Presents, Futures*, ed. Lorraine Daston (Chicago: University of Chicago Press, 2017), 311–28.

57. These computer subroutines left tell-tale traces in the simulation models of the mind advanced in the 1980s in the cognitive sciences, where they became "known as program modules, perfect for the divide-and-conquer strategy programmers often use to tackle large problems. To the computer, however, it makes no difference whether subroutines are isolated or not." Gerd Gigerenzer and Daniel Goldstein, "Mind as Computer: The Social Origin of a Metaphor," in *Adaptive Thinking: Rationality in the Real World*, ed. Gerd Gigerenzer (Oxford: Oxford University Press, 2000), 41.

58. Chris Anderson, "The End of Theory: The Data Deluge Makes the Scientific Method Obsolete," *Wired Magazine* (23 June 2008), available at archive.wired.com /science/discoveries/magazine/16-07/pb_theory, accessed 2 August 2021

59. "Root Cause: Failure to use metric units in the coding of a ground software file, 'Small Forces,' used in trajectory models." See NASA, *Mars Climate Orbiter Mishap Investigation Board Phase 1 Report* (10 November 1999), 7, available at llis.nasa .gov/llis_lib/pdf/1009464main1_0641-mr.pdf, accessed 2 August 2021.

Chapter 6. Rules and Regulations

1. Lorraine Daston and Michael Stolleis, "Nature, Law, and Natural Law in Early Modern Europe," in *Natural Laws and Laws of Nature in Early Modern Europe*, ed. Lorraine Daston and Michael Stolleis (Farnham, Surrey: Ashgate, 2008), 1–12.

2. Already in Roman law of the first century CE, jurists effectively distinguished between "law" (*lex*) and "rule" (*regula*): the latter collected ancient legal decisions into a general precept or proverb, some two hundred of which were appended to the Justinian *Digest* under the rubric *De diversis regulis juris antique*. Heinz Ohme, *Kanon ekklesiastikos: Die Bedeutung des altkirchlichen Kanonbegriffs* (Berlin: Walter de Gruyter, 1998), 51–55. Starting in the fifth century CE, the word *regulae* refers in Roman law to special rules pertaining to the church (e.g., that Christian clergy may refuse to take oaths). Ohme, *Kanon ekklesiastikos*, 1–3, 46–49.

3. Colin McEvedy, *The Penguin Atlas of Modern History (to 1815)* (Harmondsworth: Penguin, 1986), 39.

4. Jean-Jacques Rousseau, *Reveries of the Solitary Walker* (comp. 1776–78, publ. 1782), trans. Peter France (London: Penguin, 1979), 38–39.

5. For an excellent overview of the phenomenon, see Giorgio Riello and Ulinka Rublack, eds., *The Right to Dress: Sumptuary Laws in Global Perspective, c. 1200–1800* (Cambridge: Cambridge University Press, 2019). See also Daniel Roche, *The Culture of Clothing: Dress and Fashion in the Ancien Regime* (1989), trans. Jean Birrell (Cambridge: Cambridge University Press, 1994); Alan Hunt, *Governance of the Consuming Passions: A History of Sumptuary Law* (London: Macmillan, 1996).

6. Catherine Kovesi Killerby, *Sumptuary Law in Italy 1200–1500* (Oxford: Clarendon Press, 2002), 112.

7. Quoted in Frances Elizabeth Baldwin, "Sumptuary Legislation and Personal Regulation," *Johns Hopkins University Studies in Historical and Political Science* 44 (1926): 52.

8. Herzog von Sachsen-Gotha-Altenburg, Ernst I., *Fürstliche Sächsische Landes-Ordnung* (Gotha, Germany: Christoph Reyher, 1695), 541, 547.

9. Matthäus Schwarz and Veit Konrad Schwarz, *The First Book of Fashion: The Book of Clothes of Matthäus Schwarz and Veit Konrad Schwarz of Augsburg*, ed. Ulinka Rublack, Maria Hayward, and Jenny Tiramani (New York: Bloomsbury Academic, 2010).

10. Ulinka Rublack and Giorgio Riello, "Introduction," in *Right to Dress*, ed. Riello and Rublack, 5.

11. "Ordonnance contre le luxe" (1294), in P. Jacob [Paul Lacroix], *Recueil curieux de pièces originales rares ou inédites en prose et en vers sur le costume et les revolutions de la mode en France* (Paris: Administration de Librairie, 1852), 3–5.

12. "Ordonnance" (c. 1450), in Jacob [Lacroix], *Recueil curieux*, 12.

13. Catherine Kovesi Killerby, "Practical Problems in the Enforcement of Italian Sumptuary Law, 1200–1500," in *Crime, Society, and the Law in Renaissance Italy*,

ed. Trevor Dean and K.J.P. Lowe (Cambridge: Cambridge University Press, 1994), 112.

14. Maria Giuseppina Muzzarelli, "Sumptuary Laws in Italy: Financial Resources and Instrument of Rule," in *Right to Dress*, ed. Riello and Rublack, 167–85.

15. Liselotte Constanze Eisenbart, *Kleiderordnungen der deutschen Städte zwischen 1350 und 1700* (Berlin and Göttingen: Musterschmidt Verlag, 1962), 62.

16. Baldwin, "Sumptuary Legislation," 28–29.

17. Killerby, *Sumptuary Law in Italy*, 73.

18. Jacob [Lacroix], *Recueil curieux*, 40.

19. Ulinka Rublack, "The Right to Dress: Sartorial Politics in Germany, c. 1300–1750," in *Right to Dress*, ed. Riello and Rublack, 56.

20. Killerby, "Practical Problems," 105.

21. *Fürstliche Sächsische Landes-Ordnung*, 542–43.

22. "Déclaration du Roi, portant réglement pour les ouvrages et vaisselles d'or, vermeil doré et d'argent, 16 December 1689," reprinted in Jacques Peuchet, *Collection des lois, ordonnances et réglements de police, depuis le 13e siècle jusqu'à l'année 1818*, Second Series: *Police moderne de 1667–1789* (1667–1695) (Paris: Chez Lottin de Saint-Germain, 1818), 1:491–99. See also the earlier legislation on this subject issued by Louis XIV in Jacob [Lacroix], *Recueil curieux*, 1:88.

23. H. Duplès-Argier, "Ordonnance somptuaire inédite de Philippe le Hardi," *Bibliothèque de l'École des chartes*, 3rd Series, no. 5 (1854): 178.

24. "Ordinance of 1294" in Jacob [Lacroix], *Recueil curieux*, 3–4.

25. "Edict of 1661" in Jacob [Lacroix], *Recueil curieux*, 117–18.

26. Eisenbart, *Kleiderordnungen der deutschen Städte*, 69.

27. Killerby, *Sumptuary Law in Italy*, 38–39; Sara-Grace Heller, "Limiting Yardage and Changes of Clothes: Sumptuary Legislation in Thirteenth-Century France, Languedoc, and Italy," in *Medieval Fabrications: Dress, Textiles, Clothwork, and Other Cultural Imaginings*, ed. E. Jane Burns (New York: Palgrave-Macmillan, 2004), 127; Veronika Bauer, *Kleiderordnungen in Bayern vom 14. bis zum 19. Jahrhundert*, Miscellanea Bavarica Monacensia, Heft 62 (Munich: R. Wölfle, 1975), 39–78.

28. See for example Valerie Cumming, C. Willet Cunnington, and Phillis Cunnington, *The Dictionary of Fashion History* (New York: Berg, 2010).

29. Killerby, *Sumptuary Law in Italy*, 112.

30. "Edict of 17 October 1550" in Jacob [Lacroix], *Recueil curieux*, 27.

31. Killerby, "Practical Problems," 106–11. By 1330 Florence had created a special Ufficiali delle Donne with stop-and-frisk powers. Rublack and Riello, "Introduction," 17.

32. Killerby, *Sumptuary Law in Italy*, 147–49.

33. Rublack, "Right to Dress," 64–70; Killerby, *Sumptuary Law in Italy*, 120–23.

34. *Fürstliche Sächsische Landes-Ordnung*, 563.

35. Luca Molà and Giorgio Riello, "Against the Law: Sumptuary Prosecutions in Sixteenth- and Seventeenth-Century Padova," in *Right to Dress*, eds. Riello and

Rublack, 221. On exceptional occasions France also went so far as to extend regulations even to the royal family, as in the case of the 1644 edict banning gold and silver ornaments on clothing. "Edict of 1644" in Jacob [Lacroix], *Recueil curieux*, 94.

36. "Edict of 1661" in Jacob [Lacroix], *Recueil curieux*, 105. The same tendency occurs earlier in Italian cities. Killerby, *Sumptuary Law in Italy*, 37.

37. Eisenbart, *Kleiderordnungen der deutschen Städte*, 32.

38. Killerby, *Sumptuary Law in Italy*, 115.

39. "Edict of 1661" in Jacob [Lacroix], *Recueil curieux*, 17–18.

40. Molà and Riello, "Against the Law," 217; *Fürstliche Sächsische Landes-Ordnung*, 555.

41. Muzzarelli, "Sumptuary Laws in Italy," 170.

42. *Fürstliche Sächsische Landes-Ordnung*, 563–64.

43. See for example Adam Clulow, "'Splendour and Magnificence': Diplomacy and Sumptuary Codes in Early Modern Batavia," in *Right to Dress*, ed. Riello and Rublack, 299–24.

44. Rublack and Riello, "Introduction," 2.

45. "Sudan Moves to Dissolve Ex Ruling Party, Repeals Public Order Law," *New York Times*, 28 November 2019; "Le voile de la discorde," *Le Monde des religions*, no. 99, 31 December 2019.

46. D. J. [Chevalier de Jaucourt], "Règle, Règlement," in *Encyclopédie, ou Dictionnaire raisonné des sciences*, ed. Jean d'Alembert and Denis Diderot (Neufchastel: Chez Samuel Faulche, 1765), 14:20.

47. "Ordonnance de Police, qui enjoint à tous aubergistes, hôteliers, loueurs de carosses et de chevaux, et autres particuliers, de conformer aux ordonnances et réglements de police concernant la conduite des chevaux et mulets," 22 June 1732, reprinted in Peuchet, *Collection des lois*, Second Series: 6:60–62.

48. "Ordonnance de Police, concernant le nettoiement des rues de Paris," 28 November 1750, reprinted in Peuchet, *Collection des lois*, Second Series: 6:48–51.

49. "Ordonnance de Police, portant defenses de jouer dans les rues ou places publiques, au bâtonnet et aux quills, ni même d'élever des cerfs-volants et autres jeux," 3 September 1754, reprinted in Peuchet, *Collection des lois*, Second Series: 6:192–93.

50. "Édit dur Roi, portant création d'un lieutenant de police en ville, prévôte et vicomte de Paris," March 1667, reprinted in Peuchet, *Collection des lois*, Second Series: 1:119–26.

51. For a breakdown of the regulations by domain (economic, administrative, ideological, and criminal), see Jean-Claude Hervé, "L'Ordre à Paris au XVIIIe siècle: les enseignements du 'Recueil de règlements de police' du commissaire Dupré," *Revue d'histoire moderne et contemporaine* 34 (1985): 204. Only 9.9 percent of the regulations in the sample concern crimes that endanger security, in contrast to the almost 75 percent relating to maintaining economic and administrative order.

52. Heinrich Sander's 1777 impressions of Paris, quoted in Wolfgang Griep, "Die reinliche Stadt: Über fremden und eigenen Schmutz," in *Rom-Paris-London: Erfahrung und Selbsterfahrung deutscher Schriftsteller und Künstler in den fremden Metropolen,* ed. Conrad Wiedemann (Stuttgart: J. B. Metzlersche Verlagsbuchhandung, 1988), 136.

53. Louis-Sébastien Mercier, *Tableau de Paris* (1782 ; repr. Geneva: Slatkine, 1979), 1:118.

54. Louis-Sébastien Mercier, *L'An 2440: Rêve s'il en fut jamais* (London: n.p., 1771), 24. The English translator, W. Hooper, added a footnote to this passage: "This method [of keeping to the right], I am informed, has long been used in the imperial city of Vienna," suggesting that this rule was also considered novel in London at the time. Louis-Sébastien Mercier, *Memoirs of the Year Two Thousand Five Hundred,* trans. W. Hooper (London: G. Robinson, 1772), 1:27n.

55. Diderot was the editor of the *Encyclopédie,* and although the article on "Police" is signed "A.," otherwise the cipher for Antoine-Gaspard Boucher d'Argis, counselor at the Châtelet in Paris, headquarters of the Lieutenant of Police, part of the text is taken verbatim from Guillote's unpublished manuscript addressed to Louis XV. "POLICE, s.f. (*Gouvern.*)," in *Encyclopédie, ou Dictionnaire,* ed. d'Alembert and Diderot, 12:904–12, esp. 911. Guillote is usually credited with writing only one article for the *Encyclopédie,* in collaboration with Lenglet Du Fresnoy, on "Pont militaire." It is possible that Diderot, who was Guillote's neighbor in the rue Mouffetarde, may have had access to the manuscript.

56. François Guillote, *Mémoire sur la réformation de la police de France. Soumis au Roi en 1749,* ed. Jean Seznec (Paris: Hermann, 1974), 35.

57. Michel Foucault, *Surveiller et punir: Naissance de la prison* (Paris: Éditions Gallimard, 1975), 250–51.

58. See for example the description in Mercier, *Tableau de Paris,* 1:117–21.

59. The first sidewalk in Paris was on the Pont-Neuf (1607); the first street sidewalk was constructed in the rue de l'Odéon in 1781. Bernard Landau, "La fabrication des rues de Paris au XIXe siècle: Un territoire d'innovation technique et politique," *Les Annales de la recherche urbaine* 57–58 (1992): 25.

60. Daniel Vaillancourt, *Les Urbanités parisiennes au XVIIe siècle* (Quebec: Les Presses de l'Université Laval, 2009), 238–39; Bernard Landau, "La fabrication des rues de Paris," 25. Sidewalks were not installed throughout France until after the decree of 1845.

61. Leon Bernard, "Technological Innovation in Seventeenth-Century Paris," in *The Pre-Industrial Cities and Technology Reader,* ed. Colin Chant (London: Routledge, 1999), 157–62; Bernard Causse, *Les Fiacres de Paris au XVIIe et XVIIIe siècles* (Paris: Presses Universitaires de France, 1972), 38.

62. Vaillancourt, *Les Urbanités parisiennes,* 254; Bernard, "Technological Innovation," 157.

63. The grand boulevards from the Porte Sainte-Antoine to the Porte Saint-Honoré were created by Louis XIV from 1668 to 1705 and became one of the main attractions of eighteenth-century Paris, in part because rows of trees separated pedestrians from horses and carriages. See for example the police ordinance of 28 August 1751, in Peuchet, *Collection des lois*, Second Series: 6:71–74.

64. Guillote, *Mémoire sur la réformation*, 19. Major fires were indeed almost the only opportunity for early modern cities to reconstruct themselves on a grand scale, as in the transformation of medieval London after the Great Fire of London in 1666. Peter Elmer, "The Early Modern City," in *Pre-Industrial Cities and Technology*, ed. Chant and Goodman, 202.

65. Elmer, "Early Modern City," 198–211.

66. Peuchet, *Collection des lois*, Second Series: 1:119–26; Jacques Bourgeois-Gavardin, *Les Boues de Paris sous l'Ancien Régime* (Paris: EHESS, 1985), 47–51.

67. Jacques Peuchet, "Jurisprudence/ De l'exercice de la police," *Encyclopédie méthodique*, quoted in Vincent Milliot, *Un Policier des Lumières, suivi de Mémoires de J.C.P. Lenoir* (Seyssel, France: Éditions Champ Vallon, 2011), 144.

68. These regulations were collected in sixty-two bound manuscript volumes, each 300–600 pages long, by Dupré, one of the fifty police commissioners, c. 1737–1765; some volumes were lost during the French Revolution, but most are still preserved at the Bibliothèque nationale de France. Hervé, "L'Ordre à Paris au XVIIIe siècle," 185–214.

69. Peuchet, *Collection des lois*, Second Series; Jacob [Lacroix], *Recueil curieux*.

70. Charles de Secondat de Montesquieu, *Esprit des lois* (1748; repr. Paris: Firmin-Didot, 1849), Book 26, ch. 24, 415.

71. The livre tournois fluctuated in value throughout the eighteenth century, but one ounce of gold was worth roughly 90 livres; there were 20 sous to a livre. At 2019 gold prices, 300 livres would approximately be worth 12,000 euros.

72. Peuchet, *Collection des lois*, Second Series: 4:281; 6:3.

73. Peuchet, *Collection des lois*, Second Series: 4:115–17; Catherine Denys, "La Police du nettoiement au XVIIIe siècle," *Ethnologie Française* 153 (2015): 413.

74. Peuchet, *Collection des lois*, Second Series: 4:281; 6:194–95.

75. Jacob [Lacroix], *Recueil curieux*, 94; see also Nicolas de la Mare, *Traité de la police* (Paris: Jean & Pierre Cot, 1705–1738), 1:396.

76. Ordonnance de Police, pour prevenir les incendies, 10 February 1735, reprinted in Peuchet, *Collection des lois*, Second Series: 4:160–69.

77. "Déclaration du Roi, portant réglement pour les ouvrages et vaisselles d'or, vermeil doré et d'argent," 16 December 1689, reprinted in Peuchet, *Collection des lois*, Second Series: 1:491–499. See also the earlier legislation on this subject issued by Louis XIV in Jacob [Lacroix], *Recueil curieux*, 1:88.

78. Arlette Farge, *Vivre dans la rue à Paris au XVIIIe siècle* (1979 ; repr. Paris: Gallimard, 1992), 208.

79. Bourgeois-Gavardin, *Les Boues de Paris*, 68–71; Denys, "La Police," 414.

80. Elmer, "The Early Modern City," 200–207.

81. Denys, "La Police," 417.

82. Quoted in Riitta Laitinen and Dag Lindstrom, "Urban Order and Street Regulation in Seventeenth-Century Sweden," in *Cultural History of Early Modern European Streets*, ed. Riitta Laitinen and Thomas V. Cohen (Leiden: Brill, 2009), 70.

83. "Arrêt du Conseil d'État du Roi, qui fait défense d'étaler des marchandises sur les trottoirs du Pont-Neuf," 5 April 1756, reprinted in Peuchet, *Collection des lois*, Second Series: 6:236–40.

84. Albert O. Hirschman, *The Passions and the Interests: Political Arguments for Capitalism before Its Triumph* (Princeton: Princeton University Press, 1977).

85. Mercier, *L'An 2440*, ch. 5.

86. John Trusler, "Rules of Behaving of General Use, though Much Disregarded in this Populous City" (1786), quoted in Catharina Löffler, *Walking in the City. Urban Experience and Literary Psychogeography in Eighteenth-Century London* (Wiesbaden: J. B. Metzler, 2017), 84; see also John Gay's satirical poem "Trivia: Or, The Art of Walking the Streets of London," (1716), reprinted in *The Penguin Book of Eighteenth-Century English Verse*, ed. Dennis Davison (Harmondsworth: Penguin Books, 1973), 98–103.

87. Sabine Barles, "La Rue parisienne au XIXe siècle: standardisation et contrôle?" *Romantisme* 1 (2016): 26.

88. "Ordonnance de Police, concernant la police du rempart de la Porte Saint-Antoine à la Porte Saint-Honoré," 28 August 1751, Peuchet, *Collection des lois*, Second Series: 6:71–74.

89. For example, the *Almanach du commerce de Paris* (Paris: Favre, An VII [1798]), which mentions earlier such almanacs for the cities of Lyon, Marseille, Rouen, and Bordeaux. See gallica.bnf.fr/ark:/12148/bpt6k62929887/f8.item, accessed 3 August 2021.

90. Bourgeois-Gavardin, *Les Boues de Paris*, 8; "Ordonnance de Police, concernant le nettoiement des rues," 3 February 1734, Peuchet, *Collection des lois*, Second Series: 4:115–17.

91. Griep, "Die reinliche Stadt," 141–42; Denys, "La Police," 412. On belief in miasmas see Alain Corbin, *The Foul and the Fragrant. Odor and the French Social Imagination* (1982), trans. Miriam L. Cochan with Roy Porter and Christopher Prendergast (Cambridge, Mass.: Harvard University Press. 1986), 90-95.

92. "Arrêt du Conseil d'État du Roi, 21 November 1758, qui ordonne que les fonds destinés pour l'illumination et le nettoiement de la ville de Paris, seront augmenté de cinquante mille livres," reprinted in Peuchet, *Collection des lois*, Second Series: 6:349.

93. Barles, "La Rue parisienne," 27; Sabine Barles and André Guillerme, *La Congestion urbaine en France (1800–1970)* (Champs-sur-Marne, France: Laboratoire TMU/ARDU, 1998), 149–78.

94. Sabine Barle, "La Boue, la voiture et l'amuser public. Les transformations de la voirie parisienne fin XVIIIe–fin XIXe siècles," *Ethnologie française* 14 (2015): 426.

95. Elmer, "Early Modern City," 212.

96. Elmer, "Early Modern City," 201.

97. Bernard Rouleau, *Le Tracé des rues de Paris: Formation, typologie, fonctions* (Paris: Éditions du Centre National de la Recherche Scientifique, 1967), 88; Vincent Denis, "Les Parisiens, la police et les numérotages des maisons au XVIIIe siècle à l'Empire," *French Historical Studies* 38 (2015): 95.

98. Jules Verne, *Paris au XXe siècle*, ed. Piero Gondolo della Riva (Paris: Hachette, 1994), 43. The manuscript of the novel was lost after Verne's death and recovered only in the 1980s. For the convoluted history of the text, see Verne, *Paris au XXe siècle*, 11–22.

99. Hans-Werner Eroms and Horst H. Munske, *Die Rechtschreibreform, Pro und Kontra* (Berlin: Schmidt, 1997).

100. The court ruled that each of the German states (*Bundesländer*) had the right to prescribe which spelling rules would be taught in its schools and that the reforms did not violate the constitutional rights of parents and pupils. Bundesverfassungsgericht, 1BvR 1640/97, 14 July 1998, available at www.bundesverfassungsgericht.de/e /rs19980714_1bvr164097.html, accessed 21 August 2021.

101. *Scotland on Sunday*, 17 August 2008, quoted in Simon Horobin, *Does Spelling Matter?* (Oxford: Oxford University Press, 2013), 11.

102. Monika Keller, *Ein Jahrhundert Reformen der französischen Orthographie. Geschichte eines Scheiterns* (Tübingen: Stauffenberg Verlag, 1991); Académie française, "Déclaration de l'Académie française sur la 'réforme de l'orthographie,'" 11 February 2016, available at www.academie-francaise.fr/actualites/declaration-de-lacademie -francaise-sur-la-reforme-de-lorthographe, accessed 21 August 2021.

103. "Le masculin de la langue n'est pas le masculin du monde sensible," *Le Monde*, 31 May 2019. On the controversy, see Danièle Manesse and Gilles Siouffi, eds, *Le Féminin et le masculin dans la langue* (Paris: ESF sciences humaines, 2019) and, on the opposing side, Maria Candea and Laélia Véron, *Le français est à nous! Petit manuel d'émancipation linguistique* (Paris: La Découverte, 2019).

104. Horobin, *Does Spelling Matter?*, 176–77, 8.

105. Laurence de Looze, "Orthography and National Identity in the Sixteenth Century," *Sixteenth-Century Journal* 43, no. 2 (2012): 372; Giovanni Nencioni, "L'accademia della Crusca e la lingua italiana," *Historiographica Linguistica* 9, no. 3 (2012): 321–33.

106. John Hart, *Orthographie, conteyning the due order and reason, howe to write or paint thimage of mannes voice, most like to the life or nature* (1569) facsimile reprint (Amsterdam: Theatrum Orbis Terrarum, 1968), sig, Aii verso.

107. Hart, *Orthographie*, 28 recto.

108. "The Compositor to the Reader," in Hart, *Orthographie*, n.p.

109. Hart, *Orthographie*, 4 recto and verso.

110. Hart, *Orthographie*, 37 recto.

111. Richard Mulcaster, *The First Part of the Elementarie, which entreateh chieflie of the writing of our English tung* (London: Thomas Vautroullier, 1582), dedicatory epistle to Robert Dudley, Earl of Leicester, n.p.

112. T. H. Howard-Hill, "Early Modern Printers and the Standardization of English Spelling," *Modern Language Review* 101 (2000): 23.

113. "Préface du *Dictionnaire de l'Académie française*," 7th ed. (1878), reprinted in Bernard Quemada, ed., *Les Préfaces du Dictionnaire de l'Académie française 1694–1992* (Paris: Honoré Champion, 1997), 406–7.

114. *Vocabulario degli Accademici della Crusca* (Venice: Giovanni Alberto, 1612), online critical edition of Scuola normale superiore at vocabolario.sns.it/html/index .htm, accessed 20 February 2020.

115. Louis Meigret, *Traité touchāt le commvn vsage de l'escriture françoise* (Paris: Ieanne de Marnes, 1545). Meigret himself abandoned his reformed spelling in his later works. De Looze, "Orthography and National Identity," 378, 382.

116. Mulcaster, *First Part of the Elementarie*, 67, 71, 72, and 74.

117. Mulcaster, *First Part of the Elementarie*, 158.

118. See for example "Préface du *Dictionnaire de l'Académie française*," 3rd ed. (1740), reprinted in Quemada, ed., *Les Préfaces*, 169.

119. "Préface du *Dictionnaire de l'Académie française*," 7th ed. (1878), reprinted in Quemada, ed., *Les Préfaces*, 411.

120. Mulcaster, *First Part of the Elementarie*, 74, 105, 124, 156, 158.

121. Louis de L'Esclache, *Les Véritables régles de l'orthografe francéze, ov L'Art d'aprandre an peu de tams à écrire côrectement* (Paris: L'Auteur et Lavrant Rondet, 1668).

122. "Préface du *Dictionnaire de l'Académie française*," 1st ed. (1694), reprinted in Quemada, ed., *Les Préfaces*, 33.

123. Wolfgang Werner Sauer and Helmut Glück, "Norms and Reforms: Fixing the Form of the Language," in *The German Language and the Real World*, ed. Patrick Stevenson (Oxford: Clarendon Press, 1995), 75.

124. Horobin, *Does Spelling Matter?*, 13.

125. Mulcaster, *First Part of the Elementarie*, 109.

126. Samuel Johnson, "Preface," *A Dictionary of the English Language* (1755), quoted in Horobin, *Does Spelling Matter?*, 144.

127. Mulcaster, *The First Part of the Elementarie*, 164. The "Generall Table" of examples is given on 170–225; with only a few exceptions (e.g., "alwaie" vs. "always"), the spellings are modern.

128. Mulcaster, *First Part of the Elementarie*, 169.

129. Quemada, ed., *Les Préfaces*, 22.

130. Art. 24, *Statuts et règlements de l'Académie française* (1634), quoted in Quemada, ed., *Les Préfaces*, 12.

131. Jonathan Swift, *A Proposal for Correcting, Improving and Ascertaining the English Tongue*, 2nd ed. (London: Benjamin Tooke, 1712), 31.

132. "Préface du *Dictionnaire de l'Académie française*," 1st ed. (1694), reprinted in Quemada, ed., *Les Préfaces*, 28.

133. Swift, *Proposal*, 19, 28.

134. "Préface du *Dictionnaire de l'Académie française*," 3rd ed. (1740), reprinted in Quemada, ed., *Les Préfaces*, 171.

135. "Préface du *Dictionnaire de l'Académie française*," 3rd ed. (1740), reprinted in Quemada, ed., *Les Préfaces*, 169.

136. Mulcaster, *First Part of the Elementarie*, 159.

137. "Préface du *Dictionnaire de l'Académie française*," 1st ed. (1694), reprinted in Quemada, ed., *Les Préfaces*, 28.

138. De Looze, "Orthography and National Identity," 388.

139. Mulcaster, *First Part of the Elementarie*, 254. On the Académie française, see for example www.academie-francaise.fr/pitcher-un-projet, accessed 27 February 2020.

140. Noah Webster, *The American Spelling Book*, 16th ed. (Hartford: Hudson & Goodwin, n.d.), viii.

141. Horobin, *Does Spelling Matter?*, 196–98.

142. Dieter Nerius, *Deutsche Orthographie*, 4th rev. ed. (Hildesheim, Germany: Georg Olms Verlag, 2007), 302–37.

143. The correspondence relating to this conference is reproduced in Paul Grebe, ed., *Akten zur Geschichte der deutschen Einheitsschreibung 1870–1880* (Mannheim: Bibliographisches Institut, 1963).

144. Nerius, *Deutsche Orthographie*, 344–47.

145. Sauer and Glück, "Norms and Reforms," 79–82.

146. Nerius, *Deutsche Orthographie*, 373.

147. Horobin, *Does Spelling Matter?*, 8.

148. Horobin, *Does Spelling Matter?*, 157.

149. Stanislas Dehaene, *Reading in the Brain: The New Science of How We Read* (New York: Penguin, 2010), 72–76.

150. Duden, Rechtschreibregeln, available at www.duden.de/sprachwissen/rechtschreibregeln, accessed 27 February 2020.

151. *Frankfurter Allgemeine Zeitung*, 12 August 1988, quoted in Sauer and Glück, "Norms and Reforms," 86.

152. James Maguire, *American Bee: The National Spelling Bee and the Culture of Nerds* (Emmaus, Penn.: Rodale, 2006), 65–74.

153. Hannes Rackozy, Felix Warneken, and Michael Tomasello, "Sources of Normativity: Young Children's Awareness of the Normative Structure of Games," *Developmental Psychology* 44 (2008): 875–81.

Chapter 7. Natural Laws and Laws of Nature

1. Denis Cosgrove, *Apollo's Eye: A Cartographic Genealogy of the Earth in the Western Imagination* (Baltimore: Johns Hopkins University Press, 2001) surveys this tradition.

2. George Stocking, *Victorian Anthropology* (New York: Free Press, 1987); George Boas, *Primitivism and Related Ideas in the Middle Ages* (Baltimore: Johns Hopkins University Press, 1997).

3. Sophocles, *Antigone*, in David Grene, trans., *Sophocles I: Oedipus the King, Oedipus at Colonus, and Antigone* (Chicago: University of Chicago Press, 1991), 178, ll. 456–57.

4. Aristotle, *Art of Rhetoric*, trans. John Henry Freese. Loeb Classical Library (Cambridge, Mass.: Harvard University Press, 1994), I.13, 1373b6–12, 138–39.

5. Marcus Tullius Cicero, *On the Republic*, III.22, in *On the Republic and On the Laws*, trans. Clinton W. Keyes, Loeb Classical Library (Cambridge, Mass.: Harvard University Press, 1928), 211. For a general survey of ancient concepts of natural law, see Karl-Heinz Ilting, *Naturrecht und Sittlichkeit: Begriffsgeschichtliche Studien* (Stuttgart: Klett-Cotta, 1983).

6. These terms were often used interchangeably through the early modern period. Jan Schröder, "The Concept of (Natural) Law in the Doctrine of Law and Natural Law in the Early Modern Era," in *Natural Laws and Laws of Nature in Early Modern Europe*, ed. Lorraine Daston and Michael Stolleis (Farnham: Ashgate, 2008), 59.

7. *Digest*, 1.1.1.3 (Ulpian), available at www.thelatinlibrary.com/justinian/digest1 .shtml, accessed 6 July 2020.

8. Peter Stein, *Roman Law in European History* (Cambridge: Cambridge University Press, 1999), 86–88.

9. Gerard Watson, "The Natural Law and the Stoics," in *Problems in Stoicism*, ed. A. A. Long (London: Athalone Press, 1971), 228–36.

10. Thomas Aquinas, *Summa theologiae*, New Advent online edition, I–II, Qu. 93, Articles 2–5, I–II, Qu. 94, Articles 4–5, I–II, Qu. 100, Article 1, available at www .newadvent.org/summa/2093.htm, accessed 12 July 2021.

11. Jacques Chiffoleau, "Dire indicible: Remarques sur la catégorie du nefandum du XIIe au XVe siècle," *Annales ESC* 2 (May–April 1990): 289–324; Keith Wrightson, "Infanticide in European History," *Criminal Justice History* 3 (1982): 1–20; Richard van Dülmen, *Frauen vor Gericht. Kindermord in der Frühen Neuzeit* (Frankfurt am Main: Fischer Verlag, 1991), 20–26; Bernd-Ulrich Hergemöller, "Sodomiter: Erscheinungsformen und Kausalfaktoren des spätmittelalterlichen Kampfes gegen Homosexualität," in *Randgruppen der mittelalterlichen Gesellschaft*, ed. Bernd-Ulrich Hergemöller (Warendorf, Germany: Fahlbusch, 1990), 316–56; Elisabeth Pavan, "Police des moeurs, société et politique à Venise à la fin du Moyen Age," *Revue historique* 264 (1980): 241–88.

12. *Digest*, 1.1.4 (Ulpian), available at www.thelatinlibrary.com/justinian/digest1.shtml, accessed 6 July 2020.

13. Yan Thomas, "Imago Naturae: Note sur l'instituionnalité de la nature à Rome," *Théologie et droit dans la science politique de l'état moderne* (Rome: École française de Rome, 1991), 201–27.

14. Marcus Tullius Cicero, *On the Laws*, I.xv.42, in *On the Republic and On the Laws*, 345.

15. Augustine of Hippo, *Confessions*, III.8, trans. William Watts, Loeb Classical Library (Cambridge, Mass.: Harvard University Press, 1989), 1:128–129.

16. Thomas Aquinas, *Summa theologiae*, New Advent online edition, II–II, Qu. 53, Article 2, available at www.newadvent.org/summa/3053.htm#article2, accessed 12 July 2021. *Catechism of the Catholic Church*, no. 2357, 8 September 1997. The latter forbids homosexual acts as "contrary to natural law. They close the sexual act to the gift of life."

17. Seneca, *Medea*, in *Tragedies*, trans. Frank Justus Miller, Loeb Classical Library (Cambridge, Mass.: Harvard University Press, 1979), 293, 305. On the long-lived tradition of construing Medea as mad, see P. E. Easterling, "The Infanticide in Euripides' Medea," *Yale Classical Studies* 25 (1977): 177.

18. George Economou, *The Goddess Nature in Medieval Literature* (Cambridge, Mass.: Harvard University Press, 1972), 104–11; Katharine Park, "Nature in Person," in *The Moral Authority of Nature*, ed. Lorraine Daston and Fernando Vidal (Chicago: University of Chicago Press, 2004), 50–73. On the iconographic tradition, see Mechthild Modersohn, *Natura als Göttin im Mittelalter: Ikonographische Studien zu Darstellungen der personifizierten Natur* (Berlin: Akademie Verlag, 1997).

19. Augustine of Hippo, *Confessions*, III.8, trans. William Watts, Loeb Classical Library (Cambridge, Mass.: Harvard University Press, 1989), 1:128–29; Michael Stolleis, "The Legitimation of Law through God, Tradition, Will, Nature and Constitution," in *Natural Laws*, ed. Daston and Stolleis, 47.

20. On the ambiguities of the Sophist opposition between *nomos* and *physis*, see E. R. Dodds, *The Greeks and the Irrational* (Berkeley: University of California Press, 1951), 183–84.

21. Joachim Kurtz, "Autopsy of a Textual Monstrosity: Dissecting the Mingli tan (*De logica*, 1631)," in *Linguistic Changes between Europe, China, and Japan*, ed. Federica Caselin (Turin: Tiellemedia, 2008), 35–58.

22. Anthony Pagden, "Dispossessing the Barbarian: The Language of Spanish Thomism and the Debate over the Property Rights of the American Indians," in *The Languages of Political Theory in Early Modern Europe*, ed. Anthony Pagden (Cambridge: Cambridge University Press, 1987), 79–98.

23. Michel de Montaigne, *The Complete Essays*, trans. M. A. Screech (London: Penguin, 1991), I. 31: "On Cannibals," 231.

24. Pauline C. Westerman, *The Disintegration of Natural Law Theory: Aquinas to Finnis* (Leiden: Brill, 1998), 130–33.

25. Ian Hunter and David Saunders, eds., *Natural Law and Civil Sovereignty: Moral Right and State Authority in Early Modern Political Thought* (New York: Palgrave Macmillan, 2002), 2–3.

26. Hugo Grotius, *De jure belli ac pacis libri tres* (1625), trans. Francis W. Kelsey (Oxford: Clarendon Press, 1925), 2:11–13.

27. Thomas Hobbes, *Leviathan* (1651), ed. Colin B. Macpherson (London: Penguin, 1968), I.14, 189.

28. Samuel Pufendorf, *The Whole Duty of Man, According to the Law of Nature* (1673), trans. Andrew Tooke, ed. Ian Hunter and David Saunders (Indianapolis: Liberty Fund, 2003), 56.

29. Hobbes, *Leviathan*, I.14, 190; Christian Thomasius, *Institutes of Divine Jurisprudence* (1688), trans. and ed. Thomas Ahnert (Indianapolis: Liberty Fund, 2011), 180.

30. Thomasius, *Institutes of Divine Jurisprudence*, 140.

31. Grotius, *De jure belli*, 2:38.

32. René Descartes, *Principia philosophiae* (1644), II. 37–40, in *Oeuvres de Descartes*, ed. Charles Adam and Paul Tannery (Paris: J. Vrin, 1964), 8:62–66.

33. René Descartes, *Regulae ad directionem ingenii* (comp. c. 1628), in *Oeuvres de Descartes*, ed. Adam and Tannery, 10:403–6.

34. Friedrich Steinle, "The Amalgamation of a Concept: Laws of Nature in the New Sciences," in *Laws of Nature: Essays on the Philosophical, Scientific and Historical Dimensions*, ed. Friedel Weinert (Berlin: Walter de Gruyter, 1995), 316–68.

35. Grotius, *De jure belli*, 2:255.

36. René Descartes, *Discours de la méthode pour bien conduire sa raison et chercher la vérité dans les sciences* (1637), in *Oeuvres de Descartes*, ed. Adam and Tannery, 6:65–66.

37. Robert Boyle, *A Free Inquiry into the Vulgarly Received Notion of Nature* (1686), in *The Works of the Honourable Robert Boyle*, ed. Thomas Birch (Hildesheim, Germany: Georg Olms, 1966), 5:164, 170. On the sixteenth-century background to Boyle's scruples and Leibniz's response to the Latin version of Boyle's treatise, see Catherine Wilson, "*De Ipsa Naturae*: Leibniz on Substance, Force and Activity," *Studia Leibniziana* 19 (1987): 148–72.

38. Lorraine Daston, *Against Nature* (Cambridge, Mass.: MIT Press, 2019), 5–21. For overviews of the diversity of ancient Greek and medieval Latin concepts of nature, see, respectively, Geoffrey E. R. Lloyd, "Greek Antiquity: The Invention of Nature," and Alexander Murray, "Nature and Man in the Middle Ages," both in *The Concept of Nature*, ed. John Torrance (Oxford: Clarendon Press, 1992), 1–24, 25–62.

39. Francis Bacon, *Novum organum* (1620), Aphorisms II.2 and II.5, in *The Works of Francis Bacon*, ed. Basil Montagu (London: William Pickering, 1825–34), 9:287–88, 291–93; Boyle, *Free Inquiry*, 5:219.

40. Seneca, *Naturales quaestiones*, trans. Thomas H. Corcoran, Loeb Classical Library (Cambridge, Mass.: Harvard University Press, 1922), VII.25, 2:278–79; Daryn Lehoux, "Laws of Nature and Natural Laws," *Studies in History and Philosophy of Science* 37 (2006): 535–37.

41. Jane E. Ruby, "The Origins of Scientific Law," *Journal of the History of Ideas* 47 (1986): 341–59; Ian Maclean, "Expressing Nature's Regularities and their Determinations in the Late Renaissance," in *Natural Laws*, ed. Daston and Stolleis, 30.

42. Bacon, *Novum organum*, 472–74.

43. Gerd Grasshof, "Natural Law and Celestial Regularities from Copernicus to Kepler," in *Natural Laws*, ed. Daston and Stolleis, 143–61.

44. Catherine Wilson, "From Limits to Laws: The Construction of the Nomological Image of Nature in Early Modern Philosophy," in *Natural Laws*, ed. Daston and Stolleis, 13–28.

45. Isaac Newton, *The Mathematical Principles of Natural Philosophy* (1687), trans. Andrew Motte (London: Benjamin Motte, 1729), 19–21.

46. Steinle, "The Amalgamation of a Concept," 316–68.

47. Friedrich Steinle, "From Principles to Regularities: Tracing 'Laws of Nature' in Early Modern France and England," and Sophie Roux, "Controversies on Nature as Universal Legality (1680–1710)," both in *Natural Laws*, ed. Daston and Stolleis, 215–32, 199–214.

48. For a concise overview, see John Henry, "Metaphysics and the Origins of Modern Science: Descartes and the Importance of Laws of Nature," *Early Science and Medicine* 9 (2004): 73–114.

49. Catherine Larrère, "Divine dispense," *Droits* 25 (1997): 19–32.

50. Boyle, *Free Inquiry*, 5:252.

51. A. Rupert Hall, *Philosophers at War: The Quarrel between Newton and Leibniz* (Cambridge: Cambridge University Press, 1998).

52. On the political context, see Domenico Bertoloni Meli, "Caroline, Leibniz, and Clarke," *Journal of the History of Ideas* 60 (1999): 469–86.

53. Isaac Newton, *Opticks* (1704; repr. New York: Dover, 1952), Query 31, 375–406, on 398–99.

54. H. G. Alexander, ed. *The Leibniz-Clarke Correspondence* (1717), (Manchester: Manchester University Press, 1956), 12, 14, 81, 35, 114.

55. Newton, *The Mathematical Principles*, 388–92.

56. Charles-Louis de Secondat, Baron de la Brède et de Montesquieu, *De l'Esprit des lois* (1748; Paris: Firmin-Didot, 1849), 4.

57. [Antoine Gaspard Boucher d'Argis], "Droit positif," *Encyclopédie, ou Dictionnaire raisonné des arts, des sciences et des métiers*, ed. Jean d'Alembert and Denis Diderot (Paris: Briasson, David, Le Breton, and Durand, 1755), 5:134.

58. Nicolas Malebranche, *De la Recherche de la vérité* (1674–75) (Paris: Michel David, 1712), I.vii.3, 1:242.

59. Lorraine Daston and Katharine Park, *Wonders and the Order of Nature, 1150–1750* (New York: Zone Books, 1998), 334–59.

60. David Hume, "Of Miracles," *Enquiry Concerning Human Nature* (1748), ed. Eric Steinberg (Indianapolis: Hackett, 1977), 72–90.

61. Francis Bacon, *The Elements of the Common Lawes of England* (1630), in *Lord Bacon's Works*, ed. Basil Montagu (London: William Pickering, 1825–34), 13:134; Gottfried Wilhelm Leibniz, *Neue Methode, Jurisprudenz zu Lernen und zu Lehren* (1667), in *Frühere Schriften zum Naturrecht*, ed. Hans Zimmermann, trans. Hubertus Busche (Hamburg: Felix Meiner Verlag, 2003), 57.

62. Grotius, *De jure belli*, 2:192; Pufendorf, *Whole Duty of Man*, 223.

63. Boyle, *Free Inquiry*, 5:220.

64. Leibniz, *Neue Methode*, 63. See also letter from Gottfried Wilhelm Leibniz to Hermann Conring, 13/23 January 1670, in Leibniz, *Neue Methode*, 333. For further parallels between Leibniz's thinking about natural law and laws of nature, see Klaus Luig, "Leibniz's Concept of *jus naturale* and *lex naturalis*—Defined with 'Geometric Certainty,'" in *Natural Laws*, ed. Daston and Stolleis, 183–98.

65. Larrère, "Divine dispense," 19–32. See for example Thomas Aquinas on the case of whether God's instructions to the Israelites to despoil the Egyptians of their goods constituted theft. *Summa theologicae*, New Advent online edition, I–II, Qu. 100, Art. 8, available at www.newadvent.org/summa/2100.htm#article8, accessed 12 July 2021.

66. [Chevalier de Jaucourt], "Loi," *Encyclopédie*, ed. d'Alembert and Diderot, 9:643–46.

67. Lorraine Daston, "Unruly Weather: Natural Law Confronts Natural Variability," in *Natural Laws*, ed. Daston and Stolleis, 233–48.

68. Jean Domat, *Les Loix civiles dans leur ordre naturel* (1689; repr. Paris: Pierre Gandouin, 1723), 1:xxvi.

69. Stein, *Roman Law*, 101–12.

70. Montesquieu, *De l'Esprit des lois*, 5.

71. François Quesnay, *Le Droit naturel* (Paris: n. publ., 1765), 16–17.

72. Immanuel Kant, *Foundations of the Metaphysics of Morals* (1785), trans. Lewis White Beck (Indianapolis: Library of Liberal Arts, 1954), 39.

Chapter 8. Bending and Breaking Rules

1. Thomas Aquinas, *Summa theologiae*, New Advent online edition, I,-II, Qu. 100, Art. 5 https://www.newadvent.org/summa/2100.htm#article5; I,-II, Qu. 94, Art. 5. https://www.newadvent.org/summa/2094.htm#article5. Accessed 12 July 2021.

2. Samuel Pufendorf, *The Whole Duty of Man, According to the Law of Nature* (1673), trans. Andrew Tooke, ed. Ian Hunter and David Saunders (Indianapolis: Liberty Fund, 2003), 93.

3. John Locke, *Second Treatise of Government* (1690), ed. C. B. Macpherson (Indianapolis: Hackett, 1980), XIII.158, 83.

4. Plato, *Statesman—Philebus—Ion,* trans. Harold North Fowler and W.R.M. Lamb, Loeb Classical Library (Cambridge, Mass.: Harvard University Press, 1925), 294B, 135.

5. For contrasting positions, see Jeremy Waldron, "Thoughtfulness and the Rule of Law," *British Academy Review* 18 (Summer 2011): 1–11, and Frederick Schauer, *Thinking Like a Lawyer: A New Introduction to Legal Reasoning* (Cambridge, Mass.: Harvard University Press, 2009).

6. Gianna Pomata, "The Recipe and the Case: Epistemic Genres and the Dynamics of Cognitive Practices," in *Wissenschaftsgeschichte und Geschichte des Wissens im Dialog—Connecting Science and Knowledge,* ed. Kaspar von Greyerz, Silvia Flubacher, and Philipp Senn (Göttingen: Vanderhoek und Ruprecht, 2013), 131–54; Gianna Pomata, "The Medical Case Narrative in Pre-Modern Europe and China: Comparative History of an Epistemic Genre," in *A Historical Approach to Casuistry: Norms and Exceptions in a Comparative Perspective,* ed. Carlo Ginzburg with Lucio Biasiori (London: Bloomsbury Academic, 2019), 15–43.

7. Angela N. H. Creager, Elizabeth Lunbeck, and M. Norton Wise, eds., *Science without Laws: Model Systems, Cases, Exemplary Narratives* (Durham, N.C.: Duke University Press, 2007).

8. Thomas Jefferson, *A Manual of Parliamentary Practice for the Use of the Senate of the United States* (Washington City: Samuel H. Smith, 1801), n.p.

9. Colin Burrow, *Imitating Authors: From Plato to Futurity* (Oxford: Oxford University Press, 2019), 71–105.

10. Étienne Bauny, *Somme des pechez qui se commettent tous les états: De leurs conditions & qualitez, & en quelles consciences ils sont mortels, ou veniels* (1630; repr. Lyon: Simon Regaud, 1646), 227–28.

11. Margaret Sampson, "Laxity and Liberty in Seventeenth-Century Political Thought," in *Conscience and Casuistry in Early Modern Europe,* ed. Edmund Leites (Cambridge: Cambridge University Press, 2002), 88, 99.

12. John Forrester, "If P, Then What? Thinking in Cases," *History of the Human Sciences* 9 (1996): 1–25.

13. On the medical and legal collections, see Gianna Pomata, "Observation Rising: Birth of an Epistemic Genre, ca. 1500–1650," in *Histories of Scientific Observations,* ed. Lorraine Daston and Elizabeth Lunbeck (Chicago: University of Chicago Press, 2011), 45–80; Gianna Pomata, "Sharing Cases: The *Observationes* in Early Modern Medicine," *Early Science and Medicine* 15 (2010): 193–236.

14. Charlotte Furth, "Introduction: Thinking with Cases," in *Thinking with Cases: Specialist Knowledge in Chinese Cultural History,* ed. Charlotte Furth, Judith T. Zeitlin, and Ping-chen Hsiung (Honolulu: University of Hawaii Press, 2007), 1–27.

15. André Jolles, *Einfache Formen: Legende, Sage, Mythe, Rätsel, Spruch, Kasus, Memorabile, Märchen, Witz* (1930), 8th ed. (Tübingen: Max Niemeyer Verlag, 2006), 179.

16. John Arthos, "Where There Are No Rules or Systems to Guide Us: Argument from Example in a Hermeneutic Rhetoric," *Quarterly Journal of Speech* 89 (2003): 333.

17. William Perkins, *The Whole Treatise of the Cases of Conscience* (London: John Legatt, 1631), 95.

18. On the background to the polemic, see Olivier Jouslin, *La Campagne des Provinciales de Pascal. Étude d'un dialogue polémique* (Clermont-Ferrand, France: Presses Universitaires, 2007).

19. Only Letters Five through Ten deal with casuistry. The rest of the book (originally published as pamphlet installments from January 1656 to May 1627) defends Pascal's fellow Jansenist Antoine Arnauld's predestinarian doctrines against the censure of the Sorbonne and the attacks of the Jesuits.

20. Blaise Pascal, *Les Provinciales, ou Les lettres écrites par Louis de Montalte à un provincial de ses amis et aux RR. PP. Jésuites sur le sujet de la morale et de la politique de ces Pères* (1627), ed. Michel Le Guern (Paris: Gallimard, 1987), 95, 102.

21. Richard Parish, "Pascal's Lettres provinciales: From Flippancy to Fundamentals," in *The Cambridge Companion to Pascal*, ed. Nicholas Hammond (Cambridge: Cambridge University Press, 2003), 182–200; for the broader context of such religious controversies in epistolary form, see Jean-Paul Gay, "Lettres de controverse: religion, publication et espace publique en France au XVIIe siècle," *Annales: Histoire, Sciences Sociales* 68 (2013): 7–41.

22. Laxism among casuists was condemned by Pope Alexander VII in 1665 and 1666 and by Pope Innocent XI in 1679.

23. Johann P. Somerville, "The 'New Art of Lying': Equivocation, Mental Reservation, and Casuistry," in *Conscience and Casuistry*, ed. Leites, 159–84; Albert R. Jonsen and Stephen Toulmin, *The Abuse of Casuistry: A History of Moral Reasoning* (Berkeley: University of California Press, 1990). I am grateful to Professor Gianna Pomata for pointing out to me that the genre of "cases of conscience" in Catholic theology has never died out but is alive and well in medical ethics, however defamed casuistry so-termed may be.

24. Ernst Coumet, "La théorie du hasard est-elle née par hasard?" *Annales: Économies, Sociétés, Civilisations* (May–June 1970): 574–98. It is an irony of history that the theory of probabilities, of which Pascal was the co-founder, should have come to bear the name of a doctrine he detested.

25. H. D. Kittsteiner, "Kant and Casuistry," in *Conscience and Casuistry*, ed. Leites, 185–213.

26. Immanuel Kant, *Die Religion innerhalb der Grenzen der bloßen Vernunft* (1793), ed. Rudolf Malter (Ditzingen, Germany: Reclam, 2017), 247.

27. Immanuel Kant, *Die Metaphysik der Sitten*, ed. Wilhelm Weisehedel (Frankfurt am Main: Suhrkamp, 1977), 562–72/A84–A98. I am grateful to Professor Susan Nieman for drawing my attention to these passages.

28. Fatimah Hajibabaee, Soodabeh Joolaee, Mohammed al Cheraghi, Pooneh Saleri, and Patricia Rodney, "Hospital/Clinical Ethics Committees' Notion: An Overview," *Journal of Medical Ethics and History of Medicine* 19 (2016), available atwww.ncbi.nlm.nih.gov/pmc/articles/PMC5432947/, accessed 4 December 2020.

29. Kwame Anthony Appiah, "The Ethicist," *New York Times Magazine,* 3 November 2020, 20 October 2020, available at www.nytimes.com/column/the-ethicist, accessed 4 December 2020.

30. Perkins, *Whole Treatise,* 116.

31. Aristotle, *Nicomachean Ethics*, trans. H. Rackham, Loeb Classical Library (Cambridge, Mass.: Harvard University Press, 1934),V.10/1137a31–1138a2, 314–17; Christopher Horn, "*Epieikeia*: The Competence of the Perfectly Just Person in Aristotle," in *The Virtuous Life in Greek Ethics*, ed. Burkhard Reiss (Cambridge: Cambridge University Press, 2006), 142–66; Schauer, *Thinking Like a Lawyer*, 121–22.

32. Peter Stein, *Roman Law in European History* (Cambridge: Cambridge University Press, 1999), 47.

33. Mark Fortier, *The Culture of Equity in Early Modern England* (London: Routledge, 2016), 3.

34. Sarah Worthington, *Equity* (Oxford: Oxford University Press, 2003), 8–11.

35. William Perkins, *Hepieikeia, or A Treatise of Christian Equitie and Moderation* (Cambridge: John Legat, 1604), 12–13.

36. Francis Bacon, *The Elements of the Common Lawes of England* (1630), in *Lord Bacon's Works*, ed. Basil Montagu (London: William Pickering, 1825–34), 13: 153. On Bacon's defense of the court of Chancery, see Fortier, *Culture of Equity*, 74–81.

37. Jean Domat, *Les Loix civiles dans leur ordre naturel* (1689; repr. Paris: Pierre Gandouin, 1723), 1:5.

38. Aristotle, *Art of Rhetoric*, trans. John Henry Freese, Loeb Classical Library (Cambridge, Mass.: Harvard University Press, 1994), I.i.7/1354a, 5.

39. John Selden, *Table Talk* (1689), quoted in Fortier, *Culture of Equity*, 1.

40. Perkins, *Hepieikeia*, 16.

41. Plato, *Statesman*, 297A, 143.

42. Perkins, *Hepieikeia*, 19–20.

43. Worthington, *Equity*, 11.

44. Fortier, *Culture of Equity*, 12–15.

45. David Hume, *An Inquiry Concerning the Principles of Morals* (1751), ed. Charles W. Hendel (Indianapolis: Library of Liberal Arts, 1979), 39.

46. Schauer, *Thinking Like a Lawyer*, 35.

47. On the philosophical roots of modern ideals of the rule of law, see Edin Sarcevic, *Der Rechtsstaat: Modernität und Universalitätsanspruch der klassischen*

Rechtsstaatstheorien (Leipzig: Leipziger Universitätsverlag, 1996), 101–38, and (for the British and American traditions) John Phillip Reid, *The Rule of Law: The Jurisprudence of Liberty in the Seventeenth and Eighteenth Centuries* (DeKalb: Northern Illinois University Press, 2004).

48. Francis Bacon, "The Lord Keeper's Speech, in the Exchequer, to Sir John Denham, When He Was Called to Be One of the Barons of the Exchequer, 1617," in *Lord Bacon's Works,* ed. Basil Montagu (London: William Pickering, 1825–34), 7:267–68.

49. "Bill of Rights of 1689: An Act Declaring the Rights and Liberties of the Subject and Settling the Succession of the Crown," The Avalon Project: Documents in Law, History and Diplomacy, Yale Law School, available at avalon.law.yale.edu/17th _century/england.asp, accessed 7 December 2020.

50. Carl Schmitt, *Political Theology: Four Chapters on the Concept of Sovereignty* (1922), trans. George Schwab (Chicago: University of Chicago Press, 1985), 5–12.

51. Kenneth Pennington, *The Prince and the Law, 1200–1600: Sovereignty and Rights in the Western Legal Tradition* (Berkeley: University of California Press, 1993), 76–118.

52. There is an immense literature on early modern European absolutism and republicanism. For overviews, see Holger Erwin, *Machtsprüche: Das herrscherliche Gestaltungsrecht "ex plenitudine potestatis" in der Frühen Neuzeit* (Cologne: Böhlau, 2009), and Quentin Skinner, *Liberty before Liberalism* (Cambridge: Cambridge University Press, 1998).

53. Robert Filmer, *Patriarcha, or the Natural Power of Kings* (London: Richard Chiswell, 1680), 12.

54. Jean Bodin, *Les Six livres de la république* (Paris: Iacques du Puys, 1576), 16, 21.

55. Francis Bacon, "The Argument of Sir Francis Bacon, Knight, His Majesty's Solicitor-General, in the Case of the Post-Nati of Scotland," in *Lord Bacon's Works,* ed. Basil Montagu (London: William Pickering, 1825–34), 5: 110.

56. Bodin, *Les Six livres,* 126; Filmer, *Patriarcha,* 94.

57. James I, *The Workes of the Most High and Mightie Prince, James,* ed. John Montagu (London: Robert Barker and John Bill, 1616), 529, quoted in Lisa Jardine and Alan Stewart, *Hostages to Fortune: The Troubled Life of Francis Bacon* (New York: Hill and Wang, 1998), 317.

58. Mary Nyquist, *Arbitrary Rule: Slavery, Tyranny, and the Power of Life and Death* (Chicago: University of Chicago Press, 2013), 327; Locke, *Second Treatise,* XIV.172, 90.

59. J.G.A. Pocock, *The Machiavellian Moment: Florentine Political Thought and the Atlantic Republican Tradition,* rev. ed. (Princeton: Princeton University Press, 2003).

60. Locke, *Second Treatise,* XIV.172, 90, IV.22, 17, XVI.177–87, 92–97.

61. [Thomas Fuller], *The Sovereigns Prerogative, and the Subjects Priviledge* (London: Martha Harrison, 1657), Preface (n.p.), 109.

62. [John Maxwell], *Sacro-Sancta Regum Majestae: Or the Sacred and Royal Prerogative of Christian Kings* (London: Thomas Dring, 1680), sig. a recto.

63. Locke, *Second Treatise*, XIII.156–58, 81–83.

64. Francis Oakley, "Christian Theology and Newtonian Science: The Rise of the Concept of Laws of Nature," *Church History* 30 (1961): 433–57; Steven Shapin, "Of Gods and Kings: Natural Philosophy and Politics in the Leibniz-Clarke Disputes," *Isis* 72 (1984): 187–215.

65. Schmitt, *Political Theology*, 36–48, quotation on 12.

66. Noel Cox, *The Royal Prerogative and Constitutional Law: A Search for the Quintessence of Executive Power* (London: Routledge, 2021), 9–14.

67. Jeffrey Crouch, *The Presidential Pardon Power* (Lawrence: University Press of Kansas, 2009), 15–21; Harold J. Krent, *Presidential Powers* (New York: New York University Press, 2004), 189–214.

68. Andrew W. Neal, *Security as Politics: Beyond the State of Exception* (Edinburgh: Edinburgh University Press, 2019), 12–41; "Trump Pardons Two Russian Inquiry Figures and Blackwater Guards," *New York Times*, 22 December 2020.

69. Carlo Ginzburg, "Preface," in *A Historical Approach to Casuistry*, ed. Ginzburg with Biasiori, xi.

BIBLIOGRAPHY

Archival Sources

C. Pritchard to E. Mouchez, 28 March 1892. Bibliothèque de l'Observatoire de Paris, 1060-V-A-2, Boite 30, Folder Oxford (Angleterre).

Dossier Gaspard de Prony, Archives de l'Académie des sciences, Paris.

Records of the *Nautical Almanac*, Manuscript Collection. Cambridge University Library, RGO 16/Boxes 1, 17.

Published Sources

Académie francaise. *Le Dictionnaire de l'Académie française.* 2nd ed. Paris: Imprimerie royale, 1718.

———. "Déclaration de l'Académie française sur la réforme de l'orthographie." 11 February 2016. Available at www.academie-francaise.fr/actualites/declaration-de -lacademie-francaise-sur-la-reforme-de-lorthographe.

Alder, Ken. *Engineering the Revolution: Arms and Enlightenment in France, 1763–1815.* Princeton: Princeton University Press, 1997.

Alembert, Jean d', and Denis Diderot, eds. "Encyclopédie." In *Encyclopédie, ou Dictionnaire raisonné des arts, des sciences et des métiers,* 17 vols. vol. 5, 635–48. Paris: Briasson, David, Le Breton, and Durand, 1751–1765.

Alexander, Henry Gavin, ed. *The Leibniz-Clarke Correspondence* [1717]. Manchester: Manchester University Press, 1956.

Almanach du commerce de Paris. Paris: Favre, An VII [1798]. Available at gallica.bnf .fr/ark:/12148/bpt6k62929887/f8.item.

Alsted, Johann Heinrich. *Encyclopaedia* [1630]. Edited by Wilhelm Schmidt- Biggemann, 4 vols. Stuttgart-Bad Cannstatt: Fromann-Holzboog, 1989.

Anderson, Chris. "The End of Theory: The Data Deluge Makes the Scientific Method Obsolete." *Wired Magazine* (23 June 2008). Available at archive.wired.com /science/discoveries/magazine/16-07/pb_theory.

Anderson, Christy, Anne Dunlop, and Pamela Smith, eds. *The Matter of Art: Materials, Practices, Cultural Logics, c. 1250–1750*. Manchester: Manchester University Press, 2014.

[Anonymous]. *Traité de confiture, ou Le nouveau et parfait Confiturier*. Paris: Chez Thomas Guillain, 1689.

[Anonymous]. *The Forme of Cury, A Roll of Ancient English Cookery, Compiled about A.D. 1390, by the Master-Cooks of King Richard II . . . By an Antiquary*. London: J. Nichols, 1780.

Antognazza, Maria Rosa. *Leibniz: An Intellectual Biography*. Cambridge: Cambridge University Press, 2009.

Appiah, Kwame Anthony. "The Ethicist." *New York Times Magazine*, 3 November 2020 and 20 October 2020. Available at www.nytimes.com/column/the-ethicist.

Aquinas, Thomas. *Summa theologiae*, New Advent online edition, II-II, Qu. 53, Article 2, Available at www.newadvent.org/summa/3053.htm#article2.

———. *Summa theologiae*. New Advent online edition, I–II, Qu. 93, Articles 2–5, I–II, Qu. 94, Articles 4–5, I–II, Qu. 100, Article 1, Available at www.newadvent.org/summa/2093.htm.

———. *Summa theologiae*. New Advent online edition, I–II, Qu. 100, Article 5. Available at www.newadvent.org/summa/2100.htm#article5; I–II, Qu. 94, Article 5, Available at www.newadvent.org/summa/2094.htm#article5.

———. *Summa theologicae*. New Advent online edition, I–II, Qu. 100, Article 8. Available at www.newadvent.org/summa/2100.htm#article8.

Aristophanes, *The Birds*. In *The Peace—The Birds—The Frogs*, translated by Benjamin Bickley Rogers, 130–292. Loeb Classical Library. Cambridge, Mass.: Harvard University Press, 1996.

Aristotle, *Art of Rhetoric*. Translated by John Henry Freese. Loeb Classical Library. Cambridge, Mass.: Harvard University Press, 1994.

———. *Metaphysics*. Translated by Hugh Tredennick. Loeb Classical Library. Cambridge, Mass.: Harvard University Press, 1989.

———. *Nicomachean Ethics*. Translated by Harris Rackham. Loeb Classical Library. Cambridge, Mass.: Harvard University Press, 1934.

———. *Posterior Analytics*. Translated by Hugh Tredennick. Loeb Classical Library. Cambridge, Mass.: Harvard University Press, 1939.

Arthos, John. "Where There Are No Rules or Systems to Guide Us: Argument from Example in a Hermeneutic Rhetoric." *Quarterly Journal of Speech* 89 (2003): 320–44.

Ashworth, William J. "'Labour Harder Than Thrashing': John Flamsteed, Property, and Intellectual Labour in Early Nineteenth-Century England." In *Flamsteed's Stars*, edited by Frances Willmoth, 199–216. Rochester: Boydell Press, 1997.

Augustine of Hippo. *Confessions*. Vol. 3, Book 8. Translated by William Watts, Loeb Classical Library, 2 vols. Cambridge, Mass.: Harvard University Press, 1989.

Babbage, Charles. *Table of the Logarithms of Natural Numbers, from 1 to 108,000*. Stereotyped 2nd ed. London: B. Fellowes, 1831.

———. *On the Economy of Machinery and Manufactures*. London: Charles Knight, 1832.

———. *On the Economy of Machinery and Manufactures* [1832]. 4th ed. London: Charles Knight, 1835.

———. *The Ninth Bridgewater Treatise: A Fragment*. London: John Murray, 1837.

Bacher, Jutta. "Artes mechanicae." In *Erkenntnis Erfindung Konstruktion: Studien zur Bildgeschichte von Naturwissenschaften und Technik vom 16. bis zum 19. Jahrhundert*, edited by Hans Hollander, 35–50. Berlin: Gebr. Mann, 2000.

Bacon, Francis. *Novum organum* [1620]. In *The Works of Francis Bacon*, edited by Basil Montagu, 16 vols. in 17, vol. 9, 183–294. London: William Pickering, 1825–34.

———. *New Atlantis* [1627]. In *The Great Instauration and New Atlantis*, edited by J. Weinberger. Arlington Heights, Ill.: Harlan Davidson, 1989.

———. *The Elements of the Common Lawes of England* [1630]. In *The Works of Francis Bacon*, edited by Basil Montagu, 17 vols., vol. 13, 131–247. London: William Pickering, 1825–34.

Baily, Francis. "On Mr. Babbage's New Machine for Calculating and Printing Mathematical and Astronomical Tables." *Astronomische Nachrichten* 46 (1823): 347–48. Reprinted in Charles Babbage, *The Works of Charles Babbage*, edited by Martin Campbell-Kelly, 11 vols. London: Pickering & Chatto, 1989.

———. *An Account of the Revd. John Flamsteed, the First Astronomer Royal*. London: N.p., 1835.

Balansard, Anne. *Techné dans les dialogues de Platon*. Sankt Augustin, Germany: Academia Verlag, 2001.

Baldwin, Frances Elizabeth. *Sumptuary Legislation and Personal Regulation*. *Johns Hopkins University Studies in Historical and Political Science* 44 (1926): 1–282.

Balkin, Jack M. *Living Originalism*. Cambridge, Mass.: Harvard University Press, 2011.

Barker, Andrew. *Greek Musical Writings*. Vol. 2, *Harmonic and Acoustic Theory*. Cambridge: Cambridge University Press, 1989.

Barles, Sabine. "La Boue, la voiture et l'amuser public. Les transformations de la voirie parisienne fin XVIIIe—fin XIXe siècles." *Ethnologie française* 14 (2015): 421–30.

———. "La Rue parisienne au XIXe siècle: standardisation et contrôle?" *Romantisme* 1 (2016): 15–28.

Barles, Sabine, and André Guillerme. *La Congestion urbaine en France (1800–1970)*. Champs-sur-Marne, France: Laboratoire TMU/ARDU, 1998.

Bauer, Veronika. *Kleiderordnungen in Bayern vom 14. bis zum 19. Jahrhundert*. In *Miscellanea Bavarica Monacensia*, no. 62, 39–78. Munich: R. Wölfle, 1975.

Bauny, Étienne. *Somme des pechez qui se commettent tous les états. De leurs conditions & qualitez, & en quelles consciences ils sont mortels, ou veniels* [1630]. Lyon: Simon Regaud, 1646.

Belenky, Ari. "Master of the Mint: How Much Money Did Isaac Newton Save Britain?" *Journal of the Royal Statistical Society: Series A* 176 (2013): 481–98.

Berlinski, David. *The Advent of the Algorithm: The 300-Year Journey from an Idea to the Computer.* New York: Harcourt, 2000.

Bernard, Leon. "Technological Innovation in Seventeenth-Century Paris." In *The Pre-Industrial Cities and Technology Reader,* edited by Colin Chant, 157–62. London: Routledge, 1999.

Bertoloni Meli, Domenico. "Caroline, Leibniz, and Clarke." *Journal of the History of Ideas* 60 (1999): 469–86.

Bevin, Elway. *Briefe and Short Instrvction of the Art of Mvsicke, to teach how to make Discant, of all proportions that are in vse.* London: R. Young, 1631.

Bible, Revised Standard Version, Containing the Old and New Testaments. New York: New American Library, 1962.

"Bill of Rights of 1689. An Act Declaring the Rights and Liberties of the Subject and Settling the Succession of the Crown." The Avalon Project: Documents in Law, History and Diplomacy. Yale Law School. Available at avalon.law.yale.edu/17th _century/england.asp.

Binet, Alfred. *Psychologie des grands calculateurs et joueurs d'échecs.* Paris: Librairie Hachette, 1894.

Binet, Alfred, and Victor Henri. *La Fatigue intellectuelle.* Paris: Schleicher Frères, 1898.

Bion, Nicolas. *Traité de la construction et des principaux usages des instrumens de mathématique.* 4th ed. Paris: Chez C. A. Jombret, 1752.

Boas, George. *Primitivism and Related Ideas in the Middle Ages.* Baltimore: Johns Hopkins University Press, 1997.

Bodin, Jean. *Les Six livres de la république.* Paris: Iacques du Puys, 1576.

Bolle, Georges. "Note sur l'utilisation rationelle des machines à statistique." *Revue générale des chemins de fer* 48 (1929): 169–95.

Borges, Jorge Luis. "Pierre Menard, Author of the *Quixote*" [1941]. In *Collected Fictions.* Translated by Andrew Hurley, 88–95. London: Penguin, 1998.

Bourbaki, Nicolas. *Éléments de mathématique.* 38 vols. Paris: Hermann, 1939–75.

Bourgeois-Gavardin, Jacques. *Les Boues de Paris sous l'Ancien Régime.* Thèse pour le doctorat du troisième cycle. Paris: EHESS, 1985.

Boyle, Robert. *A Free Inquiry into the Vulgarly Received Notion of Nature* [1686]. In *The Works of the Honourable Robert Boyle* [1772], edited by Thomas Birch, 6 vols., vol. 5, 158–254. Hildesheim, Germany: Georg Olms, 1966.

Bozeman, Barry. *Bureaucracy and Red Tape.* Upper Saddle River, N.J.: Prentice Hall, 2000.

Brack-Bernsen, Lis. "Methods for Understanding and Reconstructing Babylonian Predicting Rules." In *Writings of Early Scholars in the Ancient Near East, Egypt, Rome, and Greece,* edited by Annette Imhausen and Tanja Pommerening, 285–87. Berlin and New York: De Gruyter, 2010.

Brundage, James A. *Medieval Canon Law*. London and New York: Longman, 1995.

Bruyère, Nelly. *Méthode et dialectique dans l'oeuvre de La Ramée: Renaissance et Âge classique*. Paris: J. Vrin, 1984.

Bundesverfassungsgericht, 1BvR 1640/97, 14 July 1998. Available at www.bundesverfassungsgericht.de/e/rs19980714_1bvr164097.html.

Burrow, Colin. *Imitating Authors: From Plato to Futurity*. Oxford: Oxford University Press, 2019.

Busa, Roberto S.J., and associates, eds. *Index Thomisticus*. Edited by Web edition by Eduardo Bernot and Enrique Marcón. Available at www.corpusthomisticum.org /it/index.age.

Busse Berger, Anna Maria. *Medieval Music and the Art of Memory*. Berkeley: University of California Press, 2005.

Campbell-Kelly, Martin. "Large-Scale Data Processing in the Prudential, 1850–1930." *Accounting, Business, and Financial History* 2 (1992): 117–40.

Campbell-Kelly, Martin, William Aspray, Nathan Ensmenger, and Jeffrey R. Yost. *Computer: A History of the Information Machine*. 3rd ed. Boulder, Colo.: Westview Press, 2014.

Candea, Maria, and Laélia Véron. *Le Français est à nous! Petit manuel d'émancipation linguistique*. Paris: La Découverte, 2019.

Capella, Martianus. *De nuptiis Philologiae et Mercurii*. [5th c. CE] (Turnhout, Belgium: Brepols, 2010).

Carruthers, Mary J. *The Book of Memory: A Study of Memory in Medieval Culture*. 2nd ed. Cambridge: Cambridge University Press, 2008.

Catechism of the Catholic Church. 2nd ed. Vatican: Libreria Editrice Vaticana, 1997.

Causse, Bernard. *Les Fiacres de Paris au XVIIe et XVIIIe siècles*. Paris: Presses Universitaires de France, 1972.

Chabert, Jean-Luc, ed. *A History of Algorithms: From the Pebble to the Microchip*. Berlin: Springer, 1999.

Chapman, Allan. "Airy's Greenwich Staff." *The Antiquarian Astronomer* 6 (2012): 4–18.

Chemla, Karine. "De l'algorithme comme liste d'opérations." *Extrême-Orient-Extrême-Occident* 12 (1990): 79–94.

———. "Résonances entre démonstrations et procédure. Remarque sur le commentaire de Liu Hui (IIIe siècle) au *Neuf Chapitres sur les Procédures Mathématiques* (Ier siècle)." *Extrême-Orient, Extrême-Occident* 14 (1992): 91–129.

———. "Le paradigme et le général. Réflexions inspirées par les textes mathématiques de la Chine ancienne." In *Penser par cas*, edited by Jean-Claude Passeron and Jacques Revel, 75–93. Paris: Éditions de l'École des Hautes Études en Sciences Sociales, 2005.

———. "Describing Texts for Algorithms: How They Prescribe Operations and Integrate Cases. Reflections Based on Ancient Chinese Mathematical Sources."

In *Texts, Textual Acts, and the History of Science*, edited by Karine Chemla and Jacques Virbel, 317–84. Heidelberg: Springer, 2015.

Chiffoleau, Jacques. "Dire indicible: Remarques sur la catégorie du nefandum du XIIe au XVe siècle." *Annales ESC*, 45-2 (May–April 1990): 289–324.

Cicero, Marcus Tullius. *On the Republic and On the Laws*. Translated by Clinton W. Keyes, Loeb Classical Library. Cambridge, Mass.: Harvard University Press, 1928.

Clark, James G. *The Benedictines in the Middle Ages*. Woodbridge, Suffolk: Boydell, 2011.

Cohen, I. Bernard. "Howard Aiken on the Number of Computers Needed for the Nation." *IEEE Annals of the History of Computing* 20 (1998): 27–32.

Colbert, Jean Baptiste. *Instruction generale donnée de l'ordre exprés du roy par Monsieur Colbert ... pour l'execution des reglemens generaux des manufactures & teintures registrez en presence de Sa Majesté au Parlement de Paris le treiziéme aoust 1669*. Grenoble: Chez Alexandre Giroud, 1693.

———. *Lettres, instructions et mémoires de Colbert*. 7 vols. Paris: Imprimerie impériale, 1861–1873.

Colebrooke, Henry Thomas. "Address on Presenting the Gold Medal of the Astronomical Society to Charles Babbage." *Memoirs of the Astronomical Society* 1 (1825): 509–12.

Collins, Harry. *Tacit and Explicit Knowledge*. Chicago: University of Chicago Press, 2010.

Condillac, Étienne Bonnot de. *La Langue des calculs*. Paris: Charles Houel, 1798.

Condorcet, M.J.A.N. *Élémens d'arithmétique et de géométrie* [1804]. *Enfance* 42 (1989): 40–58.

———. *Moyens d'apprendre à compter surement et avec facilité* [1804]. *Enfance* 42 (1989): 59–60.

Corbin, Alain. *The Foul and the Fragrant: Odor and the French Social Imagination* [1982]. Translated by Miriam L. Cochan with Roy Porter and Christopher Prendergast. Cambridge, Mass.: Harvard University Press, 1986.

Cosgrove, Denis. *Apollo's Eye: A Cartographic Genealogy of the Earth in the Western Imagination*. Baltimore: Johns Hopkins University Press, 2001.

Cotton, Charles. *The Compleate Gamester. Instructions How to Play at Billiards, Trucks, Bowls, and Chess*. London: Charles Brome, 1687.

Couffignal, Louis. *Les Machines à calculer*. Paris: Gauthier-Villars, 1933.

Coumet, Ernst. "La théorie du hasard est-elle née par hasard?" *Annales: Économies, Sociétés, Civilisations* 25-3 (May–June 1970): 574–98.

Cox, Noel. *The Royal Prerogative and Constitutional Law: A Search for the Quintessence of Executive Power*. London: Routledge, 2021.

Creager, Angela N. H., Elizabeth Lunbeck, and M. Norton Wise, eds. *Science without Laws: Model Systems, Cases, Exemplary Narratives*. Durham, N.C.: Duke University Press, 2007.

Croarken, Mary. *Early Scientific Computing in Britain.* Oxford: Oxford University Press, 1990.

———. "Human Computers in Eighteenth- and Nineteenth-century Britain." In *The Oxford Handbook of the History of Mathematics,* edited by Eleanor Robson and Jacqueline Stedall, 375–403. Oxford: Oxford University Press, 2009.

Crouch, Jeffrey. *The Presidential Pardon Power.* Lawrence: University Press of Kansas, 2009.

Daston, Lorraine. "Enlightenment Calculations." *Critical Inquiry* 21 (1994): 182–202.

———. "Unruly Weather: Natural Law Confronts Natural Variability." In *Natural Laws and Laws of Nature in Early Modern Europe,* edited by Lorraine Daston and Michael Stolleis, 233–48. Farnham, U.K.: Ashgate, 2008.

———. "Epistemic Images." In *Vision and Its Instruments: Art, Science, and Technology in Early Modern Europe,* edited by Alina Payne, 13–35. College Station: Pennsylvania State University Press, 2015.

———. "Calculation and the Division of Labor, 1750–1950." *Bulletin of the German Historical Institute* 62 (2018): 9–30.

———. *Against Nature.* Cambridge, Mass.: MIT Press, 2019.

Daston, Lorraine, and Katharine Park. *Wonders and the Order of Nature, 1150–1750.* New York: Zone Books, 1998.

Daston, Lorraine, and Michael Stolleis. "Nature, Law, and Natural Law in Early Modern Europe." In *Natural Laws and Laws of Nature in Early Modern Europe,* edited by Lorraine Daston and Michael Stolleis, 1–12. Farnham, Surrey: Ashgate, 2008.

Davis, Martin. *The Universal Computer: The Road from Leibniz to Turing.* New York: W.W. Norton, 2000.

———, ed. *The Undecidable: Basic Papers on Undecidable Propositions, Unsolvable Problems, and Computable Functions.* Hewlett, N.Y.: Raven Press, 1965.

Davison, Dennis, ed. *The Penguin Book of Eighteenth-Century English Verse.* Harmondsworth, U.K.: Penguin Books, 1973.

Deferrari, Roy J., and Sister Mary M. Inviolata Barry. *A Lexicon of Saint Thomas Aquinas* [1948]. Fitzwilliam, N.H.: Loreto Publications, 2004.

Dehaene, Stanislas. *Reading in the Brain: The New Science of How We Read.* New York: Penguin, 2010.

Denis, Vincent. "Les Parisiens, la police et les numérotages des maisons au XVIIIe siècle à l'Empire." *French Historical Studies* 38 (2015): 83–103.

Denys, Catherine. "La Police du nettoiement au XVIIIe siècle." *Ethnologie Française* 153 (2015): 411–20.

Descartes, René. *Regulae ad directionem ingenii* [c. 1628]. In *Oeuvres de Descartes,* edited by Charles Adam and Paul Tannery, 11 vols., vol. 10, 359–472. Paris: J. Vrin, 1964.

————. *Discours de la méthode pour bien conduire sa raison et chercher la vérité dans les sciences* [1637]. In *Oeuvres de Descartes*, edited by Charles Adam and Paul Tannery, 11 vols., vol. 6, 1–78. Paris: J. Vrin, 1964.

Devries, Kelly. "Sites of Military Science and Technology." In *The Cambridge History of Early Modern Science*, edited by Katharine Park and Lorraine Daston, 306–19. Cambridge: Cambridge University Press, 2006.

Digest, 1.1.1.3 (Ulpian). Available at www.thelatinlibrary.com/justinian/digest1.shtml.

Digest, 1.1.4 (Ulpian). Available at www.thelatinlibrary.com/justinian/digest1.shtml.

Digges, Leonard. *A Boke Named Tectonion*. London: John Daye, 1556.

Dionysius of Halicarnassus. *Critical Essays, Volume I: Ancient Orators*. Translated by Stephen Usher. Loeb Classical Library 465. Cambridge, Mass.: Harvard University Press, 1974.

Dodds, Eric Robertson. *The Greeks and the Irrational*. Berkeley: University of California Press, 1951.

Domat, Jean. *Les Loix civiles dans leur ordre naturel* [1689]. 3 vols. Paris: Pierre Gandouin, 1723.

Dubourg Glatigny, Pascal, and Hélène Vérin. "La réduction en art, un phénomène culturel." In *Réduire en art: La technologie de la Renaissance aux Lumières*, edited by Pascal Dubourg Glatigny and Hélène Vérin. Paris: Éditions de la Maison des sciences de l'homme, 2008.

Duden, Rechtschreibregeln. Available at www.duden.de/sprachwissen/rechtschrei bregeln.

Dülmen, Richard van. *Frauen vor Gericht: Kindermord in der Frühen Neuzeit*. Frankfurt am Main: Fischer Verlag, 1991.

Dürer, Albrecht. *Unterweysung der Messung, mit dem Zirckel und Richtscheyt, in Linien, Ebenen und gantzen corporen*. Nuremberg: Hieronymus Andreae, 1525.

Dunkin, Edwin. *A Far-Off Vision: A Cornishman at Greenwich Observatory*, edited by P. D. Hingley and T. C. Daniel. Cornwall, U.K.: Royal Institution of Cornwall, 1999.

Duplès-Argier, Henri. "Ordonnance somptuaire inédite de Philippe le Hardi." *Bibliothèque de l'École des chartes*, 3rd Series, no. 5 (1854): 176–81.

Eamon, William. *Science and the Secrets of Nature: Books of Secrets in Medieval and Early Modern Culture*. Princeton: Princeton University Press, 1994.

————. "Markets, Piazzas, and Villages." In *The Cambridge History of Early Modern Science*, edited by Katharine Park and Lorraine Daston, 206–23. Cambridge: Cambridge University Press, 2006.

Easterling, Patricia Elizabeth. "The Infanticide in Euripides' Medea." *Yale Classical Studies* 25 (1977): 177–91.

Economou, George. *The Goddess Nature in Medieval Literature*. Cambridge, Mass.: Harvard University Press, 1972.

Eisenbart, Liselotte Constanze. *Kleiderordnungen der deutschen Städte zwischen 1350 und 1700.* Berlin and Göttingen: Musterschmidt Verlag, 1962.

Elmer, Peter. "The Early Modern City." In *Pre-Industrial Cities and Technology*, edited by Colin Chant and David Goodman, 198–211. London: Routledge, 1999.

Erikson, Paul, Judy L. Klein, Lorraine Daston, Rebecca Lemov, Thomas Sturm, and Michael D. Gordin. *How Reason Almost Lost Its Mind: The Strange Career of Cold War Rationality.* Chicago: University of Chicago Press, 2013.

Eroms, Hans-Werner, and Horst H. Munske. *Die Rechtschreibreform, Pro und Kontra.* Berlin: Schmidt, 1997.

Erwin, Holger. *Machtsprüche: Das herrscherliche Gestaltungsrecht "ex plenitudine potestatis" in der Frühen Neuzeit.* Cologne: Böhlau, 2009.

L'Esclache, Louis de. *Les Véritables régles de l'ortografe francéze, ov L'Art d'aprandre an peu de tams à écrire côrectement.* Paris: L'Auteur et Lavrant Rondet, 1668.

Essinger, James. *Jacquard's Web: How a Hand-Loom Led to the Birth of the Information Age.* Oxford: Oxford University Press, 2004.

Farge, Arlette. *Vivre dans la rue à Paris au XVIIIe siècle* [1979]. Paris: Gallimard, 1992.

Favre, Adrien. *Les Origines du système métrique.* Paris: Presses universitaires de France, 1931.

Filipowski, Herschel E. *A Table of Anti-Logarithms.* 2nd ed. London: George Bell, 1851.

Filmer, Robert. *Patriarcha, or the Natural Power of Kings.* London: Richard Chiswell, 1680.

Flamsteed, John. *The Correspondence of John Flamsteed, the First Astronomer Royal.* Edited by Eric G. Forbes, Lesley Murdin, and Frances Willmoth, 3 vols. Bristol: Institute of Physics, 1995–2002.

Folkerts, Menso (with Paul Kunitzsch), eds. *Die älteste lateinische Schrift über das indische Rechnen nach al-Hwarizmi.* Munich: Verlag der Bayerischen Akademie der Wissenschaften, 1997.

Forrester, John. "If P, Then What? Thinking in Cases." *History of the Human Sciences* 9 (1996): 1–25.

Fortier, Mark. *The Culture of Equity in Early Modern England.* London: Routledge, 2016.

Foucault, Michel. *Surveiller et punir: Naissance de la prison.* Paris: Éditions Gallimard, 1975.

Fransen, Gérard. *Canones et Quaestiones: Évolution des doctrines et systèmes du droit canonique.* Goldbach, Germany: Keip Verlag, 2002.

Freudenthal, Hans. "What Is Algebra and What Has Been Its History?" *Archive for History of Exact Sciences* 16 (1977): 189–200.

Friedmann, Georges. "L'Encyclopédie et le travail humain," *Annales: Economies, Sociétés, Civilisations* 8-1 (1953): 53–61.

[Fuller, Thomas]. *The Sovereigns Prerogative, and the Subjects Priviledge*. London: Martha Harrison, 1657.

Furth, Charlotte. "Introduction: Thinking with Cases." In *Thinking with Cases: Specialist Knowledge in Chinese Cultural History*, edited by Charlotte Furth, Judith T. Zeitlin, and Ping-chen Hsiung, 1–27. Honolulu: University of Hawaii Press, 2007.

Galen, Claudius. *De temperamentis libri III*. Edited by Georg Helmreich. Leipzig: B. G. Teubner, 1904.

Galton, Francis. "Composite Portraits." *Nature* 18 (1878): 97–100.

Gardey, Delphine. *Écrire, calculer, classer: Comment une revolution de papier a transformé les sociétés contemporaines (1800–1840)*. Paris: Éditions la découverte, 2008.

Gauvain, Mary. *The Social Context of Cognitive Development*. New York: Guilford Press, 2001.

Gay, Jean-Paul. "Lettres de controverse: religion, publication et espace publique en France au XVIIe siècle." *Annales: Histoire, Sciences Sociales* 68-1 (2013): 7–41.

Gigerenzer, Gerd. *How to Stay Smart in a Smart World*. London: Penguin, 2022.

Gigerenzer, Gerd, and Daniel Goldstein. "Mind as Computer: The Social Origin of a Metaphor." In *Adaptive Thinking: Rationality in the Real World*, edited by Gerd Gigerenzer, 26–43. Oxford: Oxford University Press, 2000.

Gilbert, Neal. *Concepts of Method in the Renaissance*. New York: Columbia University Press, 1960.

Ginzburg, Carlo. "Family Resemblances and Family Trees: Two Cognitive Metaphors." *Critical Inquiry* 30 (2004): 537–56.

———. "Preface." In *A Historical Approach to Casuistry: Norms and Exceptions in a Comparative Perspective*, edited by Carlo Ginzburg with Lucio Biasiori, xi–xix. London: Bloomsbury Academic, 2019.

Gispert, Hélène, and Gert Schubring. "Societal Structure and Conceptual Changes in Mathematics Teaching: Reform Processes in France and Germany over the Twentieth Century and the International Dynamics." *Science in Context* 24 (2011): 73–106.

Glasse, Hannah. *Art of Cookery, Made Plain and Easy* [1747]. London: L. Wangford, c. 1790.

Goclenius the Elder, Rudolph. *Lexicon philosophicum*. Frankfurt: Matthias Becker, 1613.

Gödel, Kurt. "Über formal unentscheidbare Sätze der *Principia Mathematica* und verwandter Systeme." *Monatsheft für Mathematik und Physik* 38 (1931): 173–98.

Gordin, Michael D. *Scientific Babel: How Science Was Done Before and After Global English*. Chicago: University of Chicago Press, 2015.

Grasshof, Gerd. "Natural Law and Celestial Regularities from Copernicus to Kepler." In *Natural Laws and Laws of Nature in Early Modern Europe*, edited by Lorraine Daston and Michael Stolleis, 143–61. Farnham, U.K.: Ashgate, 2008.

Grattan-Guiness, Ivor. "Work for the Hairdressers: The Production of Prony's Logarithmic and Trigonometric Tables." *Annals of the History of Computing* 12 (1990): 177–85.

———. *The Search for Mathematical Roots, 1870–1940: Logic, Set Theory, and the Foundations of Mathematics from Cantor through Russell Russell to Gödel*. Princeton: Princeton University Press, 2000.

Grebe, Paul, ed., *Akten zur Geschichte der deutschen Einheitsschreibung 1870–1880*. Mannheim, Germany: Bibliographisches Institut, 1963.

Griep, Wolfgang. "Die reinliche Stadt: Über fremden und eigenen Schmutz." In *Rom-Paris-London: Erfahrung und Selbsterfahrung deutscher Schriftsteller und Künstler in den fremden Metropolen*, edited by Conrad Wiedemann, 135–54. Stuttgart: J. B. Metzlersche Verlagsbuchhandung, 1988.

Grier, David Alan. *When Computers Were Human*. Princeton: Princeton University Press, 2006.

Grotius, Hugo. *De jure belli ac pacis libri tres* [1625]. Translated by Francis W. Kelsey, 2 vols. Oxford: Clarendon Press, 1925.

Guillote, François. *Mémoire sur la réformation de la police de France: Soumis au Roi en 1749*, edited by Jean Seznec. Paris: Hermann, 1974.

Haberman, Maggie, and Michael S. Schmidt. "Trump Pardons Two Russian Inquiry Figures and Blackwater Guards." *New York Times*, December 22, 2020, updated February 21, 2021. Available at www.nytimes.com/2020/12/22/us/politics/trump-pardons.html.

Hacking, Ian. "Paradigms." In *Kuhn's Structure of Scientific Revolutions at Fifty: Reflections on a Scientific Classic*, edited by Robert J. Richards and Lorraine Daston, 96–112. Chicago: University of Chicago Press, 2016.

Hajibabaee, Fatimah, Soodabeh Joolaee, Mohammed al Cheraghi, Pooneh Saleri, and Patricia Rodney. "Hospital/Clinical Ethics Committees' Notion: An Overview." *Journal of Medical Ethics and History of Medicine* 19 (2016). Available at www.ncbi.nlm.nih.gov/pmc/articles/PMC5432947/.

Hall, A. Rupert. *Philosophers at War: The Quarrel between Newton and Leibniz*. Cambridge: Cambridge University Press, 1998.

Hart, John. *Orthographie, conteyning the due order and reason, howe to write or paint thimage of mannes voice, most like to the life or nature* [1569]. Facsimile reprint. Amsterdam: Theatrum Orbis Terrarum, 1968.

Hartley, David. *Observations on Man, His Frame, His Duty, and His Expectations* [1749]. Edited by Theodore L. Huguelet, 2 vols. Gainesville, Fla.: Scholars' Facsimile Reprints, 1966.

Havil, Julian. *John Napier: Life, Logarithms, and Legacy*. Princeton: Princeton University Press, 2014.

Heath, Thomas L. *The Thirteen Books of Euclid's Elements*, 2nd ed., 3 vols. New York: Dover, 1956.

Henning, Hans. *Die Aufmerksamkeit*. Berlin: Urban & Schwarzenberg, 1925.

Henry, John. "Metaphysics and the Origins of Modern Science: Descartes and the Importance of Laws of Nature." *Early Science and Medicine* 9 (2004): 73–114.

Hergemöller, Bernd-Ulrich. "Sodomiter. Erscheinungsformen und Kausalfaktoren des spätmittelalterlichen Kampfes gegen Homosexualität." In *Randgruppen der mittelalterlichen Gesellschaft*, edited by Bernd-Ulrich Hergemöller, 316–56. Warendorf, Germany: Fahlbusch, 1990.

Herodotus. *The History*. Translated by David Grene. Chicago: University of Chicago Press, 1987.

Hervé, Jean-Claude. "L'Ordre à Paris au XVIIIe siècle: les enseignements du 'Recueil de règlements de police' du commissaire Dupré." *Revue d'histoire moderne et contemporaine* 34 (1985): 185–214.

Hesberg, Henner von. "Greek and Roman Architects." In *The Oxford Handbook of Greek and Roman Art and Architecture,* edited by Clemente Marconi, 136–51. Oxford: Oxford University Press, 2014.

Hilbert, David. *Grundlagen der Geometrie* [1899]. 8th ed. With revisions by Paul Bernays. Stuttgart: Teubner, 1956.

Hilbert, David, and Wilhelm Ackermann. *Grundzüge der theoretischen Logik*. Berlin: Springer, 1928.

Hilliges, Marion. "Der Stadtgrundriss als Repräsentationsmedium in der Frühen Neuzeit." In *Aufsicht—Ansicht—Einsicht: Neue Perspektiven auf die Kartographie an der Schwelle zur Frühen Neuzeit*, edited by Tanja Michalsky, Felicitas Schmieder, and Gisela Engel, 351–68. Berlin: trafo Verlagsgruppe, 2009.

Hirschman, Albert O. *The Passions and the Interests: Political Arguments for Capitalism before Its Triumph*. Princeton: Princeton University Press, 1977.

Hobbes, Thomas. *Leviathan* [1651]. Edited by Colin B. Macpherson. London: Penguin, 1968.

Hoffmann, Ludwig. *Mathematisches Wörterbuch*. 7 vols. Berlin: Wiegandt und Hempel, 1858–1867.

Horn, Christopher. "*Epieikeia*: The Competence of the Perfectly Just Person in Aristotle." In *The Virtuous Life in Greek Ethics*, edited by Burkhard Reiss, 142–66. Cambridge: Cambridge University Press, 2006.

Horobin, Simon. *Does Spelling Matter?* Oxford: Oxford University Press, 2013.

Howard-Hill, Trevor H., "Early Modern Printers and the Standardization of English Spelling." *The Modern Language Review* 101 (2000): 16–29.

Howlett, David H. *Dictionary of Medieval Latin from British Sources*. Fascicule XIII: PRO-REG. Oxford: Oxford University Press, 2010.

Hoyle, Edmond. *A Short Treatise on the Game of Whist, Containing the Laws of the Game: and also Some Rules, whereby a Beginner may, with due Attention to them, attain to the Playing it well*. London: Thomas Osborne, 1748.

Høyrup, Jens. "Mathematical Justification as Non-conceptualized Practice." In *The History of Mathematical Proof*, edited by Karine Chemla, 362–83. Cambridge: Cambridge University Press, 2012.

Hume, David. "Of Miracles," *Enquiry Concerning Human Nature* [1748]. Edited by Eric Steinberg, 72–90. Indianapolis: Hackett, 1977.

———. *An Inquiry Concerning the Principles of Morals* [1751]. Edited by Charles W. Hendel. Indianapolis: Library of Liberal Arts, 1979.

Hunt, Alan. *Governance of the Consuming Passions: A History of Sumptuary Law.* London: Macmillan, 1996.

Hunter, Ian, and David Saunders, eds. *Natural Law and Civil Sovereignty: Moral Right and State Authority in Early Modern Political Thought.* New York: Palgrave Macmillan, 2002.

Hylan, John Perham. "The Fluctuation of Attention." *Psychological Review* 2 (1898): 1–78.

Ilting, Karl-Heinz. *Naturrecht und Sittlichkeit: Begriffsgeschichtliche Studien.* Stuttgart: Klett-Cotta, 1983.

Imhausen, Annette. "Calculating the Daily Bread: Rations in Theory and Practice." *Historia Mathematica* 30 (2003): 3–16.

Itard, Jean. *Les Livres arithmétiques d'Euclide.* Paris: Hermann, 1961.

Jacob, P. [Paul Lacroix]. *Recueil curieux de pièces originales rares ou inédites en prose et en vers sur le costume et les revolutions de la mode en France.* Paris: Administration de Librairie, 1852.

Jacobs, Uwe Kai. *Die Regula Benedicti als Rechtsbuch. Eine rechtshistorische und rechtstheologische Untersuchung.* Vienna: Böhlau Verlag, 1987.

James I of England, *The Workes of the Most High and Mightie Prince, James.* Edited by John Montagu. London: Robert Barker and John Bill, 1616.

Jansen-Sieben, Ria, ed. *Ars mechanicae en Europe médiévale.* Brussels: Archives et bibliothèques de Belgique, 1989.

Jardine, Lisa, and Alan Stewart. *Hostages to Fortune: The Troubled Life of Francis Bacon.* New York: Hill and Wang, 1998.

Jarvis, Charlie. *Order Out of Chaos: Linnaean Plant Names and Their Types.* London: Linnean Society of London, 2007.

[Jaucourt, Louis de Neufville, chevalier de]. "Loi." In *Encyclopédie, ou Dictionnaire raisonné des arts, des sciences et des métiers,* edited by Jean d'Alembert and Denis Diderot, vol. 9, 643–46. Neuchâtel, Switzerland: Samuel Faulche, 1765.

———. "Règle, Règlement." In *Encyclopédie, ou Dictionnaire raisonné des sciences,* edited by Jean d'Alembert and Denis Diderot, vol. 14, 20. Neuchâtel: Chez Samuel Faulche, 1765.

———. "Règle, Modèle (*Synon.*)." In *Encyclopédie, ou Dictionnaire raisonné des sciences, des arts et des métiers,* edited by Denis Diderot and Jean d'Alembert, vol. 28, 116–17. Lausanne/Berne: Les sociétés typographiques, 1780.

Jefferson, Thomas. *A Manual of Parliamentary Practice for the Use of the Senate of the United States.* Washington City: Samuel H. Smith, 1801.

Johnson, Samuel. *Dictionary of the English Language.* 1st ed. London: W. Strahan, 1755.

Jolles, André. *Einfache Formen: Legende, Sage, Mythe, Rätsel, Spruch, Kasus, Memorabile, Märchen, Witz* [1930]. 8th ed. Tübingen: Max Niemeyer Verlag, 2006.

Jones, Matthew L. *Reckoning with Matter: Calculating Machines, Innovation, and Thinking about Thinking from Pascal to Babbage.* Chicago: University of Chicago Press, 2016.

———. "Querying the Archive: Data Mining from Apriori to Page Rank." In *Science in the Archives: Pasts, Presents, Futures,* edited by Lorraine Daston, 311–28. Chicago: University of Chicago Press, 2017.

Jonsen, Albert R., and Stephen Toulmin. *The Abuse of Casuistry: A History of Moral Reasoning.* Berkeley: University of California Press, 1990.

Jouslin, Olivier. *La Campagne des Provinciales de Pascal: étude d'un dialogue polémique.* Clermont-Ferrand, France: Presses Universitaires, 2007.

Kant, Immanuel. *Foundations of the Metaphysics of Morals* [1785]. Translated by Lewis White Beck. Indianapolis: Library of Liberal Arts, 1954.

———. *Die Metaphysik der Sitten* [1797]. Edited by Wilhelm Weisehedel. Frankfurt am Main: Suhrkamp, 1977.

———. *Critique of Judgment* [1790]. Translated by Werner S. Pluhar. Indianapolis: Hackett, 1987.

———. *Erste Einleitung in die Kritik der Urteilskraft* [1790]. Edited by Gerhard Lehmann. Hamburg: Felix Meiner Verlag, 1990.

———. *Die Religion innerhalb der Grenzen der bloßen Vernunft* [1793]. Edited by Rudolf Malter. Ditzingen, Germany: Reclam, 2017.

Katz, Victor J., and Karen Hunger Parshall. *Taming the Unknown: A History of Algebra from Antiquity to the Early Twentieth Century.* Princeton: Princeton University Press, 2014.

Keller, Agathe. "Ordering Operations in Square Root Extractions, Analyzing Some Early Medieval Sanskrit Mathematical Texts with the Help of Speech Act Theory." In *Texts, Textual Acts, and the History of Science,* edited by Karine Chemla and Jacques Virbel, 189–90. Heidelberg: Springer, 2015.

Keller, Agathe, Koolakodlu Mahesh, and Clemency Montelle. "Numerical Tables in Sanskrit Sources." HAL archives-ouvertes, HAL ID: halshs-01006137 (submitted 13 June 2014), §2.1.3, n.p. Available at halshs.archives-ouvertes.fr/halshs-01006137.

Keller, Monika. *Ein Jahrhundert Reformen der französischen Orthographie: Geschichte eines Scheiterns.* Tübingen: Stauffenberg Verlag, 1991.

Edward Kennedy, "A Survey of Islamic Astronomical Tables." *Transactions of the American Philosophical Society* 46, no. 2 (1956): 1–53.

Kettilby, Mary. *A Collection of above Three Hundred Receipts in Cookery, Physick and Surgery* [1714]. 6th ed. London: W. Parker, 1746.

Killerby, Catherine Kovesi. "Practical Problems in the Enforcement of Italian Sumptuary Law, 1200–1500." In *Crime, Society, and the Law in Renaissance Italy*, edited by Trevor Dean and K.J.P. Lowe, 99–120. Cambridge: Cambridge University Press, 1994.

————. *Sumptuary Law in Italy, 1200–1500.* Oxford: Clarendon Press, 2002.

Kittsteiner, Heinz-Dieter. "Kant and Casuistry." In *Conscience and Casuistry in Early Modern Europe*, edited by Edmund Leites, 185–213. Cambridge: Cambridge University Press, 2002.

Klauwell, Otto. *Der Canon in seiner geschichtlichen Entwicklung.* Leipzig: C. F. Kahnt, 1874.

Klein, Jacob. *Greek Mathematical Thought and the Origin of Algebra* [1934]. Translated by Eva Brann. Cambridge, Mass.: MIT Press, 1968.

Knuth, Donald. *The Art of Computer Programming.* Vol. 1: *Fundamental Algorithms*, 3rd ed. Boston: Addison-Wesley, 1997.

Krent, Harold J. *Presidential Powers.* New York: New York University Press, 2004.

Kuhn, Thomas S. *The Structure of Scientific Revolutions* [1962]. 4th ed. Chicago: University of Chicago Press, 2012.

Kurtz, Joachim. "Autopsy of a Textual Monstrosity: Dissecting the Mingli tan (*De logica*, 1631)." In *Linguistic Changes between Europe, China, and Japan*, edited by Federica Caselin, 35–58. Turin: Tiellemedia, 2008.

Kusukawa, Sachiko. *Picturing the Book of Nature: Image, Text, and Argument in Sixteenth-Century Human Anatomy and Medical Body.* Chicago: University of Chicago Press, 2012.

Lahy, Jean-Maurice, and S. Korngold. "Séléction des operatrices de machines comptables." *Année psychologique* 32 (1931): 131–49.

Laitinen, Riitta, and Dag Lindstrom. "Urban Order and Street Regulation in Seventeenth-Century Sweden." In *Cultural History of Early Modern European Streets*, edited by Riitta Laitinen and Thomas V. Cohen, 63–93. Leiden: Brill, 2009.

Lamassé, Stéphane. "Calculs et marchands (XIVe–XVe siècles)." In *La juste mesure. Quantifier, évaluer, mesurer entre Orient et Occident (VIIIe–XVIIIe siècles)*, edited by Laurence Moulinier, Line Sallmann, Catherine Verna, and Nicolas Weill-Parot, 79–97. Saint-Denis, France: Presses Universitaires de Vincennes, 2005.

Landau, Bernard. "La fabrication des rues de Paris au XIXe siècle: Un territoire d'innovation technique et politique." *Les Annales de la recherche urbaine* 57–58 (1992): 24–45.

Larrère, Catherine. "Divine dispense," *Droits* 25 (1997): 19–32.

Lehoux, Daryn. "Laws of Nature and Natural Laws." *Studies in History and Philosophy of Science* 37 (2006): 527–49.

Leibniz, Gottfried Wilhelm. "Towards a Universal Characteristic [1677]." In *Leibniz Selections*, edited by Philip P. Wiener, 17–25. New York: Charles Scribner's Sons, 1951.

———. *Neue Methode, Jurisprudenz zu Lernen und zu Lehren* [1667]. Translated by Hubertus Busche. In *Frühere Schriften zum Naturrecht*, edited by Hans Zimmermann, 27–90. Hamburg: Felix Meiner Verlag, 2003.

Leong, Elaine. *Recipes and Everyday Knowledge: Medicine, Science, and the Household in Early Modern England*. Chicago: University of Chicago Press, 2018.

Lhôte, Jean-Marie. *Histoire des jeux de société*. Paris: Flammarion, 1994.

Li, Liang. "Template Tables and Computational Practices in Early Modern Chinese Calendrical Astronomy." *Centaurus* 58 (2016): 26–45.

Lindgren, Michael. *Glory and Failure: The Difference Engines of Johann Müller, Charles Babbage, and Georg and Edvard Scheutz*. Cambridge, Mass.: MIT Press, 1990.

Lloyd, Geoffrey E. R. "Greek Antiquity: The Invention of Nature." In *The Concept of Nature*, edited by John Torrance, 1–24. Oxford: Clarendon Press, 1992.

———. "What Was Mathematics in the Ancient World?" In *The Oxford Handbook of the History of Mathematics*, edited by Eleanor Robson and Jacqueline Stedall, 7–25. Oxford: Oxford University Press, 2009.

Locke, John. *Second Treatise of Government* [1690]. Edited by C. B. Macpherson. Indianapolis: Hackett, 1980.

Löffler, Catharina. *Walking in the City. Urban Experience and Literary Psychogeography in Eighteenth-Century London*. Wiesbaden: J. B. Metzler, 2017.

Long, Pamela O. *Artisan/Practitioners and the Rise of the New Science*. Corvallis: Oregon State University Press, 2011.

Long, Pamela O. "Multi-Tasking 'Pre-Professional' Architect/Engineers and Other Bricolage Practitioners as Key Figures in the Elision of Boundaries Between Practice and Learning in Sixteenth-Century Europe." In *The Structures of Practical Knowledge*, edited by Matteo Valleriani, 223–46. Cham, Switzerland: Springer, 2017.

Looze, Laurence de. "Orthography and National Identity in the Sixteenth Century." *The Sixteenth-Century Journal* 43 (2012): 371–89.

Luig, Klaus. "Leibniz's Concept of *jus naturale* and *lex naturalis*—Defined with 'Geometric Certainty.'" In *Natural Laws and Laws of Nature in Early Modern Europe*, edited by Lorraine Daston and Michael Stolleis, 183–98. Farnham, U.K.: Ashgate, 2008.

Maclean, Ian. "Expressing Nature's Regularities and their Determinations in the Late Renaissance." In *Natural Laws and Laws of Nature in Early Modern Europe*, edited by Lorraine Daston and Michael Stolleis, 29–44. Farnham, U.K.: Ashgate, 2008.

Maguire, James. *American Bee: The National Spelling Bee and the Culture of Nerds*. Emmaus, Penn.: Rodale, 2006.

Malebranche, Nicolas. *De la Recherche de la vérité* [1674–75]. 3 vols. Paris: Michel David, 1712.

Manesse, Danièle, and Gilles Siouffi, eds. *Le Féminin et le masculin dans la langue.* Paris: ESF sciences humaines, 2019.

Marguin, Jean. *Histoire des instruments à calculer: Trois siècles de mécanique pensante 1642–1942.* Paris: Hermann, 1994.

Mashaal, Maurice. *Bourbaki: Une société secrète de mathématiciens.* Paris: Pour la science, 2000.

Massey, Harrie Stewart Wilson. "Leslie John Comrie (1893–1950)." *Obituary Notices of the Fellows of the Royal Society* 8 (1952): 97–105.

Massialot, François. *Nouvelles instructions pour les confitures, les liqueurs et les fruits.* 2nd ed., 2 vols. Paris: Charles de Sercy, 1698.

Masterman, Margaret. "The Nature of a Paradigm." In *Criticism and the Growth of Knowledge,* edited by Imré Lakatos and Alan Musgrave, 59–89. Cambridge: Cambridge University Press, 1970.

[Maxwell, John]. *Sacro-Sancta Regum Majestae: Or the Sacred and Royal Prerogative of Christian Kings.* London: Thomas Dring, 1680.

May, Robert. *The Accomplisht Cook, Or the Art and Mystery of Cookery.* 3rd ed. London: J. Winter, 1671.

McClennen, Edward F. "The Rationality of Being Guided by Rules." In *The Oxford Handbook of Rationality,* edited by Alfred R. Mele and Piers Rawling, 222–39. New York: Oxford University Press, 2004.

McEvedy, Colin. *The Penguin Atlas of Modern History (to 1815).* Harmondsworth, U.K.: Penguin, 1986.

McMillan, Douglas J., and Kathryn Smith Fladenmuller, eds. *Regular Life: Monastic, Canonical, and Mendicant Rules.* Kalamazoo, Mich.: Medieval Institute, 1997.

Mehmke, Rudolf. "Numerisches Rechnen." In *Enzyklopädie der mathematischen Wissenschaften,* 6 vols., edited by Wilhelm Franz Meyer, vol. 1, part 2, 959–78. Leipzig: B. Teubner, 1898–1934.

Meigret, Louis. *Traité touchāt le commvn vsage de l'escriture françoise.* Paris: Ieanne de Marnes, 1545.

Mercier, Louis-Sébastien. *L'An 2440: Rêve s'il en fut jamais.* London: N.p., 1771.

———. *L'An 2440: Rêve s'il en fut jamais* [1771], edited by Raymond Trousson. Bordeaux: Ducros, 1971.

———. *Memoirs of the Year Two Thousand Five Hundred.* Translated by W. Hooper, 2 vols. London: G. Robinson, 1772.

———. *Tableau de Paris* [1782–88]. 2nd ed., 2 vols. Geneva: Slatkine Reprints, 1979.

Mercier, Raymond. *Πτολεμαιου Προχειροι Κανονες: Ptolemy's "Handy Tables": 1a. Tables A1–A2. Transcription and Commentary.* Publications de l'Institut Orientaliste de Louvain, 59a. Louvain-La-Neuve, Belgium: Université Catholique de Louvain/ Peeters, 2011.

Mill, John Stuart. *A System of Logic Ratiocinative and Inductive* [1843]. Edited by J. M. Robson. London: Routledge, 1996.

Miller, Naomi. *Mapping the City: The Language and Culture of Cartography in the Renaissance.* London: Continuum, 2003.

Milliot, Vincent. *Un Policier des Lumières, suivi de Mémoires de J.C.P. Lenoir.* Seyssel, France: Éditions Champ Vallon, 2011.

Modersohn, Mechthild. *Natura als Göttin im Mittelalter: Ikonographische Studien zu Darstellungen der personifizierten Natur.* Berlin: Akademie Verlag, 1997.

Montaigne, Michel de. *The Complete Essays.* Translated by M. A. Screech. London: Penguin, 1991.

Montesquieu, Charles-Louis de Secondat, Baron de la Brède et de. *De l'Esprit des lois* [1748]. Paris: Firmin-Didot, 1849.

Müller-Wille, Staffan. *Botanik und weltweiter Handel: Zur Begründung eines natürlichen Systems der Pflanzen durch Carl von Linné (1707–78).* Berlin: VWB-Verlag für Wissenschaft und Bildung, 1999.

Mulcaster, Richard. *The First Part of the Elementarie, which entreateh chieflie of the writing of our English tung.* London: Thomas Vautroullier, 1582.

Murray, Alexander. "Nature and Man in the Middle Ages." In *The Concept of Nature*, edited by John Torrance, 25–62. Oxford: Clarendon Press, 1992.

Muzzarelli, Maria Giuseppina. "Sumptuary Laws in Italy: Financial Resources and Instrument of Rule." In *The Right to Dress: Sumptuary Laws in Global Perspective, c. 1200–1800*, edited by Giorgio Riello and Ulinka Rublack, 167–85. Cambridge: Cambridge University Press, 2019.

Napier, John. *Mirifici logarithmorum canonis descriptio.* Edinburgh: A. Hart, 1614.

———. *Rabdology* (1617). Translated by William F. Richardson. Cambridge, Mass.: MIT Press, 1990.

NASA, *Mars Climate Orbiter Mishap Investigation Board Phase 1 Report.* 10 November 1999. Available at llis.nasa.gov/llis_lib/pdf/1009464main1_0641-mr.pdf.

Naux, Charles. *Histoire des logarithmes de Neper [sic] à Euler.* Paris: Blanchard, 1966.

Neal, Andrew W. *Security as Politics: Beyond the State of Exception.* Edinburgh: Edinburgh University Press, 2019.

Nencioni, Giovanni. "L'accademia della Crusca e la lingua italiana." *Historiographica Linguistica* 9 (2012): 321–33.

Nerius, Dieter. *Deutsche Orthographie.* 4th rev. ed. Hildesheim, Germany: Georg Olms Verlag, 2007.

Neugebauer, Otto. *Mathematische Keilschriften.* 3 vols. Berlin: Verlag von Julius Springer, 1935–37.

Netz, Reviel. *The Shaping of Deduction in Greek Mathematics: A Study in Cognitive History.* Cambridge: Cambridge University Press, 1999.

Newcomb, Simon. *The Reminiscences of an Astronomer.* Boston: Houghton, Mifflin, and Company, 1903.

Newell, Allen, and Herbert A. Simon. "The Logic Theory Machine: A Complex Information Processing System." *IRE Transactions on Information Theory* 1 (1956): 61–79.

Newton, Isaac. *The Mathematical Principles of Natural Philosophy* [1687]. Translated by Andrew Motte. London: Benjamin Motte, 1729.

———. *Opticks* [1704]. New York: Dover, 1952.

Niermeyer, Jan Frederik, and Co van de Kieft. *Mediae latinitatis lexicon minus: M–Z.* Darmstadt: Wissenschaftliche Buchgesellschaft, 2002.

Nyquist, Mary. *Arbitrary Rule: Slavery, Tyranny, and the Power of Life and Death.* Chicago: University of Chicago Press, 2013.

Oakley, Francis. "Christian Theology and Newtonian Science: The Rise of the Concept of Laws of Nature." *Church History* 30 (1961): 433–57.

Ocagne, Maurice d'. *Le Calcul simplifié par les procédés mécaniques et graphiques.* 2nd ed. Paris: Gauthier-Villars, 1905.

Oertzen, Christine von. "Machineries of Data Power: Manual versus Mechanical Census Compilation in Nineteenth-Century Europe." *Osiris* 32 (2017): 129–50.

Ogilvie, Brian W. *The Science of Describing: Natural History in Renaissance Europe.* Chicago: University of Chicago Press, 2006.

Ohme, Heinz. *Kanon ekklesiastikos: Die Bedeutung des altkirchlichen Kanonbegriffs.* Berlin: Walter de Gruyter, 1998.

Oppel, Herbert. *KANΩN: Zur Bedeutungsgeschichte des Wortes und seiner lateinischen Entsprechungen (Regula-Norma).* Leipzig: Dietrich'sche Verlagsbuchhandlung, 1937.

Oxford English Dictionary Online. Available at www.oed.com.

Pagden, Anthony. "Dispossessing the Barbarian: The Language of Spanish Thomism and the Debate over the Property Rights of the American Indians." In *The Languages of Political Theory in Early Modern Europe,* edited by Anthony Pagden, 79–98. Cambridge: Cambridge University Press, 1987.

Parish, Richard. "Pascal's *Lettres provinciales*: From Flippancy to Fundamentals." In *The Cambridge Companion to Pascal,* edited by Nicholas Hammond, 182–200. Cambridge: Cambridge University Press, 2003.

Park, Katharine. "Nature in Person." In *The Moral Authority of Nature,* edited by Lorraine Daston and Fernando Vidal, 50–73. Chicago: University of Chicago Press, 2004.

Pascal, Blaise. "Lettre dédicatoire à Monseigneur le Chancelier [Séguier] sur le sujet machine nouvellement inventée par le Sieur B.P. pour faire toutes sortes d'opération d'arithmétique par un mouvement réglé sans plume ni jetons" [1645]. In *Oeuvres complètes de Pascal,* edited by Louis Lafuma, 187–91. Paris: Éditions du Seuil, 1963.

———. *Les Provinciales, ou Les lettres écrites par Louis de Montalte à un provincial de ses amis et aux RR. PP. Jésuites sur le sujet de la morale et de la politique de ces Pères* [1627]. Edited by Michel Le Guern. Paris: Gallimard, 1987.

Pasch, Moritz. *Vorlesungen über neuere Geometrie.* Leipzig: B. G. Teubner, 1882.

Paulus, *On Plautius. Digest* L 17. Available at www.thelatinlibrary.com/justinian /digest50.shtml.

Pavan, Elisabeth. "Police des moeurs, société et politique à Venise à la fin du Moyen Age." *Revue historique* 264 (1980): 241–88.

Peano, Giuseppe. *Notations de logique mathématique.* Turin: Charles Guadagnigi, 1894.

Peaucelle, Jean-Louis. *Adam Smith et la division du travail. Naissance d'une idée fausse.* Paris: L'Harmattan, 2007.

Peaucelle, Jean-Louis, and Cameron Guthrie. "How Adam Smith Found Inspiration in French Texts on Pin Making in the Eighteenth Century." *History of Economic Ideas* 19 (2011): 41–67.

Pennington, Kenneth. *The Prince and the Law, 1200–1600: Sovereignty and Rights in the Western Legal Tradition.* Berkeley: University of California Press, 1993.

Perkins, William. *Hepieikeia, or a Treatise of Christian Equitie and Moderation.* Cambridge: John Legatt, 1604.

———. *The Whole Treatise of the Cases of Conscience.* London: John Legatt, 1631.

Peuchet, Jacques. *Collection des lois, ordonnances et réglements de police, depuis le 13e siècle jusqu'à l'année 1818.* Second Series: *Police moderne de 1667–1789,* vol. 1 (1667– 1695). Paris: Chez Lottin de Saint-Germain, 1818.

Pine, Nancy, and Zhenyou Yu. "Early Literacy Education in China: A Historical Overview." In *Perspectives on Teaching and Learning Chinese Literacy in China,* edited by Cynthia Leung and Jiening Ruan, 81–106. Dordrecht: Springer, 2012.

Plato. *Statesman—Philebus—Ion.* Translated by Harold North Fowler and W.R.M. Lamb, Loeb Classical Library. Cambridge, Mass.: Harvard University Press, 1925.

———. *Timaeus.* Translated by Robert G. Bury, Loeb Classical Library. Cambridge, Mass.: Harvard University Press, 1989.

———. *Republic Books VI–X.* Translated by Chris Emlyn-Jones and William Freddy, Loeb Classical Library. Cambridge, Mass.: Harvard University Press, 2013.

Pliny the Elder. *Natural History.* Translated by Harris Rackham, Loeb Classical Library. Cambridge, Mass.: Harvard University Press, 1952.

Pocock, John Greville Agard. *The Machiavellian Moment: Florentine Political Thought and the Atlantic Republican Tradition.* Rev. ed. Princeton: Princeton University Press, 2003.

Polanyi, Michael. *Personal Knowledge: Towards a Post-Critical Philosophy* [1958]. London: Routledge, 2005.

Pomata, Gianna. "Sharing Cases: The *Observationes* in Early Modern Medicine." *Early Science and Medicine* 15 (2010): 193–236.

———. "Observation Rising: Birth of an Epistemic Genre, ca. 1500–1650." In *Histories of Scientific Observation,* edited by Lorraine Daston and Elizabeth Lunbeck, 45–80. Chicago: University of Chicago Press, 2011.

———. "The Recipe and the Case: Epistemic Genres and the Dynamics of Cognitive Practices." In *Wissenschaftsgeschichte und Geschichte des Wissens im Dialog—Connecting Science and Knowledge*, edited by Kaspar von Greyerz, Silvia Flubacher, and Philipp Senn, 131–54. Göttingen: Vanderhoek und Ruprecht, 2013.

———. "The Medical Case Narrative in Pre-Modern Europe and China: Comparative History of an Epistemic Genre." In *A Historical Approach to Casuistry: Norms and Exceptions in a Comparative Perspective*, edited by Carlo Ginzburg with Lucio Biasiori, 15–43. London: Bloomsbury Academic, 2019.

Pomata, Gianna and Nancy G. Siraisi, eds. *Historia: Empiricism and Erudition in Early Modern Europe*. Cambridge, Mass.: MIT Press, 2005.

Pope, Alexander. *The Guardian*, nr. 78, 466–72 (10 June 1713).

Prony, Gaspard de. *Notices sur les grandes tables logarithmiques et trigonométriques, adaptées au nouveau système décimal*. Paris: Firmin Didot, 1824.

Proust, Christine. "Interpretation of Reverse Algorithms in Several Mesopotamian Texts." In *The History of Mathematical Proof*, edited by Karine Chemla, 384–412. Cambridge: Cambridge University Press, 2012.

Pufendorf, Samuel. *The Whole Duty of Man, According to the Law of Nature* [1673]. Translated by Andrew Tooke, edited by Ian Hunter and David Saunders. Indianapolis: Liberty Fund, 2003.

Quemada, Bernard, ed. *Les Préfaces du Dictionnaire de l'Académie française 1694–1992*. Paris: Honoré Champion, 1997.

Quesnay, François. *Le Droit naturel*. Paris: n. p., 1765.

Rackozy, Hannes, Felix Warneken, and Michael Tomasello. "Sources of Normativity: Young Children's Awareness of the Normative Structure of Games." *Developmental Psychology* 44 (2008): 875–81.

Reid, John Phillip. *The Rule of Law: The Jurisprudence of Liberty in the Seventeenth and Eighteenth Centuries*. DeKalb: Northern Illinois University Press, 2004.

Rey, Alain, ed. *Le Robert. Dictionnaire historique de la langue française*. 3 vols. Paris: Dictionnaires Le Robert, 2000.

Ribot, Théodule. *Psychologie de l'attention*. Paris: Félix Alcan, 1889.

Richards, Robert J., and Lorraine Daston. "Introduction." In *Fifty Years after Kuhn's Structure: Reflections on a Scientific Classic*, edited by Robert J. Richards and Lorraine Daston, 1–11. Chicago: University of Chicago Press, 2016.

Riello, Giorgio, and Ulinka Rublack, eds. *The Right to Dress: Sumptuary Laws in Global Perspective, c. 1200–1800*. Cambridge: Cambridge University Press, 2019.

Ritter, Jim. "Reading Strasbourg 368: A Thrice-Told Tale." In *History of Science, History of Text*, edited by Karine Chemla, 177–200. Dordrecht: Springer, 2004.

Roberts, Lissa, Simon Schaffer, and Peter Dear, eds. *The Mindful Hand: Inquiry and Invention from the Late Renaissance to Early Industrialisation*. Chicago: University of Chicago Press, 2007.

Robson, Eleanor. "Mathematics Education in an Old Babylonian Scribal School." In *The Oxford Handbook of the History of Mathematics*, edited by Eleanor Robson and Jacqueline Stedall, 99–227. Oxford and New York: Oxford University Press, 2009.

Roche, Daniel. *The Culture of Clothing: Dress and Fashion in the Ancien Regime* [1989]. Translated by Jean Birrell. Cambridge: Cambridge University Press, 1994.

Rostow, Walter W. *The Stages of Economic Growth. A Non-Communist Manifesto.* Cambridge: Cambridge University Press, 1960.

Rothrock, George A. "Introduction." In Sebastien Le Prestre de Vauban, *A Manual of Siegecraft and Fortification*, translated by George A. Rothrock, 4–6. Ann Arbor: University of Michigan Press, 1968.

Rothstein, Natalie. "Silk: The Industrial Revolution and After." In *The Cambridge History of Western Textiles*, edited by David Jenkins, 2 vols., vol. 2, 793–96. Cambridge: Cambridge University Press, 2003.

Rouleau, Bernard. *Le Tracé des rues de Paris : Formation, typologie, fonctions.* Paris: Éditions du Centre National de la Recherche Scientifique, 1967.

Rousseau, Jean-Jacques. *Reveries of the Solitary Walker* [1782]. Translated by Peter France. London: Penguin, 1979.

Roux, Sophie. "Controversies on Nature as Universal Legality (1680–1710)." In *Natural Laws and Laws of Nature in Early Modern Europe*, edited by Lorraine Daston and Michael Stolleis, 199–214. Farnham, U.K.: Ashgate, 2008.

Rublack, Ulinka. "The Right to Dress: Sartorial Politics in Germany, c. 1300–1750." In *The Right to Dress: Sumptuary Laws in Global Perspective, c. 1200–1800*, edited by Giorgio Riello and Ulinka Rublack, 37–73. Cambridge: Cambridge University Press, 2019.

Rublack, Ulinka, and Giorgio Riello, "Introduction." In *The Right to Dress: Sumptuary Laws in Global Perspective, c. 1200–1800*, edited by Giorgio Riello and Ulinka Rublack, 1–34. Cambridge: Cambridge University Press, 2019.

Ruby, Jane E. "The Origins of Scientific Law." *Journal of the History of Ideas* 47 (1986): 341–59.

Sachs, Abraham J. "Babylonian Mathematical Texts, I." *Journal of Cuneiform Studies*, 1 (1947): 219–40.

Sachsen-Gotha-Altenburg, Ernst I., Herzog von. *Fürstliche Sächsische Landes-Ordnung.* Gotha, Germany: Christoph Reyher, 1695.

Sampson, Margaret. "Laxity and Liberty in Seventeenth-Century Political Thought." In *Conscience and Casuistry in Early Modern Europe*, edited by Edmund Leites, 72–118. Cambridge: Cambridge University Press, 2002.

Sang, Edward. "Remarks on the Great Logarithmic and Trigonometrical Tables Computed in the Bureau de Cadastre under the Direction of M. Prony." *Proceedings of the Royal Society of Edinburgh* (1874–75): 1–15.

Sarcevic, Edin. *Der Rechtsstaat: Modernität und Universalitätsanspruch der klassischen Rechtsstaatstheorien.* Leipzig: Leipziger Universitätsverlag, 1996.

Sauer, Wolfgang Werner, and Helmut Glück. "Norms and Reforms: Fixing the Form of the Language." In *The German Language and the Real World*, edited by Patrick Stevenson, 69–94. Oxford: Clarendon Press, 1995.

Schaffer, Simon. "Astronomers Mark Time: Discipline and the Personal Equation." *Science in Context* 2 (1988): 115–45.

———. "Babbage's Intelligence: Calculating Engines and the Factory System." *Critical Inquiry* 21 (1994): 203–27.

Scharfe, Hartmut. *Education in Ancient India.* Boston: Brill, 2002.

Schauer, Frederick. *Thinking Like a Lawyer: A New Introduction to Legal Reasoning.* Cambridge, Mass.: Harvard University Press, 2009.

Schmitt, Carl. *Political Theology: Four Chapters on the Concept of Sovereignty* [1922]. Translated by George Schwab. Chicago: University of Chicago Press, 1985.

Schmitt, Jean-Claude. *Ghosts in The Middle Ages: The Living and Dead in Medieval Society* [1994].Translated by Teresa L. Fagan. Chicago: University of Chicago Press, 1998.

Schmitz, D. Philibert, and Christina Mohrmann, eds. *Regula monachorum Sancti Benedicti.* 2nd ed. Namur, Belgium: P. Blaimont, 1955.

Schröder, Jan. "The Concept of (Natural) Law in the Doctrine of Law and Natural Law in the Early Modern Era." In *Natural Laws and Laws of Nature in Early Modern Europe*, edited by Lorraine Daston and Michael Stolleis, 57–71. Farnham, U.K.: Ashgate, 2008.

Schwarz, Matthäus, and Veit Konrad Schwarz. *The First Book of Fashion: The Book of Clothes of Matthäus Schwarz and Veit Konrad Schwarz of Augsburg*, edited by Ulinka Rublack, Maria Hayward, and Jenny Tiramani. New York: Bloomsbury Academic, 2010.

Scott, James C. *Seeing Like a State: How Certain Schemes to Improve the Human Condition Have Failed.* New Haven: Yale University Press, 1998.

Scripture, Edward Wheeler. "Arithmetical Prodigies." *American Journal of Psychology* 4 (1891): 1–59.

Seneca. *Naturales quaestiones.* Translated by Thomas H. Corcoran, 2 vols., Loeb Classical Library. Cambridge, Mass.: Harvard University Press, 1922.

———. *Medea.* In *Tragedies,* translated by Frank Justus Miller, Loeb Classical Library. Cambridge, Mass.: Harvard University Press, 1979.

Service géographique de l'armée. *Tables des logarithmes à huit decimals.* Paris: Imprimerie Nationale, 1891.

Shanker, Stuart. *Wittgenstein's Remarks on the Foundations of AI.* London: Routledge, 1998.

Shapin, Steven. "Of Gods and Kings: Natural Philosophy and Politics in the Leibniz-Clarke Disputes." *Isis* 72 (1984): 187–215.

Simon, Herbert A. *Models of My Life*. New York: Basic Books, 1991.

Simon, Herbert A, Patrick W. Langley, and Gary L. Bradshaw. "Scientific Discovery as Problem Solving." *Synthèse* 47 (1981): 1–27.

Skinner, Quentin. *Liberty before Liberalism*. Cambridge: Cambridge University Press, 1998.

Smith, Adam. *The Wealth of Nations* [1776]. Edited by Edwin Cannan. Chicago: University of Chicago Press, 1976.

Smith, Pamela H. *The Body of the Artisan: Art and Experience in the Scientific Revolution*. Chicago: University of Chicago Press, 2004.

———. "Making Things: Techniques and Books in Early Modern Europe." In *Things*, edited by Paula Findlen, 173–203. London: Routledge, 2013.

Snyder, Laura. *The Philosophical Breakfast Club: Four Remarkable Friends Who Transformed Science and Changed the World*. New York: Broadway Books, 2011.

Sobel, Dava. *The Glass Archive: How the Ladies of the Harvard Observatory Took the Measure of the Stars*. New York: Viking, 2016.

Somerville, Johann P. "The 'New Art of Lying': Equivocation, Mental Reservation, and Casuistry." In *Conscience and Casuistry in Early Modern Europe*, edited by Edmund Leites, 159–84. Cambridge: Cambridge University Press, 2002.

Sophocles. *Antigone*. In *Sophocles I: Oedipus the King, Oedipus at Colonus, and Antigone*. Translated by David Grene. Chicago: University of Chicago Press, 1991.

Stein, Peter. *Roman Law in European History*. Cambridge: Cambridge University Press, 1999.

Steinle, Friedrich. "The Amalgamation of a Concept: Laws of Nature in the New Sciences." In *Laws of Nature: Essays on the Philosophical, Scientific and Historical Dimensions*, edited by Friedel Weinert, 316–68. Berlin: Walter de Gruyter, 1995.

———. "From Principles to Regularities: Tracing 'Laws of Nature' in Early Modern France and England." *Natural Laws and Laws of Nature in Early Modern Europe*, edited by Lorraine Daston and Michael Stolleis, 215–32. Farnham, U.K.: Ashgate, 2008.

Sternagel, Peter. *Die artes mechanicae im Mittelalter: Begriffs- und Bedeutungsgeschichte bis zum Ende des 13. Jahrhunderts*. Kallmünz, Germany: Lassleben, 1966.

Stigler, James W. "Mental Abacus: The Effect of Abacus Training on Chinese Children's Mental Calculations." *Cognitive Psychology* 16 (1986): 145–76.

Stocking, George. *Victorian Anthropology*. New York: Free Press, 1987.

Stolleis, Michael. "The Legitimation of Law through God, Tradition, Will, Nature and Constitution." In *Natural Laws and Laws of Nature in Early Modern Europe*, edited by Lorraine Daston and Michael Stolleis, 45–55. Farnham, U.K.: Ashgate, 2008.

Stroffolino, Daniela. "Rilevamento topografico e processi construttivi delle 'vedute a volo d'ucello.'" In *L'Europa moderna: Cartografia urbana e vedutismo*, edited by Cesare de Seta and Daniela Stroffolino, 57–67. Naples: Electa Napoli, 2001.

Swift, Jonathan. *A Proposal for Correcting, Improving, and Ascertaining the English Tongue*. 2nd ed. London: Benjamin Tooke, 1712.

Thomas, Yan. "Imago Naturae: Note sur l'institutionnalité de la nature à Rome." In *Théologie et droit dans la science politique de l'état moderne*. 201–27. Rome: École française de Rome, 1991.

Thomasius, Christian. *Institutes of Divine Jurisprudence* [1688]. Translated and edited by Thomas Ahnert. Indianapolis: Liberty Fund, 2011.

Tihon, Anne. *Πτολεμαιου Προχειροι Κανονες: Les "Tables Faciles" de Ptolomée: 1a. Tables A1–A2. Introduction, édition critique*. Publications de l'Institut Orientaliste de Louvain, 59a Louvain-La-Neuve, Belgium: Université Catholique de Louvain/Peeters, 2011.

Tobin, Richard. "The Canon of Polykleitos." *American Journal of Archaeology* 79 (1975): 307–21.

Unguru, Sabetai. "On the Need to Rewrite the History of Greek Mathematics." *Archive for the History of Exact Sciences* 15 (1975): 67–114.

Vaillancourt, Daniel. *Les Urbanités parisiennes au XVIIe siècle*. Quebec: Les Presses de l'Université Laval, 2009.

Valleriani, Matteo. *Galileo Engineer*. Dordrecht: Springer, 2010.

Vauban, Sebastian Le Prestre de. "Traité de l'attaque des places" [1704]. In *Les Oisivités de Monsieur de Vauban*, edited by Michèle Virol, 1157–1324. Seyssel, France: Éditions Camp Vallon, 2007.

———. "Traité de la défense des places" [comp. 1706]. In *Les Oisivités de Monsieur Vauban*, edited by Michèle Virol, 1157–1324. Seyssel, France: Éditions Champ Vallon, 2007.

———. *A Manual of Siegecraft and Fortification*. Translated by George A. Rothrock. Ann Arbor: University of Michigan Press, 1968.

Vergara, Roberto, ed. *Il compasso geometrico e militare di Galileo Galilei*. Pisa: ETS, 1992.

Vérin, Hélène. "Rédiger et réduire en art: un projet de rationalisation des pratiques." In *Réduire en art*, edited by Pascal Dubourg Glatigny and Hélène Vérin, 17–58. Paris: Éditions de la Maison des sciences de l'homme, 2008.

Verne, Jules. *Paris au XXe siècle*. Edited by Piero Gondolo della Riva. Paris: Hachette, 1994.

Virol, Michèle, ed. *Les Oisivités de Monsieur Vauban*. Seyssel, France: Éditions Champ Vallon, 2007.

Virol, Michèle. "La conduite des sièges réduite en art. Deux textes de Vauban." In *Réduire en art. La technologie de la Renaissance aux Lumières*, edited by Pascal Duborg Glatigny and Hélène Vérin. Paris: Éditions de la Maison des sciences de l'homme, 2008.

Vocabulario degli Accademici della Crusca. Venice: Giovanni Alberto, 1612. Online critical edition of Scuola normale superiore at vocabolario.sns.it/html/index .htm.

Vocabulario degli Accademici della Crusca. 4th ed., vol. 4. Florence: Domenico Maria Manni, 1729–38.

Vogel, Kurt. *Mohammed Ibn Musa Alchwarizmi's Algorismus: Das frühste Lehrbuch zum Rechnen mit indischen Ziffern: Nach der einzigen (lateinischen) Handschrift (Cambridge Un.Lib. Ms.Ii.6.5).* Aalen, Germany: Otto Zeller Verlagsbuchhandlung, 1963.

Vogüé, Adalbert de. *Les Règles monastiques anciennes (400–700).* Turnhout, Belgium: Brepols, 1985.

Waerden, Bartel L. van der. *Science Awakening.* Translated by Arnold Dresden. New York: Oxford University Press, 1961.

———. "Defense of a 'Shocking' Point of View." *Archive for History of Exact Sciences* 15 (1976): 199–210.

Wakefield, Andre. "Leibniz and the Wind Machines." *Osiris* 25 (2010): 171–88.

Walford, Cornelius, ed. *The Insurance Cyclopaedia,* 6 vols. London: C. and E. Layton, 1871–78.

Waldron, Jeremy. "Thoughtfulness and the Rule of Law." *British Academy Review* 18 (Summer 2011): 1–11.

Warnke, Martin. *The Court Artist: On the Ancestry of the Modern Artist* [1985]. Translated by David McLintock. Cambridge: Cambridge University Press, 1993.

Watson, Gerard. "The Natural Law and the Stoics." In *Problems in Stoicism,* edited by A. A. Long, 228–36. London: Athalone Press, 1971.

Webster, Noah. *American Dictionary of the English Language.* New Haven: B. L. Hamlen, 1841.

———. *The American Spelling Book.* 16th ed. Hartford: Hudson & Goodwin, n.d.

Weil, André. "Who Betrayed Euclid?" *Archive for History of Exact Sciences* 19 (1978): 91–93.

Weintraub, E. Roy. *How Economics Became a Mathematical Science.* Durham, N.C.: Duke University Press, 2002.

Westerman, Pauline C. *The Disintegration of Natural Law Theory: Aquinas to Finnis.* Leiden: Brill, 1998.

Wilson, Catherine. "*De Ipsa Naturae:* Leibniz on Substance, Force and Activity." *Studia Leibniziana* 19 (1987): 148–72.

Wilson, Catherine. "From Limits to Laws: The Construction of the Nomological Image of Nature in Early Modern Philosophy." In *Natural Laws and Laws of Nature in Early Modern Europe,* edited by Lorraine Daston and Michael Stolleis, 13–28. Farnham, U.K.: Ashgate, 2008.

Wittgenstein, Ludwig. *Philosophical Investigations* [1953]. Translated by G.E.M. Anscombe, 3rd ed. Englewood Cliffs, N.J.: Prentice Hall, 1958.

———. *Bemerkungen über die Grundlagen der Mathematik*. Edited by G.E.M. Anscombe, Rush Rhees, and G. H. von Wright. Berlin: Suhrkamp Verlag, 2015.

Worthington, Sarah. *Equity*. Oxford: Oxford University Press, 2003.

Wrightson, Keith. "Infanticide in European History." *Criminal Justice History* 3 (1982): 1–20.

Yates, Frances. *The Art of Memory*. Chicago: University of Chicago Press, 1966.

INDEX

abbots: discretion of, 34–40, 56; as exemplification of rule, 31, 33–40; Rule of Saint Benedict and, 35, 37, 39, 40, 56, 59
Abraham and Isaac, 238
Académie française, 189, 195, 198–200, 202, 204. See also *Dictionnaire de l'Académie française*
Accademia della Crusca, 191, 195
Adam and Eve, 78
Airy, George Biddell, 119, 120, 130; Edwin Dunkin and, 106, 109; "Greenwich system" of calculation, 109–10, 130, 132
algorithms, 271; in the classroom, 82–84; definitions, 85–86, 126; Euclid and, 83, 94, 96; generality, generalization(s), and, 83, 93, 94, 96, 97, 104, 105, 120; history and etymology of the term, 85; and intelligence, 142–47; overview, 85–89, 91–94; paradigms and, 6, 8, 11, 13, 15, 18, 105; teaching of, 82–84; translated into modern algebraic notation, 88. *See also* pre-modern algorithms; *specific topics*
almanac. See *Nautical Almanac*
American Spelling Book, The (Webster), 202
Amsterdam, 180–82, 185–87; map of, 177f; policing in, 176; population of, 184

Analytical Engine, 114, 115, 117, 118f, 125, 143
animal instinct, 219, 223; natural law and, 216, 217
animals, 215–17, 218f, 219, 222, 223
Antigone, 215
Antinous, statue of, 14f
Aquinas, Thomas, 37, 215, 216, 238
arbitrary power, 38, 259, 261
Aristotle: on the arts, 45–46; on equity, 39, 249; on judges, 39, 40; on laws, 39–40, 215, 239, 251; particulars and universals and, 21, 39, 67, 273; Plato and, 27, 45; vs. Plato, 47; terminology, 21, 27, 45–46, 229, 249
arithmetic, 57–59
Arithmometer, 115, 116, 128, 129f
art, 1, 54, 55, 70, 80, 191–92; "reduced to rules" (*see* reducing art to rules); rules of, 1, 53, 69, 77–81; and the understanding hand, 48–49, 51–56. See also *technê*; *specific topics*
"Art and Practice" (*Ars et usus*) (Goltzius), 50f, 51, 80–81
Arthos, John, 244–45
artificial intelligence, 145; from mechanical intelligence to, 147–50
artisans, 51–53, 55
artistic canon of body proportions. *See* canonical bodies
artists, 11. See also *specific artists*
assimilation, 100, 101

Monte Cassino, Benedictine monastery of, 31, 33
Montesquieu, 178, 232–33, 235–36
Moon, making an ephemeris of the, 131, 133
morality, 117, 182. *See also* casuistry
motion, laws of, 225–30, 232
Mulcaster, Richard, 194, 196–99, 201, 202
musical canons, 58, 59f

Napier, John, 119, 128
nations, law of, 216, 224
natural law: of animal instinct, 216, 217; customs and, 217, 222, 224–28, 234, 235; defined, 216; Enlightenment, 256, 260; God and, 151, 218f, 219–21, 224–27, 230–34, 236; as the grandest rules of all, 214; Kant and, 236–37, 253; Leibniz and, 230, 234, 260, 263; overview and nature of, 215–17, 219–25; Carl Schmitt and, 255–56, 260, 263; slavery and, 217, 226; state of nature and, 222–23
natural law theorists: Christianity and, 220–21; debates and disagreements among, 222, 224, 226; human nature and, 222, 227; reason and, 222–24; sovereign power, monarchs, and, 260; universal laws and, 214, 221, 225–26. *See also* natural law; *specific theorists*
natural philosophy and natural philosophers, 52, 214, 224–26, 228, 230, 231, 234. *See also* Bacon, Francis; Boyle, Robert; Descartes, René; Leibniz, Gottfried Wilhelm; Newton, Isaac
nature, laws of: Francis Bacon and, 226, 228–29, 234; customs and, 222, 224–28, 234, 235; defined, 222; Descartes on, 225, 226, 229, 230; God and, 151, 218f, 219–21, 224–27, 230–34, 236; as the grandest rules of all, 214; Kant and, 236–37, 253; Leibniz

and, 230–34; Newton on, 151, 230–34; overview, 222, 225–33
nature, state of, 213, 236; Hobbes on, 222; human nature and, 221–23; natural law and, 222–23; reason and, 223, 224; self-preservation and, 222, 224
Nautical Almanac: American imitation of, 109; Britain and, 129–30; calculating machines and, 129, 132–35; calculating tables for, 107, 108, 129–30, 132; nature of, 107; Simon Newcomb and, 110; office of the, 110, 144, 145
Nebrija, Antoni de, 191
Neugebauer, Otto, 91
New Testament, 35, 250
Newcomb, Simon, 109–10
Newell, Allen, 148
Newton, Isaac: on laws of nature, 151, 230–34; vs. Leibniz, 231–33; on mechanics, 78, 230; theology and, 230–34
nomos (law/custom), 28, 29
norma, 29
norms, 244; and exceptions, 265, 270; implicit, 168; regulations and, 155, 168, 185, 186, 190, 209; from rules to, 207–11, 270; spelling rules becoming, 190, 207. *See also* custom(s)

ordinances: clothing and, 156–57, 160–62 (*see also* clothing laws); Parisian, 169–70, 172, 177–79, 183, 185, 186. *See also* police ordinances in Enlightenment Paris
orthographic conferences, 201, 203–4
Orthographie (Hart), 191, 193f. *See also* Hart, John
orthography, 189–95; justifications for, 190; "physiognomic" character of, 194–95; texts on, 203, 204 (*see also* dictionaries; *Orthographie*). *See also* English orthography; French orthography; German orthography; spelling